Horticulture on the Edge

Alec Henry

Horticulture on the Edge

Copyright © Alec Henry, 2012.

Alec Henry asserts the moral right to be identified as the author of this work

ISBN 978-1-904746-77-5

First published by The Shetland Times Ltd., 2012.

A catalogue record for this book is available from the British Library.

All rights reserved.
No part of this publication may be reproduced, stored in a retrieval system, or transmitted, in any form, by any means, electronic, mechanical, photocopying, recording or otherwise, without the prior written permission of the publishers.

Printed and published by
The Shetland Times Ltd.,
Gremista, Lerwick,
Shetland ZE1 0PX.

This book is dedicated to my two lovely children, David and Julie Diane.

Contents

Acknowledgements	7
Introduction	9
Chapter 1 – Raising Plants from Seed	11
Chapter 2 – Pricking Out and Growing On	39
Chapter 3 – Plants Suitable for Shetland	59
Chapter 4 – The Shetland Environment and how it Affects Plant Growth	111
Chapter 5 – Irrigation, Feeding and the Importance of pH	131
Chapter 6 – Growth Media and Hydroponics	161
Chapter 7 – Suitable Growing Structure	173
Chapter 8 – Fruit Trees, Glasshouse Salads and Vegetables	201
Chapter 9 – Pests, Diseases and Weeds	237
Chapter 10 – Appendices	267
Jubilee Flower Park	292
Lea Gardens, Tresta	296
Adam Leslie, Gott	298
Index	301

Acknowledgements

Many people – gardeners and non-gardeners – helped to make this book possible. There are four in particular I should wish to single out; they have given a lot of their time and expertise.

James McKenzie, for making sure many of the technical details were correct. James is project officer (woodland) with Shetland Amenity Trust, and qualified with Cert of Arboriculture (RFS). James is soon to appear in a Shetland film; speak about being multitalented!

Rosa Steppanova, especially for checking the classification of the wide range of plants included in the book. Rosa has converted a bleak hill into the nationally renowned Lea Gardens at Tresta. If you live in Shetland and have not visited then you are missing out.

Fiona Morgan for proof reading and making sure it makes sense, even when she was unwell. Fiona taught alongside me in some of my science classes, and would regularly correct my grammar or vocabulary, so nothing new there.

Christine, my long-suffering wife. She helped with much of the photography, before I figured out how to use a digital camera.

I would also like to thank:- Sarah Leith for helping to demonstrate the effects of pH on mineral solubility; Angus Nicol for his knowledge and friendship; Dr Rosemary Collier from Warwick University Crop Research Centre for bringing me up to date on cabbage root fly control; Pete Glanville for his photos and advice on the 'Solar Tunnels'; Nortenergy Ltd for the information and photos regarding their 'Polycrub' tunnels; Billy Fox for providing the photos of the 'simmer dim' and dreich December day; David Henry from Yell for supplying photos of strawberry culture; Lorna Thomson for giving permission to quote from her late uncle John Copland's book 'Hardy Plants in the North'; All the gardeners mentioned throughout the book – there are a lot of talented people in Shetland; Brian Johnston and Melvyn Leask from The Shetland Times Ltd for both their professionalism and good sense of humour.

Introduction

This book came about after I had been teaching introductory horticulture for several years; with my many notes, and thirty years experience of growing plants, I felt I had useful knowledge I could pass on. Furthermore, when you teach a night class you learn a great deal from the students.

Quite what threw me into growing plants so passionately I do not know, but when I was in my twenties I was keen on the idea of being self sufficient, and concentrated on vegetables. There was a strong line of gardeners on my mother's side so that must be the source of the genes; the other line was 'died in the wool' fishermen. My first attempts were not so hot however, since, for example, I sowed some tomato seeds in a pot containing garden soil, with the first plants emerging and duly pricked out. When the plants flowered, I thought it a little strange that they were white, since even I knew tomato flowers were yellow. There were no tomatoes that season – I had pricked out chickweed. That is a true story. Am I embarrassed? Not in the least – everybody has to start somewhere. Do I still make mistakes? You bet I do – but they get fewer and fewer as time goes on.

It was only when we purchased our house at Baillister with its garden full of decent loam that my urge started to get satisfied. For many years I concentrated on the kitchen garden, but after five or so years built my first greenhouse. I usually always have a modicum of success. This is nothing to do with what many people call 'green fingers', but rather by paying careful attention to what I am doing.

Shetland can be challenging at times, but with the advances in cultivars, and the relative cheapness of polytunnels, many new kinds of plants can be grown providing you work with the environment rather than against it. Modern Shetlanders have advantages their forebears could only dream about. Hopefully this book will help you avoid the sort of errors I have made over the years. By using the proper strategies you should get good results.

Although this book deals with my own experiences relating to Shetland, it will hopefully be helpful to those many gardeners living in a similar climatic regime – there are many areas of the world with marginal northern climates.

One final important point – keep a diary and record your gardening year, and over a few years a pattern will start to emerge for your own particular site. Then you might want to write a book of your own!

Happy gardening.

Chapter 1
Raising Plants from Seed

I hope you will not be offended if I assume from the outset that you know little about plants; many of you may well be accomplished gardeners already, but I have included all the basic information for those of you who are starting 'from scratch'.

There is something particularly nice about growing a plant from seed; not only is there the excitement of browsing through the new seed catalogues to see if there is something different on offer, but there is also the buzz of when the first seedlings emerge, and then the daily watching to see the new life develop. And will your dream be realised?

Seeds are expensive, and in the last two years have risen in price again. I always choose from reliable suppliers since, as a commercial grower, I cannot afford to do otherwise. For my vegetable and flower seeds I order primarily from 'Moles Seeds', and for my perennial seeds I use 'Jelitto'; both of these are companies dealing primarily with commercial growers, but will certainly supply gardeners providing the minimum order is made. What is important is that the seeds I receive are guaranteed to be viable with a high germination rate. The consumer magazine 'Which' once did a survey on seeds and found that many of the seeds sold to amateurs were either dead or with a low germination percentage, and some of these were supplied by 'reputable companies'; so the poor amateur sows seeds and then when they do not emerge he or she thinks they have done something wrong. I recall getting one batch giving a 10% germination rate for a mixed variety cauliflower. I contacted the company and when the manager suggested maybe it was my fault, I told him rather firmly I had sown cauliflower cultivars from another outlet (Moles) and they were yielding 95% emergence. I did get my money back but they never admitted liability. Getting hold of quality seeds is imperative. Moles and Jelitto are first class.

What types of seeds to order?

Seeds come in various forms just like loaves of bread.

Raw seeds are simply that; the pips you spit out from your orange or apple are raw seeds – nothing else (save a coating of saliva). Very small seeds can be supplied as **'pelleted'**, where the seed is covered with a mineral layer that 'melts' when it gets wet; it is much easier to work with a petunia pellet than with a petunia seed, though I personally like raw seeds. Another of my suppliers sells lobelia as **'slick coated'** which looks rather like a miniature yellow pellet – easy to see and not too difficult to sow. In the past I would sometimes shake (black) onion and leek seeds with talcum powder, and this made them stand out against the dark compost – and they smelled good!

Those that are difficult to germinate can be bought as **'primed'** i.e. seeds that have been pre-germinated under ideal conditions by the seed supplier and then slightly dried back.

Some seeds such as French marigold have long 'tails' so you can buy **'de-tailed'** seeds, which are easier to sow.

Many seeds can be prone to infection or disease so another possibility is to get them pre-treated, e.g. lupins, which are often supplied **coated** in a fungicide which protects them against a disease called *Collethotricum*.

By and large you will mainly use seeds in the raw and pelleted forms.

What cultivars to order?

Hopefully this book will give an idea as to what cultivars to try out. There are a few I have had no success with (obviously there are restrictions owing to the local climate), but that leaves a huge number which thrive well. Those that are suitable are dealt with later on in Chapter 3.

How much seed to order?

When ordering from Moles or Jelitto there is no pretty picture on the packet but a large number of seeds within it. For example, the smallest packet of French marigold 'Bonita mixed', which can be ordered from Moles is 5g (grams). If carefully sown this will realise about 1200 plants so unless you are going to plant the whole of the Lang Kames (a bleak moorland found in the middle of Shetland) most of these will be surplus. Now the trick is to figure out how many plants you want (say 200), and even allowing for 30% loss you only need to sow about 1 gram. If you have one or two gardening friends then what you could do is order amongst yourselves and split up the packets.

Estimating seed numbers

Look up the Moles website, click on 'Online shop' then click on 'annuals' and then 'cultural guides'. Click on French marigolds and your answer will be somewhere in the sheet, i.e. there are about 300 seeds per gram. How do you go about measuring 1 gram? There are fairly cheap small 'spring' balances that you can obtain, however another method is to measure the volume, since it is related to mass. I did some measurements a few years ago and the table facing shows some common species and their approximate mass to volume relationships.

Above:
Seeds come in all shapes and sizes. The photo shows dianthus (1), sedum (2), cosmos (3), nasturtium (4), cabbage (5), alyssum (6), courgette (7) and to the far left yellow slik coated lobelia seeds.

Left:
Coated French marigold seeds.

Species	No of seeds	Mass	Volume
Cabbage	200	1g	1.5ml
Carrot Chantenay	1500	2g	4.3ml
Cauliflower	150	0.5g	1ml
Calendula	100	0.5g	2ml
Livingstone daisy	2000	0.5g	0.5ml
Onion	500	2g	3.5ml
Parsnip	400		6ml
Turnip	1000	2.5g	4 ml
Alyssum	750		0.5ml
Beetroot	250	5g	12ml

Using the information means you can easily measure the approximate number by pouring the seeds into either a small measuring cylinder or an empty syringe.

Another way of assessing seed numbers (using the example of French marigolds again) is to pour the whole 5 grams onto a piece of white paper and, using a knife or ruler to divide the clump, separate it into five similarly sized bunches.

Why order as much as 5 grams in the first place? Firstly, it is the smallest size of packet on offer, but the financial attraction is that the smallest packet from Moles is probably no more expensive than a small packet of the same product bought from a supermarket – and you still have 4 grams left which will last another four years if you use them at the same rate and store them properly.

Below:
Cucumber germination can be very fast. These are 20 years old seeds 12 and 24 hours after soaking in warm water.

Another example is that of lobelia seeds. A gram may not sound much but contains about 25,000 individual seeds. Even sowing these as 'bunches' you will end up with hundreds of clumps. I once read that a gram of begonia seeds was far more expensive than a gram of gold; one of these mundane facts that seems to stick in one's mind.

Storing seeds

Before we go any further, many seeds will remain viable for years providing they are kept **cool** and **dry**; remember there are seeds which have germinated despite being thousands of years old. In 2005, a Judean date palm seed retrieved from Herod the Great's Palace at Masada in Israel was successfully grown.

The worst thing you can do is to fold the packet and then stick it in the garden shed, where it will certainly absorb moisture and then undergo periods of hot and cold depending on the weather. When you have finished sowing immediately seal the packet and place in a refrigerator; be quite focused on this habit – it will eventually become second nature to you. The seeds I purchase sit in foil sealed packets and when I reseal them I use 'all-weather' tape, which can be purchased from suppliers such as Screwfix. I then put the seeds into a plastic snap lid food container and label the outside (in my case) as either annual, perennial or vegetable. I also add the date to the packet just to remind me how old it is. If you wanted to make doubly sure of the dryness you could also put a little silica gel in the box. Seeds are expensive, and sealing and keeping them cool is one of the most cost-effective things you can do.

I have cucumber seeds which are 20 years old and when sown I still get an 80-90% germination rate!

There are a few types of seeds which do not seem to store well, and the germination rate decreases with the years; those that keep less well include onions, chives, parsley, parsnip, spinach and 'Wave' petunias. The latter are very expensive so you should only order what you need and sow them all the same season.

Sowing seeds

I have been sowing seeds for some 30 years now. You should take time and care, as I do, because if you do not get this bit right then you are off to a very bad start. Remember, when you start with a seed you have a packaged plant, guaranteed pest and virus free.

A seed is a sleeping or dormant baby plant. It particularly needs three key conditions to wake it up. These are

Water
Suitable temperature
Oxygen

Seeds will not germinate without water and often, with large seeds, it pays to soak them overnight in warm (body temperature) water, say in a bowl in the kitchen. Some of these will benefit from a gentle scraping (scarification) of the outer coat to allow easier water ingress.

'Suitable temperature' is critical for some species: for instance if geranium (pelargonium) seeds are kept too hot they will 'switch off', whereas others need a minimum temperature to 'switch on'. Tomatoes will germinate at 18°C but they really take off at 28°C!

Finally, seeds and plants are no different to humans in that they also need oxygen (from the air) so the seeds must not be waterlogged when sown. This is nearly always the reason why overwatered plants die. If any one of these three conditions is not met then the seed just will not start to grow.

As a rough guide, sow the seed to the same depth as its diameter; this means the really tiny seeds such as begonia and lobelia should be surface sown; the larger seeds have a much larger starch food supply and this enables them to push up from deeper under the surface.

Follow the guidelines below and you should always have a good degree of success.

Practicalities of seed sowing

I have a dedicated sowing bench. It is not that big but strong. The two key components are a large plastic tray and lighting. The plastic tray is easily cleaned and the rim retains any seeds I inevitably drop from time to time. For lighting I have a fluorescent fitting about 1 metre above the bench, and also two spot lamps with goosenecks to illuminate the part I am focusing on. I also have a comfortable seat and the combination of sitting and using the bench to lean on keeps things very steady, as they need to be when dropping the actual seeds. Since it is situated in my 'grow room' I am always warm. Some days I may be sowing seeds for up to four hours so I need to be comfortable – my glasses are always in place and the most important thing of all – my MP3 player coupled to a nice little stereo system!

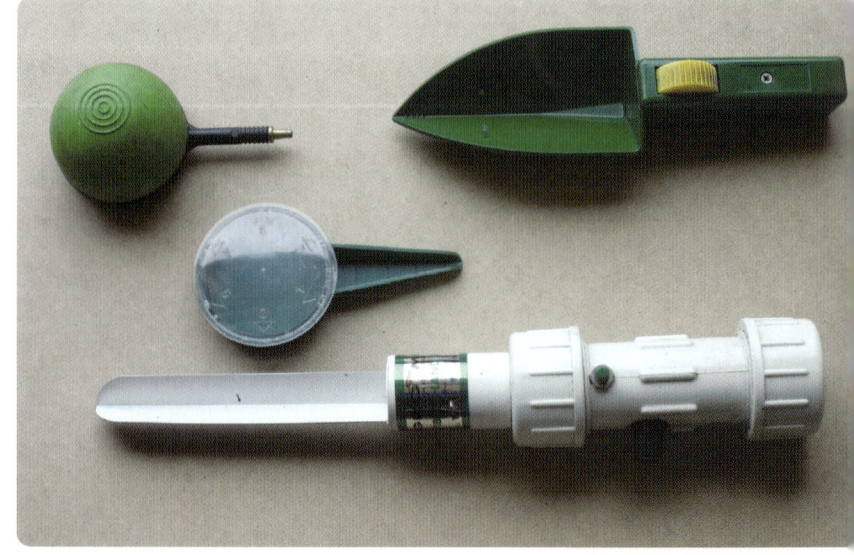

Below:
These are a selection of the many types of hand sowers on the market. My personal favourite is the one to the top right of the picture with the vibrating yellow wheel.

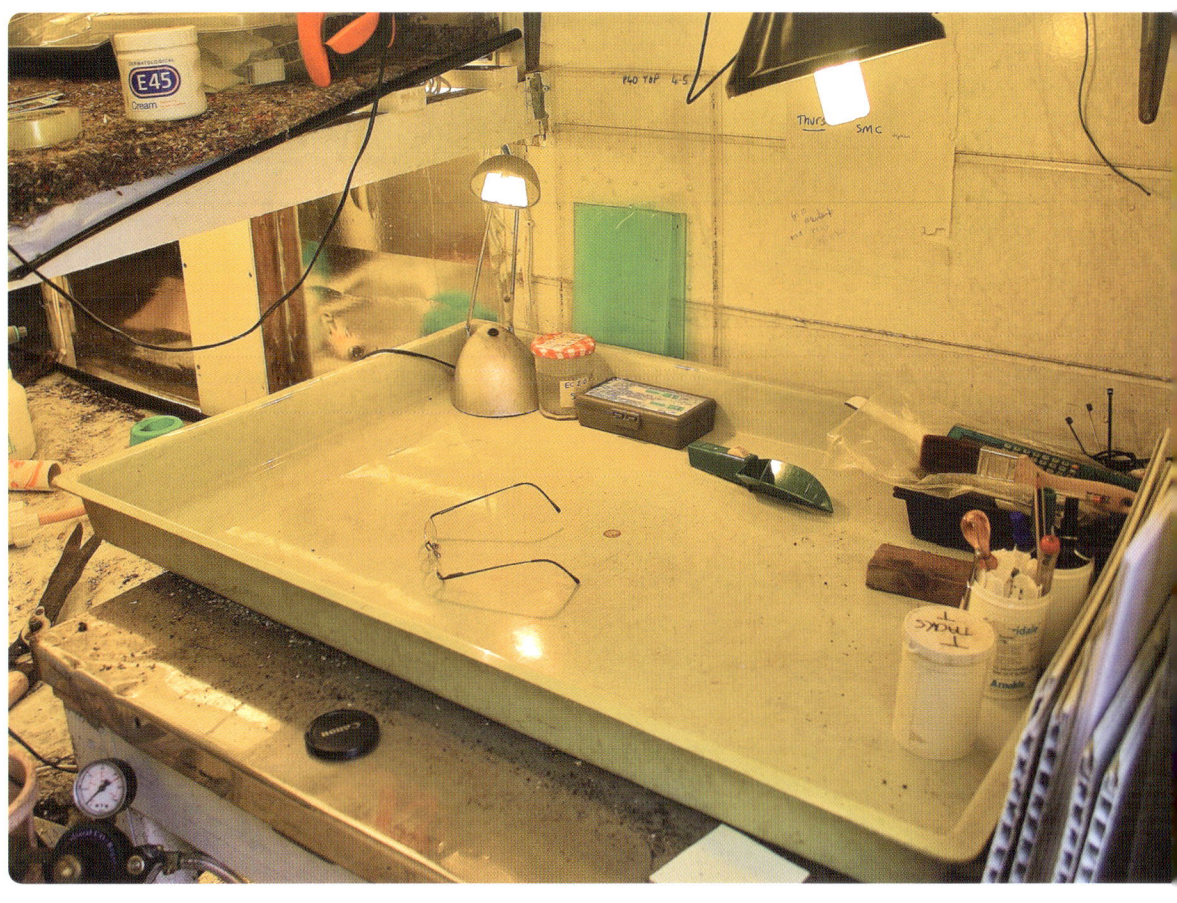

Above:
The bulk of my sowing is carried out in the tray shown. You can see there is plenty of light plus the many sundries necessary. Missing at the bottom of the picture is a large comfortable stool.

Right:
This shows the upper and lower plate used in a hand plate sower. I have deliberately put large lupin seed in the upper holes for illustration.

Obviously, large seeds such as beans and sunflowers can literally be dropped from your fingers but with small seeds and pellets it is better to use simple tools. Over the years I have developed different kinds of home made sowers. I initially tried making vacuum based devices but had tremendous problems with the static electricity generated when the air was rushing through the small pores. My preferred method, in most cases, is a vibrating hand sower. I have both manual and electric versions, but unless you are a commercial grower the former is fine. Essentially it is a case of holding the sower at an angle and then turning a wheel which vibrates the seeds, causing them to drop onto the tray of compost. It may seem quite primitive but is extremely effective; not so good if you have a hangover though! There are small vacuum seed sowers allowing you to suck up one seed at a time, but this is time consuming. Then there are commercial seed sowers which can be quite expensive.

Another excellent method of sowing lots of seeds in precisely spaced positions is by using a plate sower. I use this to sow all my brassicas and leek seeds. This method uses two perforated plates whose holes are out of line. The seeds are brushed into the holes of the upper plate, the plates placed over the seed tray, and then the two sets of holes lined up with the seeds dropping through onto the compost surface. As with the tools above you can purchase a plate sower but they are easy to construct. Details on how to build and use a plate sower are given in Appendix 4.

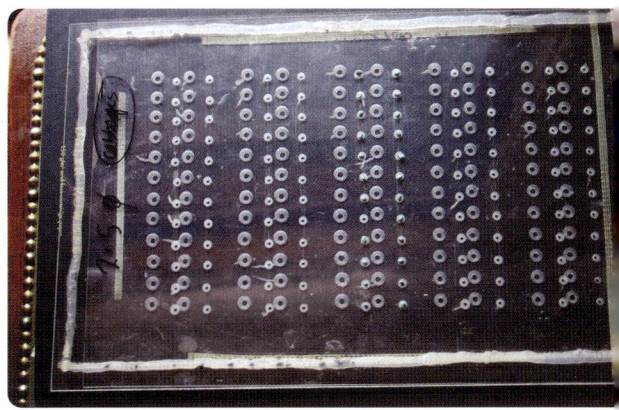

One difficulty with all these bits of plastic is the problem of static electricity. I have an antistatic brush (with carbon fibres), with which I often 'comb' the sower I am using. In the case of the plate sower, I use the carbon brush to sweep the seeds over the top plate, so killing two birds with one stone.

Guidelines for successful sowing

(a) Small seeds and pellets – surface sowing

Make sure the bench is scrupulously clean and dry. There may be spilled seeds from a previous sowing and to have several types of seedlings coming up at once could be interesting, especially if you cannot differentiate between them.

1. Fill the seed tray level with sieved seed or multipurpose compost on a separate bench. You do not want lumps amongst it (I run the compost through a garden shredder, which is a lot quicker than sieving). Level the surface with a straight piece of wood or ruler, and flatten very gently with a block of wood. I always use a stainless steel builder's float, which stays 'squeaky-clean'.

2. If you are sowing raw seed (as compared to pellets), soak the compost with warm water **before** sowing, using a watering can coupled to a fine rose, then leave a few minutes for the excess water to soak in. Do this either on the floor or on another bench, as you want to keep the seed bench bone dry.

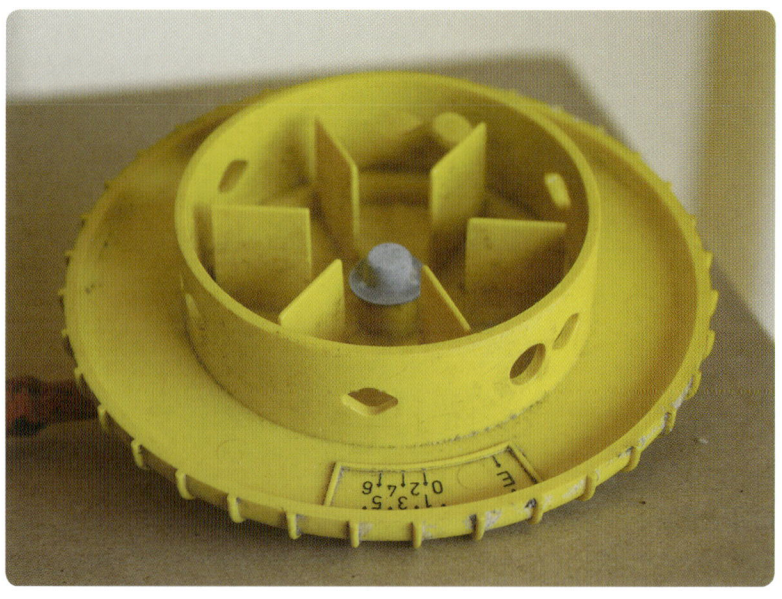

3. Work in a well-lit place and using a vibrating sprinkler/seed sower evenly spread the seeds over the damp compost. The seeds are small and you can gauge the rate of spread either by noting how quickly they leave the tip of the sower, or in some cases you can see them falling against a bright or lit background. However, do bear in mind that though small they are certainly visible. I make several parallel passes each time making sure seeds drop all over the surface i.e. not all in the middle but also along the edges. By spreading them out well the seedlings will be easy to separate when you come to prick them out. It can be surprising how evenly placed the seedlings are when they emerge. You must take care not to sow too thickly else you increase the risk of losing the seedlings to a fungal problem called 'damping off'. This is described in Chapter 9 under plant diseases.

Although pelleted seeds are easier to sow they still need to be sitting on the top of the compost. If using larger pellets I would follow stage 1 above but only water them **after** surface sowing them; if some pellets are resting too close together, they are easily moved using fine tweezers. Once the pellets get wet then they crumble when you try to lift them up.

Above:
The inside of a wheel sower; the seeds are poured into the middle chamber and then a round clear plastic cover is put in place. By carefully moving the clear outer ring you end up with an outlet suitable for a particular seed size. It is just a case of running the wheel along the row and seeds will be dispersed at regular intervals with each revolution.

a:
Livingstone daisy seeds surface sown on multi-potting compost.

b:
Three days later.

c:
Livingstone daisy seedlings have been kept too warm with stretching being the result. They could be recuperated but probably better to dump and sow again. You need to watch your seedlings every day; sometimes one day is the difference between success and failure.

d:
Leeks are erratic and you can see the stragglers. However they take such a while to grow that a few months later they all look the same size.

e:
'Slick' coated lobelia seeds surface sown on multipurpose compost.

f:
Alyssum seedlings have been sown too thick; the photo shows three days after sowing. This level of density will be very prone to damping off (described in Chapter 9).

4. Now use a waterproof marker and plastic label to write down the name of the species and insert into the compost. THIS IS VITAL!

5. Cover the seed tray with a translucent tray propagator lid, as many of these seeds **need light** to germinate. The lid also prevents the very rapid drying out which can take place, especially if the seeds are germinating under artificial lighting. Place on a propagator or heated surface, which should be set to a suitable temperature. It is **vital** you have a thermometer inserted into the middle of the sowing medium as even the best thermostats only give an approximate value.

The thermometer will give you a degree of accuracy where it really matters. You can buy cheap digital thermometers with a steel probe not unlike those used by chefs to find the temperature in the middle of a large turkey. These are much better than thermometers full of fluids and the difficulty of reading! The steel probe can easily pass through the side of the seed tray into the middle of the compost; that is where the temperature really matters. Before you start the new season it would pay you to drill fine holes in the sides of your seed trays to allow the thermometers to be easily inserted; a 5 or 6mm bit should be good for most probes.

I have at least one steel probe thermometer in each of my propagation areas so allowing me to fine tune the propagator thermostat. There is a guide to making a propagator in Appendix 2.

I have said a lot about thermometers and the point is this – accuracy means your success will dramatically increase. The alternative is just to leave it all to chance and guesswork and then you haven't got a clue as to what is going on. I would go as far as to say either do it properly or do not bother!

As a former science teacher one expression that drove me furious was when a pupil had done a mediocre piece of work, and when challenged about it, they would reply 'it will do'; these were the moments in my teaching career when I came closest to giving pupils bright red ears.

(b) Sowing larger seeds

In the case of sowing larger seeds follow the instructions above but this time compress the compost more firmly so it is sitting about 10mm under the seed tray brim. Then start to sow, making sure the seeds are well spread out. Sometimes a few will land together so have a small pair of tweezers handy to separate them.

Cover with a layer of compost taking care not to disturb the sitting seeds too much. Sometimes I will use coarse vermiculite to stop potential 'capping'; capping occurs when the surface of the compost dries out and toughens making it very difficult for the shoots to push through. When crofters cut peat for the fire they speak about a 'skin' forming on the peat after a few days drought – this is just the peat getting 'capped'. The other way to stop capping is to moisten regularly using a small hand spray gun to make sure the surface never dries out; covering the surface with a thin layer of sand will help likewise.

Place the sown tray on the floor, and using a watering can with a fine rose thoroughly and evenly water to excess with mild (20°C to 30°C) water. Allow excess water to drain, label the variety, and then cover with a layer of cling film or plastic lid. 450mm wide cling film is perfect for covering standard seed trays. The emerging seedlings will simply push the cling film upwards and once several are through the film can be removed and replaced with a lid if necessary.

Place on top of the propagator and check the temperature as described above.

Top: Essential and cheap; digital thermometers are far easier to read than 'analogue' liquid types.

Top:
Calendula seeds broadcast prior to covering in vermiculite.

Middle:
The same tray above after three days or so. Note the thermometer stuck through the tray into the compost.

Bottom:
Cosmos are very long seedlings so it is wise to prick them out and give them cooler growing conditions as soon as possible.

21

> **Full culture notes.** The advice I am giving in this book is basic; to get concise details go to the **Moles** website and click on 'Cultural Guides', and then on the plant you wish to grow. Another great site is **Ball Horticulture**; open it up and click on 'Growers' on the top menu bar – open and you will see a menu; click on 'Culture Focus Sheets' and open the one of interest. Note that the culture notes relate to those needing a bit more care during propagation, so there are no French marigold or calendula culture notes, for instance. I mention the **Jelitto** website later on in this chapter for guidance with perennial plants. The attraction of going online to get this information is that it will be up to date with modern ideas, and if the culture sheet from one company does not make complete sense then you can check with another.

Remember to seal the packet of remaining seeds with all weather tape and return to the refrigerator for using next season.

In Appendix 3, section 10, you will find germination times for some of the hundreds of cultivars I have attempted to grow. If there is no emergence within a day or two of these times there is something wrong. Double-check the temperature in the middle of the compost. Did you remember to put the seeds in place? Were the seeds fresh? Did you wave your magic wand? (Joking!)

One or two other things to watch out for are:

(a) Sometimes if birds get into the greenhouse they can pull the seedlings out and use them for nest material. Birds in a greenhouse are always bad news.

(b) You sometimes get 'rogue' snails in the greenhouse, these easily crawl up the bench legs and along to the seed trays. I sometimes sprinkle a few slug pellets over the bench before setting the seed trays down. A large slug can play absolute havoc with small seedlings. If the seed trays are to be placed in a cold frame then slug pellets are **imperative**. If you buy slug pellets in bulk the unit costs are very cheap. 25kg will last for several years.

Labelling

You will only forget to label the trays once and then never again. It is sometimes easy to identify a seedling but most cultivars are near identical. Since I grow commercially, I become almost paranoid when it comes to producing lobelia (for example) since I sow trailing blue, trailing mixed, compact blue and compact mixed all at the same time. With lobelia I actually label twice – once with a white plastic insert, and secondly with a small sticky address label. Sticky labels can easily be produced on any computer. However it is vital to print the labels using a **laser** printer, as inkjet will wash away at the first irrigation. Likewise with white plastic insert labels where there is no option but to use waterproof ink. Very soon labelling will become instinctive.

In my own situation, double labelling means if one is lost then there is another to fall back on.

Shredder or sieve, and why

When sowing seeds you really want a fine compost media, which flows well and can easily fill the cells if you are producing plugs. Most compost is certain to have lumps and these give little problem when you are filling up larger pots. However when you use a cell tray such as a P180 with cells only about 10cm^3 volume problems are guaranteed.

You can get garden sieves fairly cheaply and they are splendid for small volumes, but for fairly large quantities it is much better to use a garden shredder. I use an electric one (pictured below) and it saves a lot of time; I did slightly modify it so it sits on a stand, meaning I can hook a bag on the output to catch the fine compost.

For really fast work then you could use a petrol shredder – they will blast through an 80-litre bag of compost in around two minutes. If you are going to use a shredder of any sort then goggles and earplugs are vital.

Right:
If you are properly organised, a shredder can process a lot of compost in an hour.

Growing your own plugs

Since seeds such as lobelia are relatively cheap and the tiny seedlings too small to easily handle, it makes sense to grow little bunches in sectioned trays producing clumps of seedlings whose roots are separated from each other – these are known as 'plugs'. It is not dissimilar to eggs sitting in an egg carton. Many plants such as lobelia and alyssum lend themselves ideally to being grown in this way, and it is also often an advantage to sow the more expensive vegetable seeds likewise so as to prevent root damage when removing for planting. You will certainly have seen plugs advertised for sale in many magazines. The one thing to note about ordering plug plants is that they can often be tiny; a larger plug plant gets you off to a better start, but many gardeners seem to get on quite well with these smaller ones, though they will have to wait longer for the plant to reach maturity.

There are lots of different plug formats. Those I regularly use are called P24s and P40s – very simply the cells are of a size so that either 24 or 40 units will fill a seed tray. A photo of some common types is shown below alongside seed trays and 11cm and 13cm pots.

Below:
Some of the commoner tray and cell units used in propagation. The standard seed tray sits at the front right, with the 180-cell unit immediately behind. Also shown are 24 and 40-cell units, and 13cm and 11cm pots.

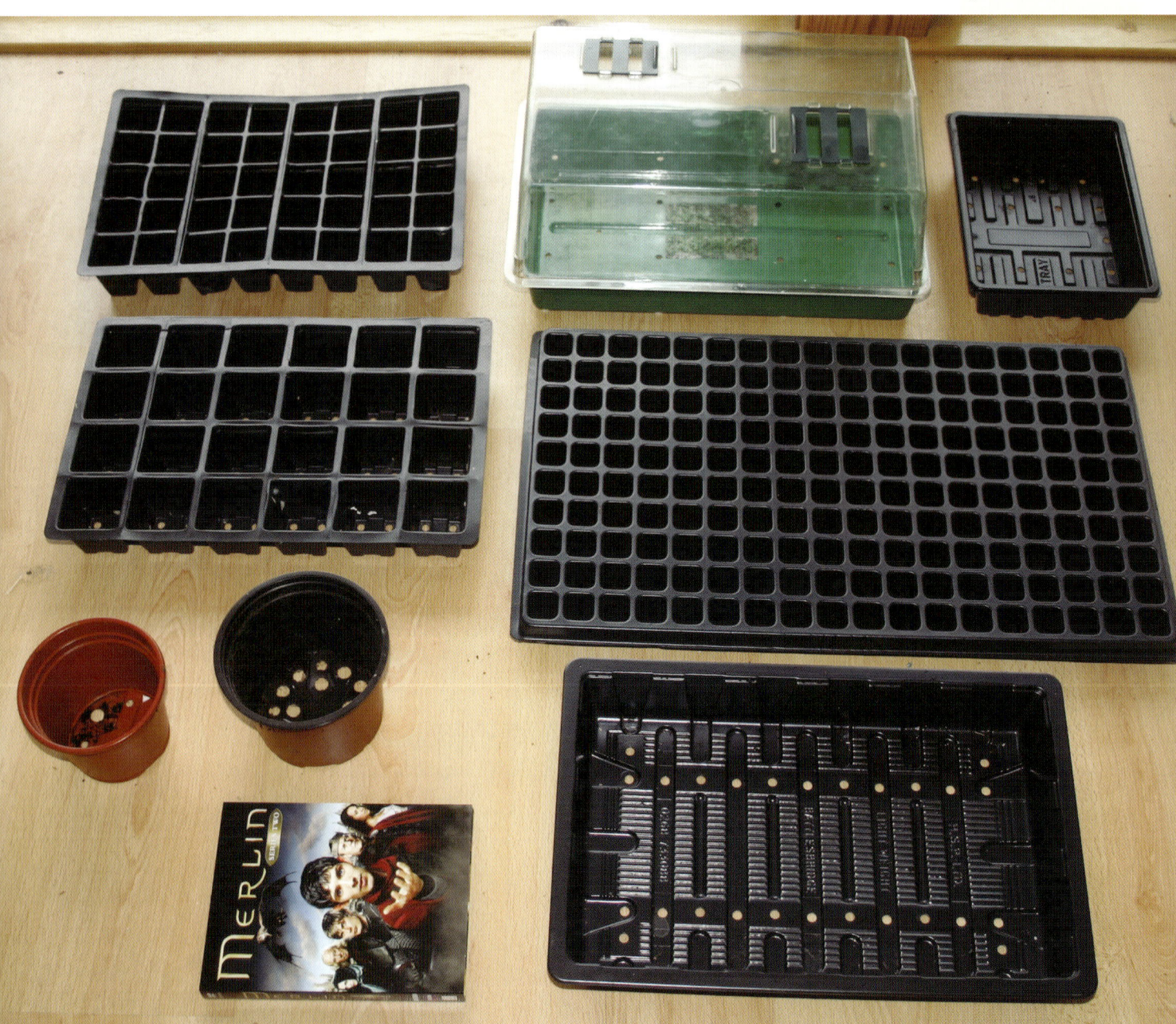

Time and experience will enable you to determine what works best for your own regime, but what is important is the actual cell volume since this determines root size. The root volume of a P24 cell is 100cm^3 whereas for the P40 it is 50cm^3. I once used plates with really tiny cells of about 3.3cm^3 but since they dried out so quickly, they became a nightmare to monitor and were quickly abandoned. As a rule of thumb the larger and more vigorous the seedling the larger the cell you would want to use. So lupins would be better started in P15s (225cm^3) whereas lobelia and alyssum are more suited to P40s. Just out of interest, a standard seed tray contains just a little over 3 litres; there are of course 1000cm^3 in a litre.

Plug growing procedure

Naturally the first stage is to actually fill the plug pack with compost. With the smaller cells you can see why it is vital to have lump-free compost. The process of sieving or shredding has already been mentioned.

Fill the plug tray with the compost but now gently drop the tray on the bench from a height of about 30cm. This will help to drive the compost into the bottom of the tapered cells. Cover the plug tray with more compost and repeat the dropping process before finally using a straight edge to scrape over the plug unit surface to remove the surplus.

At this stage it is a good idea to gently make small indents on the cell surface so that the seeds or pellets are sitting **below the rim** and do not stick to the cling film which finally covers the tray.

From top:

Stage one is to fill the cell tray with compost, whilst making a small dimple on the surface. This is a 20-cell tray

Stage two shows the compost (which has been wetted) with small bunches of alyssum seed placed in the middle of each dimple.

After two days at around 25°C you can see there is active germination taking place.

The alyssum seedlings close up.

The alyssum plants in the left tray growing towards the light (phototropic). You often see this with plants grown near a window.

If you are sowing small raw seeds or pellets then soak with tepid water beforehand. It is very easy to accidentally sow two pellets into a cell; what I do, especially with expensive cultivars like 'Wave' petunia, is to transfer the extra pellets using a long nail – the damp pellet will stick to it and can easily be taken to a spare cell.

If you are sowing larger seeds such as dahlia or lupins in bigger cells then of course you can push the seed under, cover with a little compost, water in and cover with cling film.

The notes below describe the methods I use for some of the more popular species. Try them out and see how you get on. You may wish to improve the process with your own modifications. One thing I find interesting is that you often get different recommendations from different sources as to what is the best way to grow plants. Lobelia is a good example where I have seen different sources suggesting germination temperatures ranging from 20°C to 26°C. I always use the higher value since it gets the seeds through fast and then you can ease back on the heat.

Typical sowing dates for common species in Shetland

A table with recommended sowing dates is given at the end of this chapter.

Petunia

Always choose the most suitable cultivars – in 2010 I used 'Storm' as my preferred variety; it has grandiflora sized flowers with multiflora type characteristics. My colleague Angus Nicol likes 'Storm' for its durability in the Shetland weather. For the small flowered milliflora version I used 'Picobella', which is an improvement on 'Fantasy'.

In the case of petunia I prefer to use the raw seed despite it being more difficult to handle; the raw seed always gets off to a quicker start. Pellets are fine and in the case of the larger 'Wave' series, only pellets are available. Make sure before sowing that the compost has been watered and a 'dimple' formed to keep the seedling below the level of the cling film. If you accidentally drop two pellets then transfer one with a nail as mentioned above. Remember the 'Wave' seeds are very short lived so you need to sow the whole packet the same season – and they are expensive!

As soon as bursting (of the pellets) or chitting of the seeds begins then start to vent the trays. This involves either opening the covering lid vents, puncturing holes or turning the cling film over for a day or two. When the bulk emerge then either vent the lid further or remove it; if you decide on the latter, make sure to keep the relative humidity (RH) high, i.e. the surrounding air moist. If you are growing in a larger chamber the humidity needs to be at least 50% RH. Check twice daily and spray mist the surface if necessary. Since they should still be sitting on a propagator, the roots will start to develop fast. What always amazes me regarding petunia seedlings (and other surface sown species) is how there are tiny pilot hairs which emerge before the main root – these hold onto the surface enabling the main root to push into the compost.

Initial emergence and growing on is one of the most difficult operations in raising seedlings. If there is too much moisture there will be problems with disease and mineral uptake, but if it is too dry then quick wilting and possible plant loss follows. As the seedling's roots get deeper into the compost there is less danger of it drying out. I deal with the importance of moisture and relative humidity later on.

Try to grow on at an air temperature of about 15°C and a root temperature a little higher at, say, 18-20°C; this will allow roots to form without the plants getting too stretched. You need to balance root growth against the danger of the warmed compost drying out too quickly; regular monitoring is the only way to succeed with this (difficult) stage. After a few weeks, the root mass will be well formed, and the shoots will rapidly develop. I regularly eject the odd plug partly to see how the roots are progressing but also to make sure there is no drying out at the bottom of the small cells. At this stage you can pot them up into an intermediate container (I use 11cm pots) prior to the final planter or basket. If you are pushed for time you can cool them down for a few days, but better to get them potted up. Now you can bring them on with even less heat, with around 10°C yielding a well-branched plant. As spring progresses the temperatures will rise and, once above 12°C and there is longer day length, flower production will start.

You can give them a boost at this stage by feeding them with a balanced fertiliser at weekly intervals.

As a commercial grower I sometimes resorted to using a growth regulant called Daminozide (B9), which helped to keep the plants from getting too sprawly, although it has to be stopped before the flower buds develop. It is very expensive but you can avoid stretching by ensuring the glasshouse temperatures do not get too high and by trying to follow the culture notes mentioned earlier on.

The plants are relatively pest free but can be susceptible to various fungal diseases so good hygiene is essential.

Amateur growers will have difficulty in maintaining all these parameters precisely but it gives an indication of roughly what you should be aiming for, and there is always leeway. Incidentally, I do not keep all this information in my head and always have culture guides to hand.

Spreading Petunia i.e. 'Wave' types

Very similar to the normal petunias with the only difference being that when you are growing on the seedlings you can use a slightly higher air temperature of 16-18°C and feed with every second or third watering, i.e. these plants can be 'driven' a bit harder.

From top:

Single pelleted seeds sown individually into a 180-cell tray with indents in the peat surface.

Here we can see the seedling bursting out of the pellet.

A day later we can see the seedling sitting upright.

Impatiens (Busy Lizzies)

Always use fresh seed for this species. In 2010 I used the variety F1 'Desire', however F1 'Expo' or F1 'Accent' should do well.

Sieve compost into P40 cells and water well.

Sow the seed. The seeds are quite large so it should be easy to spread them out over the compost surface. Give either no cover or a **thin** covering of medium vermiculite.

Expose the seeds to one day of low-level light – as little as one hour of 108 lux (dim light) is sufficient. Then cover in the dark and keep the RH high. Keep germinating seeds moist at all times. Set the temperature in the region 22-25°C but really watch you do not exceed these values otherwise germination will be reduced.

If you decide just to 'broadcast' (by hand) impatiens seeds onto the compost surface, then prick out as soon as possible before the main root branches form since untangling these will slow you right down.

Lobelia

Fill up a P40 cell tray with sieved compost, tap and repeat.

Make 'dimples' to get the compost below the cling film level.

Water thoroughly; I add a little fungicide at this stage.

Spot-drop raw seed at a density of 10-20 seeds per cell, or pellets at about 6-10 per cell.

Cover with cling film so there is good overlap and tightness. Remember cling film is relatively cheap. Lobelia is slow to germinate but if the temperature is kept high (no less than 25°C and up to 28°C) the seedlings should appear within three to four days. I would remove the cling film after 8-10 days. Once the cling film has been removed you should cover with a lid and gradually vent until the roots are well developed; I sometimes look at the bottom of the cells to see if the roots have appeared, or push a plug out to see how they are progressing. With correct conditions roots will be running through the plugs after 15-16 days. Do bear in mind, a plant will only do as well as its roots allow; healthy roots nearly always being **white**, by the way. And do have patience – very little will happen above the compost surface until the roots are well grown underground.

I give a once weekly feeding with a half strength solution (about CF12 measured with a conductivity meter; the higher the CF the more concentrated the fertiliser solution).

Watch that the seedlings are not kept in too moist an environment or else they will succumb to 'damping off'.

Above:

Here we can see lobelia 'Fountain Mix' plugs growing with around 8-10 seeds sown per cell.

Bacopa

The trick for dealing with pelleted bacopa is to try to maintain high humidity (95% + RH) at the start of the germination process; this will soften the pellet and the coating will dissolve. This means keeping a propagator lid or cling film on top of the seed tray. Have a minimum temperature of 20°C and do not cover with compost – this is not necessary. When plants start to emerge then spray the tops regularly with a fine spray of mild water; this will soften any stuck pellets and allow the leaves to break out. Once the true leaves are beginning to grow you should feed them weekly at a CF 10, i.e. a weak feed solution. The term CF is explained in Chapter 5.

I would try to keep the seedlings in a warm place (18-20°C) for as long as possible, making sure there is enough light. In an unheated glasshouse you may struggle to get these temperatures, but this will simply result in your crop being a bit later. I found them quite easy to grow. Two interesting features of bacopa is that the pellets supplied are multiseeded; with a little care it is possible to split up the seedling bunch into individual plants, and I have certainly done this in the past if I thought I was running a little low in plant numbers.

Once potted into small 11cm pots they will grow fine with a night temperature of down to 12°C. Bacopa have vigorous roots, and on occasions I have had to 'tear' the roots from the underlying capillary matting, due to the roots going straight through the pot drainage holes into the mat. The white bacopa is considerably more vigorous than the blue variety.

Hopefully these examples will keep you on the right track. The four plants given above are not the easiest, and you could experiment initially with less difficult plants such as white alyssum or Livingstone daisies. What should be obvious to you is that sowing seeds and bringing on seedlings requires a great deal of attention, and though it is easy for me (since this is my livelihood), it will not be so handy if you are working all day and do not have anyone who can monitor what is going on.

Right:
Bacopa pellets germinating. Each pellet contains 5-10 seeds thus producing the uneven results shown

Seedling growth

Very often a seedling emerges and seems to sit around for a while and you think nothing is happening; and then all of a sudden it seems to 'take off'. Many people think that plants only consist of the bit above the ground since that is all that can be seen. However, a plant is only as good as its roots, and you cannot have a plant with little or no root. When the seedling emerges and you seem to have a 'dormant period' the plant is actually pushing down roots like mad to sustain the part above ground. Horticulturalists will very often use the terms 'balanced plant' or 'balanced growth'; what they are meaning is that the roots are able to support the shoot and vice versa. I will be saying more about roots later on.

Vegetable and herb seeds

If you have a lot of these to sow then you would certainly be better using a plate sower whose construction is given in Appendix 4. A decent plate sower enables you to sow the seeds at precisely spaced intervals so reducing competition and optimising growth. The F1 vegetable seeds such as those of the brassica (cabbage) family tend to be expensive and are usually graded by the seed supplier to about the same diametre, therefore graded seeds are ideal if using a plate sower.

I have mentioned Moles seeds earlier on; for my line of work with edibles they are very good. They are continually introducing new cultivars and all seeds conform to EEC standards. I have five packets sitting in front of me just now fresh from the fridge. The first thing to notice is that on the back of the packet it states "*this hermetically sealed foil pack is designed to protect seed germination and maintain vitality and vigour*".

On the front we get the name of the seed, the amount, and each label ends with the seed code and batch number.

The five labels have more information:

    Celeriac 'Giant Prague' 10g

    Melon F1 'Angel' 50sds

    Lettuce 'Catalogna Verde' 5g

    Cabbage F1 'Tundra' 100sds Grade H

    Parsnip F1 'Palace' (primed and graded) 1000sds Wakil XL + Metalaxyl + Cymoaxonil + Fludioxonil Primed seed.

It should be obvious what the first three are saying, however when we come to the cabbage, we see that it has been graded with a value of H. This means that the seeds, on average, fit within the diameters 1.75 to 2 mm. In effect the seeds have been sieved to remove the smaller (and usually less viable) seeds so that those left can be more easily sown mechanically. The parsnip has also been graded and the seed 'primed'. Those of you who have grown parsnips before know it takes forever for them to appear at the soil surface, but primed seed has been 'kicked into germination at the seedhouse' and then dried back so it is 'raring to go'. Always buy primed seed if it is available. I remember sowing primed and unprimed primrose seed once and the difference was like day and night. The parsnip seed has also been treated with various fungicides, essentially giving the seed protection against disease once it has been sown. These seed treatments are superb tools and should be grabbed with both hands.

I say more about seed cultivars in Chapter 9 when I consider plant diseases.

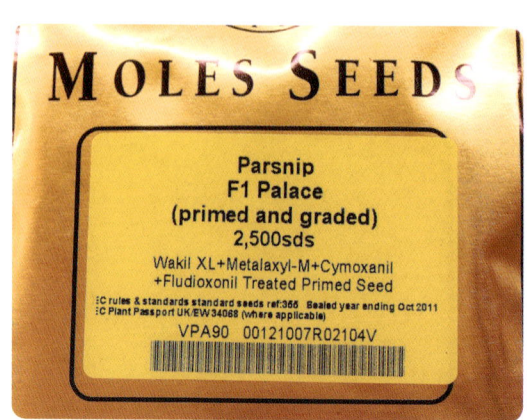

Left:
A typical seed packet containing lots of information about the seeds inside.

Brassicas. By this I mean all the cabbages, cauliflowers, brussel sprouts and their ilk. The first thing is to get them sown and germinated. I sow with the plate sower mentioned earlier, with around 24 seeds per P5 strip producing an average of 20 plants. My germination area (top shelf) sits at about 25°C, so once they are sown, they emerge quickly. Most of them are through in four days, almost to the hour. What I then do is immediately get them out to the cold frames and leave them to progress at a slow steady speed. Initially you just need to keep the compost moist since they take a while to bulk up. Once they are large enough I look for a decent weather window and get them out of the frames until sale time. Once out of the cold frames there are two things you must do. The first is to keep feeding once a week with a balanced feed at about CF 15. The second is far more important. The stage when you have decent plants with large leaves coincides with early May, when often you can get a very dry sunny period. You have to watch like a hawk in case they dry out; I often have to water twice a day around this period. With 20 large plants to a P5 strip there is a huge amount of transpiration (leaf sweating) going on. There must be protection against rabbits at all times.

I produce very healthy strong compact plants this way. The sowing dates are quite important and mid-March is about right. You could sow different types of cauliflower in succession up to early May to try to extend the harvesting period. I had little luck in the past with succession sowing, but since then there have been huge changes to the cultivars available.

Leeks and onions. The earlier sown the better. Therefore I usually kick them off around mid-January, once again using a plate sower, though it is not so accurate due to the crinkled nature of the seeds. Growth is usually very slow and steady, but once the calendar hits mid-April I start to feed them alternately with balanced and high nitrogen feed every two or three days. As we approach May they start to fill up and the stems become much more chunky. If you do not get a long period of seedling growth, you will really miss the season. In the case of onions you might want to use 'sets' (i.e. baby bulbs) but if you were sowing leeks, then onions would be ideal as a partner. Compared to sets, onion seed is very cheap, and you could then choose from a huge range of cultivars.

Right:
Baby leeks nearly ready for transplanting.

Celery. Really very easy to grow providing you remember they are frost susceptible and you must sow them very thinly – it takes a long time before they are ready to prick out. I usually sow them about mid-February, certainly no later than mid-March, as they are relatively slow growers.

Parsley. Parsley seed is cheap but is slow to emerge. I sow as little bunches, cover with compost and then cover with cling film. They will take around 10-12 days to appear assuming the temperature is around 20°C. Once the cling film is starting to push up then remove it and have the parsley sitting on a warm surface for at least a week to complete germination.

Herbs. Many herb seeds are simple to deal with and species such as marjoram, chamomile, peppermint, coriander, chives and sage will grow effortlessly. Basil is not easy and the trick is not to sow too early in spring but wait until the temperature warms up; and even then it is not a guaranteed success.

Sowing vegetable seeds directly into the soil

Unless you have cloches or are starting plants off underneath black plastic sitting on the soil, you should not be sowing directly into the soil until around mid-May. As I say later on, May can be a difficult month for plants, especially if it is sunny, cool and dry. If you have these conditions then **hold back** until the milder and moister southerly winds come back into force. Another good pointer as to when conditions are right is to carefully look at the soil surface; you will see millions of tiny (weed) seedlings forming at the surface. If the soil temperature is sufficient for weeds to germinate it will also be suitable for your carrots and turnips etc.

For those of you who are organic growers, Moles seeds also offer a decent selection of organically produced seeds.

Perennial seeds

Perennial seeds are a totally different kettle of fish compared to many of the fast growing annuals. Many perennials are much slower growing; for instance I am currently (late September) pricking out small *campanula* plants (*C. cochlearifolia* and *C. carpatica*), which were sown at the start of August i.e. it has taken nearly eight weeks just to get the seedling big enough to handle; when it comes to saxifrages you can be waiting another four or five weeks. Some perennial seeds need chilling before they will start; some wait a year and so on. Those which I have found easy to grow from **seed** include the following; *Arenaria, Armeria, Arabis* (the pink form is that bit more tender), *Achillea, Alyssum montanum, Alchemilla*, some of the *Alliums, Anacyclus, Anthemiis*, some of the *Artemisia* cultivars, *Aubrietia, Aquilegia, Bellis perennis*, most of the commoner *Campanula, Centranthus*, the 'Shasta daisy' *Chrysanthemums, Calamintha*, most of the perennial *Dianthus, Doronicum, Erigeron, Erodium manescavii*, certain *Eucalyptus*, many of the *Euphorbia* cultivars, many of the perennial *Geraniums* (cranesbill), a lot of the grasses (*Cannabis sativa* excluded), *Gypsophila*, the dwarf *lupins* 'Gallery' and 'Lulu', *Heuchera* cultivars, some of the *Ranunculus* (buttercup) cultivars, *mossy saxifrage, mimulus*, many of the poppies especially *P. orientale*, many of the *Polyanthus* and *Primrose* cultivars, *Potentilla, Saponaria*, some of the *Silenes*, many of the *Sedum, Trollius, Verbascum, Viola soraria*, and some of the *Veronica*. The bulk of these are fairly quick growing; I am afraid I have not got the patience for some of the slow germinators – some of them needing up to two years. I am not a perennial specialist, and I have tried many others which have not done well including some of the *Penstemons, Rudbeckia*, many of the perennial *Salvias* and so on. I know Rosa Steppanova (one of Scotland's top perennial growers based on the west side of Shetland) did not succeed with these so that is a pretty good indication that they are not for Shetland, or at least for wet, peaty soil.

'Primed seeds' are specially treated (vernalised) to break dormancy in certain cultivars. I regularly use 'primed seeds' with a good deal of success. As for quantities, unless you are a larger commercial grower, get the smaller 'p' (portion) packets, which will yield from 100 to 200 seedlings.

I recall once visiting Angus Nicol and he was very excited about something. Once I had established that it was not winning the lottery, he took me to a cool part of his greenhouse and showed me some tiny seedlings. He said, "These are paeonia plants and they have taken two years to emerge"; if I sow seeds and they do not emerge within three weeks I get fed up!

Controlling humidity

Humidity means how damp the air is. On a misty day in Shetland everything is damp and the relative humidity (RH) would be around 100%. On a sunny day in a greenhouse it might be 30-40% and in the Sahara at noon probably 2 or 3%. Unless you are growing cacti, plants dislike low RH since it puts them under stress. With germinating seeds and tiny seedlings it can be a disaster.

Never ever have these directly in the sun since they can dry out in the blink of an eye; fortunately many seeds are sown in early spring when this will be less of a problem but you have to watch out from early March onwards. If you are really organised you could use a shed or store with overhead or supplementary lighting; I shall say more about this later on. Once the seedling has become established with decent roots it is then far better able to survive the varying conditions found in a greenhouse.

Certainly with very small seedlings you really need to have a lid or something similar over the top of the tray so they are surrounded by their own moist enclosure; once the roots are well down then gradually increase the ventilation until eventually the cover is removed completely. This is not an easy procedure and I only succeed as a result of many years' experience.

The simplest way to increase RH in the glasshouse itself is by 'damping down' which simply means you soak the floor, with the evaporating water making the air 'buoyant'. You can go one step further, i.e. have lots of cloth lying about which can absorb a lot of water like a sponge and so evaporates over several hours. The cloth I use is called 'capillary matting' and the manufacturer will specify its absorption capacity. Most matting will hold at least 3 litres of water per m^2 and some as much as 5l. I should imagine carpet underlay (the cloth type) or old bedsheets would be nearly as good. It is a good idea to buy several humidity meters and have them placed at strategic points to see what the humidity levels are. I always have at least two in each of my own growing areas. I shall be saying much more about humidity and plant growth later on.

Water temperature

I have measured the temperature of the water coming out of the cold-water tap in January and February and it can be as low as 4°C. This means if it were four degrees cooler there would be ice cubes coming out of the spout. I dare you to have a cold-water shower in early spring; do take a photo before and after! If you water seedlings or plants with this level of chill, the roots will not grow or may die. In summer it is quite easy to have two barrels full of water in the glasshouse or tunnel and when you are using one the other is warming up. The problem with early spring is that there is no real strength in the sun. It needs a great deal of energy (about 3000 watts) to warm up even a kettle full of water. If you have a purpose built grow room like I do then you can simply keep the barrels in it, but a better solution is to have a thermostatic aquarium heater sitting in the barrel. If you have access to low tariff electricity then the heater could be linked to a time switch. In any case you are only looking at a maximum of 100 watts; if electricity costs, say, 20p per unit then you are speaking about 50p per day or under £4 per week. You simply have to do something like this otherwise the plants are not going to grow or thrive, and it is a relatively small running cost in the process of producing possibly thousands of seedlings. Once you get to late April/May then the greenhouse will start to be warming up and there may be less need to use the heater.

Obviously you want to minimise the heat loss gained when the heater is in place and there are a few simple ways to encourage this:

- Use a plastic barrel as a container;
- Have the barrel sitting on any insulator to isolate it from the (concrete) floor;
- You can also wrap the barrel in loft insulation, which is relatively cheap and has high thermal resistance;
- Obviously you will want a lid, partly to keep the convecting heat in, but also to stop dirt falling in and clogging up your watering can roses.

If the watering can has some warm water sitting in it simply rest it on the propagator surface if there is space and it will keep warm for your next watering.

I will stress once again – **never ever** use water straight from the cold tap.

Temperature guidelines for germination

Be sure to read the guidelines for the plant you are going to sow. Most do well at 15°C to 20°C, but there are exceptions.

Below is a list of temperature **guidelines** for some typical plants you may wish to germinate. The more detailed table in Appendix 3 states how long they take to emerge. The days to germinate are taken from my own experience and I am continually taking notes for reference each season and adding to my databases. One extremely handy device I use constantly is a large magnifying glass. This lets me see the smaller seeds easily and I can see how they are progressing.

Different crops have different optimal temperatures. Take care not to induce thermodormancy; this is when the incorrect temperature sends the seed embryo into a 'sleep' mode.

19°C (67°F)
Pansy and Viola, Dahlia.

22°C (72°F)
Aster, calendula, carnation, chrysanthemum, cosmos, dianthus, cineraria (foliage), kale/cabbage, gazania, geranium, French marigold, Shasta daisy, snapdragon and stock.

25°C (77°F)
Ageratum, alyssum, begonia (both fibrous and tuberous), coleus, impatiens (25°C max), lobelia, pepper, petunia (25°C max), salvia and tomato.

MAKE SURE YOU HAVE A METAL PROBE THERMOMETER STUCK INTO THE MIDDLE OF THE COMPOST SO YOU KNOW YOU ARE ACHIEVING THE CORRECT GERMINATION TEMPERATURE

Light requiring

Those seeds needing light to germinate include begonia, gerbera, impatiens (just one hour of light is all that is needed) petunia, primula and antirrhinum. Even relatively low light levels are enough to kick-start the embryos into growth.

Once the seedling emerges

So far so good. The seedling has emerged from its cocoon but remember, some seeds will have been sown as early as January or February; for example to get decent sized leeks a January sowing is highly desirable, and for plants such as petunias, pansies, dahlias and bacopa you really have to sow in February. Many of these plants grow much better in a cool greenhouse over a longer season. Forcing many plants on in a 'hothouse' is both expensive and leads to a poor quality 'stretched' plant. Now two important statements regarding both seedlings and plants:

Plants grown in too warm a temperature and without enough light will become thin and leggy, and very prone to disease;

Plants grown with plenty of light and cool air temperatures will become hard, dark green and sometimes bluish or stunted. So would you!

What you want is **plenty of light** and **decent air temperatures** to produce bright green and sturdy strong plants which transplant easily and are resistant to disease.

Anyone living in Shetland will generally always say the same thing about January – it is a long, dark cold month. However, there is a very easy way to satisfy the needs of seedlings to enable them both to keep warm and also get enough light – artificial lighting. To stop the greenhouse from freezing all you need (assuming your greenhouse is not the size of an aircraft hanger) is a small tube heater; a 100-watt version is cheap to run and is sufficient to take the chill off the air, particularly at night-time. As for getting enough light to grow, you can easily give them supplementary lighting in the form of white or (better) warm white fluorescent tubes. This is dealt with in much more detail in Chapter 4. All I would say now is that it is highly cost effective.

Recommended sowing dates

The table below is a guide to when to sow various annuals to be ready for a June planting in the garden. This is assuming you have some lighting and heating to hand. If not, then add on two or three weeks and assume your crop will be later. Certainly sow no earlier than the dates given below. If you find the crop is maybe coming on too fast then you can always slow it down – far easier to do that than try to force them on.

Species	Recommended sowing date
Allysum rose	early March
Allysum white	early March
Antirrhinum 'Appeal' mix	early February
Bacopa	mid February
Beet chard	end March
Broccoli purple sprouting	mid March
Brussel sprout	mid March
Cabbages	mid March
Calendula 'Fiesta'	mid March
Cauliflower	end March
Chives	early February
Cosmos	mid March
Courgette	mid April
Cucumber	mid April
Dahlia	mid February
Gazania 'Kiss'	mid February
Geranium 'Video'	third week February
Leek	early February
Lettuce	mid April
Livingstone daisy	early March
Lobelia	mid February
Marigold African	end March
Marigold French	end March
Mimulus	early February
Nasturtium	mid March
Onion	early February
Pansy	early February
Parsley	mid February
Pepper bell	early March
Petunia	third week February
Sage	early March
Salvia	start April
Sweetcorn	mid April
Tagetes	start April
Tomatoes	end March

Summary of seed sowing

- Before sowing seeds make sure to read the instructions on the packet.

- Take care and make sure everything is clean and tidy.

- Fill the seed tray to the surface with fine or sieved compost.

- Decide how many seeds to sow; do you really want 5000 alyssum plants?

- If the seed is to be **surface sown** then water compost thoroughly with **warm** water and allow draining; scatter the seeds evenly and over the whole surface of the tray. If you are using pellets you can surface sow then gently water afterwards.

- Cover with a clear-vented lid and place in suitable light and temperature.

- **Label the tray.**

- If the seed is larger and to be **covered**, compress the compost gently, scatter the seeds evenly over the whole surface of the tray, and cover with a thin layer of compost. Water thoroughly with **warm** water and allow it to drain.

- Cover with a vented lid (or you can use cling film), and place on a propagator at a suitable temperature.

- Remember many surface sown seeds need some light to germinate.

- Watch carefully for signs of germination; if conditions are good they may well emerge quicker than stated on the packet.

- Once through, increase the ventilation gradually until the lid or cling film can be removed.

- Make sure to keep a diary so you can fine-tune the sowing date for another year.

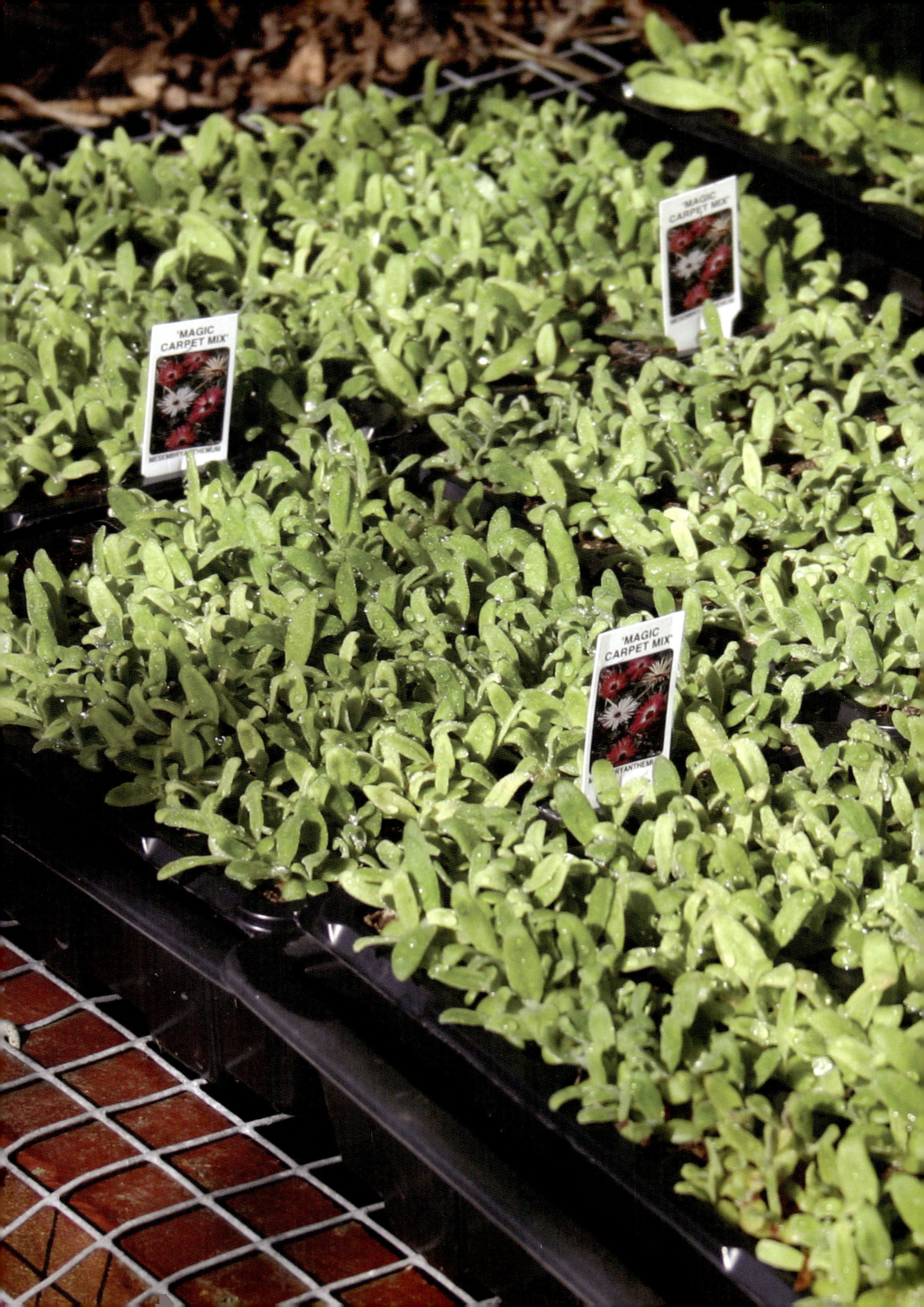
'MAGIC CARPET MIX'
'MAGIC CARPET MIX'
'MAGIC CARPET MIX'

Chapter 2
Pricking Out and Growing On

Once the seedlings are through, check them at least once daily. Although the seed companies quote 'germination times' what they give is usually the average time. Some seedlings can appear before this and if not given enough light can become stretched. Once your seedlings are through and big enough to handle then it is really important to get them out of the seed tray as soon as is practical, otherwise the roots will grow, spread and then have to be torn apart. Leave it too long and your plants will suffer damage or endure a growth check; teasing the seedlings out of the seed tray is a process called 'pricking out'. When to prick out comes with experience but generally, large, quick growing plants can be pricked out after a few days, whereas plants like begonia and petunia, which produce tiny seedlings, need to be left and grown on for a long time. As a rule of thumb, prick out when the seedlings are large enough to handle.

Below: Calendula seedlings just starting to emerge.

NEVER WATER PRIOR TO PRICKING OUT OR EVERYTHING GETS REALLY STICKY

The critical part of pricking out is to extract the seedling from the seed tray trying not to damage the roots too much, but **not damaging the stem** at all costs. One can lose a little root and even a bit of leaf but if the stem gets damaged then it should be dumped; the stem contains the main transport system delivering materials from roots to leaves and vice versa. The critical thing is to hold the seedling by the tiny seed leaves, but do not attempt to clean the compost from the roots or you will damage the tiny root hairs that are vital for root function.

When pricking out you have to decide what size of container they are going into. I normally use P24s, P40s or P15s as an intermediary before planting into the final container; it never pays to grow a tiny seedling in a very large pot.

Guidelines for pricking out

Remember **NOT** to water the seedlings that morning – they must be dry for you to easily handle.

Put some sieved compost into the cell tray, drop the tray carefully onto the bench to enable the media to settle, then add some more compost and level with a straight edge.

Extract the seedling; I tend to use a 100mm galvanised nail to do this but I know some people who use a fork (kitchen, not garden!) just as easily. What is important is that you take great care when extracting the root to minimise damage, and hold the seedling by the small leaves, **not** the stem. To repeat what I said before, if the stem gets damaged the plant will struggle and possibly die. Sometimes there might be too much compost stuck to the roots. If so some of it can be carefully tapped off, allowing you to more easily insert the plant into the cell.

Make a small hole in the cell or pot using your finger, nail or dibber, and let the roots 'tumble' into it; they will mix with the compost when watered in. You do not need to carefully pack the compost around the sides of the plant; this is time consuming and you run the risk of stem damage. And, you do not need to have the plant sitting absolutely vertical – it knows where 'up' and 'down' is. What you will find with experience is that certain seedlings are easy to deal with – immediately French marigolds and calendula come to mind. However, others are quite tricky; nemesia for instance is a very delicate little seedling, and I would never attempt to prick out alyssum or lobelia. Another tricky character is *Campanula cochlearifolia*, which I now sow directly into a plug cell at around six or seven seeds per plug. I have mentioned elsewhere to be alert when you are working with nasturtium or sweet pea seedlings – once you see the shoot, then the root will already be a mile long, so act quickly. As you work with more and more seedlings the whole process will become second nature to you.

When the tray of cells or small pots has been transplanted then rest the tray on the floor and thoroughly water with **tepid** water. Depending on conditions, they should not need watering for at least another week and this will encourage the roots to grow through the compost. If there is an abundance of water then the roots will become 'lazy' with no need to grow through the compost to seek water. Once watered, some of the seedlings will tend to 'fall over'; do not worry, as they will soon sit up once the surface has dried out somewhat.

Then label – very important.

Water extremely gently and **carefully**, almost keeping the young growing plants on the dry side. A good guide to knowing when to water is to feel the weight of the tray. If you are growing them under artificial lighting then you will certainly have to check them possibly daily since the surface will dry out more quickly. In many ways seedling care is rather a trying episode for the grower since there is little scope for error; once they are in a larger pot then even missing one day's watering would not be so serious.

Sometimes growers can have a problem if the seedlings are getting too large and they do not have time to prick them out. What you should do is set the seedlings aside somewhere light and **COOL**. This will slow them down but you should try to avoid this if possible (unless you are going on your honeymoon – no, forget that, the seedlings are more important)!

When to prick out

Some plants can be pricked out immediately; for instance sweet peas, sweetcorn and nasturtiums should be done **as soon as they appear**. For most plants however, the best time is as soon as they are easy to handle. Certainly many seedlings can be handled soon after sowing; for instance French and Scotch marigolds produce large seedlings with decent roots. I find that the latter can be pricked out six days after sowing, with French after four to five days. The important thing is if it is a vigorous seedling the roots will quickly form and tangle, and you will be completely slowed down. On the other hand, some seedlings such as saxifrage and campanula take ages to become manageable and you are looking at about two month's growth before handling. This slow growth, plus the overwintering, is one reason why perennials are more expensive than annuals; on the other hand, many perennials will often survive for several years so are a better investment in the long run. Some varieties of plants such as *Campanula cochlearifolia*, alyssum, lobelia and the saxifrages are much better off to be direct-sown into small plug cells, with these eventually being potted on into either a larger cell or the final pot.

At the end of the day, you need seedlings whose seed leaves are large enough to be handled and not too delicate.

Optimum root zone temperatures

Different roots will grow at different speeds and have preferred temperatures. By and large I aim to have roots at about 15°C to 18°C and it is just a case of tweaking the thermostat coupled to the soil warming cables. The Farm Energy Centre suggests most vegetable seedlings do best at 18°C to 20°C, with tomatoes and peppers 21°C to 25°C, and for bedding plants in the region of 20°C to 25°C. I operate a lower temperature because at the higher levels I find the smaller plugs drying out too quickly, i.e. it is a matter of compromise.

Above:
Some seedlings produce positively giant roots just even when they are emerging. We can see this with the sweetcorn compared to the calendula and cosmos. You have to prick out sweetcorn and nasturtium the instant the shoot pops through the surface.

However, one very important fact is that for most species it is desirable to maintain a root temperature a little above the air temperature. Once again, as stated in Chapter 1, make sure the thermometer is inserted into the medium to check the precise root temperature.

Summary of pricking out seedlings

1. **DO NOT WATER** THE SEEDLINGS ON THE DAY YOU INTEND TO PRICK THEM OUT.

2. Choose a suitable container for the small plants. This might be a tiny pot or a smaller structure, which is called a cell. Commonly used cells are P40s and P24s which means either 40 or 24 exactly fill a seed tray.

43

3. Fill the cells up with finely shredded or sieved compost.

4. Using a nail or a kitchen fork prise below the roots to lever the seedling out, holding the plant by its **leaves** and not its **stem**.

5. Make a small hole in the cell and slip the root in, and carefully push a little compost around the small plant.

When the cells are all full, water well and then try to water as little as possible for the next week or two to encourage root growth.

Potting up

Before I describe the potting-up process, I would recommend you build an extremely strong potting bench. The three I use in my work are able to carry three or four bags of compost at one end, allowing me to pull the compost along for potting at the other end. In the grand scheme of things wood is not that expensive and by getting it right first time it will give years of efficient work. I have included my very 'basic' design in Appendix 12.

Left:

One of my larger potting benches. It is extremely strong (able to hold six or seven bags of compost) with a rim around the edge to stop the compost falling on to the floor. Note the fluorescent lamp sitting over it for use on duller days.

As the seedling grows you will quickly realise that its home is too small. A general rule is to move the small plant into the larger pot once the roots are well grown through the compost of the smaller pot, but not to the state that the plant roots are really dense and the plant has become 'rootbound'. If you are careful, you can put your fingers at either side of the plant, turn it upside down and give a tap, and the 'sandcastle' showing root development will sit in your hand and let you know the roots are progressing. For many of the larger plants such as lupins, I germinate the seed in a P40, and once properly developed, pot up into a 13cm pot for overwintering and then into a 2-litre pot in early spring. I start a great number of my plants off in 40s then move them into the 11cm or straight into the 13cm (litre) final pot. Up to a point the pot determines the final size of the plant. When I was less experienced I sowed some godetia rather too early and potted on and on until each gigantic plant was in a 3-litre container and you can see the result in the picture below. I have never sown godetia since!

Below:
Godetia sown too early and ending up being huge in 3-litre pots.

If you were potting up a lot of plants I would strongly advise using latex gloves for skin protection. Latex can irritate some skin types, and alternatives are those made from polythene, vinyl and nitrile. I originally used my bare hands but the combination of breaking up the lumps, coupled with the fertiliser in the compost, led to my skin splitting open and actually bleeding at times, not to mention being rather sore. Sometimes, if my hands are a bit dodgy, I will also apply a hand cream with the latex gloves going on the outside.

(Once again) never water plants prior to potting up otherwise everything gets really sticky.

Be careful not to over firm the compost around the roots but, rather, rely on watering to settle them in. It is never a good idea to compress any compost as you will reduce the air spaces and this can bring multiple problems. Air space (capacity) is dealt with later on in Chapter 6 dealing with growth media.

Potting up baskets and pots

This is easy. With containers, simply fill with compost and plant the large seedlings into it. Water in, and then hold back on watering as long as possible to encourage root growth through the media. As for baskets, remove the handle and repeat as with containers, then reattach handles once planted. For summer grown plants you may wish to add some slow release fertiliser, in which case you will need to know the volume of compost. I would only add half the recommended rate of slow release coupled with liquid feeding. This is discussed later in Chapter 5.

Growth regulators

I seldom use these but they can be handy. One of the key problems with growing bedding plants, in particular, is that if conditions get too hot they can stretch. By slow, cool growing I avoid this, but it can be difficult. Many commercial growers use specialised chemicals that avoid this problem. These substances interfere with the plant's metabolism and hormone production. This aspect of horticulture is well researched. Two of the regulators I sometimes use are Daminozide (Alar or B9) and Chlormequat (Cycocel); the former is very expensive and you would need a good reason to purchase it.

Types of pots

Clay pots have little advantage unless in special circumstances where you either need stability or the cooling effect caused when the water evaporates through the walls; and stones at the bottom have been proven to be a waste of time unless you do not want the pot to blow over. What is attractive with the plastic brands is that they are light, cheap and not brittle; by shopping around you can realise large savings, especially if you buy them by the hundred.

The main categories of pots I use are 11cm, 13cm (1 litre), 2-litres and 3-litres, but primarily the first three. Carrying lots of pots around can be a logistical nightmare so I use 'Empot' carriers, each of which can carry 15x11cm, 12x13cm or 8x2 litre pots. So by having a tray in each hand I can carry a total of 24 x litre pots at one go. Usually I move these with a double-decker trolley enabling me to move a total of six or eight full trays fairly easily.

Below:
An 'Empot 12 tray' able to contain a dozen 13cm pots.

Bottom:
The 'Empot 15 Tray's.

46

Hardening off

Taking a plant from a warm glasshouse and setting outside is just asking for trouble, with the plant needing to be 'weaned' from one to the other. If the plants are reasonably tough then I sometimes wait for a decent break in the weather, but more often I will go through an intermediate process using cold frames, which can be opened on better days and vice versa. The hardening-off process is quite complex but once a plant sits outside in moving air lots of physical changes take place, making the plant tougher, with the leaves becoming almost leathery in some cases. Frost is obviously to be avoided but I have had lobelia damage simply as a result of tender plants sitting in very heavy rain. Once the leaves have toughened up they can endure the bulk of the elements. Shetland is fortunate in not having hard frosts but if you have a lot of susceptible plants sitting outside then you should cover them with fleece or similar in an emergency. Generally in Shetland we only get frosts in reasonably calm conditions so the fleece will sit reasonably still but you will still have to fasten it down. The hardening-off process should not need much more than two weeks but obviously you need to check the changes in the plants and still only have them fully exposed when there is a suitable weather window.

Potting up summary

1. If the compost is lumpy, break it up by rubbing it between your hands

2. Approximately half fill the pot with compost; if you intend to grow the plant in it for two or more months you could consider adding some slow release fertiliser, but use a type with the correct life span and still carry out some liquid feeding.

3. Place the roots onto the compost then fill up the pot, **gently** firming the compost so the plant is held in place, but on no account compress since this will reduce the oxygen available for root survival.

4. Give a good watering with **tepid** water, then water as little as possible for as long as possible until the roots start to appear at the pot sides and grow through the drainage holes. If the roots are intense and crowded the pot will become root bound and plant growth restricted. At this stage you would repot into a larger pot, unless you want the plant to remain small.

Unless you are certain what the plant is and know how to recognise it, make sure to label it.

Growing on

Now your plants have either been pricked out or potted on, you want to grow them on into larger plants in readiness for going into the garden, container or house. To understand how particular aspects of culture enhance growth I am firstly going to say a little about the basics of plant structure (anatomy) and secondly explain how they work (physiology).

Plant structure

Plants, like animals, are built from cells. Though both types of cells have a nucleus and many other identical structures, they are different in that the plant cell wall is made of cellulose (hence the reason why a carrot is crunchy), the cells are also full of little green structures called chloroplasts, and finally they have a 'water sac' called a vacuole, inside. If there is plenty of water available and the vacuole is 'full' then the plant is said to be 'turgid', which is just the opposite of 'wilted'. The chloroplasts are able to move around the cell and they are responsible for photosynthesis in the plant.

Everyone knows that there are four key parts to a plant, namely the roots, stem, leaves and flowers.

Roots

These play a role both in keeping the plant stable and with searching for water and minerals in the soil. The roots (which are nearly always white when healthy) contain channels which bring substances up to the leaves and vice versa. These tubes run from the roots up through the stems to finally end up in the veins of the leaves; the water and mineral transport tubes only carry substances upwards, but the 'food' tubes start off from the leaves and carry the products of photosynthesis throughout the whole of the plant.

One of the most significant features of root anatomy is the fact that the finer root strands are covered in millions of tiny root 'hairs', these being only one cell thick. This elaborate structure of 'fluff' is critical for root function, not only greatly increasing the surface area required for water and mineral absorption, but their delicate structure easily enables diffusion of the water and minerals into the root fibre and thus into the plant.

Above:
A nasturtium plant showing healthy white roots filling the space of a 24-cell unit.

Left:
The same nasturtium root in more detail; can you see all the white 'furry' root hairs. These hairs are critical to enable normal root function.

Stems

Stems normally support the plant, keeping it aloft and assisting it in receiving maximum light. The stems of many plants consist simply of a cellulose tube with a ring of transport tubes around its outside. In some plants these tubes deposit a layer of lignin on the inside and this results in a 'woody' plant, i.e., a tree or a bush.

Leaves

Leaves are the chemical factories of plants and the key area for photosynthesis. A typical leaf consists of two layers, the upper surface often shiny with a dark green tissue of cells (the result of high concentrations of chloroplasts). The duller underside of the leaf is riddled with thousands of tiny little breathing pores called stomata; these pores lead into air spaces inside the bottom of the leaf, often described as being 'spongy'

Flowers

Flowers contain the reproductive organs of plants – in essence the function of a flower is to produce seeds. And, of course, it is the flower which is often the whole reason for a gardener growing a particular plant. Most of you will be aware that for most plants to produce seeds, pollination is involved.

How plants work

Gardeners are keen to promote good growth whether this results in a brighter show of flowers or a greater yield of fruit; not only is growth wanted but equally important is quality. I want to summarise some of the key processes taking place in active growing plants; if you can understand this and think like a plant, you will better understand how to achieve optimal growing conditions.

Photosynthesis

Plants are the starting point (primary producers) of any food chain, i.e. a flow of energy from one organism to the next. Plants trap energy from the sun and convert two common substances, water and carbon dioxide, into energy storage compounds that we call foods – this is **photosynthesis.** The process of photosynthesis is shown in the simplified diagram below.

Below: Photosynthesis.

Since this process takes place in the plant's leaves, any loss of foliage will reduce productivity. It should also be obvious that over a range of brightness photosynthetic production will be directly proportional to the amount of light hitting the plant. However, the leaves can only trap so much of the light available, and on a bright sunny day only around 10% of the light is used. Photosynthesis will also readily take place during dull conditions, with slower growth on these days, more the result of lower greenhouse temperatures, or high humidity (such as on a misty or foggy day).

Now for the bit that matters. The diagram below shows a simple leaf with photosynthesis taking place.

Hopefully you can understand that there are two scenarios at work. The first is on the top surface of the leaf where the sun's rays are being absorbed by the dark green chloroplasts. On duller days the more light getting through to hit this surface the better, hence the obsession of commercial growers with high light transmission, achieved by keeping the glass sparkling clean or using larger panes with relatively less structural components. Providing there is sufficient water and carbon dioxide, then for every 1% increase in light we get a 1% increase in the plant's mass. Photosynthesis is cumulative, so if the daylength is 10 hours rather than five, you will end up with twice the chemistry taking place and twice the growth.

The second process is the exchange of materials on the underside of the leaf, with carbon dioxide being absorbed and oxygen and water vapour being released, all through the tiny stomatal pores. If these substances are not moving in or out then the chemistry of growth just stops. No different from a car running out of fuel. Photosynthesis is further complicated because, what the diagram shows is the 'day' reaction, and you can immediately guess there is also a 'night' reaction. This is one of the reasons that it pays to have a little warmth in the glasshouse overnight because growth is just as dependent on the night reaction as that taking place during the day. All chemical reactions are temperature dependent; a well-known scientific fact is that for biochemical processes an increase of 10°C doubles the speed of reaction (sometimes referred to as Q_{10}). For biochemical reactions involving enzymes the rate increases are a little more complex but the same principle applies.

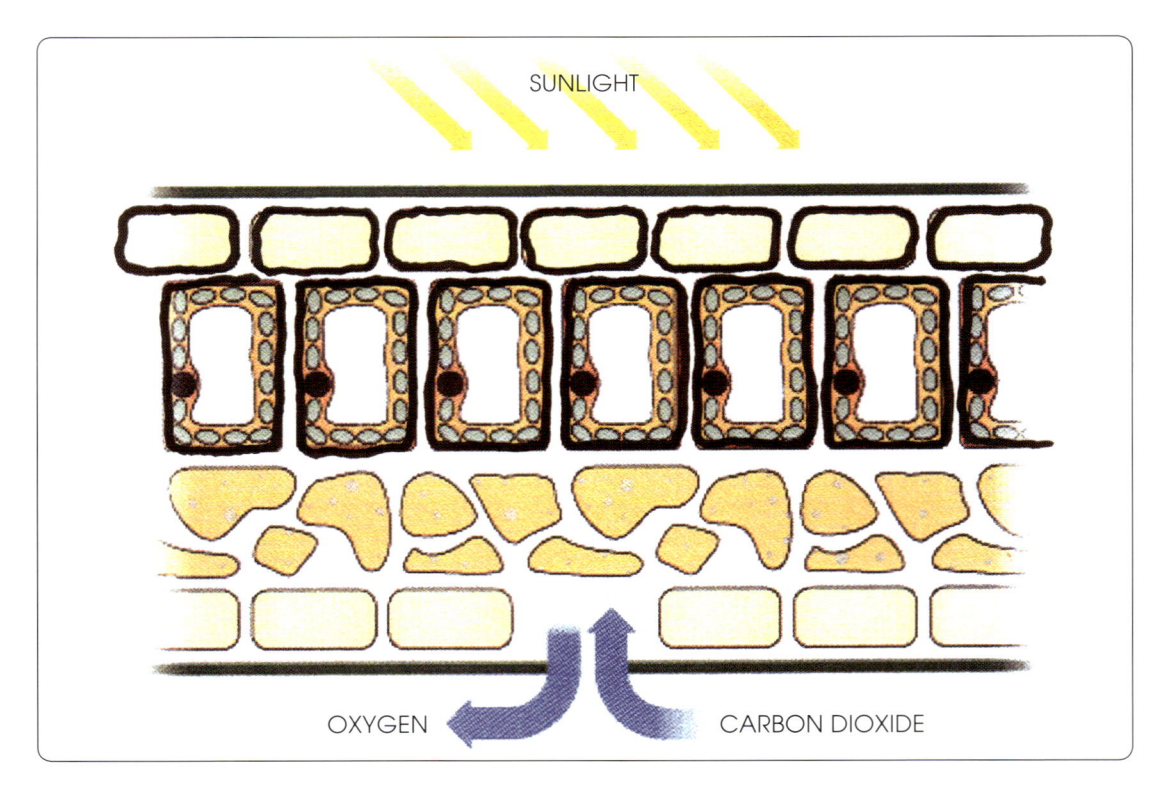

Left:
Cross section of a leaf showing photosynthesis taking place.

Lack of air movement around the plants is dire. Why do sheets on the washing line never dry out on a calm day? Though you cannot see it, next to the sheet surface there is a tiny layer of moist air forming a barrier, preventing other water molecules escaping from the cloth. Once a breeze picks up this layer of mist is blown away, so allowing more water to evaporate from the sheet and so on. This is almost identical to calm conditions around a leaf. Once again a barrier forms preventing both carbon dioxide absorption plus water and oxygen release; a gentle breeze removes this barrier and growth can then charge on. **Still conditions are bad news for growing plants.** As if the stopping of photosynthesis was not bad enough, still conditions bring the added problems of mineral deficiency, overheating and disease. Water lost from the leaf is replaced by water being pulled up from the roots via the stem. But this water is also a mineral carrier, taking nitrates, phosphates, potash and other essential chemicals from the growing medium. No water movement and suddenly minerals are missing. Water evaporation from a leaf surface is no different from humans sweating to keep cool; no leaf evaporation leads to overheating and tissue damage. This is why plants can be unaffected even on very hot days as long as they can 'sweat'. Finally, continual dampness when the foliage does not dry out is a guaranteed recipe for disease onset.

The horticultural term used to describe water loss by the 'sweating' of a leaf is **transpiration**; it is one word worth knowing and understanding.

Mineral and water absorption

Water is taken into the plant's root hairs by a process called osmosis. You get osmosis taking place every time you put a limp lettuce into fresh water and the absorbed water makes the lettuce crisp again. You get osmosis in the reverse direction when you 'salt' herring, as many of the older fishermen used to do. I recall my late father putting a layer of salt in a wooden barrel followed by a layer of herring and so on. After a few days the whole barrel was full of brine, i.e. water had moved out of the fish and dissolved the salt; the herring were 'pickled'.

Without boring you with the science of osmosis (I taught it often enough), just accept that osmotic water movement will take place through a cell wall providing the water inside the cell is slightly 'saltier' than the water outside; the word 'salt' is being used in its broadest sense.

Look at the diagram (overleaf) of some tiny root hairs a single cell thick. In a nutshell, the very dilute (light blue) water on the outside will (by the laws of physics) want to move in through the cell wall to join with the 'saltier' solution inside the cell. This natural process works splendidly until the grower does something daft and unnatural. One example is when you decide to be 'smart' and boost the fertiliser levels in the soil; then the salt level outside the root hair is higher than that inside so instead of water moving into the plant, the reverse takes place, and the whole structure starts to wilt. This often leads to root hair damage coupled with the possible onset of root rot, simply because you were trying to be 'too kind'. I return to this idea in Chapter 5 when I deal with feed levels.

With hydroponic culture you can do just as much harm if you suddenly change from supplying feed solution to the plants to giving them plain water. In this situation the water will rush into the root hairs so fast they will expand and burst; they will grow back, but that may take a week or two.

And how does this apply to practical horticulture? Be careful when feeding plants and make sure you are sticking with the manufacturer's instructions regarding optimal concentrations. I deal with measuring feed levels later on.

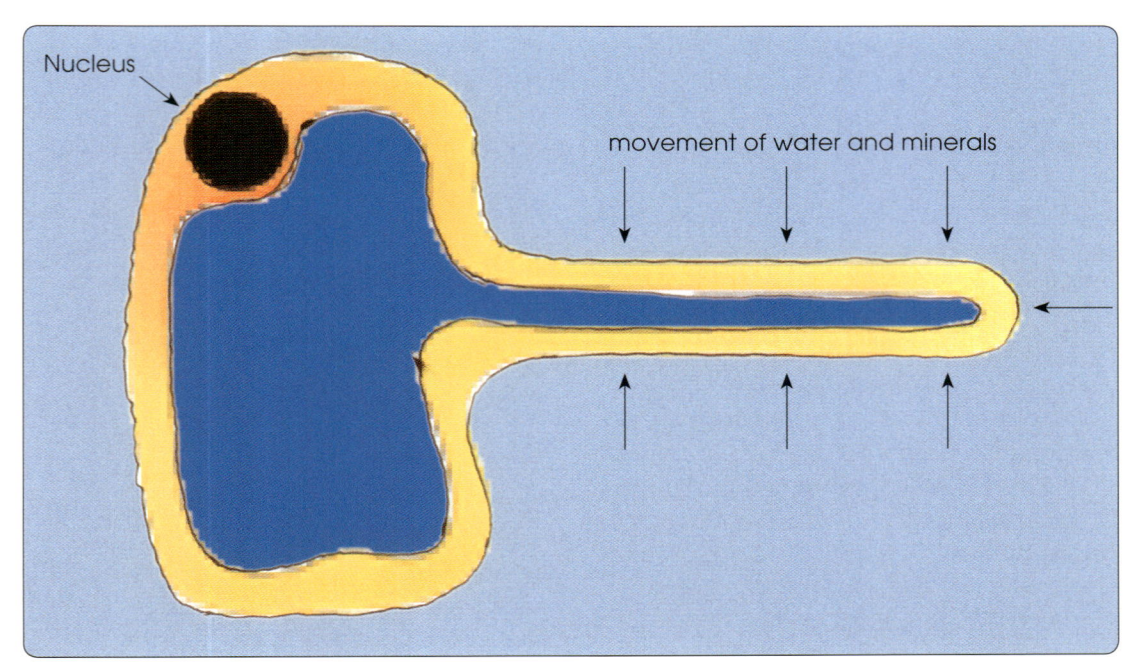

Left:
Drawing of root hair showing diffusion in and out of cells.

Below:
The root had salt solution trickled down the left hand side. Can you see the root hairs are absent having been destroyed by the osmotic effect of the salt? You will likewise scorch the root hairs of most plants if you apply too strong a fertiliser solution.

Flowering

I grow many types of plants and although I will sell a few foliage varieties and vegetable transplants, it is all about flowers. I have put plants to market with the bud nearly bursting but they just do not sell. If I put the plant out a few days later with the flower peaking through, they fly off the shelves; I jokingly say to some people that I have glued those in bud so they will **never** open, though I am careful to whom I repeat this!

Flowers are there to produce seeds, and certain conditions are necessary for flower bud initiation in different plants. There are several triggering actions; some of these are fairly obvious, others less so.

Stage of growth

Sometimes this is called 'juvenility' but really means that before a plant will flower it has to be fairly well developed with a specified number of leaves. This 'critical leaf number' varies, ranging from as little as four to five in some species of campanula, to as many as 60 in plants like the *Digitalis obscura* cultivars. The whole idea of juvenility is important to me when it comes to growing bedding plants. For instance, it has been well established that pansies growing in cooler conditions take around 100 days from sowing to flowering. In my case I sow around 100 days before I want them in bloom. In many ways sowing dates for bedding plants are based on the optimal time for sales, which tends to be primarily mid-May to mid-June.

Vernalisation (chilling). Many perennial plants need a cold period to initiate flowering; some seeds need the same. This is an environmental switch telling them that winter has passed, and there is weather more favourable for germination or starting to flower. There are three groups of plants in this section:

- Those with no cold requirement;
- Those with (obligate) cold requirement;
- Cold beneficial plants.

There are huge lists of plants falling into the three groups. Irrespective of which group a plant belongs to, it is safer to assume all require cold treatment since it will not do any harm even to those needing no cold requirement.

Commercially, this allows me to sow certain perennials in early spring (without cold treatment) and still get flowering for certain species of lupins, *Campanula carpatica* and *Armeria*. I still prefer to have them sown in autumn and then overwinter.

The 'obligate' cold group need cold or flowering will not take place, and includes many of the aquilegias, astilbes and primulas. I recall overlooking the sowing of *Saponaria* one year so I started them off in January. I ended up with large plants by early summer and not a flower in sight!

And how cold should it get? The general consensus seems to be that you would not want exceedingly cold temperatures in case of root damage, but temperatures in the range 3°C to 7°C work well. Researchers suggest 6 to 10 weeks as being fine, in a typical Shetland winter we get many weeks in winter at this level, and the bulk of the plants I overwinter flower without problems.

Light requirement. Light has multiple effects on living systems; it establishes the seasons and the various responses from many organisms, be it hares turning white in the winter, salmon migrating upstream in autumn, sheep coming into heat and birds flying away in autumn to sunnier climes. Light in nature acts as a biological clock and switch. So far I have only mentioned light with regard to its importance in photosynthesis and growth, but the duration of light (daylength or photoperiod) has the key role of triggering flower production, when conditions are suitable to allow pollination and seed production. Flowers have been split into three photoperiodic groups:

- The majority of (commercially grown) perennials are 'long day' plants, needing a minimum of 13 hours to start. Many of the campanulas fit into this bracket;
- A few plants are said to be 'short day' – these are plants typically flowering in autumn;
- Finally, a number of plants are said to be 'day neutral'. In the next chapter you will see that (where possible) I prefer to use day neutral cultivars hence my choosing *Salvia* 'Salsa' series, and African marigold 'Antigua'.

Many growers force their plants into early flowering simply by artificially creating long days, but unless you are a commercial grower and wanted to target, say, Mother's day, this is not to be pursued.

Purely out of interest, in 2010, I sowed *Chrysanthemum paludosum* 'Mini Marguerite' in January using supplementary 24-hour lighting. These annual plants were in flower by late April, far earlier than the normal July flowering, and just when the market was keenest; I shall certainly be repeating this in successive years.

The glasshouse environment

Once you are experienced you can just go into the glasshouse and know immediately if conditions are conducive to plant growth. What you want is the glasshouse air to be warm, not too dry or wet, and (critically) some air movement. Within-limits temperature is not the 'Holy Grail', but you would neither want the plants to cook during the day nor freeze at night. In early spring, if it is dull, wet or both, I just leave the fluorescent lights on and this keeps it bright, gives a little temperature lift, and helps to dry the air a little. On a 'normal' bright/cloudy day I want to ventilate even at the expense of dropping the air temperature. You produce an infinitely better plant though it might grow a little slower; more to the point is that you will get 'quality' growth. If you do not vent you are destined for all sorts of trouble.

Venting lets the moist warm air out through the top of the house, to be replaced by cooler drier air. You must try to drive the humidity (RH) down; if it stays high the leaves cannot transpire. As I mentioned earlier, transpiration is the means by which a plant can pull water and minerals up from the roots to be used for the key metabolic processes. If the RH is too high then the lack of transpiration means the leaves can overheat (possibly scorch), and vital minerals do not move through the plant. For example, tomatoes need calcium to help make the cells of their fruit. Lack of calcium leads to cell collapse and we get classic 'blossom end rot' often found in tomatoes sitting in an unfavourable growing environment. On a 'normal' day in the glasshouse the windows **should be clear and dry**; if they are damp or steamy, problems will literally start queuing up.

One of the worst scenarios is when there is a bright sunny day with cold outside air. Here you have to try to have a balance between reducing the humidity whilst not having the glasshouse absolutely freezing.

Above:
Early spring in the glasshouse. There are many plants growing; the pots very largely contain dahlias and the baskets primarily petunias.

Right:
What a super device. You can get both the temperature and relative humidity at one go.

Another difficult situation is later in the season when you get 'dawn to dusk' blue skies. Obviously you will vent to drive the temperature down, but this will take the RH to a very low level, putting the plants under stress. If the RH gets too low then the stomata (pores) in the leaves start closing, there will be reduced gas exchange, and photosynthesis slows down. It is a little ironic that bright sun and its 'drying power' in a greenhouse can cause slowing down in growth. I mentioned earlier that my benches are covered with capillary matting. What I do is soak both the floor and all the matting; this helps to increase the humidity somewhat and give the atmosphere a bit more 'buoyancy'.

With time and experience you will just walk into the glasshouse and know instinctively if it feels right; in the meantime, have thermometers and RH meters at strategic points but do not get paranoid and look at them twenty times a day!

With a little night warmth and vent control during the daytime there is very little you could not easily grow in Shetland, though you would be daft to try things like bananas; you do not want to try competing with Africa!

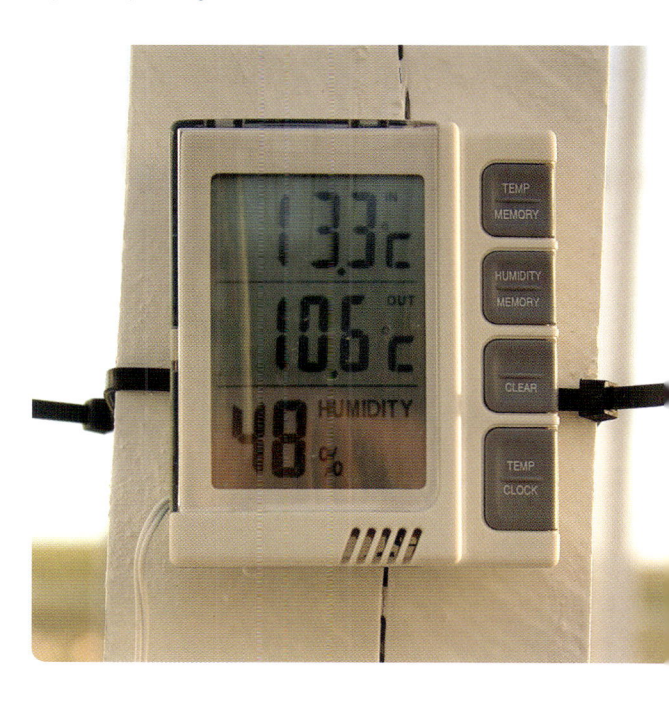

The polytunnel environment

Tunnels and greenhouses are very different beasts, with each having advantages over the other. In many ways the tunnel climate is closer to what you get outside, with slightly warmer days and generally not such cold nights, but there are circumstances when the tunnel can be very hot in the day and very cold at night. Tunnels in Shetland mimic the climate you would find outside in southern England. Outdoors we are always going to struggle with runner beans and courgettes (for instance) but the tunnel changes all that. For some crops such as tomatoes, indoor cucumbers and peppers, a glasshouse will always be better. I recall one year planting the same variety of tomato in both the greenhouse and the tunnel at the same time. The glasshouse growth was infinitely better with much earlier ripening and much better quality fruit. I think that some plants do not like the extremities you can get in a tunnel, compared to the temperature buffering and control achieved in a glasshouse.

Tunnels are particularly good for a wide range of fruit and cool salad crops. I use one of my tunnels to overwinter some of the potted perennials which otherwise might succumb to the winter rains, and also for giving some temperature lift in early spring when I am potting up plug plants such as the annual dianthus and violas.

Below:
One of my 'Clovis Lande' tunnels in early spring. As well as the viola baskets there are flowering arabis, poppies and annual dianthus growing.

pricking out and growing on

The one snag with tunnels is the ventilation since (in Shetland anyway) you cannot have roof vents. You get tunnels with side vents but sometimes you encounter a calm sunny (or worse, a calm misty) day when neither heat nor moisture can get out. As I said earlier, still air is bad news. One way around this is to have your tunnels on a slope, and via the process of convection the hot air will exit at the top and the cool air be dragged in the bottom. Another possibility is to have extractor fans sitting at the end of the tunnel, but to get serious air movement you will need a large machine and all that entails. You could have some circulatory fans moving the air inside but that does not really get rid of the heat and moisture, it merely moves it around. We have not had a week of fog or mist for a few years now but when it comes, look out!

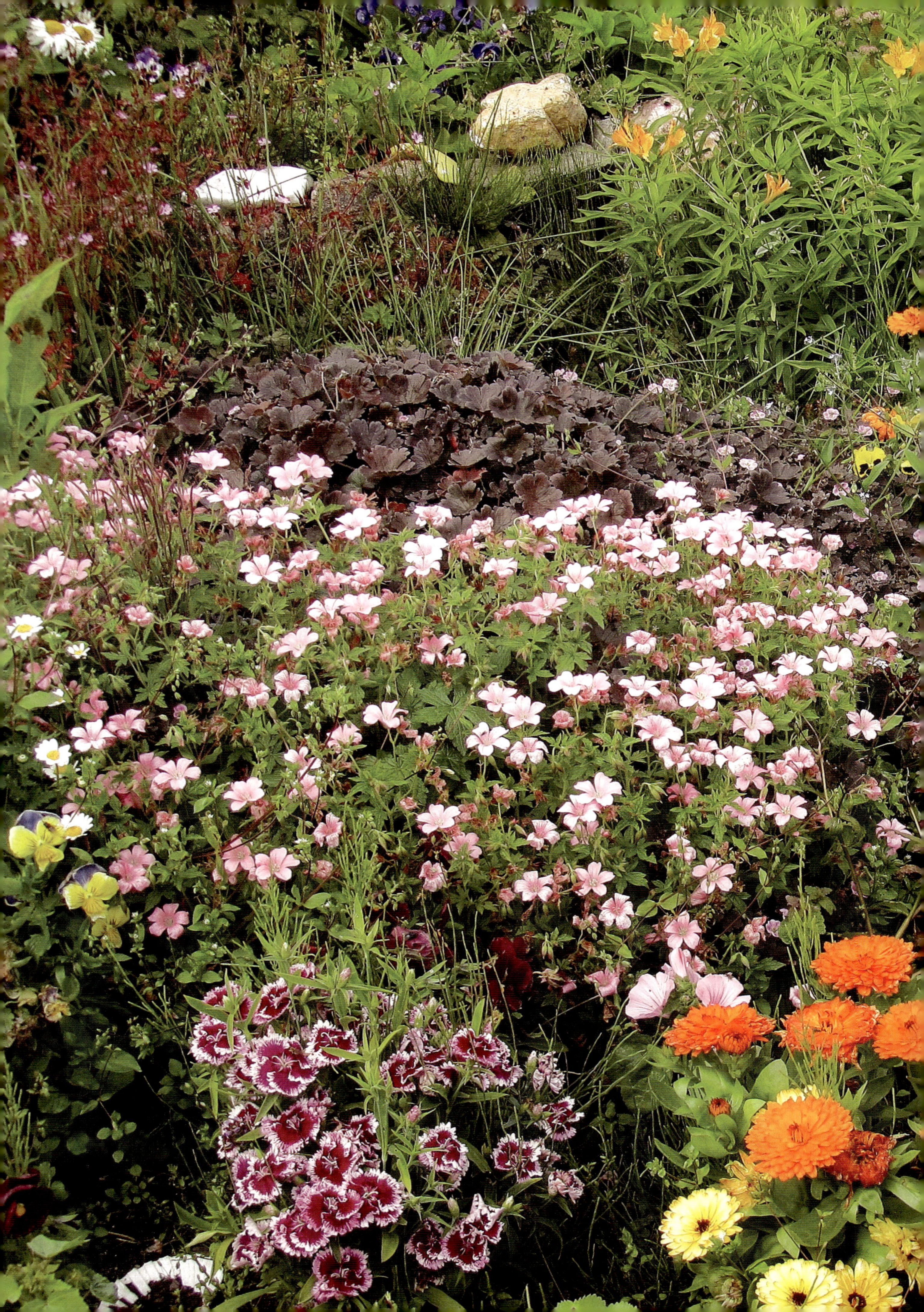

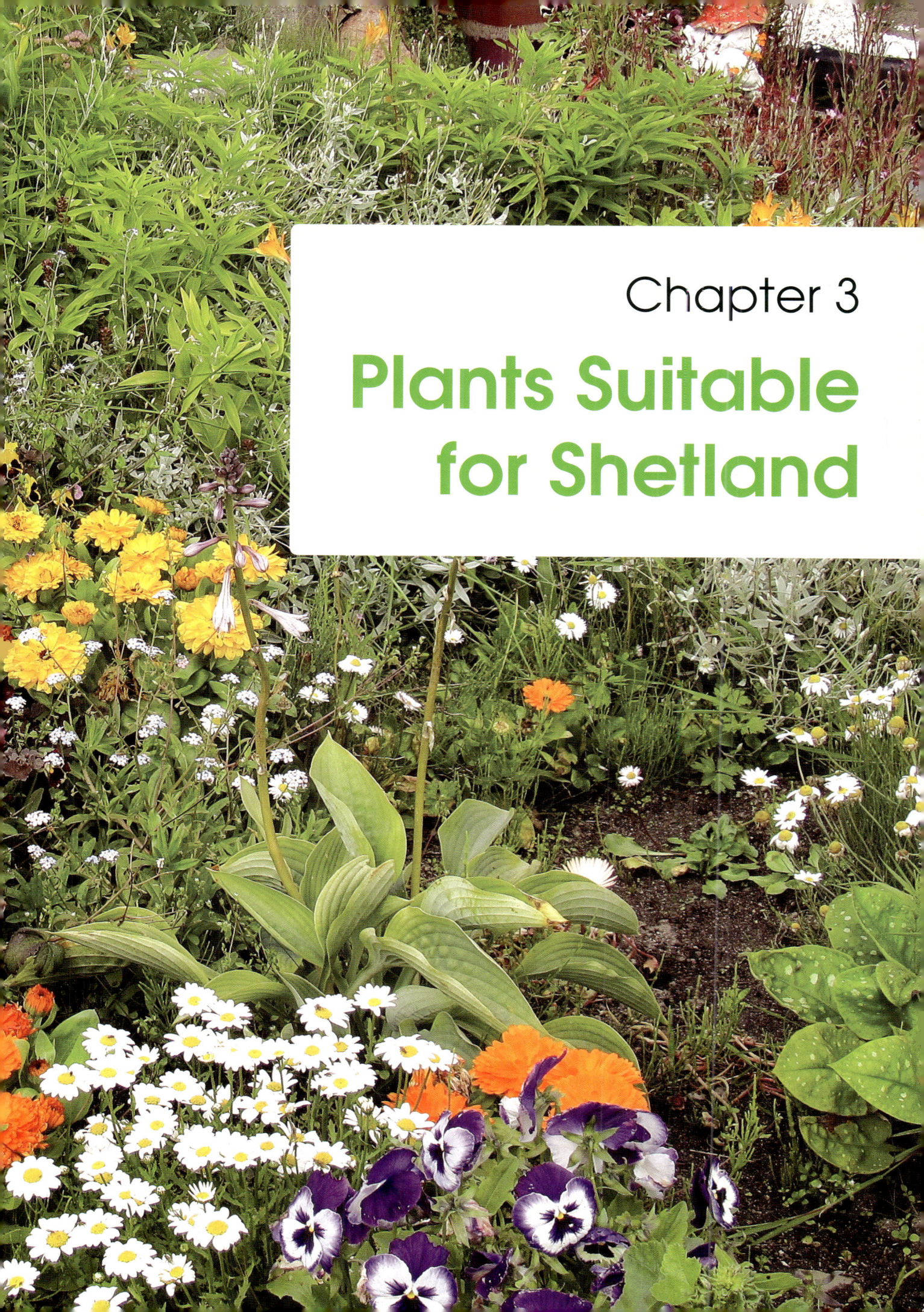

Chapter 3
Plants Suitable for Shetland

Introduction

Shetland's weather plays a part when choosing what to grow. Although the islands never get too cold, the reverse is also true. But the key feature to any island group sitting in the middle of nowhere is the prevailing wind. Dead calm days in Shetland are a novelty and certainly explain why the local windmills are so productive. Being a coastal area also means that the islands have higher levels of rain and greater humidity than elsewhere, being at its extreme when there is a week of fog in summer – and everything gets soaked. Providing you are not growing on the top of an exposed hill, tall plants can survive remarkably well though many people will opt for the dwarf cultivars.

I remember growing some beautiful delphiniums once and having to stake each individually, which rather detracted from their impact; they would have been fine at any other spot in my garden but I 'chose' to grow them where the wind funnelled – not very smart!

There are several plants where it is important to take into account water tolerance, e.g., the 'veined' type petunias are more rain resistant than the non-veined. Then there is the problem with the short winter days and very long days of mid-summer; the net effect being to give the Shetland garden a shorter season. Some plants need a certain number of daylight hours for flower initiation so I always choose (where available) the 'daylength neutral' cultivars.

As far as frost is concerned we get off relatively lightly compared to, say, the Highlands of Scotland where temperatures can dip below -20°C; at our worst it gets to -8°C, though in the winter of 2009/2010 temperatures did dip to -13°C. Nevertheless, frost must be considered when putting plants outside. It would be wise not to put the more sensitive species outside before the start of June; and be fully aware of the combination of northerly winds plus clear nights with the resulting chill factor.

So how 'limited' are we when it comes to growing plants in the Northern Isles? Bearing in mind that Lea Gardens contains 1500+ species and cultivars alone and the owner, Rosa Steppanova, uses virtually no annuals and bedding, you can see things are not that bad. Though the south of England may have a bigger range, there are many plants which thrive in cooler climes.

Before considering the different kinds of plants in more detail, I want to say a little about the symbol 'F1'. This is a genetic term used to describe an organism which has inherited favourable characteristics from two different parents. For instance, there are lots of cultivars of tomatoes; you will certainly have met cherry, beef, yellow, plum shaped types and so on. Tomato plants are susceptible to many root rots, but those with resistant roots do not produce particularly good fruit. If the plant breeder brushes the pollen from the rot resistant variety and fertilises the flower of the high fruiting variety, the resulting seeds will yield a 'crossbred' plant (or hybrid), hopefully with strong roots and decent yields. This must not be confused with a genetically modified (GM) plant. Every person on this earth is really a hybrid, i.e., the results of combination of genes from a different mother and father.

Without going into punnet squares and other genetic terminology, you simply cannot take the seeds produced by an F1 hybrid and expect to get more of the same – the plant is no longer 'true'; by definition an F1 is the cross between two named parents.

The consequences of plant breeding have been enormous right through the history of Man, leading to huge increases either in yields, colours, shapes and a whole lot of other features. One example is that of wheat where the yield has gone from 750kg (per hectare) in 1950 to 2750 kg in 2004. Increased milk production in cattle is another giant leap. Agriculture today is light years ahead of what it used to be. This is what makes the arrival of new seed catalogues so exciting; what have the breeders generated this season?

There are also F2 cultivars but the genes in these have been further 'diluted', and you do not get such a good plant.

Hopefully the above paragraph will explain why the F1 hybrids are more expensive, but, as they say, you get what you pay for. The F2 will give a show but the F1 'Wave' is in a league of its own. Indoor cucumbers are another example; in Shetland if you do not use an F1 plant with mildew resistance you are wasting your time, since after the first few misty days in summer your plants will look as though they have been sitting in a snow blizzard.

VARIETIES OF PLANTS WHICH HAVE PROVEN TO DO WELL IN SHETLAND

Part A: Annuals

You may find this strange but many people mix up annuals and perennials; they think that because 'The Broons' and 'Oor Wullie' come out every year, annual plants must do likewise. Amusing and understandable! To clarify – annuals are for one year only. And why are they so popular? They have a long flowering season compared to many of the perennials. There are a few tender perennials only surviving one season and they tend to be categorised as annuals, e.g., the modern cultivars of *Bellis perennis* and *Myosotis*.

*Below:
A lovely display of annuals in Lerwick's Jubilee park.*

Top:
The attractive and more traditional garden created by Ruby Gray from Skeld.

Below:
White alyssum – producing a wonderful perfume.

Ageratum. This is a very attractive plant but not popular. I personally do not like the white, but the blue gives a good show when fed properly. Do not sow too early – early March would be about right. With the aid of the growing rig lighting (see Chapter 4) I used to start them around mid–February. Commercially they did not sell so I gave up on them.

Alyssum (Lobularia). I adore the perfume alyssum produces. The white version is a tough plant with the advantage of being frost hardy, though it is still essential to put the plants through the hardening-off process. Alyssum is always best grown as plugs as they are difficult to prick out, and also prone to 'damping off' (see Chapter 9). 'Snowdrift' is inexpensive and attractive though you can get new cultivars such as the 'Crystal' series, which are described as being 'tetraploid'. You and I are diploid (we received a set of chromosomes from each of our parents); the effect of two extra sets of chromosomes results in a tetraploid plant with larger flowers and increased vigour better able to cope with a cooler climate. If you were an alyssum fanatic these would seem ideal.

Pink alyssum is more tender than the white, and I always hold it indoors far longer than the white prior to hardening off.

63

Antirrhinum (Snapdragon). There is little alternative to using the dwarf cultivars for the windy climate. F1 'Appeal', 'Chimes' and F2 'Cheerio' are reliable – all being attractive with a nice scent. The difficult part regarding antirrhinum culture is getting them to the pricking out stage; the trick is to grow them on the 'dry' side. Fortunately, in early spring watering is rarely needed. I do lose the odd plant, but probably no more than five per 1000.

Bacopa (Sutera). Since I raise all my plants from seed I am rather 'stuck' with the cultivars 'Snowtopia' and 'Bluetopia'. However, bacopa are primarily grown vegetatively from cuttings and amongst those available we get the 'Scopia' range, the double flowered 'Copa', the 'Abunda' group, all in a wide spectrum of colours. I mention this later in the book but you must ensure the plants do not dry out. I have seen this happen and overnight the plants drop their petals; you could not get a greater contrast of before and after. They are not too difficult to grow from seed, these being supplied as multiseed pellets.

Begonia. I used to grow a lot of begonia in the past and, though rather a long haul from seed, they do thrive. The seeds are small and the seedlings seem to hang around for a while, but eventually the roots get down and the foliage start to kick in. Be careful not to transplant shallow rooted seedlings too deeply. There are many fibrous rooted cultivars to choose from and they should all do well. As for the tuberous variety, the one to go for is the F1 'Non-stop' series. They really are as pretty as the pictures in the books. They enjoy decent light but not direct sun, from which they easily get leaf scorch. There can be a strong sun under glass even as early as March. Once they have reached a decent size then feed regularly with a weak balanced feed. I have also grown the cascading cultivars for baskets and had good results by doing likewise. Unless you have a lot of patience, you would be as well to grow begonias from plugs.

If you decide to grow from seeds then read the full cultural notes since there are a number of little pointers to be wary of, particularly with regard to feeding and pricking out.

Above:
A nice bacopa grown by Adam Leslie of Gott.

Below:
Begonia 'Non-stop'. They really are as nice as the photo.

Bellis perennis. Though I always succeed with bellis they can be difficult if conditions are not right. I find the watering rather tricky; I overwinter them as large plugs (watching out for botrytis in particular) then pot them up in early spring. There are some wonderful cultivars and I especially like the 'Tasso' variants, having less success with the 'Rominettes'. With proper high potcsh feeding they can look brilliant.

Bidens. I grew these many years ago, sowing at the start of March. The two things that I recall about them are that they were liable to stretching so were grown cool, and were unusually prone to greenfly. In Shetland these plants have been superseded by bacopa.

Brachycome (Swan river daisy). Virtually the same comments apply here as for bidens.

Calendula (Scotch marigold). What a cracking plant! Long seasoned and brightly flowered with the bonus that it is frost hardy and cheap. I have only grown the variety 'Fiesta Gitana'. They are a prime example of the expression "if it ain't broke why fix it".

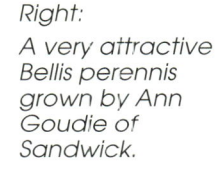

Right:
A very attractive Bellis perennis grown by Ann Goudie of Sandwick.

Below:
Troughs containing both calendula (at the back) and dahlias. I think this is a lovely combination.

Celosia. These are nice looking and not that difficult to grow, but really for a cool porch. Sometimes I think of them more as a novelty plant; those I grew looked less exciting than the pictures in the seed catalogues.

Chrysanthemum parthenium 'Santana'. I grew these many years ago, and though easily cultured, they came to be too late in flowering for a Shetland annual. Possibly they could be kicked into flowering by using artificial lighting. They were attractive but nothing to die for. Manipulation of daylength is a big feature of those commercial growers supplying the cut flower market, particularly with cut chrysanthemums. I now grow marguerites instead.

Chrysanthemum paludosum (Marguerite). A complex name but the cultivar 'Mini-Marguerite' should get some of you excited. I start these off in early January as plugs and keep them under the lights for several weeks. They are very early to flower and my 24-hour lighting regime initiates flower production. I wish the seed companies could provide a wide range of colours.

Chrysanthemum carinatum. This cultivar is called 'Bright Eyes', an attractive plant grown in Lerwick's Jubilee Park.

Cineraria (foliage type). An easy plant to grow and it looks good in the flowerbed when contrasted with something different. 'Silver Dust' has been around for a while, and I am attracted to the description of 'Cirrus', said to be weather resistant, dwarf and compact. Sounds great for Shetland!

Cosmos. Not such a well-known plant but I have sold quite a few over the years. Though tall, it is tough though I would not grow it on top of a hill. There are several cultivars including 'Cosmic' and 'Sonata'. I had much more success with 'Cosmic' despite it being four times cheaper. This plant thrives in poor soils; if the soil is too rich then the plant grows large with few flowers. I sow it around the end of March. Do not sow it too early, as it dislikes the coldness you get with an unheated glasshouse in early spring.

From top:

A nice display of Marguerites still actively growing in October in Helen Sandison's garden.

Chrysanthemum carinatum 'Bright Eyes' from Jubilee Park.

This shows how nice cineraria is when contrasted with a 'brighter' companion.

This beautiful Cosmos was growing in Helen Sandison's garden in Lerwick.

Right and below:
Just two of the dozens of Dahlia cultivars available for your garden. Both of them were grown in the central mainland.

Dahlia. All dahlias are, in theory, perennials, however some cultivars are treated as annuals. I particularly like 'Figaro', while Angus Nicol prefers 'Redskin' with its deep bronze green foliage. They are easy to grow but frost sensitive and need a longer growing season compared with some bedding plants. Dahlia interplanted with Calendula gives a great combination with both plants having the advantage of not needing sun to burst into flower. Sowing dates are critical with my 'Figaro' seeds being sown about the 10th February. I always find a few plants growing 'blind', i.e. with no buds, so always sow around 25% extra to make up for this. I give them a balanced feed weekly two weeks after potting up, and then twice weekly as market time approaches. Try to plant in soil with a good nutrient content at the beginning of June. Plants are sturdy and will not need support. They are very attractive to greenfly and positively 'haute cuisine' for slugs.

At the end of the season you will find little dahlia tubers sitting under the withered plants. I have never overwintered these to grow in spring but they should be viable.

67

Dianthus (annual). What a stunning group of plants with more and more cultivars being added each season, and a huge colour range. There are two species called *Dianthus chinensis* and *D. barbatus* (Sweet William) but what is essential for the Shetland climate is the **hybrid,** i.e. *chinensis x barbatus* – very tough. I have had great success with the cultivars F1 'Festival' and F1 'Ideal' series. You can grow these from a January sowing, but I prefer to start them off in August, prick them into P24s and overwinter them. In early spring I give the plants a good 'haircut', then move them into 11cm pots for June flowering. Growing these cool is a must. Grow on at around 15°C until they are nicely established, then the temperature can be dropped back to around 10°C. I feed them twice weekly with a medium strength high potash solution once the buds appear until they are ready to go to market. They are fairly pest free, with aphids the only thing to watch for; these only become a real pest once the weather warms up.

Dianthus caryophyllus (Carnation). I used to grow the annual variety F1 'Lillipot' but found it late in flowering, hence my reason for switching to the annual dianthus mentioned above. I do recall the scent being heavenly.

Gaillardia. The photo below shows a cutivar called 'Arizona Sun' grown in Adam Leslie's garden in 2011.

Left:
You can understand the great affection gardeners have for pinks. They were certainly one of my best sellers; this is one of Helen Sandison's bowls.

Below:
Adam Leslie's 'Arizona Sun'.

Gazania. Easy to grow but sun dependent, i.e., no sun no flower. Stick with the naturally compact F1 'Kiss' series; these do not need to be treated with growth regulators. I find it strange that Livingstone daisies are so popular locally yet gazanias seem to have a very limited market. I recall overproducing one year and a visitor said to me how much she liked gazanias. I replied "this is your lucky day, come back with a lorry". I had no problems with disease or pests. They are not difficult to grow.

Geranium (Pelargonium). This has limited interest locally but those who grow them seem to do well. There are many cultivars and most should be fine; I had little problem growing the more compact F1 'Video'. When germinating try to keep a constant value in the range 20-23°C, but on no account let it rise above 24°C otherwise you will induce thermodormancy (too much heat putting the seeds into sleep mode). Trailing types such as 'Summer Showers' are likewise easily cultured but sprawly. Many local growers bring their plants inside for overwintering, which is the smart thing to do and therefore the plant becomes a perennial. Geraniums are hungry beasts so need regular feeding to help them look their best. One problem is that they can become rather lush and sprawly, and many growers overcome this by using chemicals called growth regulators. For many cultivars the substance 'Cycocel' (Chlormequat) is normally used. This ensures a compact habit, and leaf zoning patterns also become stronger. I have used this in the past but prefer now to choose naturally compact cultivars. F1 'Video Mixed' has such a compact habit that growth regulator is unnecessary. In 2010 I tried F1 'Palladium' and it seemed to grow very nicely. One 'problem' is that cultivars are continually being improved so this year my main suppliers do not offer F1 'Video' at all.

You can use F2 cultivars if you want to save money but there are limited colours, flowering is later and you do not get such an attractive plant. I regularly see geraniums that have been passed down the various generations from Adam (husband of Eve); you know, the tall ugly looking plant, really just an elongated stem, with very few leaves or flowers, and having never been pruned. Throw them out. A plant freshly grown from seed is gorgeous in comparison.

Heliotrope. This is a tender plant and one to keep in a cool porch or next to your front door. The only reason I am including it is that its perfume is breathtaking. Sometimes it is called 'Cherry Pie' for whatever reason; they smell nothing like cherries! I grew them about 15 years ago and do not recall any problems with its culture. I love perfumed plants – but then I suppose everyone does.

Isotoma (Laurentia). These are stunning plants but with a very long culture period. Even when I was sowing them in January, there were not many flowers until mid-June. One year I sowed them in late autumn but they did not overwinter too well. This is a plant I will return to some day. Be aware that the seeds can be expensive. When you sow them (surface sown) do keep them in the dark for the first seven days then get them into subdued light till they emerge. I found that the pink was earlier to flower than the blue, though it was the latter I found most attractive. If you grow it, check the culture sheets for more details.

*Left:
Impatiens; I have completely forgotten what the cultivar was; there are new ones appearing every year.*

*Below:
Lavaterra 'Mount Blanc'.*

*Bottom:
Lavaterra 'Hot Pink'.*

Impatiens (Busy Lizzie). In a nice summer with decent shelter these will give a bright display. Most people in Shetland tend to grow them in a cool porch unlike in the southern UK, where huge outdoor displays are commonplace. One problem is that of petal drop leading to a lot of regular sweeping up. The cultivars keep improving and I have recently grown the F1 'Dezire', 'Expo', and 'Accent' series. The culture notes state "Keep the germinating seedlings moist at all times; temperatures below 21°C may cause tip abortion and seedling loss, above 24°C may cause thermo-dormancy of the seed". I grow my plants with little trouble keeping the temperature just a little above 20°C. I normally pot the plugs into 1.5 or 2-litre bowls and grow them reasonably dry, with very little feeding. This helps flowering and keeps the plant more compact. I found them to be both pest and disease free

Lavaterra. Lavaterra are relatively easy to grow, and I grew them several years ago. The two photos to the right were taken in the Lerwick Jubilee gardens.

Lobelia (annual). Well-grown lobelia is a beautiful plant. You probably know there are two types, the compact for edging and bedding schemes, and the trailing primarily for baskets and planters. Seed prices vary depending on what you want; essentially you pay more for the earlier flowering cultivars. For the trailing types I have found that the 'Fountain' and 'Regatta' series give good results, and for the compact types, 'String of Pearls mixed' and 'Cambridge Blue'. The compact group 'Riviera' are three times more expensive but flower up to two weeks earlier. They are not the easiest to grow from seed and hopefully my notes in chapter one will help you to succeed.

Mesembryanthemum (Livingstone daisy). These are tremendously popular in Shetland and with a good display on a sunny day you can understand why; the downside is that in a dull summer the flowers stay shut. They are easy to grow from seed, surface sown in clumps or as plugs, minding that you only need 15°C or so to get germination.

Top:
Lobelia baskets grown in Lerwick by Helen Sandison. I like the addition of the red agryanthemum giving an attractive contrast.

Right:
These Livingstone daisies were growing at the roadside near Weisdale. You can understand why they are one of my most popular plug plants.

71

Myosotis (Forget-me–not). I have seen some beautiful forget-me-nots throughout the more marshy parts of Shetland. The modern hybrids are radically different from the wild *M. palustris,* with groups such as the 'Victoria', 'Magnum' and 'Sylva' series being compact with tight heads of flowers. I found the latter botrytis-prone; 'Magnum' fared much better. Good ventilation is essential.

Nasturtium (Tom thumbs). Many gardeners incorporate these into their hanging baskets. Easy to grow; I germinate them on the floor of the grow room at a temperature of around 12-15°C. Prick them out as soon as they appear above the surface as the roots are extremely vigorous; P15 type cells or small pots will be fine to bring them on prior to planting in your basket. There are many cultivars though I just stick with 'Double Gleam Hybrids'. I would take care not to overfeed them otherwise they might grab you by the legs.

Nemesia. These are not the easiest to propagate, with the seedlings in particular being delicate little threads. However, they give a great splash of colour. I used to grow 'Carnival' mixed but there are many cultivars including 'Danish Flag', and 'KLM' – with the colours of Royal Dutch Airlines; presumably you get a buttonhole when you board the aircraft!

Osteospermum. These used to belong to the genus *Dimorphotheca* but now have been put together in a separate genus (*Osteospermum*) with around 50 different species. These produce big bright gorgeous flowers, but the seed can be expensive. There is a limited colour range. I have spoken to growers who have had very mixed germination results, though I was achieving 95% – possibly the seeds enjoy the steadier temperature found in the grow room. They certainly are pretty plants with some of the colours being particularly vigorous. Strictly speaking they are tender perennials but generally considered annuals.

Petunia. One of my seed catalogues has 16 pages relating to petunia cultivars, and the other one 12. I gave some advice regarding the sowing in Chapter 1. Most cultivars do fairly well and some are superb. For ordinary 'run of the mill' petunias one of the most suitable for Shetland's climate is the F1 'Storm' cultivar. Get those with veined petals; for whatever reason, the veined petal forms withstand damp conditions better. If you like the smaller flowered, more compact 'junior' types, you should be using F1 'Picobella' which stays compact without growth regulators; it produced nice bowls for me during 2010. Though I have growth regulators I am reluctant to use them, but if you are an obsessive petunia grower then the substance to employ is called daminozide (dazide or B-Nine); correctly used, this will produce more 'breaks' (i.e. shoots) helping to keep the whole thing more compact. One useful piece of advice I read was that prior to planting the plugs, you should immerse them in **feed** solution; this gets them off to a good start once in the larger pot. When you pot them on give a good watering to settle them in – this helps to give the plug more intimate contact with the compost so encouraging root growth.

I mentioned earlier that petunias thrive much better in a wet/dry regime, in other words let them dry back somewhat before watering; they have to be really dry before you lose them altogether. I would strongly advise the use of weak feed solutions (high potash) for every irrigation. Those of you who have been through Lerwick's town centre will have noticed the hanging baskets grown by Angus Nicol. These are fed at every watering with a dilute solution of the tomato feed mixtures A and B given in Appendix 7. How do I know? I made up the solutions! A particularly attractive feature of petunias is that they are relatively pest free; I have never seen a petunia with aphids yet.

Below:
One of Angus Nicol's petunia baskets growing in Commercial Street, Lerwick. Angus is a particularly good grower and highly sought after for landscaping.

Although it does not really affect Shetland growers, petunias are daylength dependent, with most of them needing between 10 and 12 hours light for flowering to be initiated; locally we are getting much more than that even by the time we get to early May. Petunias have a classification all to themselves, which I never have and never will understand!

Then there are the 'Wave' petunias. Each season sees the introduction of more and more versions; currently the ones available are 'Shock Wave', 'Easy Wave', 'Wonderwave' and 'Tidal Wave'. The last produces a mound shaped plant whereas 'Wonderwave' has a spreading habit. I have never timed these but the seed manufacturers quote the length from sowing to flowering as 'Easy Wave' 7-10 weeks, 'Wonderwave' 9-16 weeks and 'Tidal Wave' 14-19 weeks. With Shetland's limited season it would be best to use 'Easy Wave' to get maximum value.

One point to note regarding their culture is that the Easy Wave petunias require more fertiliser than is usually recommended for the ordinary petunias. Use a high potash feriliser at a concentration of CF 20 every other irrigation, or feed during every irrigation at about CF 12. This measurement of fertiliser concentration is explained fully in Chapter 5.

Ideally petunias should be grown on at between 16°C to 20°C during the daytime, which is easily achieved in a glasshouse even in Shetland. What might not be so easy would be to achieve the optimal night values of 14°C-18°C; an unheated greenhouse will fail in this respect. However, they will still grow at a (night) low of 10°C, which is not difficult to maintain in late spring – all that happens is that the crop takes longer to flower.

73

Salvia splendens. Some gardeners are keen on these and I personally find the bright red ones attractive. Sowing time is critical – too early and it struggles to develop in a cool glasshouse but too late results in losing some of the flowering season. I always sow the first week in April and use a daylength neutral variety called 'Salsa' (the scarlet form). Well-grown salvia is attractive and copes fine with Shetland's weather. They are salt sensitive so take care not to make the feeding solution too strong.

Above:
Another of Angus Nicol's petunia baskets growing in Commercial Street, Lerwick.

Left:
Salvias are bright and surprisingly tough in Shetland.

Tagetes erecta (African marigold). These are the types with the big pom-pom heads. Not too difficult to grow but relatively tender, so watch the frost. I would suggest you stick with 'Antigua', a daylength neutral cultivar. They can be prone to botrytis so you may have to spray if there is balmy weather. I would advise against sowing before the middle of March or else you will struggle with the cool spring temperatures; they certainly benefit from being grown on a warm bed initially, and this does wonders for root growth.

Top:
Sweet Pea cupid.

Right:
One attractive feature about all marigolds is that they normally produce a very even crop.

75

Tagetes patula (French marigold). There are so many types of French marigold that it is difficult to know what to suggest, but I cannot recall having any real problems. My most recent sowings include 'Hero', 'Bonanza' and the 'Royal Crested' series. However, if you are keen on these plants you must try the triploid cultivars, such as 'Zenith', and the very recent 'Sunburst' cultivars. As I said earlier, most organisms have two sets of chromosomes, in our case 23 from Mum and 23 from Dad. By tweaking certain cells, plant biologists have been able to develop a variety with three sets. This results in more flowers that last longer, are seedless, require less deadheading and are not daylength sensitive. They are big and bright, and one of my more popular products is to have three of these growing in a 1-litre pot. Regular feeding is essential but boy are they bright.

Tagetes signata (*T. tenuifolia*). This is rather like a tall, very small flowered French marigold. A few people like them but I find them difficult to keep compact, and they are very late flowering. I use the 'Gem' series. Seed is cheap and fast to emerge.

Verbena. Though I have grown these in the past I would suggest you avoid them; they are particularly attractive to greenfly, and often bothered with mildew though the 'Quartz' series are supposed to be mildew tolerant. There are other more attractive plants into which you should put your efforts.

*Below:
Triploid French marigolds. With decent nutrition they stay this bright all summer.*

Viola. In the Northern Isles violas are even more popular than pansies, partly because of their slightly earlier flowering time but also due to their compactness. There are two you should consider; one is called F1 'Avalanche' and the other F1 'Sorbet'. I sow the former in early autumn then overwinter them in P24 plugs ready for a spring potting into large bowls. The blues are by far the most vigorous but I have had mixed results with the others. This is typical of many flowers – once you start to breed away from the original true strain, problems can arise. The blue 'Avalanche' viola in full bloom is a lovely sight. The other form of viola, the F1 'Sorbet' is available in a large spectrum of beautiful colours. Viola culture is almost identical to that of pansy. Just to make life more interesting the breeders have crossed a pansy with a viola to give what is called 'Panola'; I have grown them but found they stretched somewhat compared to their parents.

Violas do particularly well in Shetland, with many gardeners appreciating their compactness. The cultivar below is a trailer called 'Avalanche'.

Viola × wittrockiana (Pansy). Where do you even start when it comes to pansies? There are so many cultivars and gardens without their presence are scarce. The hundreds of cultivars include the F1 types 'Matrix', 'Mystique', 'Plentifall' (a trailing pansy), 'Panola' (a pansy-viola cross), 'Purple Rain', 'Whiskers', 'Ultima supreme', 'Dynamite' and 'Joker'. All of these are good though the ones I have been recently using are 'Matrix' and 'Ultima Supreme'. The first is gorgeous, but the second that little bit earlier to flower. I shall not bother naming the F2s. Pansies take around 100 days from sowing to flowering, so if you sow in April, they may not be flowering until August which is too late; I sow mid-January and the plants come into flower late April/early May, just when the gardeners are looking for them. Seeds can be expensive but the F1s have a high hit rate in excess of 90%. Sowing and germinating is no big deal providing the temperature is kept around or just below 20°C. I initially grow them under the growing rig in P180 cell units, resting them on large heat mats to encourage root growth. Once there is a decent root mass I then insert the small plugs into whatever container I am using, grow them on till the roots have spread through the compost, then put them out to the cold frames. The cool conditions are a **must** otherwise you can easily end up with stretched leggy plants – you do not want to be using growth regulators if possible. Pansies keep going and going and have the advantage of being completely frost hardy, though you still need to harden off prior to putting outside. The plants are prone to root pests; if you have problems with these then you must either treat the plants with an insecticide drench (such as 'Provado' with the active ingredient Thiacloprid) or grow them in containers with fresh compost. The seeds do not store so well with approximately 10% decrease in germination with each successive season.

Sometimes I have to contact the seed companies for advice and a few years ago I had a query regarding daylength neutrality. The company I called said that as far as they were aware there was no cultivar actually daylength neutral – all pansies and violas being daylength sensitive to differing degrees. They agreed that 'Ultima' was one of the quickest to flower in late winter/early spring – under low light/short day conditions. The other series they recommended as being less daylength sensitive was the 'Panola' series being comparable timing-wise to 'Ultima' in their trials. They also suggested the 'Matrix' series as being one of the quickest flowering, large flowered pansy series.

Above:
A beautiful pansy grown by Ruby Ann Gray from Skeld.

Below:
A collection of pansy blooms.

Zinnia. The only reason I mention zinnia is to warn you not to even think about going there. I tried them for two or three seasons and did everything including taking them to bed with me, and still they perished! The damp climate here coupled with their susceptibility to various fungal pathogens proved too much, despite spraying them with a plethora of different fungicides.

These photos show two aspects of Adam Leslie's garden at Gott, which should inspire everyone reading this book.

Part B: Pot plants

The notes below give a little guidance regarding the few cultivars I used to grow. Some are relatively easy and others rather more testing

Coleus. Once coleus seeds have germinated and the first true leaves have formed you will know exactly which ones to keep. With proper feeding (high potash) you can end up with bright and stunning plants, but if the feeding or watering regime is wrong they will look terrible. Been there, done it! The cultivar I used was called 'Wizard'.

Cuphea ignea. An easy-to-grow novelty plant. It is the type of plant you just grow once, rather nice first time round but not leaving a burning desire to grow it again.

Cyclamen persicum. Now for something much more challenging! I grew cyclamen for a number of years primarily for the Christmas market and they were stunning, especially the perfumed cultivars. They are not easy but if you follow these guidelines you should have some success. Part of the problem is that they are a 'long haul' crop. The seed companies say that 'Laser' takes 26-28 weeks from sowing to flowering, with 'Sierra' being 30-32; I sowed the seed mid-March so as to generate a lot of growth during the brighter months, and could slow them down later to catch the Christmas market. I found 'Laser' had an emergence of 90% compared to 75% with 'Sierra'. When sowing, cover with vermiculite or compost and ensure the temperature does not get above 18°C – keep a thermometer permanently in place for easy monitoring. Use an unvented lid and cover with perforated black film so light is totally excluded. Emergence gets going five to six weeks later. Keep the humidity high even once emergence starts. You may need to spray the seedlings occasionally with tepid water to help the seedling slip out of its seed case. Prick the seedlings into medium sized cells – I found the P15 about right. Ideally they should be grown in a cool glasshouse whilst sitting on a warm propagator surface to speed up root growth. You will find each plant generates a little corm at the leaf base; do not bury this corm either when pricking out or potting up. Grow them on in the small cell until the roots are well developed, and then you can be thinking about potting up; this will be about eight to 10 weeks after sowing. Be gentle when you pot them up leaving about 1/3 of the corm exposed after watering in. I used 13cm (1-litre) pots though it takes a long season to achieve a quality plant. I contacted a seed company regarding feeding and they recommended I start with high nitrogen (2-1-1) once five true leaves had formed, and then move onto high potash once the leaves had "covered the pot". The logic here is that by using high nitrogen it encouraged leaf/vegetative growth and you can then encourage the plants to initiate flowering. Prior to this advice my plants did not have as many large leaves as I would have wished – and you need the leaf/flower contrast for stunning plants. I used slow release fertiliser in the past but due to its unpredictability I ended up liquid feeding for my last two seasons. I say a lot more about feeding in Chapter 5.

Grow them on rather dry but avoid wilting. Water early in the day to avoid foliage lying wet overnight. Excessive watering is disastrous, and **slight** midday wilting in hot weather is acceptable. Good ventilation is essential.

Above: This coleus is not too bad but there are some really ugly ones.

Try to maintain 18°C during seedling growth and transplanting periods, and then 12°C -15°C at final potting. With the combination of Shetland's cool summer and sensible ventilation it is easy to maintain this warm but not excessively hot temperature. Imagine the problems the growers in the warmer regions have in summer with cool grown crops.

As for pests and diseases, there were two key problems I have encountered. One was botrytis (grey mould) so I took care not to water late in the day or during misty periods, and always tried to have air circulating. The second was the vine weevil, whose grubs love cyclamen roots. I say more about vine weevil in Chapter 9 but the best option for the amateur is to use Provado as a vine weevil preventative.

You need to be keen and patient to succeed but the bonus is that once the season is finished, the corms will go on to produce flowers for many seasons. If you are determined to try these, then also refer to the culture notes. If I ever do cyclamen in the future I will purchase plug plants; small growers can never mimic the ideal conditions used by the very large operators who may be bringing on several million cyclamen at once. The only snag is that you will probably need to order a minimum of 100 plugs.

Gloxinia sinningia hybrid. This is a stunning plant and a fairly easy one to grow, needing plenty of light to germinate. You should be sowing them around late March/April. They will certainly brighten up a dull porch. Although they are perennial they are usually grown as annual.

Schizanthus. This is also known as 'Poor Man's Orchid'. I have grown them fairly easily in the past and though rather pretty, I tend to think of them as more of a 'novelty' plant. When I sent them to market they fairly flew off the shelves. They are prone to stretching so watch the temperatures.

Senecio cruentus (Cineraria). These are not to be confused with the grey foliage cineraria, and are beautiful plants giving a kaleidoscopic display in the heart of winter. The sowing time is critical since, if you do not get the bulk of the vegetative growth done in late summer/autumn, there will not be much hope once November starts. I sowed my seeds around the start of July and had good results with the cultivars 'Cindy' and F1 'Jester'. The seed should be surface sown, keeping the humidity high or covering with a thin layer of fine vermiculite. Germinate at a temperature of around 20°C and there will be emergence after five days. After three weeks or so the seedlings are ready to be pricked into P24s or F15s depending on the size of the plant. I potted them up into 13cm pots about the 10th August. Once potted, keep them at 8-12°C – cool growing conditions are a must, as is regular feeding. They are prone to greenfly so have a suitable treatment to hand. Avoid watering in damp conditions, and make sure there is plenty of air movement or botrytis will plague them.

Right:
Cineraria is a stunning plant but cool growing is paramount.

81

Solanum pseudocapsicum (Christmas cherry). I grew these about 20 years ago; I do not recall any significant problems with the culture but I did have a lot of problems with mice. I recall one crop full of berries – then I must have blinked for a few days and it suddenly dawned on me that the berries were diminishing by the hour. By the time I had figured out what the problem was it was too late. If you grow them, remember that the berries are poisonous, but not to mice!

Streptocarpus. Streptocarpus, also called Cape primrose, is a relatively easy plant to grow and will thrive in a cool greenhouse or conservatory.

Part C: Perennials

Let me state emphatically that I am not a perennial specialist; Rosa Steppanova, Angus Nicol and the late John Copland (who wrote the little gem of a book 'Hardy Plants in the North') are far more knowledgeable. This is one of the problems with being a commercial grower – you focus on the 'bread and butter' items. I shall probably get lynched for saying this, but though there are outstanding perennials like lupins, columbines and campanula, there are many I would never bother with. I find some downright ugly! Some can be very sparse with their flowers; maybe I am growing the wrong variety, but verbascum hardly knocks me over – such a small flower spike on such a large plant. And the *Ranunculus* genus – most of them are just glorified buttercups but that is probably me just being a Philistine!

Here are a few notes regarding some of the easier seed-derived cultivars I have succeeded with, along with my own reflections. I have said little about the culture; advice is readily available elsewhere. There are many plants not mentioned, especially those needing specialist growth media. Being a one-man business, I do not have the time to produce the many different types of 'composts' required. I know many perennials do much better with the John Innes soil-based types, but if a variety does not thrive in my regular potting compost I do not grow it again.

I contacted a technical advisor from one of the seed companies regarding some problems I was having, and the gist of the reply is given below.

"All the varieties you have said you are having problems with are those which like an open, free draining soil. You should look at growing in an alternative substrate like a 'John Innes' type; this would ensure water was not sitting in the pots. Another alternative could be to add a good proportion of bark or sand/grit to your peat substrate – this would open the compost up again and make it more free draining."

Above: Streptocarpus.

Here are a few general comments about perennials based on my own experience.

A number of basic species overwinter well outside in pots providing they have some shelter and are 'rabbit proofed'. These include *Saponaria ocymoides*, *Alyssum montanum* 'Mountain Gold', *Arenaria montana* 'Avalanche', *Cerastium tomentosum var. columnae* 'Silberteppich' (snow in summer), *Aethionema grandiflorum*, *Arabis blepharophylla* 'Rote Sensation' and *A. procurrens* 'Glacier', *Lychnis alpina*, *Veronica officinalis*, *Gypsophila repens* and *G. cerastoides*, *Dianthus deltoides* 'Arctic fire', *Uncinia rubra*, *Luzula sylvatica* and *Armeria*; pretty well all the sedums and sedges. It is vital that you have a good root mass built up over summer/autumn to better help the plant overwinter. (There is more about overwintering in Chapter 4).

Some do well from a January sowing such as *Saponaria ocymoides Delosperma sutherlandii*, *Heuchera sanguinea*, sedums, *Campanula carpatica* and *Campanula cochlearifolia*. Some of the larger campanulas need to be summer-sown such as *Campanula glomerata*, and *Campanula punctata*. It makes sense to grow as many as possible in summer then overwinter them in P24 or P15 plugs.

The following list contains many of the perennials I have grown easily and successfully using **peat-based** compost. As stated above, some of them, particularly the alpines, will probably grow even better in a loam-based compost.

Achillea (Yarrow). Easy to grow. There are numerous *Achillea* species and numerous *A. millefolium* cultivars, but one I did like was *A. sibirica* whose attractive leaves give a great contrast with the flowers. I had no luck with *A. clypeolata*.

Aethionema. I have grown the species '*A. grandiflorum*'. It was easy and looked good. I am not sure as to its longevity in Shetland.

Alchemilla (Lady's mantle). *Alchemilla mollis* is very easy to grow; the only drawback with the Alchemilla genus is that they only come in shades of yellow. I never rated these plants as anything special until I saw them sitting next to Weisdale church interplanted with potentillas and (perennial) geraniums. Rosa Steppanova designed this planting and it shows emphatically how important contrast is in bringing out the best in any plant. I found *A. mollis* 'Thriller' to be strong-growing.

Allium. I grew some perennial onions last year, including *Allium obliquum*. Despite growing well and looking good I sold none. I only found out after dumping them that they can be used as a garlic substitute. Drat!

Alyssum (perennial). Easy to grow and, despite yellow not being my favourite flower colour, they sparkle if you give them the occasional drench of high potash feed. The cultivars 'Gold Ball' and 'Mountain Gold' are strong players, though I had no luck overwintering 'Luna', and found *A. sulphureum* very erratic.

Anacyclus pyrethrum var. depressus. Very easy to grow but I can think of perennials with much more abundant flowers, e.g., the Shasta daisy. It is small and neat which might be to some people's taste, but the expression 'glorified lawn daisy' does come to mind! I would not bother with it.

Anaphalis margaritacea 'New Snow' (Pearl everlasting). This plant is easy to grow; in the proper context it can look good.

Anthemis. *A. tinctoria* and its cultivar 'Sancti-Johannis' is easily grown though rather tall. The former has orange flowers and is very attractive. I am not sure as to their longevity; they did not last long for John Copland. *Anthemis carpatica* produces white flowers but I found them rather thin on the ground (they always look better in the seed catalogues!).

Aquilegia (Columbine). This is a huge genus with some 65 individual species and goodness knows how many cultivars. The cheaper *A. caerulea* mixtures 'Biedermeier' and 'Dragonfly' hybrids are easily grown though I sow early to ensure a good crown and root system to withstand overwintering and guarantee subsequent flowering. There are some expensive cultivars available such as the *A. caerulea* F1 'Origami' series, supposed to be first year flowering, but unless you have sophisticated growing facilities and are willing to run up large electric bills for supplementary lighting, it is just not going to happen. Columbines are certainly one of the highlights of the perennial range in Shetland gardens.

Arabis. These plants are both easy to grow and attractive. The pinks tend to be less hardy than the whites and more susceptible to waterlogging; I have found *A. blepharophylla* 'Red Sensation' fairly successful with some winter protection, and for the whites I am fond of the evergreen *A. procurrens* 'Glacier'.

Arenaria montana. This has the double advantage of being both an attractive white flowering plant and it is easy to grow. You can get these as gold nugget (GN) seed.

Above:
Anthemis – some people just treat is as an annual.

Left:
Pink arabis in early spring.

Armeria (Sea pink). There are over 100 cultivars and they have come a long way from the tiny pink morsel found on the cliff edge. There are whites and various colours of pink, and one very attractive group of hybrids called the 'Joystick Series', which come in white, lilac and red forms. The armerias are easy to grow from seed, and their toughness makes them popular locally. They become almost luminous after a soaking of potash-based feed.

Aubrietia x cultorum series. Easy to grow from seed though its winter survival in Shetland is somewhat mixed, and certainly related both to soil type and drainage. I know of talented Shetland growers who cannot get them to survive at all, yet others who have positively huge masses of aubrietia in spring. I generally grow the 'Cascade' cultivars.

Calamintha. I have only grown *C. grandiflora* 'Elphin Purple' and found no problem. Although the flowers are not exactly out of this world the plants are nicely perfumed, being related to the catmints.

Campanula (Bellflowers) I should imagine everyone finds the campanulas attractive. I have a book solely devoted to them; the genus has approximately 300 species found worldwide and there are goodness knows how many cultivars. Providing you have time and patience they are not too difficult to grow. You may have to wait two to three months before they can be pricked out, and during that time they must not be allowed to go dry. Some books advocate sowing them in cold frames but then you have your slug problems – they can soon graze a campanula crop of small seedlings. I once was caught out like this with primula seedlings – with the larger slugs being voracious eaters. If you have the seedlings inside on a shelf in a cool area of the glasshouse then you are less likely to overlook checking them. The easiest method of propagation for some of them is to simply divide the roots and I have resorted to this if running low on a particular variety.

Right:
A nice campanula growing in Debbie Scott's garden in mid November.

Amongst the more popular ones is *C. carpatica* in its white and various blue forms; I normally grow the cultivar 'Pearl', being compact and quicker to flower. Then there is *C. garganica*, a pretty little thing with neat star-shaped blossom. To say that the species *C. poscharskyana* is vigorous is a bit of an understatement; it has large bright blue flowers, but does look a bit sprawly. *C. persicifolia,* has tall flower spikes and tends to be very late in flowering. *C. punctata* and *C. takesimana* produce large delicate stunning flowers but do need decent shelter from the wind. *C.cochlearifolia* (*pusilla*) is small and neat. This campanula gave me rather a headache when trying to prick it out, but now I just sow a few seeds per cell and grow them as plugs. I have never grown *C. rotundifolia* (Harebell). Most of the campanula seeds tend to be relatively cheap, though you have to ask yourself how many you want to grow.

Another positive feature regarding the campanula genus is that, bar slugs (and snails), they are pretty well trouble free, with no interest to greenfly. Apparently they can be prone to fungal 'rusts' – although if you maintain good culture the problem should not arise.

Catanache caerulea. I found these reasonably easy to grow but thought the flowers were rather disappointing.

Centranthus ruber (Red valerian). Easy to grow, with red and white forms available; I personally did not find them particularly attractive.

Above:
These pots containing the white form of Campanula carpatica were in flower in mid-July.

Dianthus (Pinks). Another large and popular group of plants – there are around 300 species alone. I have grown a few cultivars from seed and by and large found them to be easy. *D. deltoides* 'Arctic Fire' has to be one of the nicest and toughest. *D. alpinus* is a small neater plant and rather attractive, whereas the *D. plumarius* group tend to grow large and chunky. *D. spiculifolius* gives rise to fringed white flowers with a red eye, pretty but rather sparse. *D. knappii* is the odd one out with yellow flowers and, bar the novelty factor, not really worth pursuing. I adore the strongly perfumed types. There are thousands of species and cultivars and you could spend the rest of your life growing nothing else; remember I only grow the seed grown cultivars, but even more are only available as cuttings. I have a very attractive book called 'Perennials' by Roger Phillips and Martyn Rix, with Volume 2 dealing with late perennials; in the section labelled 'Dianthus' there are stunning pictures of some of the various cultivars including double-flowered pinks, single and semi-double pinks and modern garden pinks. Remember this group includes the carnations.

Digitalis (Foxglove). This is a genus of plants I have never tried but I have several friends who grow it regularly.

Doronicum orientale 'Little Leo'. I have just tried the one variety. It is easy and attractive if you like yellow flowers (which I do not).

Erigeron speciosus 'Azure Fairy' (Fleabane). I have grown this cultivar but it did not really appeal.

Erodium manescavii I found it easy to grow; it produces pinkish attractive flowers.

Erysimum. This is a 'new' name for Cheiranthus, the wallflower genus. I have grown two cultivars, one is *E. allioni*; the orange form is nice but has to be grown cool to avoid stretching. The other is *E. helveticum,* which is much more compact. Both have amazing perfume.

Right:
Dianthus alpinus is certainly not miserable with its flower display.

Euphorbia. I have grown some of these in the past but they did not sell particularly well so I dropped them. From what I can remember, *E. polychroma* and *E. rigida* were easily grown and I recall dumping surplus plants. I also mixed up the labels and Rosa Steppanova promptly corrected my mistake!

Fuchsia. Yes, you can grow these from seed but it is a long haul; been there, done it – but never again. Far quicker to take fuchsia cuttings; also with a cutting you know what you are getting. You are no doubt aware that there are thousands of fuchsia cultivars.

Gentiana. I tried various Gentian species including *G. sino-ornata* and *G. septemfida* with no success, but they can grow extremely well in Shetland providing the conditions are right.

Top:
A nice fuchsia growing in Adam Leslie's garden.

Above:
I found the leaf colour of this variegated fuchsia very attractive.

Left:
A fuchsia grown by Angus Nicol; spot the solitary greenfly!

*Above:
I found this geranium growing in the Jubilee Park. Cultivar – haven't a clue!*

Geraniums (perennial Cranesbill). I used to grow *G. sanguineum* with no problems. Geraniums form a large attractive genus; my key reason for ignoring them is that Angus Nicol was already growing them commercially.

Geum. I used to grow the cultivars *G. chiloense* 'Mrs. Bradshaw' and 'Lady Stratheden' with little problems, yielding yellow and reddish colour flowers respectively.

Gypsophila (Baby's breath). A nice looking plant, and easy to grow. I normally grow *G. repens rosea*, however *G. cerastoides* is compact and extremely pretty.

Heuchera. This is another large genus with the modern cultivars grown primarily for their foliage. I grew a few of these for many years, including *H. americana* 'Dale's Strain' and *H. sanguinea* 'Ruby Bells'. I cannot remember much about the former but the latter grew fairly easily; the reddish flowers were nothing to write home about. I am not sure as to their longevity.

Kniphofia (Red-hot pokers). I have grown *K. hirsuta* 'Firedance' and *K. uvaria* 'Border Ballet' in the past from seed but it is a long haul; much quicker and easier to grow from root cuttings. They are tough and popular and are found in many Shetland gardens. Some species are extremely tricky and need specialist treatment.

Leucanthemum (Shasta daisies or perennial Chrysanthemum). These are very popular and do well throughout Shetland. I have grown several cultivars but the two outstanding ones are *Leucanthemum* 'White Knight' and *L. maximus* 'Dwarf Snow Lady'. These are both dwarf growing to around 30 and 20cm respectively. They have a high germination rate, and relative ease of culture. Rosa Steppanova tells me the best cultivars can only be reproduced vegetatively.

Lupinus. An old fashioned plant making a great comeback and why ever not. Stick to the dwarf Russell 'Gallery' and 'Lulu' series, or the taller ones if your garden is extremely well sheltered. I mentioned earlier that the non-blue colours are less vigorous and tend to die out leaving the blues to maintain dominance. I also tried growing *L. arboreus* and *L. littoralis* but they disliked the peat-based compost.

Lychnis. Some of these are easy to grow such as *L. flos-cuculi* (Ragged Robin), but I did not find them attractive. I have also grown the cultivar *L. arkwrightii* 'Orange Zwerg' but it totally failed to overwinter.

Lysimachia. I have only grown one cultivar of this genus, the *L. atropurpurea* 'Beaujolais', and though the flowers were a bit tall, I thought they looked nice.

Mimulus (Monkey flower). Both *M. cupreus* and *M. luteus* are easy and fast growing. The watering is tricky since you have to strike a balance between having it too wet and too dry. A good root will overwinter with ease.

Papaver (Poppies). Many of the oriental poppies do well in Shetland and there are some wonderful strains available. I only started to experiment with them last year, and am experimenting with more cultivars this season. One particularly nice plant was *P. orientale* 'Royal Wedding', a stunning white with black centre. I recall with some amusement a story told to me by the chief gardener of the Lerwick parks department, Tommy Sinclair. He was showing me the latest blooms in Jubilee Park, when I noticed some poppies with large seed heads and I suggested (jokingly) that these looked like *P. somniferum* (the opium poppy). To my surprise he said "absolutely correct" and that he "had to chase certain characters out of the parks as they were removing the seed heads for processing"! Incidentally, *P. somniferum* is an annual.

Penstemon. A number of years back I tried several cultivars including *P. alpinus*, *P. heterophyllus* 'Zuriblau', *P x mexicale* 'Sunburst Amethyst', *P. x mexicale* 'Sunburst Ruby' and *P. strictus* – the germination went well but the plants only seemed to thrive in the tunnel. Rosa Steppanova cheered me up by saying they were not for outdoors in Shetland but rather a cool porch or greenhouse.

Left:
Unless you are really close to the sea, lupins are almost failsafe.

Below:
Mixed sedum growing at my nursery.

Bottom:
Sedum S. spectabile growing in Lerwick.

Potentilla. These are easy from seed; I grew some plants for a friend once and it was no big deal. These included *P. atrosanguinea* var. *argyrophylla, P. nepalensis* 'Helen Jane', *P. nepalensis* 'Miss Wilmott, *P. nepalensis* 'Ron McBeath', *P. nepalensis* 'Shogran' and *P. neumanniana (verna)*.

Primula. What a lovely group of plants. Many different kinds do well in Shetland and I have only tried a few. They are generally not difficult to grow, but are difficult to grow well! Ideally you want a plant with dark green leaves so that the flowers give the contrast. Always use primed or gold nugget seed wherever possible and watch out for slugs, vine weevil and aphids, not to mention botrytis. If you can achieve a decent growing regime with regular feeding you will be well on the way.

For many of them it is rather a 'waiting game' with the seeds and seedlings being very small. Those which have done well for me include the primrose *P. vulgaris* 'Arctic Series' (classed as an annual), *P. x pubescens* 'Exhibition Series' auriculas, the candelabras *P. beesiana* and *P. bulleyana* and their hybrids, *P. denticulata, P. japonica* 'Appleblossom' and finally (about butterfly sized at the moment) *P. viallii* which look not unlike miniature red hot pokers.

Saponaria (Tumbling Ted). I have grown *S. ocymoides* in its pink form, and also *S. ocymoides* 'Snow Tip'; the latter plant was disappointing. You need to ensure that these plants get chilled over winter (vernalized), otherwise no flowers will be produced.

Saxifraga. There are many types of saxifrage. The only ones I have grown are the mossy *S. arendsii* cultivars, in three different colours. They are slow initially, and you have to be sparse with feeding or else they grow like cabbages (which I discovered to my dismay a few years ago; it may not surprise you to know that cabbages taste better)!

Sedum (Stonecrops). The bulk of these are easy to grow with some attractive ones available. Those I have grown include *S. acre* 'Oktoberfest', *S. aizoon* (a taller type), *S. hybridum* 'Czar's Gold', *S. kamtschaticum, S. oreganum, S. pulchellum* (did not overwinter), and *S. selskianum,* several of the 'spurium' cultivars, *S. telephium* and *S. reflexum*. My favourite has to be the *S. kamtschaticum* with *S. oreganum* a close second. Some of them, especially *S. spuriums* cultivars, are as tough as old boots. In my library I have a book called 'Sedum; Cultivated Stonecrops' by Stephenson, which explains how to identify the 400 or so stonecrops in cultivation. Gulp!

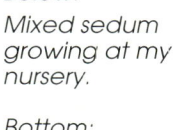

Sempervivum (House leeks). These are easy to grow and rather attractive. Do try to keep them dry overwinter otherwise they can fall prey to botrytis. Why on earth they are called house leeks I cannot imagine.

Silene. These are related to *Lychnis*. Some are attractive and easily cultured, such as *S. schafta*, and *S. uniflora*, which includes 'Robin Whitebreast'. Do not grow *S. caroliniana;* it is rather tender and dies with the winter wet.

Verbascum (Mullein). Easy to grow – I grew *V. chaixii* 'Sixteen Candles' and 'Wedding Candles' but as I said earlier, these give rise to such a small (though attractive) flower spike to be sitting on such a large plant. The plants come through the winter with ease.

Verbena. I have only grown the species *V. tenuisecta*; I recall it was easy to grow but failed to overwinter.

Heathers (Calluna and Erica). With my house sitting in the middle of a hill surrounded by miles of heather there is not a great incentive to grow them. However, they can grow well and look beautiful as my aunt Reneé from Scalloway shows. Although many types of heather must have acid soil, there are a number which do not.

Above:
A nice mixed bowl of house leeks.

Below:
My Aunt Reneé's splendid collection of heathers near the fisheries college at Scalloway.

Above:
Once you get close to heather flowers you can see how attractive they are.

Below:
Adam Leslie's attractive panorama of differently coloured grasses.

Grasses

I recall a few years ago sending out a questionnaire to various groups asking them what they would like me to grow. I had a good response, and amongst the suggestions there was a keen interest in ornamental grasses. Anyway, I produced grasses 'by the million' for the first few years, then demand dwindled. I have had some nice plants at one of my outlets but they were not selling. I toyed with the idea of amending the label stating "best smoked before teatime to have maximum effect" but I thought the better of it. Most grasses are very easy and amongst them I would include *Festuca*, some *Carex* (sedges), *Cortaderia* (pampas grasses), *Corynephorus canescens*, *Luzula* 'Lucius' and *L. sylvatica* 'Select' (Starmaker) and some *Stipas,* including *S. capillata* (Lace Veil, Bridal Veil) and *S. tenuissima* (Pony Tails). There are thousands of different kinds of grasses; they may not look very impressive individually but can give a very attractive show when strategically placed together

A synthesis of what perennials other Shetland growers have found successful

What plants do well in Shetland? I have already stated that the climate is too harsh for certain genera such as penstemon and rudbeckia. Many perennials will grow, but of course, if they do not overwinter they are really no more than an expensive annual. Shetland may be small but is no different to any other region in having a multiplicity of plant habitats, ranging from high and exposed to low and sheltered, north facing and south facing, sea swept and so on. Then we come to soil types ranging from peaty through the loams and ending up with, well, gravel. Though the pH is predominantly acidic there are pockets of limestone such as in the Tingwall valley. So virtually every location in Shetland has its own geology as well as its own microclimate.

I have contacted a number of friends who are keen gardeners and asked them what has worked for them. They were all more than forthcoming with their experiences, and what I have done is analyse what they told me and identify common themes and trends.

Following is a list of those who have contributed, alongside a small comment about their garden and its location. I have not included Rosa Steppanova from Lea Gardens since her book 'The Impossible Garden' contains a huge amount of detailed information relating to her own success.

I have mentioned this before, but if anyone asks me what he or she should grow I always say, "What grows well in your neighbour's garden?"

Do bear in mind that some of the species we grow in our gardens are already either native and/or naturalised here already. A casual glance at 'The Flowering Plants and Ferns of the Shetland Islands', by Scalloway botanist Walter Scott and Richard Palmer (Oxford), shows in the region of 15 different species of ferns, as well as several *Alchemilla, Alstroemeria aurantiaca* (Peruvian lily), *Anchusa arvensis, Digitalis purpurea* (Foxglove), *Tropaeolum speciosum* (Flame nasturtium), various *Poppies, Hesperus matronalis, Inula helenium* (Elecampane) and a number of the *Geraniaceae* (Crane's bill) family.

So in theory you should easily be able to grow all of these but in practice you may not, since of course it depends on the various environmental factors mentioned above.

John Copland (1914-1991). I visited the late John Copland many years ago at his garden 'Armeria' in Northmavine. I was a complete amateur then, but two things stood out, namely that he was exceedingly knowledgeable and also a modest person, a real gentleman. Since then, cultivars and cultural methods may have changed, but for many plants the same key rules apply. I have incorporated some of his comments as they are just as relevant today as they were in the past. His garden lies in a sheltered spot in the north mainland of Shetland surrounded by very large hills.

John was one of Shetland's first serious horticulturalists and did a lot of pioneering work with perennials. His book, 'Hardy Plants in the North', is a little gem, and one I often refer to. He also discovered two new varieties of plants unique to Shetland, which he named *Silene acaulis* 'Frances' and *Calluna vulgaris* 'Ronas Hill'. Frances is his wife's name.

Joanna Forsyth. Joanna is a very competent gardener and though her garden is at Semblister, on the west side of Shetland, anyone visiting the main street in the village of Scalloway during the last two decades would have seen the beautiful display just next to the Burn Beach for which Joanna is responsible. The garden at Semblister faces the north-east and is relatively close to the sea; it is a clay loam and quite acidic. At the top of the slope the soil is thin and stony but improving into a deeper, better quality medium down near the bottom.

Ruby Anne Gray. My cousin Ruby Anne lives in Skeld on the west side. There are a few houses sitting around a voe (sea inlet). Her house sits half way up a hill, having some shelter from the prevailing south-westerly wind but getting hit hard by the easterlies. She is a regular winner in the various country shows, which take place in autumn.

Ruby Jamieson. Ruby is a good friend and lives in the small village of Scalloway. Its main feature is a natural harbour and its own castle. Ruby's garden is situated in the middle of the village and consists of a number of planters and large pots, coupled with soil grown annuals and perennials. Her greenhouse is very small (about 2 metres x 1.5 metres) and is the most productive unit of its size I have ever seen.

Kit Mowat. Kit is a friend who obviously took her love of gardening from her father, the late John Williamson, who was passionate about and successful with growing fruit. She is based in Ollaberry, a remote area in the north mainland. I once recall giving Kit a few spare plants and she was positively bubbling with excitement; it is lovely to see spontaneous enthusiasm.

Helen Sandison. Helen has a gorgeous garden in Westerloch, Lerwick, with the advantage of a lot of shelter. She is particularly keen on pink colours, and her garden supports a very broad range of plants indeed. One day when I was having a cup of tea with her, she said, "Watch this", cut an apple in two and stuck the pieces onto two canes outside her living room window. Within five minutes there were several waxwings feeding voraciously; when you see them that close you know how they got their name!

John and Bertha Walterson. John and Bertha live in Scalloway right on top of a large embankment situated in the middle of the village. Their garden is spacious with part of it extending down the slope to the west and so facing the prevailing south-westerly wind. They have regularly won awards, with their garden having been continually improved over the many years they have lived there.

Diane Inkster and Liam Anderson. Diane and Liam are the gardeners in charge of the Lerwick parks Jubilee Park, sitting in the middle of Lerwick near the Town Hall, is an inspiration whether it is early in the year with the bulbs on display or later in high summer with bedding plants and roses particularly eye-catching. The park has a lot of shelter. They are passionate about their work and highly skilled in many aspects of horticulture.

Adam Leslie. Adam has the most wonderful garden sitting near Strand Loch at Gott, five miles from Lerwick. His garden is sitting on the edge of a low hill, but by planning it strategically, he has converted the hill stream into a feature running through his garden, and focused on shelterbelts from day one. His garden is testament to a huge amount of hard work. I recall speaking to Adam one day when he said, "You know, my garden is not really typical," and I immediately replied, "Yes, and that is why you keep winning prizes."

Left:
One view of Adam Leslie's garden.

The list of species and cultivars below shows some of what is available for Shetland's gardeners to experiment with. The plants below have succeeded for the growers mentioned before, and even if only half of the plants did well in your own particular niche, you would still end up with a very rich outcome.

Achillea (Millfoil; Yarrow). These were mentioned as being easy to grow and hardy by some of the gardeners. Amongst the cultivars mentioned were *A. millefolium* 'Summer Pastels', *A. millefolium* 'Summer Berries' and *A. millefolium* 'Cassis'. One grower had *A. sibirica camtschatica* 'Love Parade' growing well and not minding some shade. Some growers said they were easily grown from seed, but would need some support in more exposed areas. *A. filipendulina* 'Gold Plate' was found to be long lasting but likewise needing support. Another whose garden is not so well drained stated that as a result of a number of wet winters they had all died out.

Aconitum (Monkshood). Several of the growers speak highly of these, and say many species and cultivars do well in Shetland. John Copland said it "was so dependable that no old Shetland garden lacked it"; a common species is *A. napellus*. They would need support in more exposed gardens, and benefit from dividing every few years. The plants are poisonous so best not to have them for breakfast!

Ajuga (Bugle). This genus seems to do well with many species and cultivars being successful. John Copland liked *Ajuga pyramidalis,* and *A. reptans* has been mentioned. They tend to spread and make a good ground cover, but can be quite invasive. *A. reptans* 'Burgundy Glow' has spectacular colour.

Alchemilla. Is very popular locally though one of the gardeners called it a 'thug'. Another grower deadheaded the plants as a result of prolific self-seeding. Many of them do well including *A. mollis* 'Thriller', *A. alpina* and *A. robustica*. *A. mollis* is the common one which tends to self-seed.

Allium. Those doing well include *A. triquetrum* (apparently very invasive), *A. ostrowskianum*, *A. christophii* (Star of Persia), *A. aflatunense* and *A. moly*.

Alyssum. Many growers spoke highly of *A. montanum* 'Mountain Gold', while *A. saxatile* 'Gold Queen' survived several winters.

Anchusa azurea (italica). Good comments all round. The variety 'Loddon Royalist' lasts well but needs staking.

Anemone (Windflower). I know Rosa Steppanova is successful with many of the lesser-known anemones, but many of the growers have had some degree of success with *A. hupehensis (japonica)* regularly mentioned – said to be really good for autumn gaps. John Copland spoke highly of *A. blanda,* which is a spring bulb. Rosa likes *A. nemorosa* in all its many forms.

Top:
I thought this was a very attractive cultivar of achillea.

Right:
Aconitum are tall but yield an attractive blue colour; these were growing in the Jubilee Park in Lerwick.

Anthemis. The cultivars *A. tinctoria* 'Kelwayi' and 'Sauce Hollandaise' grew well although both were found to be short-lived.

Anthriscus sylvestris (Cow parsley). This grew well in Helen Sandison's garden in Lerwick.

Aquilegia (Columbine). These are certainly for Shetland, with everyone saying how well they did. Amongst those mentioned were *A. caerulea* 'Origami' series, *A. alpina*, *A. buergeriana* 'Calimero', *A. flabellata* and *A. vulgaris* var. *stellata* 'Barlow Series' to name a few. Most seemed to overwinter well, and for Shetland this is really the mark of a good perennial. Also giving good results are *A. vulgaris* var *stellata* 'Greenapples', *A. chrysantha* and *A.* 'McKana', the latter slow to grow initially but yielding large spurred flowers. One thing to bear in mind is their final heights if you have an exposed garden; dwarf cultivars include *A.* 'Musik' and *A.* 'Spring Magic Series', *A. flabellata* 'Cameo Series' (only 10cm or so high), *A. vulgaris* 'Winky' series and *A. caerulea* 'Biedermeier'.

Arabis. Many of the cultivars of arabis do well though it would seem that the whites are more vigorous than the coloured. Amongst those mentioned are *A. blepharophylla* 'Red Sensation' and *A. procurrens* 'Glacier'. One grower did well with *A. alpina* 'Snowcloud', finding it very hardy.

Armeria (Sea pink). The sea pinks are both popular and good for overwintering; one grower stated that the white form *A. maritima* 'Alba' did particularly well.

Aster (Michaelmas daisy). Some of these are not strong performers in Shetland with the consensus being that they cannot cope with the winters, probably due to the high rainfall, and can be very prone to mildew. Nonetheless, I have seen outstanding plants at Lea Gardens demonstrating how important it is to choose the correct cultivar. John Copland certainly sang the praises of *A. novi belgii* 'Alice Haslam', a dwarf variety, which he described as being 'faultless', but described many others collectively as being a source of great disappointment. *Aster* 'Alice Haslam' is propagated from cuttings.

Astilbe (Goatsbeard). These do well in Shetland with species such as *A. chinensis* var. *pumila* and *A. japonica* hybrids being mentioned. They prefer moist or boggy conditions and some can grow in half shade. Many hybrids are available in various shades from deep red to white; they can be divided every few years and benefit from a (garden) compost dressing.

Astrantia. This plant survives in Shetland although it is not well known; the cultivars mentioned are *A. major* and *A. maxima* (masterwort).

Left:
Astilbe chinensis.

Aubrietia. We get a mixed bag of results for this plant, with some growers struggling and others finding it overwintering really well. Once again the best remedy is to get hold of a plant and see how it does in your own particular niche. *A. x culturum* 'Cascade' and *A. deltoidea* are both mentioned. The blue cultivars seemed to last longer.

Bergenia (Elephant's ears). These seem to do fine although not very popular. One grower said *B. stracheyi* 'Sunningdale' had lasted for several years, growing in moist soil and half shade. Their large leaves catch the wind so need to be sheltered to look good, and vine weevil feed on the foliage.

Buphthalmum *B. speciosum.* (also called *Telekia speciosa*) described as being a very good performer, doing fine in shade; some growers could not get it to overwinter at all; it grows well in the Faeroe Islands.

Camassia. This lesser known plant is a true bulb and was apparently used as a food by some of the American Indians. Several species grow well in Lerwick, namely *C. quamash, C. leichtlinii ssp suksdorfii* 'Caerulea Group' and *C. leichtlinii* (the white form). Very worthwhile in early spring; the latter species flowers later and helps to extend the season.

Campanula (Bellflower). A popular group of plants, with many species and cultivars mentioned positively. The species doing well include *C. alpestris, C. carpatica, C.cochlearifolia, C. glomerata, C. lactiflora, C. latifolia, C.persicifolia, C.latiloba, C.portenschlagiana, C.poscharskyana, C.rapunculoides, C. rotundifolia, C. turbinata* and *C. trachelium* all mentioned. If you like blue you should certainly find something to suit your taste as many of the contributors obviously did. Once again, check the heights as they range from ground cover to three feet tall.

Carex (Sedge). Most of the cultivars of this group of grasses are strong players in Shetland. One grower stated that *C. coman* 'Frosted Curls' deserved a mention; another grew them in pots since some can be quite invasive and difficult to dig out.

Catanache. This plant can do well in Shetland but only in certain soil types. *C. caerulea* did well in Jubilee Park (in Lerwick) in both the blue and white forms.

Centaurea. Two species in this genus are mentioned regularly, namely *C. dealbata* and *C. montana*, the latter appearing to be very hardy. It particularly likes light soils where it spreads easily. They may require staking in windier locations.

Centranthus. *C. ruber* cultivars 'Snowcloud' and 'Pretty Betsy' are both mentioned as being successful.

Cerastium (Snow in summer). *C. tomentosum* overwinters well and is popular throughout the Islands. It can spread out of control somewhat. There is a beautiful 'fleece' of this plant hanging over one of the walls just when one comes into Scalloway – very striking! Benefits greatly from a good 'haircut' after flowering.

Chiastophyllum oppositifolium (Lamb's tails). Seems to do well in Shetland. I did grow it once from seed but it took two years before it started flowering (one and a half years too long for me!). One grower said it grew happily amongst gravel.

Coreopsis. Only mentioned here as a group of plants **not** for Shetland; several growers have tried and failed to get them to overwinter – enough said.

Corydalis. There was a favourable response here, with *C. lutea* the one to experiment with initially – it self-seeds very easily; also mentioned is *C. solida* in red to white shades, and the blue *C. flexuosa* which has a wonderful perfume, and can grow in most places. Rosa Steppanova describes it as a "wonderful genus for Shetland, one I am only just discovering".

Crocosmia (Montbretia). A group of plants giving a positive response, with *C.* 'Lucifer' (red) a strong candidate. One of the growers said that it "can spread spectacularly in the garden," and does well in the Lerwick parks. One grower stated that plants were best divided when the clumps become too dense. This seemed to help flowering vigour.

Above:
Though I do not like yellow, I was particularly taken with this corydalis in the Jubilee Park with its neat little flowers.

Left:
An attractive Montbretia growing in Joyce Gear's garden in Lerwick; this was the day after a severe gale hence its bedraggled look.

Dianthus (Pink). Surprisingly these were not mentioned by many of the gardeners, suggesting they are not as popular as you might think, or winter losses are high. Although I sell *D. deltoides* 'Arctic Fire' and *D. alpinus*, I shift large numbers of the annual dianthus – and these are spectacular. There is possibly a move away from perennials over to the bedding cultivars. There are lots of perennial cultivars to choose from. I personally find the winter hardiness of the *D. deltoides* very mixed, with 'Arctic Fire' the one sure-fire item, and *D. plumarius* a good second. One grower spoke positively about *D. deltoides* 'Vampire' as being very robust, with a striking red pink colour. Good drainage is certainly a factor affecting their survival.

Delphinium. Popular; I know some growers who have had great success with these and others not. They certainly do well in the Lerwick parks with the dwarf cultivars being chosen; the taller cultivars certainly need staking and prefer sunny locations. They can overwinter if the garden is well drained.

Dicentra. Widely grown with the two cultivars regularly mentioned being *D.* 'Pearl Drops' and *D.* 'Bountiful'. They can be a bit invasive but give fine early colour, and can cope with half shade. They seem to be quite hardy.

Digitalis (Foxglove). These plants are commonly grown with the *D. purpurea* cultivars being the plants of choice, including 'The Shirley', *D purpurea albiflora* 'Suttons Apricot', 'Pam's Choice' and 'Primrose Carousel'. The cultivar 'Candy Mountain' is not so tall and is easily raised from seed. They seem to do well in half shaded areas amongst trees. One grower had little success with *D. parviflora*. *D. purpurea* cultivars tend to be biennial and several of them will self-sow. One grower said that once the first flush of flowers had finished you could cut them away and get a second display, so extending the season.

Doronicum (Leopard's bane). Not popular; I found these overwintered fine – pity they look rather like dandelions! Several growers liked them since they were 'cheerful', giving a display in April when little else was happening; although very hardy they are prone to slug damage.

Echinops. Two or three growers mentioned these as growing well, it being a huge favourite with bees and butterflies. The variety *E. bannaticus* 'Blue Globe' had the praises of one grower.

Eremurus (Foxtail lily). The species *E. robustus* seemed to do well. *E. stenophyllus* was not so successful. These can be grown from seed or bulbs.

Erigeron. The one species regularly mentioned here was *E. speciosus* with the cultivars 'Azure Fairy' and 'Pink Jewel' being favoured. Some growers found they did not overwinter particularly well so you should experiment with one or two initially.

Erodium (Heron's bill). John Copland said a lot about these in his book and spoke highly of *E. chrysantha*, *E. macradenum*, *E. manescavii* (which I have easily grown from seed) and *E. reichardii*.

Eryngium (Sea holly). These are popular, with the species *E. alpinum*, *E. agavifolium*, *E. bourgatii* and *E. variifolium* all mentioned. Seem to do better in sunny locations.

Erysimum. Cultivars include 'Jenny Brook', 'Constant Cheer' and 'Bowles Mauve'.

Euphorbia (Spurge). John Copland was keen on these, and I know Rosa Steppanova grows several species. I grew several one year but they carried little interest. One grower had good results with *E. amygdalciaes* 'Robbiae' and *E. x martini*.

Francoa sonchifolia. Reliable, showy and apparently easy to grow.

Gaillardia. Only mentioned here as one group of plants **not** to bother with.

Gentiana. On a recent visit to Lea Gardens I saw some stunning gentians in full flower. Rosa Steppanova said she has had them in her garden for around 30 years. She said they were not that difficult to grow, with the G. sino-ornata revelling in damp peaty soil and one of the few plants to flower into November.

Geranium (Cranesbill). One grower said to me, "All are popular and do well in Shetland." That matches what Angus Nicol says – he is a keen advocate. Amongst the species mentioned are G. sanguineum, G. psilostemon, G. macrorrhizum, and G. phaeum and G. subcaulenscens,. Amongst the cultivars mentioned there are G. 'Orion', G. pratense 'Striatum (Splish-splash)', 'Mrs. Kendall Clark', G. x cantabrigiense 'St. Ola', Geranium x riversleaianum 'Mavis Simpson' and 'Russel Prichard', Geranium cinereum 'Ballerina', 'Lawrence Flatman', G. sanguineum 'Max Frei' and goodness knows how many more. They can range from ground cover to alpines, up to tall bushy plants.

Geum. This is a popular genus, with G. chiloense 'Mrs. Bradshaw' and 'Lady Stratheden' mentioned most frequently, with the consensus being that it overwinters fine; does best in sunny positions with moist soil. G. rivale (a Shetland native) and G. coccineum are also mentioned. One grower found G. 'Oranges and Lemons' a long lasting plant with the advantage of flowering in its first year.

I photographed these gorgeous gentians at Lea Gardens in October 2011. The darker plant (above) is Gentiana sino-ornata and the lighter one (top) Gentiana 'Strathmore'.

Gunnera. A less well-known genus but the species *G. manicata* with its huge leaves does well in Shetland. Apparently they are having serious problems with the invasiveness of some other species in Ireland and 'gangs of people' are involved in clearing large areas where it is a problem.

Helleborus. These seem to grow well in woodland type gardens and seem quite hardy. They are long flowering from late winter into spring. Those mentioned include *H. orientalis* hybrids, *H. niger* (Xmas rose) and *H. corsicus*. One grower said that *H. niger* only yielded four or five flowers around Christmas time, though Rosa Steppanova said this was the result of the plants being starved (she mulches her plants with peat/wood ash which supplies potash).

Hesperis matronalis (Sweet rocket). Several growers have mentioned this less well-known plant; it is very hardy. It releases a wonderful perfume, especially in the evening, and comes in both the pink and white forms.

Heuchera. Some are grown for their foliage and some for their flowers. Those doing well include *H. americana* 'Melting Fire' and *H. sanguinea*. One grower liked the cultivar 'Purple Petticoat' in particular; another mentioned 'Metallica'. This is another plant favoured by vine weevils.

Hosta. Many of these are popular and do well in Shetland. There is one outside our bedroom window and it has emerged from its winter sleep for many years now. They are prone to slug damage. They do best in moist soil with a bit of shade.

Iberis (Candytuft). Those spoken about favourably include the species *I. aurosica* and *I. sempervirens*. I personally never found them looking as attractive as the pictures in the books.

Incarvillea. I tried *I. delavayi* 'Deli Rose' and *I. mairei* without success. Rosa Steppanova said that this plant is better being grown hard and slow in a free draining compost (including grit and vermiculite), and she has ancient plants still growing strong and flowering freely. They have taproots like carrots and take a number of years to reach flowering size.

Inula. Spoken about favourably including *I. orientalis* 'Grandiflora' and *I. ensifolia*, with the very tall *I. helenium* found growing wild in places. There are nice ones in the Weisdale community garden. *I. hookeri* is also mentioned as being a reliable hardy plant with striking yellow flowers.

Iris. The following species were mentioned positively: *I. chrysographes*, *I. sibirica*, *I. pumila* and *I. setosa*. One grower said that *I. reticulata*, of which there are several cultivars, gave very early spring flowering from the bulb. There are many more which could have been included.

Knautia macedonica. One grower said this was a very hardy plant that seems to do well in Shetland.

Kniphofia (Red hot poker). Spoken highly of by many of the gardeners. After a few years they can be divided to increase the stock. Smaller cultivars include *K. hirsuta* 'Traffic Lights' and *K.* 'Flamenco'

Lamium. When someone describes these as 'thugs' you know they do well locally! One grower tried the cultivar *L. maculatum* 'White Nancy' successfully. Another said that with hindsight it would not have been grown at all in her garden. Seem to do better with some shading.

Lavendula. Nice plant and smells great, but take inside for overwintering; Rosa Steppanova told me she manages to get *L. stoechas* ('French lavender') to survive outside; very good winter drainage is needed.

Leucanthemum (Shasta daisy). These are popular plants, with *L vulgare* 'White Knight' and *L. x superbum* cultivars 'Alaska' and 'Crazy Daisy' being mentioned as long lasting. Shasta daisies are found all over Shetland.

Linaria (Toadflax). These seem to be popular, with *L. purpurea* and *L. alpina* all doing well. I once grew *L. aeruginea* very easily from seed but it was sold and I am unsure as to how well it did.

Lupinus. Great plant; regaining popularity – stick to the dwarf *Russell* cultivars 'Gallery' and 'Lulu'.

Lychnis. *L. coronaria* and *L. coronaria* 'Alba' are both mentioned as being easy to grow, being vigorous and good in dry shaded locations. Another grower spoke highly of *L. chalcedonica*, describing it as being very hardy.

Meconopsis. The two popularly mentioned are *M. cambrica* (the Welsh poppy), and the china blue *M. betonicifolia*. It is vital with the former to dead head before the seeds mature, as it is a prolific spreader.

Mimulus (Monkey flower). These are bright, moisture loving plants. The two most successful species are *M. cupreus* and *M. luteus*. Very often you will find stragglers growing wild in Shetland, presumably their owners were fed up with them so threw them out. One grower found the variety *M. luteus* 'Malibu Orange' to be very hardy.

Monarda didyma (Bergamot). This is easily grown from seed and will last several seasons but the flowering depends on the weather.

Myosotis (Forget-me-not). The wild forget-me-not, *M. scorpioides*, is common; there is always a nice crop near the head of the Weisdale Voe. There were mixed comments regarding the modern types, but John and Bertha Walterson said they found the cultivars 'Blue Sylva' and 'Magnum' very hardy, though I found them rather prone to botrytis; possibly there was not enough air movement through my crop. It is a pity that the wild *scorpioides* is so sprawly when grown from seed.

Nerine. These are grown from bulbs and very attractive additions to the garden.

Nepeta (Catnip). Some of these grow well but make sure you like the perfume and do not have cats; John Copland spoke highly of *Nepeta racemosa* (originally *mussinii*), which is totally hardy and flowering over a long period.

Osteospermum. This was mentioned by one of the Lerwick growers who said that the species *O. jucundum* (African daisy) was very hardy; it must not be confused with the annual plant *Dimorphotheca* (also called 'Star of the Veldt').

Left:

Angus Nicol grew this nerine.

Oxalis. One grower mentioned the Chilean oxalis *O. adenophylla*, and John Copland spoke highly of *O. floribunda* and *O. enneaphylla*. These plants are all grown from bulbs.

Papaver. These do well and are very popular, though there could be a lot of room for experimenting with new cultivars. *P. orientale* is available in a number of single and mixed colours; these plants are very hardy and long-lived. Amongst the variety of others mentioned are *P. alpinum*, and *P. rupifragum* which John Copland sang the praises of.

Penstemon. Another group of plants **not** to bother with; not for Shetland.

Persicaria (Knotweed). The one mentioned here is the species *P. affine*, with one grower being fond of the cultivars 'Donald Lowndes', and another finding 'Darjeeling Red' as being very hardy; just out of interest this genus is related to the common dock.

Physalis. Helen Sandison in Lerwick grew *P. alkekengi* successfully "in a container to restrict its rapid spread".

Polemonium (Jacob's ladder). These get a good set of reports, in particular *P. caeruleum* in its various colours such as 'White Pearl' and 'Blue Pearl', as does *P. carneum*. They seem to be very hardy with a tendency to self-seed all over the place. One grower mentioned *P. yezoense* 'Purple Rain' as being a strong grower with nice purple leaves.

Potentilla. These are found in many Shetland gardens. Amongst the more popular are *P. crantzii*, *P. megalantha*, and various cultivars of *P. nepalensis* including 'Miss Willmott', 'Ron McBeath', and *P. x tonguei* 'Yellow Queen'.

Primula. A very large number of primula do well locally, not a together surprising since some are most happy with wet feet. I shall not mention all the species and cultivars but amongst the successful ones are *P. acaulis* (the Arctic series are as tough as they come), the *P. elatior* hybrids (polyanthus), *P. auricula*, as well as *P. beesiana*, *P. bulleyana*, *P. x bulleesiana* *P. japonica*, *P. pulverulenta*, (candelabras), *P. denticulata*, *P. integrifolia*, *P. juliae*, *P. luteola*. *P. prolifera*, *P. x pubescens* (auricula strain), *P. rosea* and *P. veris*. I have grown many of these from seed; they start off small but steadily come away. You have to take great care not to let them dry out – not easy if you happen to start them off in summer. One grower said the flowers were attractive to wild birds. And watch the slugs!

Pulmonaria (Lungwort). Constantly mentioned is *P. officinals* 'Cambridge Blue Group'. It is very hardy and dependable, and apparently favoured by bumble bees. The foliage gives a very nice contrast with selected plants.

Pulsatilla vulgaris. Rosa Steppanova told me that these need a lime rich soil as a suitable growing media, hence the failure to thrive with me.

Ranunculus (Buttercup). Has no appeal for me but one noted was *R. aconitifolius* 'Flore Pleno' ('Bachelor's buttons'), a popular old garden plant, and which Rosa Steppanova said could only be propagated by division. Another species mentioned is *R. gramineus*.

Rosmarinus. The species *R. officinalis* does grow but needs to be protected over the winter.

Rudbeckia. Another one not to bother with in Shetland; Rosa Steppanova said that 'Goldstrum' needs long warm summers to be truly perennial and then dislikes the winter wet. She has never managed to keep them more than a year or two.

Saponaria (Soapwort). *S. ocymoides* is one species which could do well depending on your location, being very hardy and low growing. Another is *S. officinalis* although it can be a bit invasive. Make sure it has good drainage and is in a sunny position; give it a good haircut in autumn.

Saxifraga. Very popular. The *arendsii* cross in its various colours is easy to grow though a little patience is needed. It prefers decent drainage and good light. Another one cited as doing well is the Shetland native *S. oppositifolia*. If you are keen on saxifrages then I recommend that you read the information in John Copland's book.

Scabiosa. A mixed bag here with varied success, though they seem to do well in Lerwick.

Schizostylis coccinea. This plant is grown more easily from the bulb; one grower found that *S. coccinea* cultivars were very hardy and robust, preferring sun and moist soil.

Sedums (Stonecrop). I have already mentioned many from my own experiences. My gardening colleagues mentioned the following: S. *acre* 'Oktoberfest', *S. aizoon* (a taller type), S. *album*, S. *cauticola*, S. *dasyphyllum*, S. *hybridum* 'Czar's Gold', S. *kamtschaticum*, S. *middendorffianum*, S. *oreganum*, S. *selskianum*, S. *spathulifolium*, several of the forms of 'S. *spurium*', S. *telephium* and S. *reflexum*. Many do well in the rock garden thriving even in very thin soils. One grower particularly liked the 'ice plant', S. *spectabile*. I mentioned S. *pulchellum* earlier, which did not overwinter for me.

Sidalcea. Some good reports for these flowers with S. *candida* 'Bianca', S. *malviflora* hybrids 'Purpetta' and 'Rosanna' strong growing and thriving in some Shetland gardens.

Silene. Some of the silene group grow well and those mentioned are: S. *maritima* 'Robin whitebreast', S. *acaulis* (moss campion), S. *schafta* and S. *uniflorum*.

Sisyrinchium augustifolium. Also called 'Blue eyed grass' and said to grow well. One grower who became so fed up with their self-seeding said, "they are now confined to growing through the garden paths".

Solidago. Favourable reports. Tough and hardy.

Stachys. Some of those doing well include *S. macrantha* (Grandiflora) which can be almost rampant in some gardens; Rosa Steppanova speaks highly of *S. macrantha* 'Robusta', *S. officinalis* 'Rosea' and *S. officinalis* 'Superba'. Another grower also did well with the latter; this is a shorter plant, growing around 30cm tall, unlike the taller 40-45cm, *S. macrantha*.

Tanacetum. The classification of these plants seems to overlap with the Chrysanthemum and is a bit confusing. *T. haradjanii* did well for Helen Sandison, and *T. densum* ssp *amani* for John Copland. They are tough with decent drainage (in winter) being the key ingredient for their survival.

Thalictrum. *T. aquilegifolium* (meadow rue) was mentioned by one grower, being hardy once fully grown.

Thymus. Thyme seems to thrive with the species *T. serpyllum* (wild thyme) spoken highly of. Prefers good drainage and a sunny location. Adored by bees.

Tiarella (Foamflower). Helen Sandison has succeeded with the variety *T. polyphylla* 'Filligran'. I have never heard of it before!

Trollius. This is a popular and reliable group with the following all seeming to do well; *T.* x *hybridus*, *T. chinensis* 'Golden Queen', *T.* x *cultorum* 'Orange Globe' and *T. pumilus*. They are all part of the buttercup family.

Tropaeolum speciosum. One or two growers seemed to find that this creeper did well for them; one complained that it "never appeared where it was planted but turned up some distance away". Another said not to plant too deeply and give it some shade. It can be difficult to establish.

Veronica. There was positive feedback with regard to the species *V. gentianoides*, *V. officinalis*, *V. prostrata* and *V. spicata*.

Viola. This group seemed to yield mixed results with one of the growers finding *V. cornuta* such a vigorous plant that "it could be overly", while others found it very short lived. Some are easy to culture, and I had no problems growing *V. soraria* from Jelitto gold nugget seeds. Rosa Steppanova said that *V. odorata* is best grown in a cool greenhouse since it does not thrive outdoors in Shetland.

Taking Cuttings

This is a great way to increase perennials, as the best cultivars do not come true from seed. This is dealt with later on in Chapter 10, Appendix 9

Below:
A very attractive rhododendron, 'Linda', grown at Frakkafield.

Trees and shrubs

Despite my own fairly large garden having lots of trees and shrubs present, these are types of plants I know little about. However, those doing really well for me (and in other areas of Shetland) include the trees *Salix udensis* 'Sekka' (the Dragon willow), the poplar *Populus trichocarpa* 'Black cottonwood' and *Alnus sinuata* (Sitka alder).

The Dragon willow is so easy to grow from cuttings, is vigorous and dense, and has the most attractive bright green leaves, contrasting with a reddish stem. It also has a strange feature in having flattened or 'fasciated' stems. This is a brilliant plant for shelter and has a long season of leaf presence.

The poplar Black cottonwood is also easy to grow from cuttings and yields a tall chunky tree containing a wonderful smelling aromatic resin, which fills the air especially during summer evenings. It has the advantage of being fairly rabbit proof – presumably they do not like the sticky resin found in the bark.

The Sitka alder is fast growing and just looks really good; it has the advantage of coping well in moist soils.

Artemisia abrotanum. This shrub is the well-known Southernwood found in many Shetland gardens. When the leaves are squashed they release a very sweet perfume. I recall bushes of these around our house at Baillister when we moved to live here in the 1970s. This silver foliage plant does well in drained soil and facing the sun.

Above: Dragon willow grown in my garden.

*Right:
A nice bacopa grown by Adam Leslie. The attractive blossom indicates careful watering.*

109

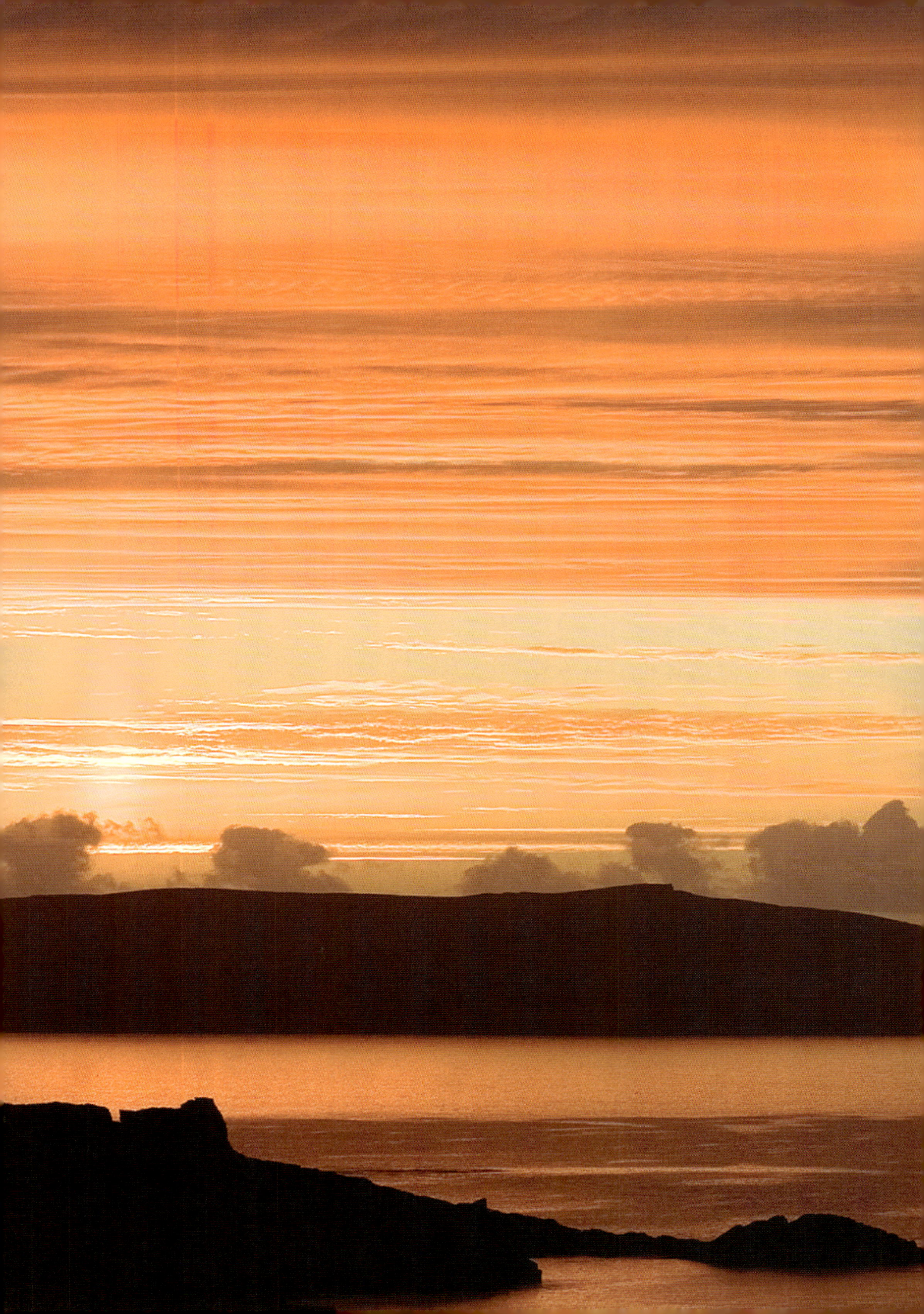

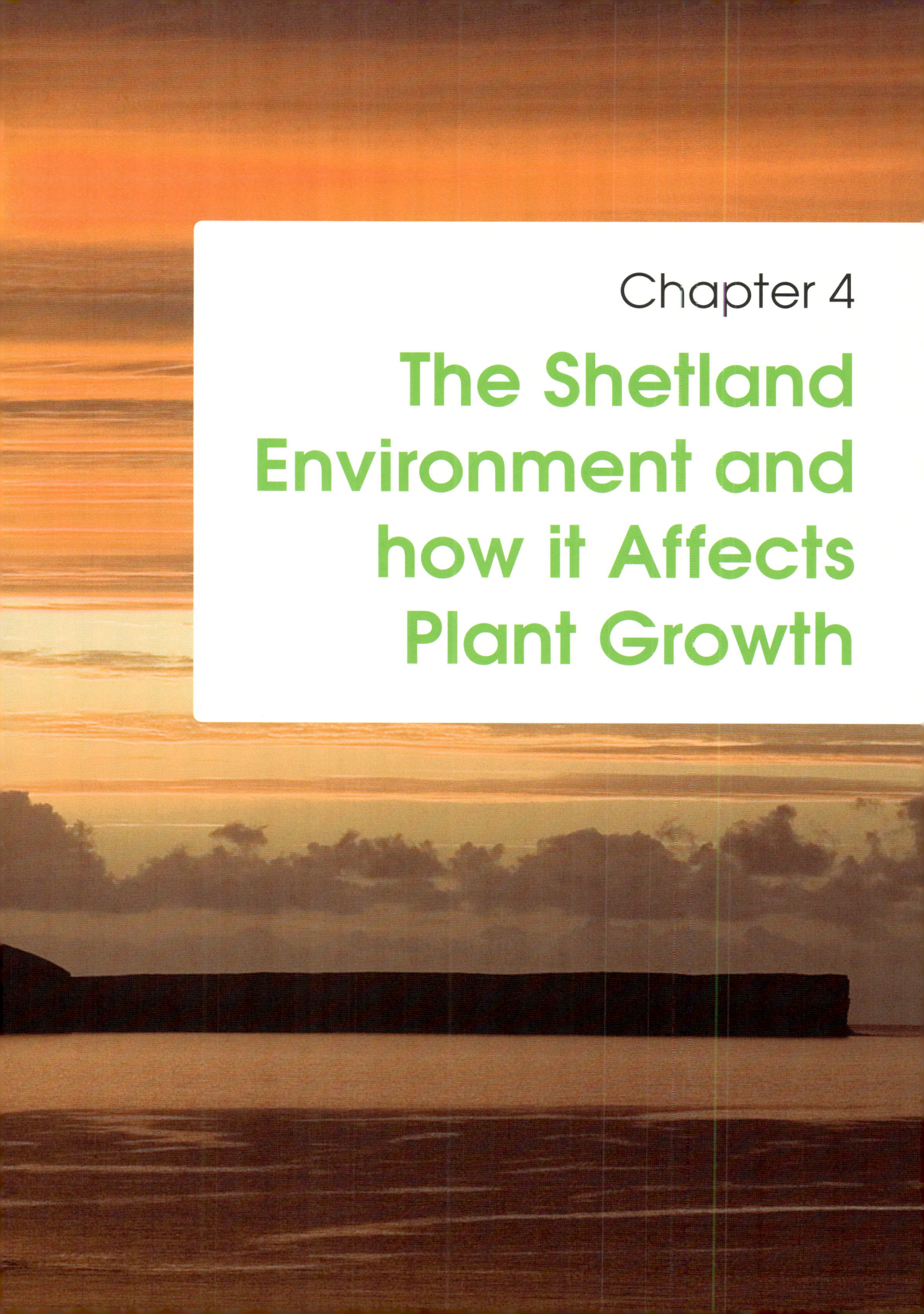

Chapter 4
The Shetland Environment and how it Affects Plant Growth

the shetland environment

The small map above shows the position of Shetland with respect to both the UK mainland and Scandinavia – completely out on a limb and surrounded by ocean. Furthermore, Shetland is positioned on latitude of some 60° North meaning it is in line with both the southern tip of Greenland and Hudson Bay in Canada.

Shetland suffers from four main geographical problems linked to growing plants.

Compressed season

Ours is a northerly latitude, and this leads to a shorter growing season. The following graph (not to scale) shows why.

You can see at the equator there is a steady 12-hour day and 12-hour night all season; dark at 6pm and light at 6am. In England we start to see longer summer days and shorter winter nights, but in Shetland the situation is even more exaggerated, with the almost constant daylight in the middle of June (locally called the 'simmer dim') and the reverse with limited poor quality light on a dull December's day. Though we get more hours of sunlight in the middle of summer, Shetland is way behind, say, southern England. Without churning out pages of meteorological summaries, the average annual sunshine for Shetland is 1038 hours as compared to Greenwich with 1417 hours.

Shetland only starts to receive 'quality' light around the beginning of March. That is one quarter of the year gone, but growth up to this point can be promoted very effectively and efficiently with the careful and cost-effective use of lighting. This allows growers to produce small but healthy seedlings so they can be potted up just when decent light is coming on stream. Remember that a seedling or plug plant might look small, but it is enormous compared with the seed it originated from. Many plants undergo exponential growth, which is another way of saying they double in size at regular intervals till they are nearly fully grown, so a decent seedling will often quickly fill a pot.

Consider a plant doubling in size each week. If we imagine a plant initially 2cm tall, then a week later it would be 4cm. At the end of week two the plant would be 8cm and extrapolating, then after a month it would be 32cm. After eight weeks it would be about 4.8 metres tall and you would probably need either to raise the glasshouse roof or punch a hole through it to let the plant through.

113

Left:
About 2am during a mid-June morning over Bressay.

Below:
A January afternoon.

Photographs taken by Billy Fox.

Now, the previous scenario is a little exaggerated since it assumes both perfect growing conditions and husbandry, but you know from your own experience that a plant will get to a certain size then 'take off'. The bottom line is that a plant nurtured by lights is at a perfect stage to take advantage of the quality light emerging in early March.

I have already mentioned the problems of daylength with regard to 'day neutral varieties', and also its effect on reducing the season in Shetland for cauliflowers.

Cooler temperatures

One effect of the sea surrounding Shetland is to delay the spring somewhat and so we have to plant later. A glasshouse avoids this by using a little heat, but it would be unwise to plant, say, tomatoes, before the start of April or the heating could become prohibitive. The July/August average temperature for Shetland is around 14°C, as compared to Greenwich with nearly 23°C. One commonly experienced problem takes place in late spring, when we get what is called locally 'the Gabs o' May'. This is the result of an anticyclone to the north of Shetland, near the Arctic Circle, generating a cool and very dry northerly wind which seems to scorch everything in its path. Take note of the weather forecasts and avoid planting if you see this situation arising. Most bedding plants should not be going in to the ground before early June unless they are hardy varieties and your garden is well sheltered. The cooler summer prohibits us from growing plants we often see discussed on the television, such as penstemon and runner beans, unless we use polytunnels or something similar.

Conversely, the sea's moderating effect means we do not get the very cold temperatures some other parts of the UK can get in winter. For Shetland a thermometer reading of -9°C is a rare event.

The whole of the UK had a very cold winter spell at the end of 2010, and I read that in the very fertile Wash region of the east of England one farm alone had lost 85% of its crop and was in the process (in mid-February) of ploughing one million frost damaged purple sprouting broccoli back into the ground to prevent disease spread. What finished the crop were the days in December when the mercury plunged to -18°C, well below the temperature even this winter hardy vegetable can stand. Wind chill made those temperatures plummet even lower, with the result that the plants started to rot after frost got into the stalk. The spring cauliflower crop was likewise more or less written off.

The big problem in Shetland during the winter is not the temperature but the precipitation. I say more about over-wintering plants later on.

Moister air

Since Shetland is surrounded by the sea, there is a higher ambient humidity, and this is at its worst when we get a week of mist in summer. In particular, this can lead to fungal diseases in the glasshouse environment. At these times venting and a little night heat is essential, merely to keep the air dry. This will be dealt with in more detail when we consider the greenhouse environment, pests and disease. Not only can the moisture be a problem but also this moisture can often be carrying salty sea spray so making things even tougher. I often say that if you have a scenic view in Shetland then creating a decent garden will not be easy, and vice versa. We get much of our precipitation in the winter and this is one of the main causes of plant loss; this can be exacerbated when the plant is sitting in a pot (rather than in well drained soil). Most potted plants are much better sitting under a shelter, and most of my over-wintered perennials spend their time sitting in a polytunnel or under a cold frame.

As far as hard data is concerned, Shetland gets 1003mm of rain per year compared to Greenwich with its 585mm, i.e. we get something like double the volume of rain compared to the south of England.

More wind

Shetland is windy, but considering it is sitting in the middle of the ocean this should come as no surprise; very soon Shetland may be the home of a large wind turbine project. Fortunately, many of the plants you might fancy growing come in dwarf sizes, with *Lupinus* 'Gallery' just to mention one. I will be saying more about shelter and its provision later on.

Shetland is certainly not the easiest of places to grow plants but if you stick to some basic rules and monitor your crop regularly then you should be able to achieve extremely good results. The best attitude is not to focus on what you cannot grow here, but rather think of the many thousands of types of plants you can. Because of the climate's challenging nature, many Shetland growers probably get even more satisfaction with a quality plant. I remember being down in Somerset staying with a student friend. His father, Murdo Chisholm, came from the Black Isle and was a keen gardener. When I asked him if he had any success growing plants, he replied, "Down here you just need to scratch the surface and it will grow". I replied that it was certainly not like that in Shetland!

You may be interested to see the Shetland weather summary in Appendix 10.

The importance of lighting for plant growth

If you are trying to grow plants in a dark cupboard and not succeeding then pay attention!

Shetland has two particularly dull months, namely December and January (though snowy weather can brighten things up). We start to get good light levels from early March to early October. However, if you sow your seeds in March, then by the time the seedling is a reasonable size we have reached mid-April and your effective season has been reduced by around six weeks.

The solution is 'artificial' lighting. There are several ways of providing extra light in early spring and the basic details are given below. One point to note is that you do not need a light intensity greater than 2000 lux; any more than this is really a waste of energy.

Fluorescent tubes

This is the cheapest way of producing large quantities of healthy baby plants. One of the best ways to achieve this is to build what is called a **growing rig**, simply an array of tubes 300mm (1 foot) apart, with the tubes suspended about 600mm (2ft) above the seedlings. Use 'warm white', which produces a spectrum of 'colour' that is most similar to wavelengths allowing maximum photosynthesis, i.e. most similar to sunlight. The modern slimline tubes are 1200mm long (4ft) and 35 watt. Remember there will be the bonus of a small amount of heat released which helps to raise the temperature. Do make sure to get the types of fittings containing what are known as 'starterless' ballasts. They are more expensive but you do not have all the ensuing problems when the starters start to fail.

At the simplest level you could simply have a fluorescent fitting mounted above the seedling trays in the greenhouse. The diagram shows a light fitting screwed underneath a wooden bench in the glasshouse; this can be repeated two or three times depending on the number of shelves you have.

Top:
Supplementary lighting as carried out by Ruby Jamieson of Scalloway; very simply, fluorescent tubes fixed underneath her greenhouse shelves.

Right:
Some of my growing rigs showing the lights in the 'up' position; they would normally be off in this situation.

Unless you know what you are doing, you **must** contact an electrician who will almost certainly fit RCD fittings for safety. These are super sensitive fuses, which 'trip out' if anything causes a current surge – you have probably seen these fitted to electric lawn mowers and hedge trimmers.

The fittings are cheap if you shop around, and the running costs low. If you are at home and it is a bright day then, of course, you can switch them off, but otherwise they can be left on 24 hours per day. Sometimes this set up is called **supplementary** lighting since it 'supplements' the ambient light. My friend Ruby Jamieson in Scalloway uses this very effectively and produces huge numbers of plants from a very small glasshouse. At this stage it is worth noting that it is essential to keep a low level of heat in the glasshouse; for bedding plants this need only be a minimum of between 10 and 12°C. Photosynthesis is a chemical reaction and temperature dependent – all the light in the world will not make the plants grow if the air temperature is too cold. It is a good idea to hang a thermometer in a shaded part of the greenhouse to see exactly what the value is.

The dimensions of the above rig are 1200mm x 600mm (8ft by 4ft). Bear in mind that the tubes are connected to 'switchgear' (ballasts), which is kept inside the metal fitting. My switchgear sits on a separate plywood board and the tubes are connected to these by lengths of wires. This helps keep the roof of the rig less heavy and by having the roof hinged it is then very easy on sunny days to raise the roof, allowing the plants access to normal daylight. Be aware that there is no artificial lighting that can remotely match the sun, which gives both intense and quality light. However, artificial lighting is a very useful aid in early spring.

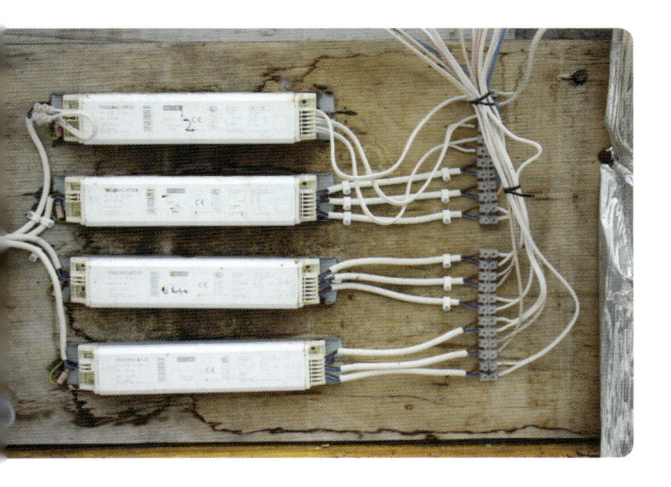

Grow room

I realised that it was not too difficult to take the second stage above one step further, and make a propagation or 'grow room'. A photo of the room is shown right, but essentially it is a large chamber with alternate rows of lights and shelves, each layer being 600mm apart. There is a high level of insulation; the floor, walls and roof are all clad with 50mm Kingspan – I chose this instead of polystyrene primarily because it is fire resistant. The walls and roof are further clad with twin wall sheet plastic, and the roof also covered with insulation. All the heat is trapped, though I have to circulate the air to avoid the temperature rising too much near the roof. Even in the coldest spring weather the grow room warms up; not only does it gain from the warmth being radiated from the fluorescent tubes, but it also retains the heat generated in the tube ballasts sitting underneath each of the shelves. Heat is not expensive – it only becomes so when it is allowed to escape. I also keep a barrel of water in the grow room.

Above:
The rig tubes in the down and active position.

Left:
The ballasts switchgear, which enables the lights to work. They are very heavy compared to the tubes so I just fix them as groups on the adjacent wall.

Right:
The grow room showing three levels of lighting. The black boxes are thermostats to keep the temperature constant, and are linked to 100-watt tubular heaters near the floor.

Finally, the warm shelves of the grow room are brilliant for assisting quick rooting of various cuttings taken in spring.

The combination of steady temperature, 24-hour lighting, proper nutrition and careful watering can lead to very fast seedling growth indeed. The great attraction about this level of control is that you are independent of the outside weather, and you can sow a seed on any particular day and know when it will be ready for pricking out or potting up. And the grow-room can hold an enormous number of plants at one go, as many as 200 standard seed trays.

From a commercial point of view, the propagation room is the difference between my business being profitable and not.

*Above:
A closer look at one of the levels of lighting.*

Other lighting options

1. **High pressure sodium lamps.** I would recommend these as excellent for **supplementary** lighting if you are really serious. The one I use has a 400-watt bulb called the 'SON-T agro' and it is almost tailor made for the Northern Isles, where we have a slight blue deficiency in the colour spectrum earlier in the season as a result of our 60 degrees north latitude. Not only does this bulb supply abundant radiation in the orange-red, but also tops up with the requisite blue. My bulb is situated above the crop and I only switch it on when the day is drab or misty. My lamp has been designed so it can hang down from the greenhouse roof close to the plants yet give a good spread of light. When I ordered it the supplier carried out a computer analysis to give me the optimum height and position to maximise the light distribution. You would not want it on during sunny days and there are light sensors designed to switch it off in such instances. Since light gain and photosynthesis is accumulative, these lights will enable plants to grow during the night, and there could be situations when this could be very useful, such as if you felt a crop was getting behind schedule.

2. **LEDs.** This is a relatively new development. You will certainly be aware of LED (light emitting diode) torches which have LEDs instead of bulbs; there is very little heat produced, so the batteries last for ages. Horticultural scientists have gone one step further, producing large lamps containing arrays of these diodes generating a lot of light with very little heat. Furthermore, they can produce different colours to suit certain crops. They are still being developed and rather expensive but this will be the way forward, certainly for commercial growers.

3. **Ordinary light bulbs** as used in your house. So poor you would be better using a candle!!

There are a large number of other methods of lighting available such as mercury fluorescent (MBF), metal halide (MBI), but the amateur should stick with fluorescent, and if really keen possibly the high-pressure sodium.

Below:
The sodium lamp has an orange yellow emission.

The economics of fluorescent lighting

1. Assume that each unit of electricity costs 15p (based on June 2010 price) per day and 7p per night. A rig has an output of 8 x 1.2 metre tubes x 35w = 260w, or about quarter (0.25) of a kilowatt

2. So the daily running cost for each rig equals (15p x 0.25Kw x16hrs) + (7p x 0.25Kw x 8hrs)

3. Comes to be 60p + 14p = 74p per day = around £20 per month

4. If the rig contains around 26 trays or 1000 PP40 plugs, then over one month this will cost 2p per plug for electricity. Add on 0.5p for heating cable = 2.5p.

5. The figures above show the running costs only, and exclude the depreciation.

Remember this is a whole month of lighting switched on 24 hours per day. In reality there will be many days when the rig can be raised for six or seven hours so the lights will be off during the expensive tariff. Many plants will not need as much as a month and you will end up with a chunky plug, ready to race ahead when potted on.

Summary of lighting

- The most cost effective method of the hobby grower to bring the small seedlings on quickly in early spring is to use fluorescent lights (warm white or white) placed 1.5 to 2ft above the seedlings.

- If you use a small room or cupboard you have the advantage that you are also trapping the heat, and if the temperature can be brought up to 20°C then most plants will germinate and grow well, although you will have to watch that certain seedlings do not stretch.

- Leave the lights on 24 hours per day.

- If, on the other hand, you have the tubes sitting under the shelves in the greenhouse, you have the advantage that on a sunny day the lights can be switched off. The tubes will also keep the greenhouse frost-free on a cold clear night.

- **Make sure to get help from an electrician**

- Remember, plants kept warm without light will stretch, fall over and become diseased. Plants given plenty of light but kept cold will stay stunted and go a bluish colour.

When you deal with lighting, heating or whatever, you need to design a system, which can be suited to your own needs.

There are many useful booklets, many of which I have used to set up my own systems. These include:

1. Notes for application of photoperiodic lighting techniques in horticulture – TN 21;

2. Electrical aspects of micro propagation – TN 23;

3. Germination cabinets and rooms – TN 46;

4. Quartz linear lamps for horticulture – TN 54;

5. Horticultural produce cooling – TN 55;

6. Soil warming in horticulture – heating cable & mat systems – TN 56;

7. Electric heating for horticultural applications – TN 57

Carbon dioxide enrichment

A further refinement to my grow room (since it is more or less a sealed box) was to provide carbon dioxide enrichment. By increasing the normal levels of carbon dioxide to 1000 parts per million (300ppm), photosynthesis (and subsequent plant growth) can be further speeded up. A monitor checks the CO_2 levels every minute. If the amount present drops below a particular set point, a signal is sent to the gas cylinder causing a relay to open and release the gas. I mentioned above about the need to recirculate the air; this air movement also spreads the CO_2 and it is important to try to keep the air moving over the leaf canopy so you do not end up with a shortage of carbon dioxide next to the leaf stomata (pores). You will have to purchase CO_2 cylinders – typically I find one lasts three days and they are easily refillable. If you are a wine or a beer maker then leave your demi-johns in the room since they release CO_2 during the fermentation process. Since I do the bulk of my sowing and pricking out in the grow room then the CO_2 I breathe out helps the enrichment. I once asked my wife, Christine, if I could tether our two cats there and she was not keen on this at all – cannot think why!

It is also possible to generate CO_2 by burning a suitable hydrocarbon with one kilogram of propane or butane yielding three kilograms of CO_2; I would be reluctant to go down this path with the possible danger of fire, and the combustion process will also produce water vapour. A sealed grow room would certainly start to overheat so you would have to vent, leading to CO_2 loss and suddenly everything is getting very complicated. One source has even said if you had a compost heap in the grow room the decomposition process would release CO_2; I would not advise this!

Above:
The black and green box is the carbon dioxide controller. An infrared sensor feeds the value into the processor and an electronic switch releases carbon dioxide from the cylinder.

Overwintering plants in Shetland

Plants sitting in pots are more difficult to keep through the winter than those growing in the soil. Surprisingly, frost and snow are not the problem since our winters are not particularly hard; our bugbears are the wind and particularly the rain. The annual rainfall for Shetland is somewhere in the region of 1 metre (nearly 40 inches) and you can guess when most of it lands.

Wind damage

It goes without saying that windbreaks and shelterbelts are vital to help buffer the plants from the winter gales. Shelterbelt construction is explained in detail below.

Waterlogging

Plants overwintering in a pot are quite confined compared to those actually growing in the soil. There is much more risk of pots getting excessively wet, leading to the inevitable root rots and death. I keep the bulk of my potted perennial plants under cover but make sure they are well ventilated to keep the foliage dry and the humidity at bay. I do not let them dry out but restrict the watering, and make sure they are either on a bench or sitting on sloping ground to allow water to drain. If you did not have a tunnel or cold frame then you would really want to be using free draining compost, possibly incorporating grit or perlite, and have the pots sitting on gravel beds or some similar material, even coarse sand.

If there is no decent ventilation you almost certainly will end up getting botrytis, especially with plants like *Myosotis* and *Bellis*; even with decent ventilation I use a fungicide called 'Switch' which is particularly good in dealing with the disease.

Desiccation

One other aspect to consider is drying out when cold northerlies appear. In a few species you can have the awful scenario of water getting sucked out of the leaves, but if the pot is frozen obviously no water is going to move into the roots to replace it. To combat this scenario I make sure that the cold frames and tunnels have some degree of windbreak netting so there is ventilation but not a gale passing through the structures.

Frost protection

Fortunately, we do not have the serious frosts found on the UK mainland – I mentioned earlier about the farmers having to dig in their brassica crops. In 2010/11 it did go down to -9°C in Shetland, very unusual considering the relatively mild winters of the last decade. It is unusual for plants sitting in a tunnel, for instance, to be frozen through, but I do recall one spring potting up primula whose roots were solid lumps of ice. They yielded a good crop later on that same spring, but you would not want to do that normally. You can also reduce frost damage by standing the plants close to each other, rather as you would find in a penguin nursery. This cuts down the 'wind chill' factor.

If there were a period of very hard frosts and you were worried, there is always the option of covering the plants with bubble wrap film; but do not keep it in place any longer than is necessary otherwise you will end up with disease initiation. Another option could be to cover the plants with a fleece.

Hardening off

Perennials will stand a better chance of overwintering if they can be naturally hardened off prior to winter; so you would avoid giving fertiliser late in the growing season and cut back on the watering from late September/early October onwards to try to encourage the acclimatisation process.

Even if you follow all the guidance above you will still find that certain plants are hard to overwinter; for instance, I never manage to get lavender to overwinter in pots, yet I know Rosa Steppanova manages to get *Lavendula stoechas* to survive outside, though she has it positioned on a well drained slope.

Rabbits

A page dedicated to rabbits – surely not! In particular, the winter of 2009/2010 was 'the year of the rabbit'. The rabbit population has been increasing lately and of course the 09/10 winter was one of the worst the UK has had for decades. Shetland had a long period of lying snow, so with thousands of starving rabbits on the hills, any vegetation was fair game – it needs a lot of snow to bury a tree! I spoke to someone from the village of Aith on the west side of the Mainland, and she said that not only were her bushes and trees now reduced to stumps, but when the gritters had been spreading salt the grass along the verges was exposed as the snow melted. She said one night she was returning home and was amazed to drive past literally thousands of pairs of eyes along the roadside. She had never seen this in her life before. There are only two solutions to rabbits and shooting is not one of them!

1. Try growing plants which rabbits do not like. I was pleased they were not keen on the black cottonwood which I am very fond of; I think they do not like the scented sticky resin found in the bark – not so good to chew into. They also did not seem too keen on Sitka alder. However, everything else was up for grabs, particularly the willows, whitebeam and buddleia. Rosa Steppanova said they were not so keen on birches, or lodgepole pine with its soft needles, but readily stripped Sitka spruce and fir (Abies) of their needles and twigs.

2. In reality rabbits like just about everything if they are hungry enough. In spring 2010, they were even eating the tops of my armeria (sea pinks), which they have never done before. The only sensible solution is to physically protect the plants. I had no trouble with the plants in the cold frames since I made sure the doors were closed. The tunnel was fine since the plants were sitting on benches.

With the rest, closing off the garden with galvanised wire mesh is the only sensible answer. One neighbour told me cattle grids are no use as they have figured out how to get over them. Another form of physical protection, certainly for your trees, is to wrap the stems with spiral tree guards, particularly the younger ones. A company called LBS sells these at around £60 per 250 of the 38mm diametre variety, 600mm (2ft) long. They certainly worked with the trees I wrapped them round. I did enquire about a substance animals apparently find distasteful (Aaprotect) but it has been discontinued, and I was told the results were a bit dubious!

Right:
This is NOT rabbit damage but the results of our cats using this particular tree as a scratching post. With the bark being destroyed it is just as devastating.

3. Shelterbelts

Whenever someone asks me about establishing a garden in Shetland the first thing I say is that they need to get some shelter. I would always suggest this particular sequence:

1. Get the fence in place;
2. Get a windbreak fixed to the fence;
3. Establish fast-growing trees round the perimetre;
4. Once these have established then concentrate on the ornamentals.

The following notes explain what has certainly worked for me throughout the years.

Get the fence in place

Unless you are a crofter or a farmer, you would be much quicker getting a fencing contractor to do this. I decided to hire them recently and they put it up quick, straight and strong. Leave it to the experts – you will have enough to do and there is nothing more ugly than a DIY fence! I recall a lady once asking me to look at her DIY kitchen, which she said "only cost £500". I had a look and thought, "Yes, looks like a £500 kitchen!"

Fix the windbreak

The windbreak I use is strong and woven together in a special way so that if you do get a hole in the material it will not spread. The important thing is the actual fixing to the fenceposts. First of all you have to fix it to the fence posts on the opposite side of the wire, i.e. so that the netting is getting pressed evenly against the smooth wood. In 2008 I put in place some very long runs of this material – some 300 metres or so.

Top:
This is rabbit damage to an expensive tree which we tried to save without success. The ringbarking is very clear.

Left:
A plastic spiral guard which will protect against both cats and rabbits.

Wait for a calm day. I remember getting up one day around 6.30 in the morning, when it was dead calm, and installing some 200 metres of mesh by 9am! This is how I did it:

1. Using a large stapler, fasten the top of the windbreak along the tops of the fence posts; you only need to do every second or third one, but you do have to apply some tension to keep it straight.

2. Before you start, get some 25 x 50mm treated wood cut to the correct length, and staple some rubber-glazing strip to it; this will apply even pressure on the net. Fix this strapping to the fence posts with the netting getting trapped in the middle. Use good quality screws as they will give a tremendous grip. Ensure they are stainless steel, and then they can easily be removed in future. With a drill driver and four screws per post, you can get through this very quickly providing you are organised. Properly put up, this relatively cheap net will last for at least 10+ years. If it is put up tightly and evenly it will look smart.

Below:
A wooden strip (with glazing strip fixed to the inside) pressing against the windbreak. Stainless steel screws were used to give even pressure.

Right:
The bracing posts strengthening the fence from the prevailing wind.

Establish fast growing trees round the perimeter

There are some slow movers but others are really fast, particularly many of the willows; my favourite tree is 'black cottonwood', with Sitka alder coming a close second. It will take two or three years for these plants to give proper shelter; do keep abreast of the rabbit problem, especially with willows. Taking cuttings of willows and black cottonwood is both cheap and quick – there are a few basic notes regarding taking cuttings in Appendix 9.

Get the ornamentals in place

Lawn problems

This is only mentioned since some people have occasionally contacted me with 'balding' patches in their lawns. In nine cases out of ten the problem is due to nothing more than 'stoorie worm', i.e. the larvae of the crane fly (daddy long legs). For whatever reason there are enormous quantities of these grubs in Shetland, so much that the council actually gives grants to crofters to combat them. If you have a problem with these larvae then treat the ground with a product called 'Cyren'. Apply this as a drench at 1 in 500, or 2ml per litre; you should be able to get this from any agricultural supplier. Do bear in mind that this is a **highly toxic** anticholinesterase organophosphate compound and it would be better getting someone qualified to apply it. **Under no circumstances allow skin contact.**

Right:
Plants growing during the day with the lights in the 'up' position.

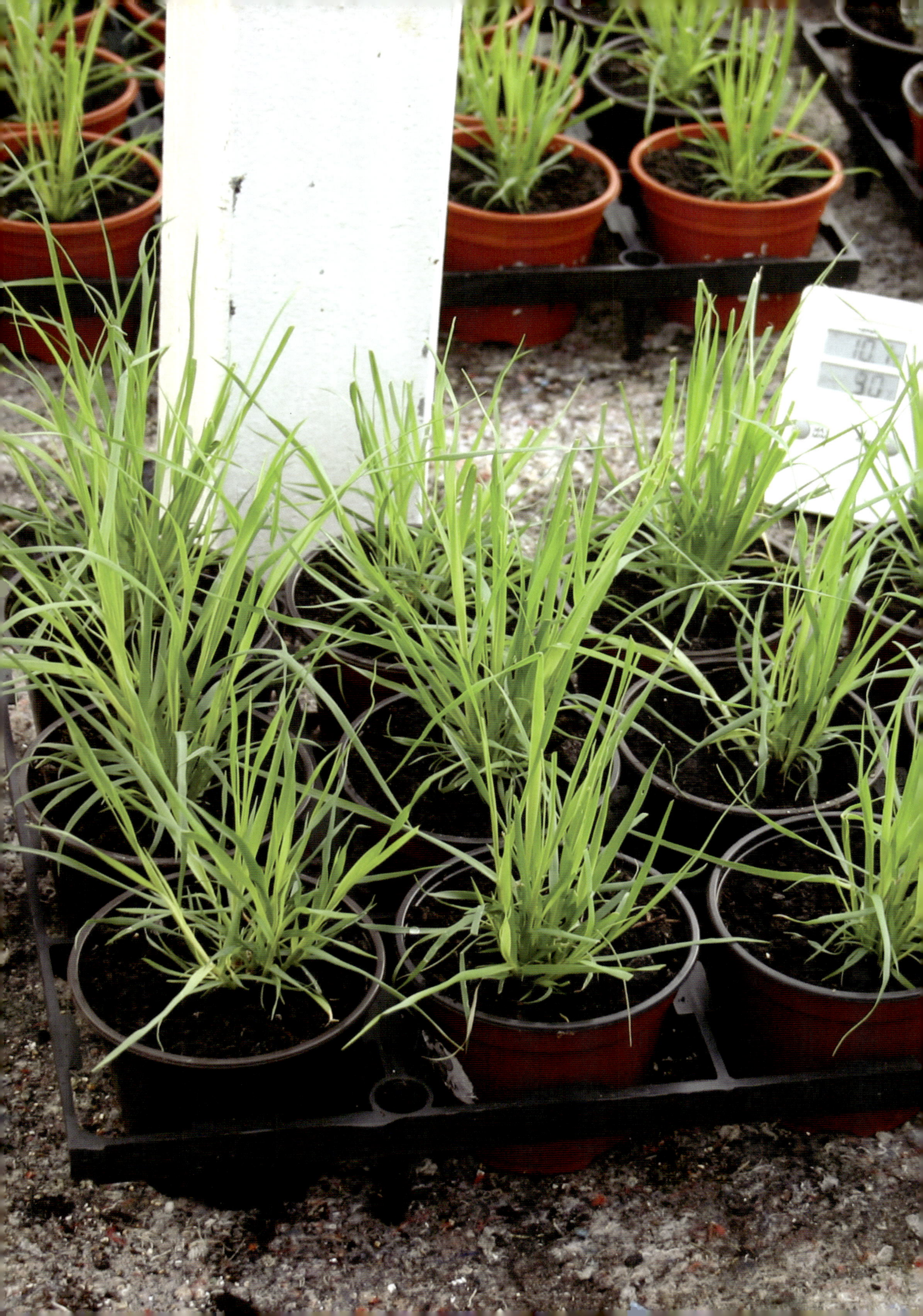

Chapter 5

Irrigation, Feeding and the Importance of pH

Watering plants

I am reluctant to let anybody else water my plants. At peak season I can take as long as 4 hours daily to get through it, especially if it is a 'blue sky' day.

The water requirements of plants are not that dissimilar to those of humans; it depends on weather and a whole lot of other factors. Unless you grow plants hydroponically it is impossible to get it exactly right, but you also want neither to over nor underwater excessively. One often used rule is 'little and often'. It is easy enough to check if plants grown in peat-based compost need water – you just have to lift the pot and feel the weight, but plants grown in heavier soil-based John Innes composts are more difficult to assess. Generally, it is better to err on the dry side rather than on the wet. The problem with soil-based compost is that they feel heavy whether dry or wet. Soil moisture levels can be tested using a moisture meter but this is time consuming. There are a few species intolerant of peat-based medium, but more to the point there are many which like them. When you have worked with one type of medium for a number of years then you instinctively get a feel for it. This is why I stick with the same brand of compost (with the same physical and chemical characteristics) so leaving fewer things to chance. I use composts made by a company called 'Westland'; they are moderately priced and give a decent performance.

Overwatering over a period of time is fatal

If you overwater then you drive out the air and oxygen, the roots die and rot, diseases set in and the rotting accelerates with even less water absorption – you have initiated a vicious cycle. The compost has become stagnant for want of a better word. Just because they do not have a set of lungs does not mean their dependency on oxygen is any less than ours.

Some plants can stand a considerable amount of dryness, and even survive wilting, but eventually we get to permanent wilting point (PWP) and then it is 'game over'! I take irrigation very seriously, especially in summer. Because there is such a large variety of plants at different sizes and stages, I will invariably lose the odd one due to either under or (more likely) to overwatering. I cannot lift all of them to check the weight! One of the problems with just looking at a pot is that it might be 'surface dry' yet be quite wet underneath. The compost surface dries very quickly on a sunny day. If I see a plant whose leaves are going yellowish with other odd colours starting to appear, I lift it (normally finding it very heavy) and place it apart from the others, sometimes on a shelf, and that gives a signal to miss it out during the next few waterings.

What makes life a bit more complicated is that some plants like to be wet most of the time whereas others prefer being alternately wet and dry. Two common examples are bacopa and petunia. The former needs to be kept at least damp otherwise the petals will drop like confetti, whereas the latter prefers to be wetted and then dried back alternately.

Right:
This pink bacopa has been carefully watered in order to give such a good display.

133

This can be tricky to manage, and I have spent more than a few minutes some days feeling the weights of petunia hanging baskets to see what the water regime is like.

There are so many varieties of plants with different requirements that you should study the culture notes from the seed house, and try to grow a few of your favourite plants well, rather than trying to cope with too many. No matter what you do, if you are not regularly picking up a selection of your pots to feel their weights you will not succeed in producing quality plants.

A few years ago I was struggling with some of my crops on long sunny days, as the leafy ones were removing the water as quickly as I could supply it – and there was the difficulty of re-wetting some of the pots once they had dried out. I eventually found the answer, namely white polydrip trays.

These were ordered from the USA and have multiple advantages. Essentially they catch the bulk of the water or feed solution, leaving a small reservoir which can then be absorbed by the pot over a period of time. They reflect light, and since the pot is sitting on a plastic surface the roots do not get entangled, as is the case with capillary matting. These trays come in three different formats accommodating different sizes of pots. The saving in time is enormous and they enable me to produce a better quality plant. I find them especially useful for the annual dianthus – trying to water some 800 11cm pots individually was soul destroying, but with the tray system irrigation is speeded up enormously. They can be used satisfactorily with overhead sprinkler systems, though I am not a keen advocate of 'giving everything a drink whether it wants it or not', since with the whole place drenched there is the potential threat of disease.

Left:
Polydrip trays play a large part in my water management. The bacopas look quite happy.

Over time I have built up a lot of notes relating to watering, and the list below shows some of the key issues to be considered. Some are more than obvious.

- The water characteristics in an enclosed pot are very different from those in the garden soil.

- The medium must hold enough water for a reasonable period yet also have an air supply.

- The trick is to water just before wilting or suffering water stress – this is difficult even for good growers; plants do go dull before wilting – better to feel the weight of the pot.

- Overwatering occurs when plants are watered too frequently, not by applying too much at a single watering.

- Although I generally apply the rule 'little and often', at least once a week during decent weather I give the pots a really good soaking, even if this means double watering. The pot will be fully soaked and the excess will simply run away through the bottom. In sunny weather, and adopting a 'little and often' strategy, there is the danger that the water never really gets to the bottom of the pot. I have seen pots looking wet at the top yet being quite dry at the bottom, with potential for root damage. Even if the pot was soaking, on a sunny day the plant would soon 'dry it out', but this would not be a good scenario in a damp misty spell, i.e., in dull weather be extra careful.

I grow a wide range of crops in different settings, and during peak production time often have to compromise.

Capillary matting

The bulk of my benches are covered with a layer of plastic on which rests 'capillary matting' (not unlike carpet underlay). In the early days of horticulture, sand beds were often used – nothing wrong with that bar the enormous weight and logistics of replacing and cleaning. Although the water trays mentioned above are superb, matting has many advantages. You can think of the matting acting as a spongy reservoir with the water absorbed by capillary action through the pot's perforated base. So you just fire the water at the plants and the surplus sits in the mat. This saves a lot of time. To get the maximum benefit it is important that your benches are fairly level.

One big advantage of the matting is during sunny days when the air is getting very dry (low RH). At these times I soak virtually all the matting and the evaporation helps to both reduce the temperature and raise the humidity. This very much more 'buoyant' atmosphere is conducive to good growth and reduces the stress caused by the 'desert-like' conditions. As I said earlier, low RH leads to stomatal closure, so curtailing photosynthesis and growth.

Matting does have its problems – roots just love getting into it and during 2010 I had to literally tear the bacopa from it by actually twisting the pot, so good was the root growth. The bacopa are destined for the polydrip trays next season. Another problem is the build up of algae, especially if you are applying feed solution. Many growers cover the matting with black perforated polythene; as well as blocking out the light, so reducing the amount of algal growth, it also reduces plant root growth into the matting.

Irrigation summary

- With exceptions, it is probably better that the compost is on the dry side (not to Sahara Desert levels!) rather than wet. The best way to judge is to feel the weight of the pot. LITTLE AND OFTEN should be the rule.

- If you find a plant that is really wet and suffering, put the pot somewhere aside so it does not get watered with the bulk of the plants.

- A newly potted plant is certainly better kept on the dry side. Keeping it dry will also help to encourage the roots to search for water. Once the roots are established then the shoot growth will really take off.

- Never ever use chilled tap water, especially in spring.

Feeding

Of all the words used in horticulture 'feeding' must be the most inappropriate. When humans eat they are primarily securing an energy supply; we are consumers and need an energy supply. Plants, however, get their energy from the sun and convert its energy into sugars, ultimately helping the plant to grow. This is the process of photosynthesis mentioned earlier; plants are producers and store energy.

When we speak about 'feeding' plants we are actually meaning supplying them with minerals. We also need **minerals**, and you will certainly know that calcium is required for bones and iron for blood. During the rest of this chapter, bear in mind that if I use the words 'feed' or 'feeding' I mean supplying the plants with a supply of suitable minerals or nutrients, normally in the form of simple inorganic compounds called fertilisers.

Above:
Pampas grass and house leeks sitting on the capillary matting.

Feeds are often described as '2-1-5' or some other combination of ratios. These three numbers describe the **Macronutrients** or key minerals, and the relative amounts of **N**, **P** and **K** present; so '2-1-5' means that for every two parts of nitrogen there is one part of phosphorus and five parts of potassium. **N** is the symbol for nitrogen, which encourages leaf and foliage growth and makes the plant green. Plants that are fed too much nitrogen often become excessively lush, soft, and difficult to manage. **P** is the symbol for phosphorus, whose main role in plant growth is that of root formation, so feeds lacking this element will not help the plant thrive, as the roots are a hidden but critical part of the equation. **K** is the symbol for potassium and its key role in plant growth is for the formation of flowers and fruit, so tomato feeds like 'Tomorite' will contain lots of potash (an abbreviated potassium). Sometimes the label or bag will give the percentage of these elements present. The elements are always supplied in the form of compounds and some of the more common ones are potassium nitrate (KNO_3) containing K and N, ammonium nitrate also called nitram (NH_4NO_3), and monoammonium phosphate (($NH_4)_2PO_4$) with both N and P.

A complete feed will also contain what are known as **trace elements**, needed in tiny amounts, but absolutely essential if the plant is going to survive. These include elements such as iron, magnesium, zinc, copper and molybdenum. The amounts of trace elements that are needed may be small but if they are missing the effects can be devastating, just like humans developing a vitamin deficiency. For instance, when I make up tomato feed I use around 1.2 grams (quarter a teaspoon) of molybdenum per 50,000 gallons of feed solution. You might think that if it was left out the plants would not notice, but they certainly do, and you would see deficiency symptoms appearing.

The actual identification of individual mineral deficiencies in plants is very difficult indeed, and though you might hazard a guess that a plant with the bottom leaves starting to turn yellow was suffering a nitrogen shortage, it could also be due to root damage or as the result of a whole host of insect, fungal or bacterial pathogens. This, coupled with the fact that a deficiency of one element is often linked to another, makes the situation even more problematic – for instance shortage of manganese induces a shortage of iron and so on. The only way to be certain what deficiency is present is to request a sap (or tissue) analysis. Collect a reasonable mass of affected leaves, send it off to a chemical laboratory, and with the use of modern analytical instruments, such as spectrometers and photometers, they can pinpoint what is missing. I have had the occasional leaf analysis carried out, the only problem being that it takes a few days to complete, and when the plants are looking bad, you want a result immediately. Many years ago I invested in what is known as a flame photometer, which enabled me to determine very quickly the levels of potassium, calcium and sodium in the growbag solution.

If you ensure that all the key elements are present, these problems can be avoided, though the formulations (which can be found in commercial horticulture books) have been carefully evolved over many years. If you are using a proper feed, a reasonable medium pH (explained later in this chapter), and half decent growing conditions, you will be unlikely to have mineral deficiency problems.

Plants grown in soil or soil based composts need far less 'feeding' than those grown in peat based medium; the latter have to be supplied with minerals soon after the roots have reached the edge of the pot. Some plants, like the heavy fruit bearers, need lots of feed, whereas others need very little.

Half decent loam has a large fertiliser supply, very much to do with the interaction of clay and other components of the soil crumbs. There is a very complex relationship between the chemical and physical components of soil. It would require a large textbook just to explain even the basics. If you wanted to find out a bit more about the soil, you could not do better than read a copy of 'The World of the Soil' by Sir E. John Russell, one of the New Naturalist series (ISBN-10: 0002132559).

Some plants cannot cope well when there are lots of minerals present. This can inadvertently happen if there is a lot of dry, hot weather and you are rather 'keen' with the feed packet. What happens is that the plant takes up the water (via transpiration, i.e. 'sweating' through its leaves) in preference to the fertiliser, and so the latter increases in concentration with the medium becoming quite 'salty'. A simple experiment can show the effect of this: take a small carrot and cut it long ways into quarter sections, put one of these into very salty water and the other into plain; after about 30 minutes remove them from the liquids and you will see the one in salty water has become limp – a process called 'osmosis' has removed the water. If the limp carrot is put back into fresh water it will recover. Unfortunately this does not work with tiny delicate root hairs; very 'salty' situations kill the roots of plants. I have already said a bit about this in Chapter 2 when dealing with root structure.

Be very wary of feeding the plants and soaking the foliage on a sunny day, as the water will evaporate leaving the fertiliser behind, and the leaves then become scorched. Under such conditions, I always give the foliage a quick spray of fresh water to remove the remnants.

If you are unsure as to the concentration and the frequency follow the instructions on the manufacturer's packet.

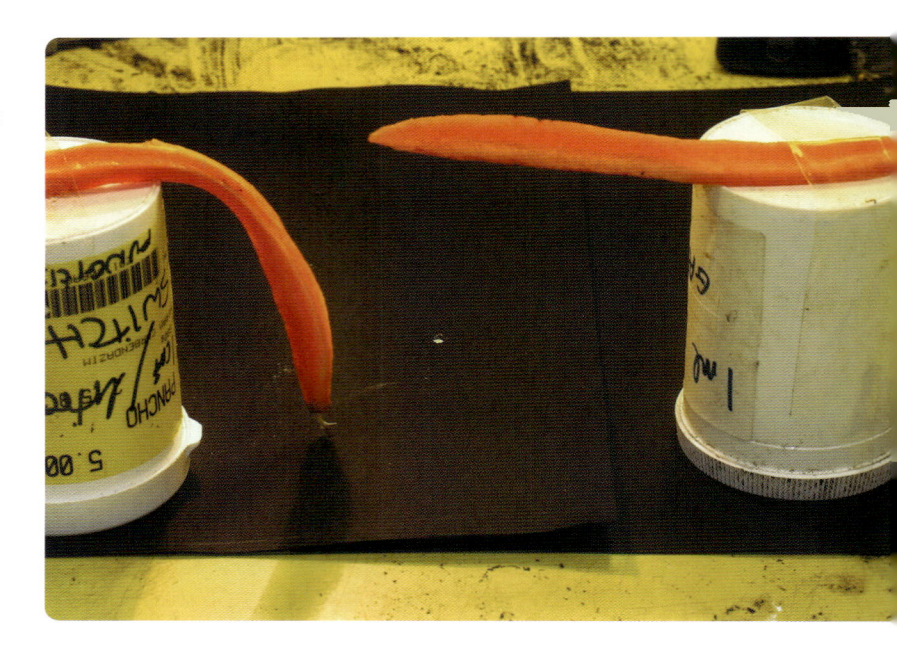

If you make up your own feed solutions, as I do, you can measure its concentration by using a **conductivity meter**; basically the more salty the higher the conductivity. I say more about conductivity meters later on.

Types of feed

1. Proprietary

This includes such feeds as Phostrogen, Tomorite, Baby-Bio, Chempak and a whole lot more I know nothing about since I never use them. There is nothing wrong with them, providing you follow the instructions. To save money, never buy fertiliser in liquid form if possible, but as powders. Generally, the bigger the pack, the cheaper per unit. If you are a small commercial grower then you could be looking at something like the Vitafeed range which includes such ratios as 1-0-1+TE (no phosphorus), 1-0-2+TE (higher in potassium), 3-0-1+TE, 2-1-4+TE (all three present but with higher potassium), and 1-1-1+TE being a balanced fertiliser. The TE stands for trace elements. Vitafeed is reasonably cheap and purchasing the pack saves the hassle of weighing chemicals, with the potential for error.

Above:
Carrot strips having been soaked in salty and fresh water for half an hour. Osmosis has sucked the water out of the left hand strip.

The Vitafeed 4-1-2 label states: "A high nitrogen feed beneficial where plants have become pot-bound or starved". On the back it starts with the description, "NPK Fertiliser 28-7-14" then states: "Total Nitrogen 28.0%, Phosphorus 7%, Potassium 14%", and so on with the other elements. It advises you to make the concentrated stock at 1kg per 10 litres, or if you want to mix it diluted then a 1-200 dilution corresponds to 1kg per 2000 litres. It also says it can be stored indefinitely, but do keep it dry as it is hygroscopic (absorbs water from the air).

There is a great deal more to plant nutrition than the basics above.

2. Formulated

You can make most basic feeds using three chemicals – potassium nitrate, mono-ammonium phosphate and ammonium nitrate. In the long term this yields extremely cheap mixes but you do have the initial outlay for the 25kg sacks of the raw ingredients. I grow a lot of plants so this saves me money, although my favourite is a high potash tomato recipe which has the added advantage of containing all the trace elements (although these have to be carefully weighed out).

During its manufacture, peat based compost is 'charged' with the key minerals, and these will only last the plants possibly four to five weeks. For most gardeners there are two options to 'keep the plant going', either liquid feeding or incorporating slow release fertilisers.

Liquid feeding is just what it says. Most people will just mix some powder into a watering can at the recommended dosage, and add to the pots. As a rule of thumb, feed weekly if the plant is in active growth, or twice weekly if it is vigorous such as petunia. Tomatoes should be fed at every watering once the first fruits are pea size, though on a hot day extra waterings should be water only.

If you want to keep the cost down, shop around and buy a powdered feed such as Phostrogen in as large a packet as possible. It can last for years providing it is kept dry. Some simple arithmetic will determine the cost per gallon of feed solution. For fruit or plants in flower you should be looking at a product with high potash. For leafy plants such as lettuce or spinach you might want to use a high nitrogen formula. Stick to the recommended dosage; if you try to be smart and give more than stated it will suffer and could die.

3. Making your own

I make up all my own feed solutions and have two groups, namely the 'short haul' and the 'long haul' formulations.

I use the 'short haul' feeds for crops that are going to be potted on into larger pots, or those soon to be planted into the garden, e.g. bedding plants. By using various combinations of monoammonium phosphate, ammonium nitrate and potassium nitrate, I can make up any ratio of the key nutrients needed. So it is easy to make up 4-1-2 (4 parts nitrogen to 1 part phosphorus to 2 parts potassium) by having a mix with a greater proportion of ammonium nitrate (35% nitrogen) added. The formula 2-1-5 would be a high potash mix with a greater proportion of potassium nitrate being used. Making your own is easy and cheaper but you do have to buy the chemicals (called 'straights') in 25kg quantities. The recipes for these are given in Appendix 7.

It goes without saying that the 'short haul' mixes do not contain any calcium, magnesium or the micronutrients (or trace elements) such as iron, copper, zinc, manganese and molybdenum. If you are growing tomato plants, for instance, which may be in the pot for up to nine months, the deficiencies will soon appear like the spectre at the feast. For these I use 'long haul' feed solutions made by the combination of two separate solutions; it is vital that the phosphate and calcium are kept separate when in concentrated form – if not, they react to make calcium phosphate which precipitate out, and will not only be unavailable to the plants but will also lead to blockages when using drip irrigation. One interesting point about the traces is that the iron used is in chelated form (EDTA), since 'normal' iron salts such as iron carbonate will react immediately with the compost and be unavailable to the plant. EDTA is a complex organic molecule which wraps round an iron atom (chelate means 'claw') and releases it to the plant's roots when required. Very clever!

The recipes for long haul crops are also given in Appendix 7.

Unless you are familiar with chemistry, or grow plants on a larger scale, it would be easier to stick with known brands.

Some fertilisers have special formulae to compensate if the medium's pH tends to become acidic, and others try to neutralise any drift in an alkaline direction. This is complicated, and way beyond the scope of this book; the fact that Shetland's water is so soft removes much of this problem.

The recipes enabling you to make up your own bedding plant feeds are given in Appendix 7.

4. Slow release (or controlled release fertiliser, CRF)

Slow release fertiliser is a little package of chemicals wrapped in a plastic coat. The plastic has the virtue of allowing the feed to seep out, but what is really smart is the seepage is quicker at a warmer temperature, and of course this normally fits in with the plant's requirements.

By adjusting the type of plastic coat the minerals can be released at different rates so you can get four to five month, six to nine month, 18-month release and so on.

In theory, the steady release of minerals takes away a lot of the problems of when and when not to feed. You add the slow release when you are potting up the plants, so when I am working with 3-litre petunias hanging baskets, I add 6 grams of 6-month slow release. To quickly measure this amount I use an empty hypodermic syringe (minus needle) cut at the relevant mark as a 'scoop', and mix it into the compost. You can also mix slow release with the compost in a cement mixer, making sure you use it within a few weeks since the minerals will start releasing immediately.

Having told you all this I actually rarely use slow release now, save for some of the summer baskets and bowls; another local grower recently told me he had given up on it as well. The main problem is that the cooler temperatures in Shetland seem to be under the threshold enabling decent mineral release. When I do use slow release I keep the quantity low and feed at least once a week, but for most crops I directly liquid feed on a regular basis depending on the crop size and weather conditions. This way I know what they are getting and how much they are getting. With my young leek plants, for instance, I start them off with a balanced feed but as we get closer to planting, I alternate with high nitrogen.

5. Organic fertilisers such as manure or nettle soup

The great problem here is the rate of nutrition release and the amount available. With hoof and horn or manure you have very little idea, with the outcome being you will never achieve the optimal release rate. Compare throwing some nettle juice at a tomato plant with giving it a solution you know definitely contains 300mg of potassium per litre of tomato fertiliser. A potassium ion (K+) is a potassium ion whether it comes from cow manure or from Tomorite – it will make no odds to the root hair trying to absorb it. Similarly with phosphates, nitrates and so on. There is absolutely nothing wrong with feeding organically but for most plants you will never achieve the potential yield. However, where I strongly support organic practice is with pest control, where I will not spray edibles with anything other than natural insecticides.

Angus Nicol is a great believer in using cow manure, and he always tries to get me to do likewise. I normally reply, "But Angus, I don't have a cow!"

6. Seaweed

At this point I must make mention of my Uncle Tommy Goodlad from Scalloway, who grows positively the largest onions I have seen in Shetland. What he does is to get a plastic drum and bore a hole in the bottom. He then fills it up with seaweed and pours a bucket of water in at the top. Here is the smart bit – he puts another bucket underneath the drum and the juice percolates down through. Once the bucket is full, he then pours it into the top of the drum again and so on. Of course, the juice gets more and more concentrated, and he uses this brew to feed his plants; he says that as more seaweed is added the mixture 'melts', with the volume greatly decreasing. Eventually thick gelatinous liquid starts to drip out through the holes in the bottom of the drum, this being a sign that everything is working fine. After a while the liquid emerging starts to become more 'water-like' and at that stage he then starts off another batch. He says he makes a new batch every month or so in summer.

I buy a commercial drum of the same extract, but must find time to get myself more organised. I have a trailer, I have a spare drum, and I know where the beach is! I recall staying with my Grandfather at Elie (in Fife) in the 1950s and both of us dragging 'tang' from the beach to the compost heap; he was a successful grower, as was his father. I mention further benefits of seaweed later when dealing with plant diseases.

Below:
A plastic drum full of seaweed starting to rot down.

Angus Nicol throws seaweed straight on to his garden, and this summer showed me one of his potatoes. Not many growers can boast about peeling one tattie yielding a meal for four!

Why is seaweed so good? The first thing to note is that it is not a fertiliser. A much better name for it is 'biostimulant'. Biostimulants are mixtures of complex organic chemicals conferring multiple benefits on plant growth. In the case of seaweed, the key compounds are cytokinins (a plant hormone promoting cell division in plant roots and shoots) and betaines – these are used in plant cells for protection against drought, high salinity or high temperature.

Tests carried out using seaweed extracts claim not only increased foliage growth and greater yields, but also extended growing season and better flower and fruit setting. As if that was not enough, the scientists also state that leaves become greener (due to increased chlorophyll production), there is reduced stress, better biological control, and seaweed helps the plant develop resistance/tolerance to pests and diseases. It also has a role in stimulating beneficial soil organisms. Finally, it can help plants more quickly acclimatise to frost, helping them tolerate even colder conditions than they would normally endure. I was so impressed with its potential I rubbed a little on to my bald patch – no sign of hair growth but it did get a nice tan!

Out of interest, seaweed has long featured in Shetland's agricultural practices. James R. Nicolson, in his book 'Traditional Life in Shetland', said that the crofting year began in the depths of winter, with heavy seas piling seaweed on exposed beaches, and I quote: *"This was a crop that never failed, and one that was extremely important to the crofter, for when it rotted it made excellent manure"*. During these winter days men and women piled the seaweed in mounds above the high water mark; this was described as "laying up the waar".

Above:
The extract is allowed to seep through the rotting seaweed several times, each time getting more concentrated and effective.

7. Generate

This is a product I use on selected crops in early spring – a concentrated form of zinc ammonium acetate (combined with an organic wetter). Only one application is needed and is claimed has the effect of stimulating the production of chlorophyll, so speeding up photosynthesis. It has been discontinued, as some growers were dubious about its benefits.

8. Biosept

This is a broad-spectrum plant stimulant carefully formulated with a mixture of grapefruit oil, natural plant extracts and other essential oils that activate plant flavonoids. 'Flavonoids' is a general name given to more than 5000 compounds with many of these having antioxidant effects. The manufacturers claim that regular use of Biosept stimulates growth and builds up immunity against fungal and bacterial diseases. I doubt this substance would be any better than seaweed extract but if you were an organic grower the product might be worth considering. I have only included this to show there is more than just seaweed available.

9. Other biostimulants

As well as seaweed there are many other substances in this category, including coral extracts, ground crab and shrimp shells, and fish extracts containing high concentrations of oils and lipids (fats).

There are certainly hundreds of other biostimulant products out there – I come across many quite regularly. Many of them are questionable, and I would suggest in the first instance to stick to seaweed which has a known track record, and then possibly experiment with the others if you feel they could be of further benefit.

10. Garden compost

By this I mean rotted plant and animal tissue, as compared to peat based compost. This is an excellent example of a slow release organic fertiliser and superb if you are a dedicated organic grower. However, if you try to make compost, then make sure to carry out some research to ensure success.

Some pointers include:

- You must have a big enough pile to generate enough heat in the middle of the pile, partly to ensure proper breakdown but also to kill the unavoidable weed seeds. Because Shetland is cooler there will be a greater heat loss, and a small pile will have a greater surface to volume ratio so exacerbating the problem;
- Try to make sure that air (oxygen) can get into the centre of the pile so as to allow the aerobic micro-organisms a chance to carry out their part of the process;
- It does need to be turned from time to time, which can be heavy work.

Delivering the goods

Plants need to be watered and at the same time have the minerals delivered. Water moving through plants is not dissimilar to blood through humans, i.e. substances are transported around the tissues; and remember water is a key ingredient for photosynthesis.

1. Watering cans

It is really worthwhile getting a good watering can with a fine spray brass rose. One thing to beware is that occasionally the rose will come off accidentally, and the surge of water is unfortunate if you are working with seedlings. What I now do is fasten the rose to the can spout using a little all-weather tape. If you take feed from a barrel of solution, make sure it is covered, since insects and whatever else fall in and eventually block the rose pores. One way to dislodge the rubbish is to take the rose and connect it directly to a tap and use mains pressure to unblock it. This works quite well for bits of green slime. If you use cans or sprayers for applying weed killers always have them separated and properly labelled. Despite having now 20 or so watering cans it is amazing how often I cannot find one.

I use a small 1-litre version for watering tiny seedlings such as germinating petunias. Another option is to use a large syringe. The nice thing about a watering can is that you can be quite selective. Do watch out for the dribble at the end!

2. Hose and lance/gun

Sometimes growers prefer to use an extended gun called a lance; if you purchase one of these be wary of those with aluminium tubes as these can slowly corrode when using liquid feed solution.

Previously, I would couple the hoses, lances and guns together. There are other companies that make these, but it is a good idea to stick to one brand and then you can be sure that all the components will be compatible. When you get a lance make sure it has a trigger switch, and obtain one with a simple rose head; you do not need those which give different sprays (they are also a lot more expensive).

I have at least one full size hose with connected lance in each of my growing areas. If you have a lot of plants then watering cans are impractical. Even with hoses and lances to hand it can take me three to four hours to water at peak times. Watering is something you just cannot rush.

Below:
A typical water pump used in irrigation, and many of the Hozelock fittings for hoses, as well as watering lances.

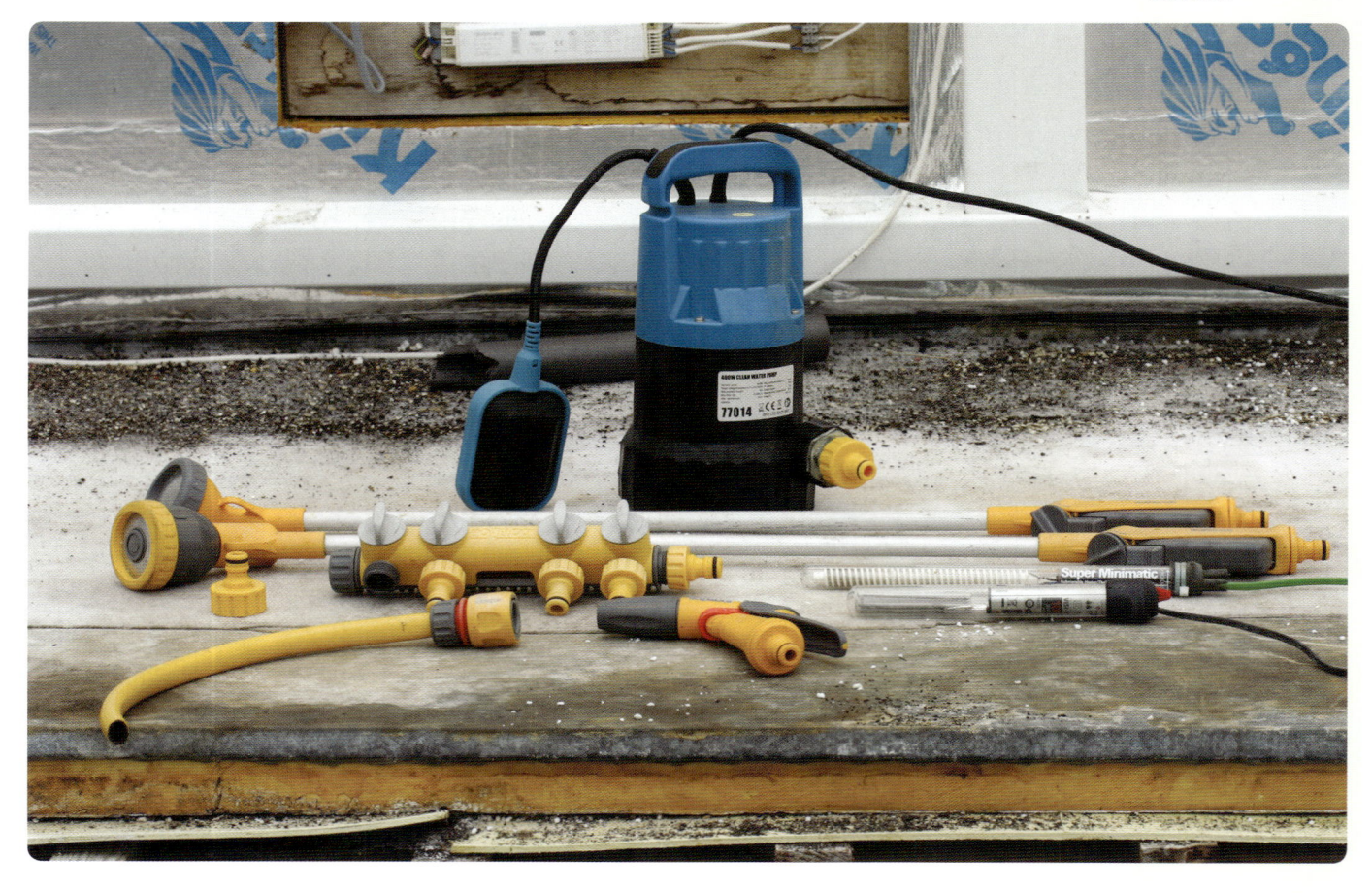

Finally, with all these lances lying around it is easy to accidentally leave them outside. Make sure to get them in before the winter as they will just burst open if ice forms inside them. I lost one lance this way a few years ago, and was more than annoyed about it.

3. Drip irrigation

I used to have containers and pots all over the place in my garden. On a fine sunny day these needed up to 100 gallons, which meant a lot of running around. I had them all connected to 'drips', i.e. tiny little tubes plugged into a long pipe. The individual drips have a flow rate of so many litres per hour, and the pipe is made of a cheap form of thin plastic, namely LDPE (or low density polyethylene). Plugged into this are 5mm drip tubes and the actual dripper plus stake. One thing to note is that for them to work the water or feed solution needs to be pumped out **under pressure**, so I use an electric pump connected to a time switch. They will not function if you simply try to 'gravity feed' by having the feed solution barrel high up on a bench.

Once you get your pipe (12mm diameter will do) you can then send it to where you want by using a variety of barbed fittings which can allow you to take a right angle bend, allow you to insert a valve and so on. If you want to be really smart you can then incorporate manifolds. The simplest method is to speak to the supplier and discuss your needs with them.

The drips I currently use are 'Aquaplast', 2-litres per hour pressure compensated, and this means that if I want the pot to get one litre I leave it switched on for 30 minutes. I could not possibly cope otherwise, with watering taking place usually at least every second day in summer. The 'pressure compensation' means that, even for a long run of pipe, the release rate is the same at each drip.

Finally, it is vital you incorporate an in-line filter between the barrel of solution and the delivery LDPE pipe. The drips are essentially small tubes bored to a precise diameter, and they are very difficult to unblock.

Below: Drip assembly.

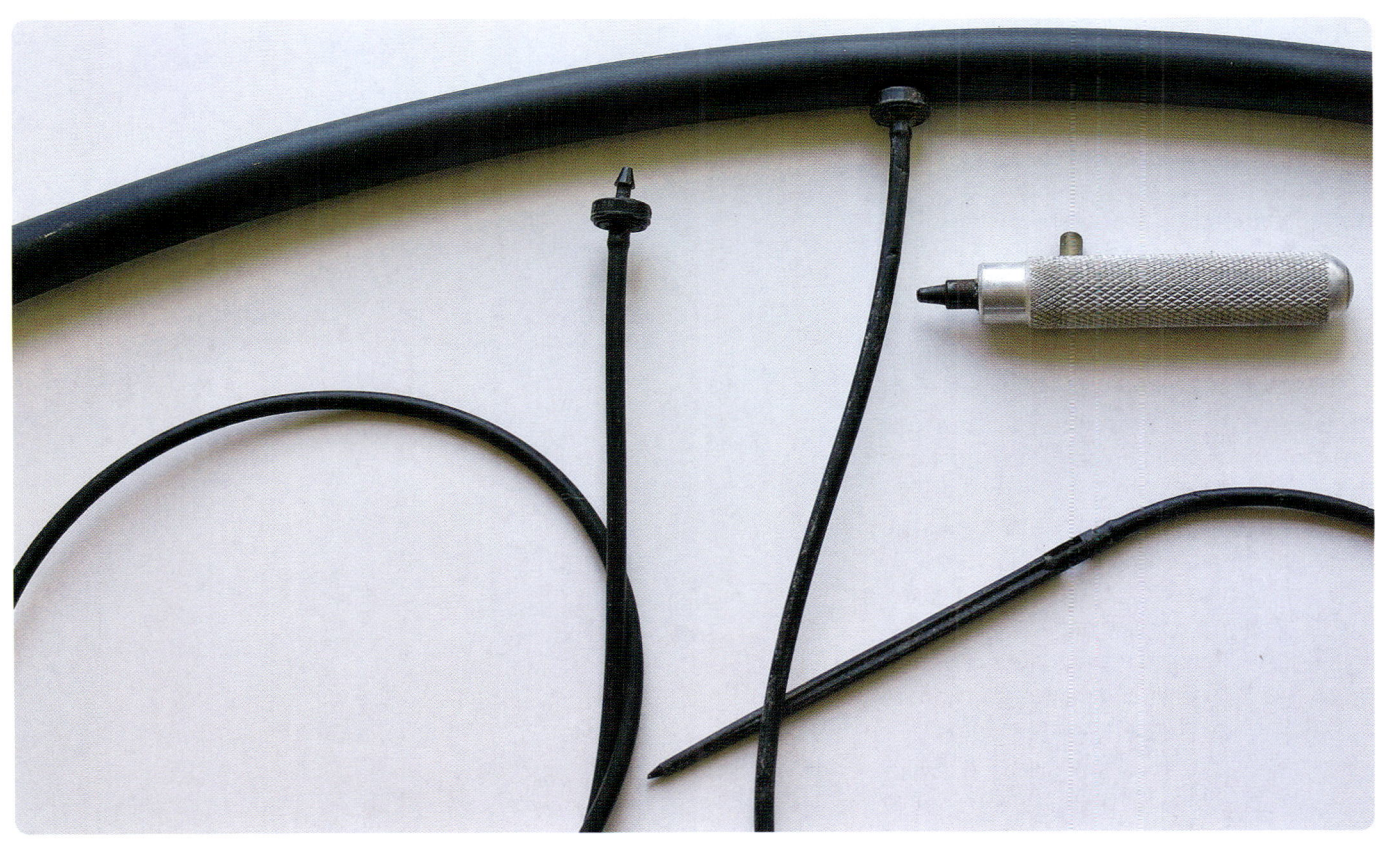

Mixing up the feed solution

It is very important that the plants get the minerals at the correct concentration. It was mentioned earlier about the danger of high salt levels and root hair damage. Here are some of the options:

1. **Mix the feed directly in the barrel and pump out.** To get an accurate concentration use a conductivity meter and make sure you stir the feed solution well. I let the pump do the mixing. I just add the concentrate, switch on the pump, and come back five minutes later. I need to pump the solution to get enough pressure, particularly with drip irrigation. There are superb water pumps available but make sure they have float switches.

Left:
I found this very smart irrigation system in a polytunnel at Whiteness; they still have to connect the electric to the solenoids (electric switches).

Below:
A water tank, supplied from the fresh tap via a ballcock. You can see the cable running down to the pump, which pushes the feed solution out via a hose. In early spring there is always an aquarium heater sitting at the bottom.

Water storage

The days of free water are over. There is nothing quite like water meters to help remind customers to turn the taps off. One way for growers to keep their costs down is to catch roof 'run off'. Many gardeners do this in a small way with 'water butts', but those with larger water requirements have to increase storage greatly. The most common method is to use circular galvanised tanks with a rubber lining; make sure there are decent foundations or solid ground underneath. You will still need to buy mains water since the bulk of the rainfall hitting Shetland is during winter, and often during May I have thought it would never rain again. But of course it does (eventually, and how)!

2. **Use a diluter.** This is a canister filled with feed concentrate. It operates by a combination of suction and pressure, with the feed being diluted as it is sucked into the fast moving water stream, often at 100 or 200:1 dilution, depending on the type of jet used.

   If your concentrate in the diluter has blue dye mixed in it then as the concentrate is displaced, you can see the blue layer in the diluter dropping. These work fine with lances and guns but fail with drip irrigation, and you must take care they do not fall over or else the concentration is affected. I believe you can get simple ones which simply connect to the end of the hose; I have not used them so cannot comment.

   I would recommend mixing in a barrel before using a diluter I am not impressed with diluters. Far better to mix in a barrel then pump out. If you have so many plants that mixing in a barrel is impractical, then I would strongly advise purchasing an injector.

3. **Use an injector.** I have used injectors in the past; they are effective but expensive. If you want to use this form of feeding then you should be looking at a smaller model which can deliver up to 2500 litres per hour. Providing they are maintained properly they give high accuracy. Sometimes they are called proportional injectors since they actively 'pump' the concentrate into the water stream. In other words, the faster the water flow the quicker the injector pump squirts fertiliser into the water stream. Injectors are commonly used by many small commercial growers, and certainly save a lot of bulk tank mixing.

Top:
This type of diluter is better than nothing; only just!

Right:
Serious growers with many plants to water and feed should be considering the Dosatron (compliments of Hingerose Ltd.).

4. Timing

Timers are almost essential because you can activate pumps exactly when you want. I use an electronic one and it can be set to the nearest minute; manual ones are only accurate to the nearest quarter of an hour. If you plan to irrigate different areas of a larger greenhouse then you can use a multi-timer connected to solenoids linked to different pipes. There are simple electronic taps available which could be useful if you want your plants watered in the middle of the day when you are not at home. Once again, take great care when fitting electrics of any sort in the glasshouse. Feed and salty solutions are highly conductive.

Using a conductivity meter

If you are serious about growing plants, a conductivity meter is highly desirable, and absolutely essential when it comes to hydroponics. You can test how much chemical is dissolved in a solution by seeing how easily electricity passes through it (or is conducted). Salt water allows electricity to pass through it more easily than fresh; this is the main reason that fishing boats operating in a marine environment are equipped with low voltage electricity, as wet, salty hands would be disastrous near faulty electrical connections. Any type of inorganic salt solution will be a good conductor of electricity because the salt, once dissolved, splits into lots of charged particles. These little particles (or ions) carry the electricity through the solution extremely easily. Many of the soluble fertilisers used by gardeners readily

Below:
This photo shows two types of electronic timer. There is also some LDPE fittings as well as a water filter with a yellow inlet and outlet.

Above:
I use all of these conductivity meters but my favourite is the top one with its bright display.

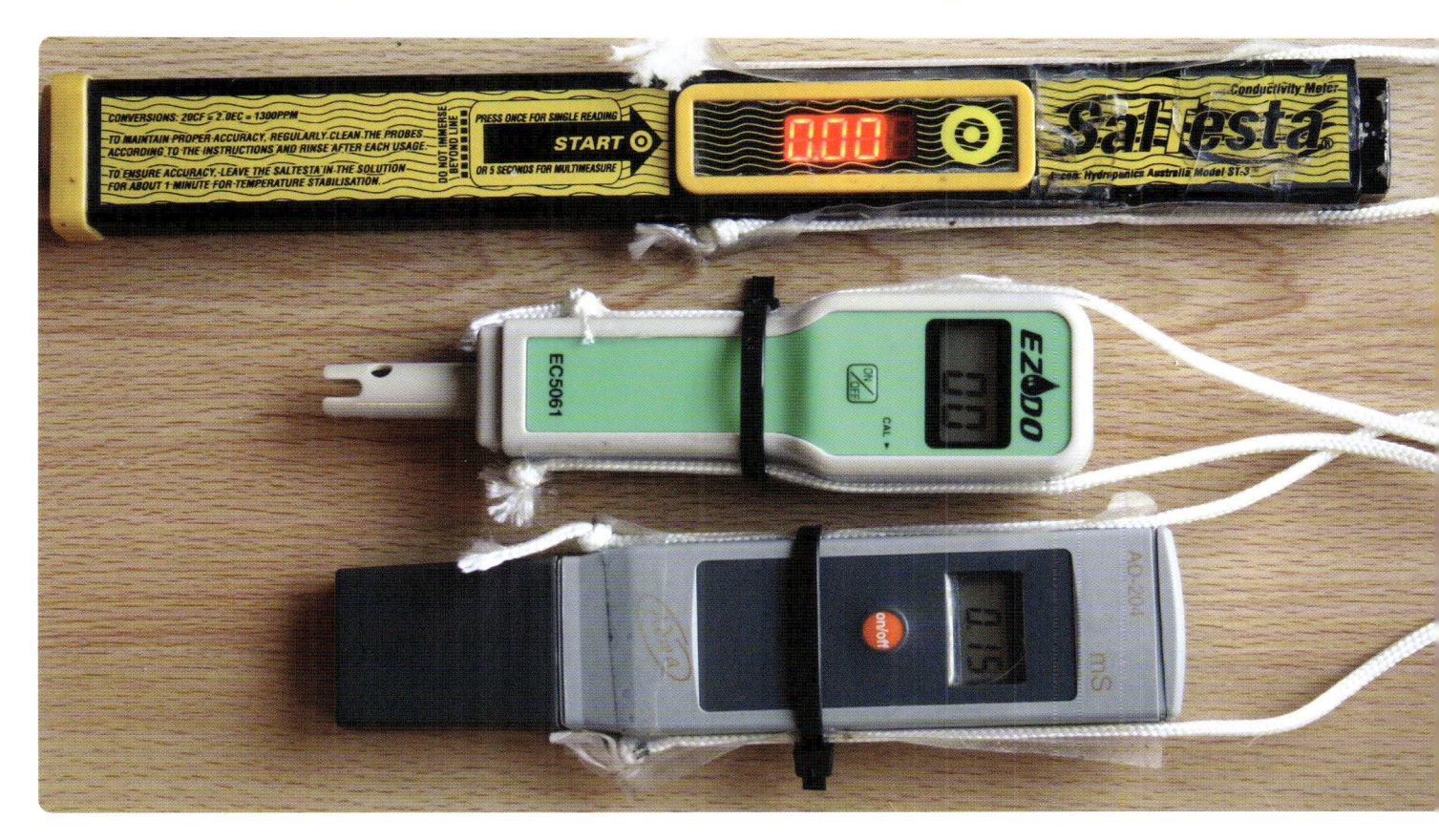

form ions in solution such as nitrates, phosphates, potassium and various other salts. When a chef refers to salt in his kitchen, he means sodium chloride; when a horticulturalist speaks about salt he is referring to a large number of chemical compounds including inorganic fertilisers, i.e. he is using the chemist's definition of 'salt' (a substance produced by the neutralisation of an acid with an alkali or base).

It should be obvious that as the solution gets saltier and saltier it becomes even more conductive as there are even more ions available to do the conducting.

The units used in conductivity

This can get very complicated, so I will keep it simple. The main ones are EC, which simply means electrical conductivity (measured in units of ms/cm, milliSiemens per centimetre), and CF meaning conductivity factor. Essentially CF is just EC without the decimal point; some countries prefer CF since its value is a whole number, though it is old fashioned.

Distilled water is pure and so will give a reading of EC = 0.0

Shetland tap water contains a little amount of dissolved minerals and when tested gives a reading of EC = 0.4; or you could just as easily say it had a CF = 4. You might want to feed your tomatoes with Tomorite at a value of EC = 2.5; this is just the same as CF = 25.

For my day-to-day work I use the CF scale; whole numbers are easier to write down – as simple as that!

A conductivity meter has fewer applications for a soil grower because many of the nutrients present are said to be 'organic'. Substances such as fishmeal or hoof and horn will dissolve but do not form charged particles (or ions), so do not register on a concuctivity meter.

Other terms commonly used in the measurement of plant nutrition are ppm and TDS. The first of these, ppm, simply means parts per million (or milligrams per litre, i.e. mg/l); the second refers to 'Total Dissolved Solids'. This is a very accurate measurement of nutrient availability but the technique required is outside the scope of this book.

Some conductivity have the advantage of a bright illuminated readout and automatic switch off.

To calibrate your meter, simply acquire some anhydrous calcium sulphate (ask a school science lab for a little – it is cheap), put several spoons into a jam jar full of distilled water and shake. Check next day – there should be some powder at the bottom, i.e. the solution is 'saturated'. If not, then add some more and shake again until you are left with white sediment at the bottom of the jar. This gives a CF of 20 at room temperature (20°C).

Another method is to add table salt (sodium chloride) to distilled water; if you can get someone to accurately measure out 2.1 grams of table salt and dissolve this in 1 litre of distilled water then your meter should read CF = 30 (equivalent to EC 3.0)

If you can chat up someone who works in a science laboratory, ask if they can make up a small bottle of 0.01 N potassium chloride in distilled water; this makes a standard giving you a CF of 14 at 25°C (equivalent to an EC of 1.4). A box of chocolates should be a fair payment.

Finally, you can order standard calibration solutions from virtually all the conductivity meter manufacturers.

Shetland has good quality tap water but it is not 'pure' since it contains small quantities of natural minerals that dissolve out of the landscape. These include sodium chloride and other less well-known compounds. So when you test the conductivity of a jar of tap water you get a reading round about CF = 3, sometimes described as the 'background' CF. If I wanted to feed my bedding plants at CF 15 then I would actually apply it at CF = 18, i.e. the 15 desired value plus the value 3 already existing in the water.

If you are growing 'long haul' crops such as house plants, then over time the background salt from the water supply will start to build up in the compost; when you carry out medium analysis you get a decent reading but a lot of it is due to background remnants such as sodium chloride, which the plant does not really want. For this reason, every now and again, it is worthwhile irrigating your plants **to excess** with plain water to flush some of these unwanted minerals away. This is much easier said than carried out in real life! Once again Shetland has soft water so background build-up will not be the issue it would be for growers in the chalky regions of south England.

Below:
One of these meters needs a slight adjustment. They are both sitting in the same solution, with the left one reading CF 79 and the other reading EC7.5, i.e. CF = 10x EC.

When you read culture notes relating to different plants, they will give the concentration and frequency of feeding. Some plants need a lot of feeding and others much less.

Testing the fertiliser level in your compost

There are various ways to test the feed levels present in the growing medium, with the 'Pour Thru' probably being the easiest to carry out. This test was developed in the USA.

1. Water the plants one or two days before you normally give them their weekly feed.

2. About an hour after this watering, set the pot into a plastic saucer. Add enough distilled water to the surface of the compost to produce about 40ml liquid seeping into the saucer. Ideally you should be taking the samples from five pots and either doing them individually and taking the average, or mixing them together and taking the mix reading.

3. For all extractions it is better to use distilled water since tap water will contain its own natural salts, although, as I said earlier, this tends to be at a low level in Shetland.

4. There are a number of other extraction methods but what makes this one so attractive is that it signals the fertiliser level actually experienced by the roots.

The following information indicates the 'Pour Thru' results you should be expecting with different crops.

Light feeders

With the following plants you should be looking at a Pour Thru EC of 1.0 to 2.6, the same as CF 10 to 26:

Ageratum, Begonia (fibrous), Begonia (tuberous), Cineraria, Coleus, Cosmos, Cuttings (during rooting), Cyclamen, Geranium (seed), Impatiens, Marigold, Pansy, Plugs, Primula, Salvia, Snapdragon

Medium feeders

With the medium feeders you should be looking at a Pour Thru EC of 2.0 to 3.5, the same as CF 20 to 35:

Alyssum, Calendula, Campanula, Carnation, Dahlia, Dianthus, Cineraria (foliage), Geranium (cutting), Larkspur, Lobelia, Onion, Pepper, Petunia, Rose, Sunflower (potted), Tomato, Verbena

It is so easy to add concentrated fertiliser solution, and before you know it you have pickled the root hairs, and instead of going one step forward you go ten in reverse. Some plants are very sensitive to high salt levels, and others less so. Whether I am simply adding a watering can full of fertiliser solution to a few trays of plug plants, or mixing a 250-litre barrel full for pumping out, I always double check the CF level. Before I even start I test the value of the water supply, and if the reading is not between 3 and 4 I then get another conductivity meter to double check; it may be the battery is getting low. So the first line of defence against burning the root hairs is to know what level of feed you **want** to supply and checking the **precise** solution value.

Another fatal error is to jump from a weak feed solution to a strong one too quickly (though it is tempting to do so). For instance, you might be feeding tomatoes at a CF of, say, 18. Then the first truss sets, so you want to take the feed level up to CF 26. All you need to do is simply raise the feed level by a value CF= 2 to CF = 20 at the next feeding, then two days after that increase to CF = 22 and so on. This lets the roots gradually adjust to the feed level and stronger growth will ensue.

Bill Argo and Paul Fisher, in their series of articles 'Understanding Plant Nutrition: Managing Medium EC' suggest the following fertiliser concentrations as a starting point for feeding:

50-75 ppm N for plugs;

75-150 ppm N for bedding plants;

200-250 ppm N for pot plants and larger containers.

The numbers describe parts per million (mg per litre) nitrogen in the mix. These values correspond to conductivity values of EC = <0.7 (CF < 7) for plugs, EC 0.6 to 1.1 (CF 6 to 11) for bedding and EC1.5 to 1.8 (CF 15 to 18) for pot plants and larger containers if using balanced feed.

My own feeding regime

With so many different crops on the go at once, and many at different stages of growth, I have to compromise. Except for leeks, which I feed alternately with high nitrogen feed, the bulk of my plants are fed with the hydroponic high potash recipe developed at the Scottish Crops Research Institute (SCRI) based at Auchincruive.

For plug plants, depending on the variety, I will feed either once or twice a week at a reduced level of around CF 8 to 10. They will be achieving steady growth under the lighting rigs.

When I prick out the seedlings or pot them up, there is enough feed in the potting mix to keep them going for the first two or three weeks. Once the 'better' weather comes during early March, I will then commence feeding. Since 90%+ of my plants are sold in flower, I use the high potash recipe two to three times weekly at a CF of around 18 (having added on the CF = 3 already in the mains water) depending on the weather conditions. Immediately after feeding I reconnect to the fresh water and rinse away the traces of feed solution from the plant leaves. If this feed solution is allowed to sit on the leaves on a sunny day, the water evaporates and the concentrated fertiliser scorches and burns holes in the leaves. That is a recipe for disaster!

I am not saying that my husbandry is perfect but most plants sparkle with regular nutrition. As for the perennials (bar the saxifrage and alpines), I give them a once-weekly feed with the same high potash recipe.

Above and left: I raised these primroses from seed a number of years back; with proper nutrition they show great contrast between the flower and the leaves.

Summary of plant feeding

- There are three main (macro) elements, namely Nitrogen (N), Phosphorus (P) and Potassium (K). If a ratio is given on a pack of fertiliser then it will always be in the order NPK, e.g. 2-1-5 is a fertiliser rich in potassium but with plenty of nitrogen and phosphorus.

- It might be better sticking to liquid feeding as the cool temperatures make slow release fertiliser rather unpredictable.

- As well as the macro elements there are the micro elements such as iron, magnesium, calcium, copper and so on.

- When buying fertilisers shop around with the idea of the 'bigger the cheaper' and use powders which are more cost effective.

- Peat-based compost has a much lower fertiliser reserve than loam.

- Generally you should start feeding plants growing in potting compost when the roots hit the side of the pot.

- Most plants will be happy with two feeds per week, with the exception of tomatoes and other heavy fruit bearers which should be fed at every watering.

- Always stick to the manufacturer's recommendations.

pH and plants

We meet 'pH' regularly in life whether it relates to toothpaste or shampoo, and this chemical concept has great relevance to horticulture.

The symbol pH tells us how many charged hydrogen ion particles (H+) are present in water-based solutions, and consequently we can also deduce the numbers of another particle called the hydroxyl ion (OH-) present. Put simply, if there are lots of hydrogen ions there will be very few hydroxyls and we therefore have a strong acid, such as you would find in a car battery. Conversely, if there are few hydrogen ions there will be many hydroxyl ions present, and you have a strong alkali such as caustic soda. When the amounts of the two particles are equal then we end up with a **neutral** solution, the best example being pure water. Both hydrogen and hydroxyl ions are aggressively active and if there are too many of either, we end up with corrosive and dangerous solutions.

The pH scale used to measure acidity ranges from 1 to 14. What is confusing is that the lower the number the more acidic the solution. So at value 1 we have a very strong acid, at 14 we have a very strong alkali and at value 7 we have a neutral solution.

So –

$$H^+ \; H^+ \; H^+ \; H^+ \; H^+ \; H^+ \; H^+ \; H^+ \; H^+$$
$$OH^- \; H^+ \; H^+ \; H^+ \; H^+ \; H^+$$
$$H^+ \; H^+ \; H^+ \; H^+ \; H^+ \; OH^- \; H^+$$

This would be very acidic, i.e. lots of **H+**

The pH scale is logarithmic meaning that pH 4 contains 10 times more hydrogen ions than pH 5, 100 times more than pH 6, 1000 times more than pH 7 and so on; in other words, plants which grow fine at pH 5 might positively struggle at pH 4. The scales we normally use, such as measuring a length with a ruler, are said to be linear.

Left:
The pH of these liquids are all different, ranging from acidic (red) through neutral (green) to alkali (blue).

Importance in horticulture

The pH value is critical as this controls the ability of the soil or compost to release minerals and make them available to the plant for absorption. There could be sufficient minerals in the medium but if the pH is wrong they will be 'bound up' and unavailable to the roots. The diagram right shows the solubility of different elements at different pH values – essentially the thicker the band the more available it becomes. At around pH 4 in soil most minerals start to become very soluble and will get washed out, and then soluble aluminium appears. Even at value 5 we have problems with phosphate availability. However, at the other end of the scale (above 7.5), we get reduced availability of phosphate, potassium and many traces. Every plant has its optimal (most suitable) pH. In the case of a loam-based medium, most plants do well with a reading about pH 6 to 7 with 6.5 probably the ideal value for the vegetable garden. If you grow brassicas and have problems with the fungus clubroot you could even push this a bit higher to pH 6.5 to 7. However, some plants prefer acidic conditions at 4.5 to 5, e.g. heathers, azaleas and rhododendrons, so these must be grown in an acid soil or using an ericaceous (lime free) compost. Purely out of interest, hydrangea flowers turn white in soil of high pH and purple in soil that is acidic.

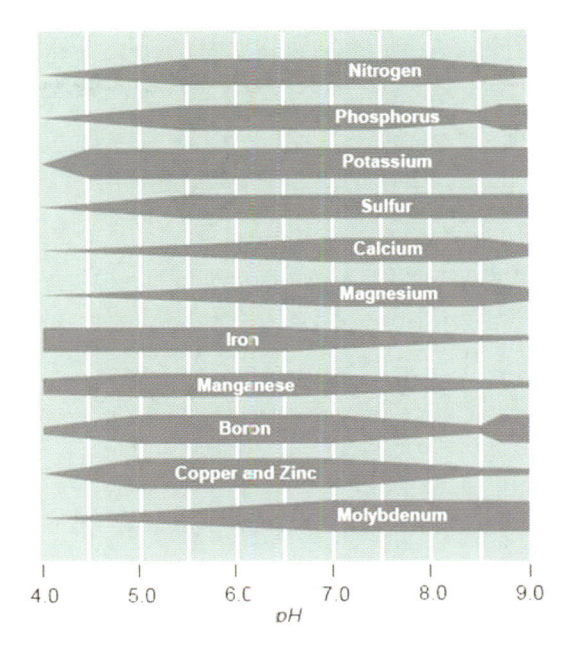

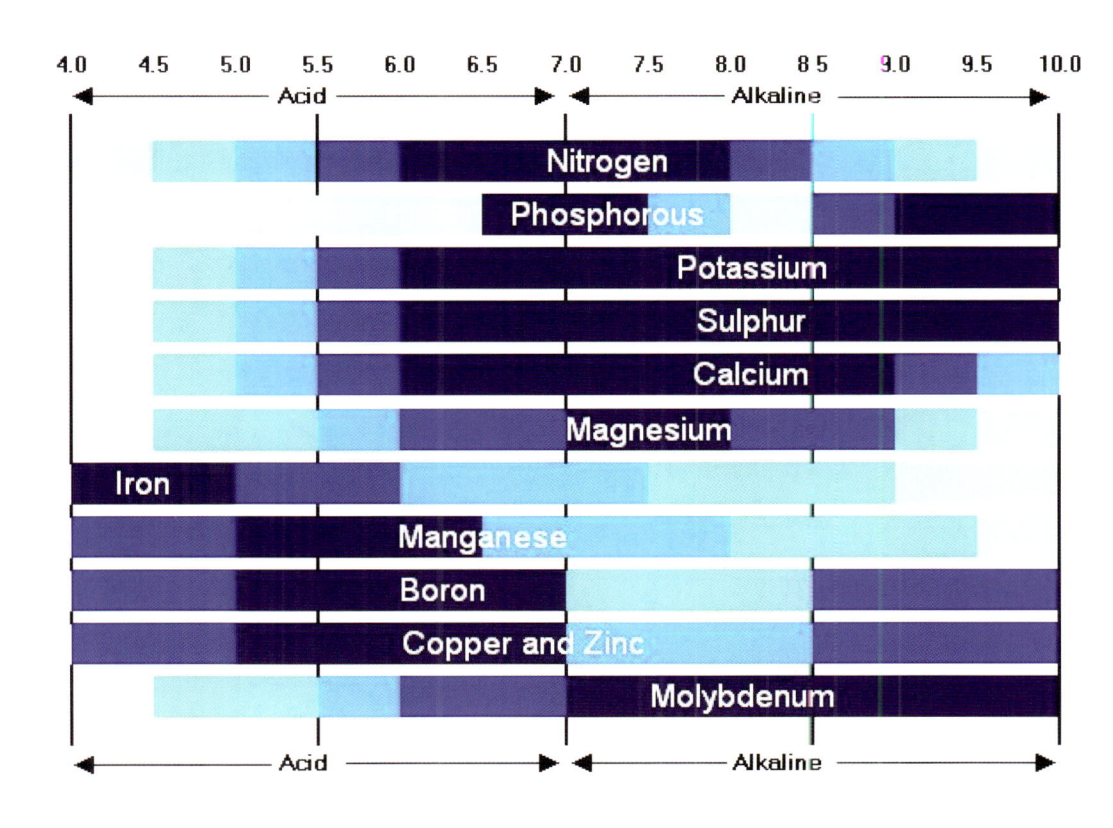

Top:
This shows the amount of mineral released at different pH values. Essentially the thicker the band the greater the release. For instance at pH value 4.0 there is virtually no molybdenum available.

Right:
This is another way of looking at mineral release; it is based on a diagram produced by Micromix Ltd.

A peat-based medium (your 'normal' potting compost) is completely different. The bands of availability tend to be increased at the lower levels in peat (as compared to soil) with the optimal pH being in the range 5.0-5.5. One good example is that of phosphorus (essential for good root growth) which at pH 7 is abundant in loam but very scarce in peaty compost.

Bear in mind that the soil in your garden has completely different physical and chemical characteristics compared to peat-based compost, and even a whole book devoted to this subject would just skim the surface.

Water quality

Shetland's local water supply is excellent for feeding plants, particularly if you are a hydroponic grower.

I contacted Scottish Water early in 2008 regarding water quality and was told that Lerwick's water is classed as 'moderately soft'. They told me that there are a number of ways of expressing hardness. In my case the water had "28.6 mg/l as calcium **or** 71.5 mg/l as calcium carbonate **or** 0.7 millimoles calcium **or** 14.9mg per litre bicarbonate **or** 5.0 Clarke Degrees," and so on. All that matters is that there is very little calcium present, hence our kettles and pipes never 'fur up' with scale as they do in the south coast of England. Another water analysis a few years earlier stated: "Your water is of excellent quality particularly for hydroponics". Water containing high levels of calcium creates a pH increase of the growing medium, and then the chemistry gets complicated. We do not have that problem here.

If your plants do not grow properly then do not blame the water!

Above:
The blue copper and brown iron compounds have no difficulty in dissolving in the left hand side acid solutions, but sit unchanged in the alkali.

Testing pH

You can test the pH either by using your tongue (joking), a pH meter or pH paper. Unless you are a chemist, avoid pH meters. They are quick and accurate but quite unstable and notoriously difficult to calibrate. It is much easier is to use pH paper or an indicator solution. You should try to use narrow range pH paper, which will give a fairly accurate value. The paper will last for years providing you keep it cool and dry.

Testing soil pH

Take several small eggcup samples from different parts of your garden.

Add two volumes of water for every volume of soil plus a small pinch of calcium chloride and stir for five minutes so that you end up with a brown 'soup'.

Allow the solids to settle for at least five minutes.

Filter the top layer of brown solution into a clean jar (do not filter the sludge at the bottom).

Insert a small piece of pH paper into the solution for about five seconds, remove, and compare the colour with the scale.

If using a pH meter, then make sure to clean the probe before and after use.

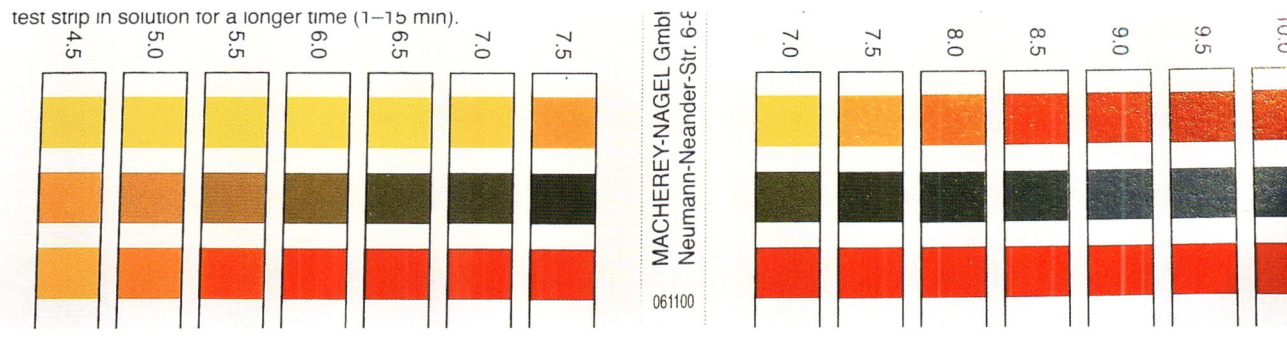

Above:

Can you match the top six test strips with the key? I would have said that the second one had a value of around pH = 9.0

Adjusting pH

If your soil is acidic you can neutralise it by adding an alkali. So the OH- joins with the H+ from the acid and, bingo, you end up with water, i.e. neutralisation.

$$H^+ + OH^- \longrightarrow H_2O$$

This happens every time you cure indigestion due to excess acid being produced in your stomach. When you take milk of magnesia ($Mg(OH)_2$) you are swallowing an alkali to neutralise an acid. Purely out of interest, honey bee stings are acidic whereas wasp stings are alkali. If a wasp stings you then get out the vinegar; if it is a bee then treat with detergent.

Shetland is largely clad in acid soil, and this explains the predominance of heather. Chalky or other calcium rich substances have the effect of increasing pH, and locally the farmers deliberately add calcium in the form of lime which, when dissolved, yields the alkaline solution calcium hydroxide. By using rock lime (a slower dissolving form of the mineral) reduced acidity can be sustained over a number of years, but does have to be replenished eventually.

By knowing the pH of a particular soil an analyst can easily determine the mass of lime required, although it does also depend on the soil type.

Unless you are a crofter-cum-gardener you will obviously not be interested in the liming requirements of the hills of Shetland, but the table above gives the general idea.

If, on the other hand, you want to make your soil acidic then you can consider adding either flowers of sulphur (which is converted to acid by microbial action), or alternatively aluminium sulphate.

If you are a keen gardener and have a soil whose nutrition status is uncertain you must get a full chemical analysis carried out. I always use the Scottish Agricultural College (SAC) based at the Agricultural Centre in Lerwick; they carry out an accurate pH and test the levels of two of the three key nutrients, P and K. What is far more important than the actual testing is their recommendations. I have had SAC soil analysis carried out two or three times. One of my results is shown below, along with the excellent advice given by the analyst

Initial pH Of Loam	Volume Lime Added (Kg Per m^3)
6.3 and over	Nil
6.0	1.25
5.5	2.50
5.0	4.50
4.5	6.25

The cost is very reasonable and would more than pay for itself even in the short term. Consider the 'law of limiting factors' – this states that all the key nutrients have to be there in the correct quantities for the plant to grow at its optimum. You might have plenty of N and P but if there is insufficient K your crop will just not thrive. No different from you or I not getting enough vitamin C! One of my first analyses, when we moved to our present house around thirty years ago, indicated a shortage of phosphorus and I remember spreading 'basic slag' (slow release form of mineral rock phosphate) on my vegetable patch; who could forget a name like that!

Summary of pH and its effects on Plant Growth

- When we speak about soil acidity we are referring to a value known as its pH. The pH value is part of a scale which ranges from 1 to 14 with the middle number 7 being said to be 'neutral'.

- The solutions **below** 7 are acidic whereas those **above** 7 are alkaline. A lower or higher number corresponds to a greater acidity or alkalinity.

- If the pH is wrong, then even if there are sufficient nutrients present these will be bound up in the soil and unavailable for the plant.

irrigation, feeding and pH

100 years Supporting the land-based industries 1904 - 2004

SAC

Pure Shetland
C/O Alec Henry
Baillster
Gott
Shetland
ZE2 9SH

Our Ref: gjf/wmc/adv/soil

Date 22/04/2004

Dear Alec,

Subject: Soil Analysis

Enclosed are the analysis results for the soil sample you submitted, Lab Ref No 24004136.

Everything analysed is high including the pH, which is extremely high at 7.9. Has excessive lime or sand been applied in the past?

With a pH of 7.9 your crops may be prone to trace element deficiencies such as manganese, boron and iron. Either use a general foliar feed containing trace elements or treat the specific problems. For example brassicas may require a boronated fertiliser to prevent problems.

Farmyard manure is probably all that is required as a fertiliser but if unavailable you could use a general fertiliser such as 20:10:10 at 30-40 grams/m².

Yours sincerely,

Graham Fraser

G J Fraser
Senior Consultant

SAC
Farm Business Services Division
Agricultural Marketing Centre
Staneyhill, Lerwick
Shetland ZE1 0RN

Direct Tel Line: +44 (01 395 693420)
Direct Fax Line: +44 (01 395 693450)

Summary of Results

For: **Pure Shetland**
c/o Alec Henry
Bailister
Gott

Batch Number: S32378

Farm sampled:-

Notes: a) VL=Very low, L=Low, M=Moderate
H=High, EH=Excessively high
b) P=Phosphorus, K=Potassium
Mg=Magnesium

ASD Ref	Field name/ref.	pH	Lime required Arable t/ha	Grass	P	Extractable K mg/l	Mg
24004136	Vegetable Plot	7.9	0	0	32.2(H)	224(H)	792(H)

- The optimum value for peat compost is 5 to 5.5 whereas for soil it is 6 to 6.5.

- Some plants like moderately acid conditions; one should grow these in what is called ericaceous compost or lime-free soil.

The big trick to successful horticulture is to remove the guesswork and be rigorous and systematic. There is no such thing as green fingers. Never guess, if you have an instrument or technique that can give you a measured value.

Correspondence from the Scottish Agricultural College regarding soil samples taken from my garden.

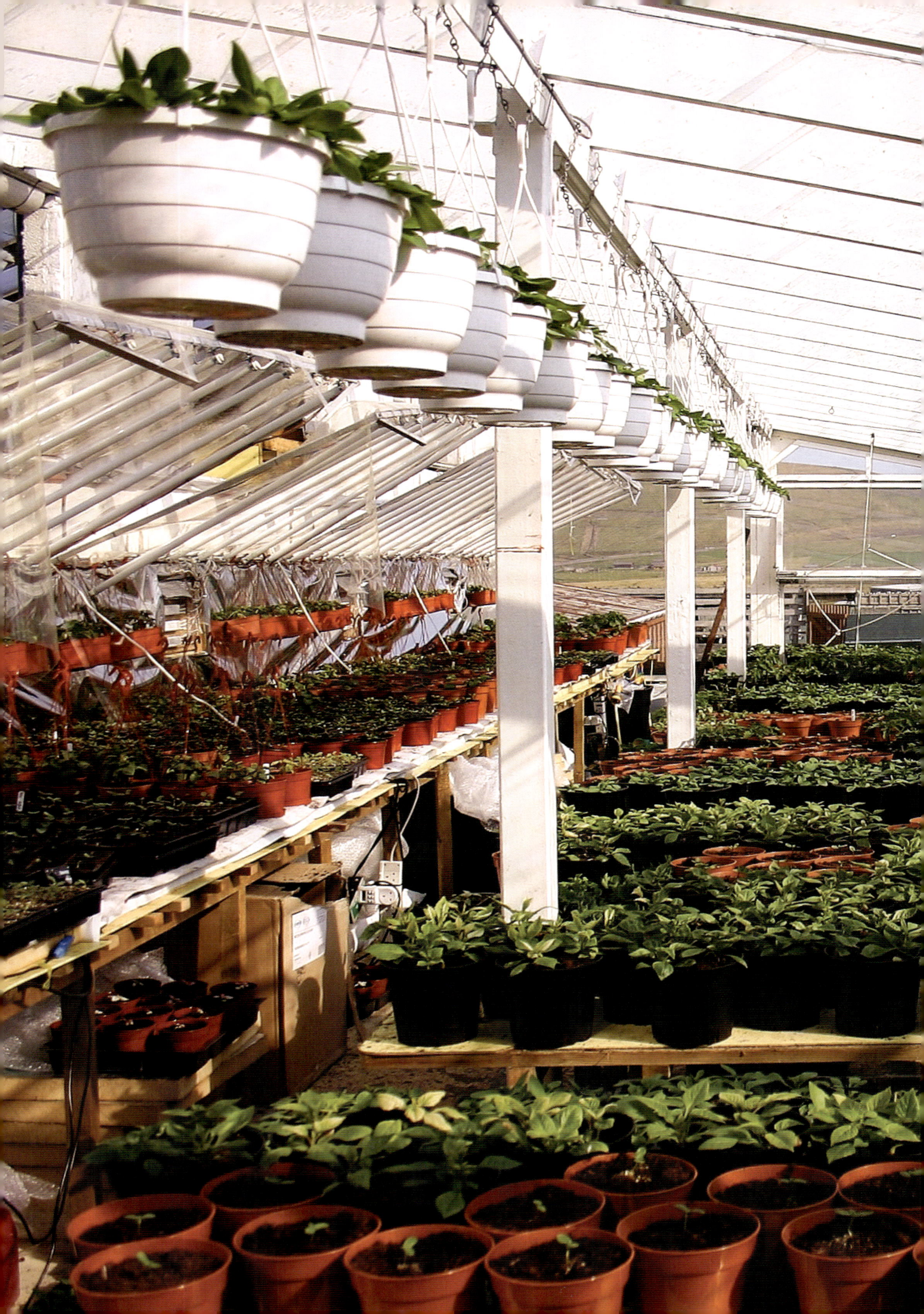

Chapter 6
Growth Media and Hydroponics

Plants can be grown in a huge number of different materials (growth media) ranging from soil to sand and straw, but they must all have certain key features or they will not be effective.

The key features are **air and water holding capacity**, and roots must be able to penetrate and grow. So a wet brick will not do, despite being full of air and water. It is also desirable that a store of minerals is held in reserve, though these can be delivered in solution, as is the case with hydroponics.

What makes a good growth medium?

Whenever you add water to a pot plant you drive the air out (like soaking a sponge) but of course you can replace the air by drying it out again. This is not practical and does not make sense. An ideal medium is one that you can water and is relatively free-draining so that the air can once more be replaced, but still leave a reservoir of water available for the plants. A good analogy is 'the sponge' model. If you take a sponge, saturate it and then let it drain, you find the following:

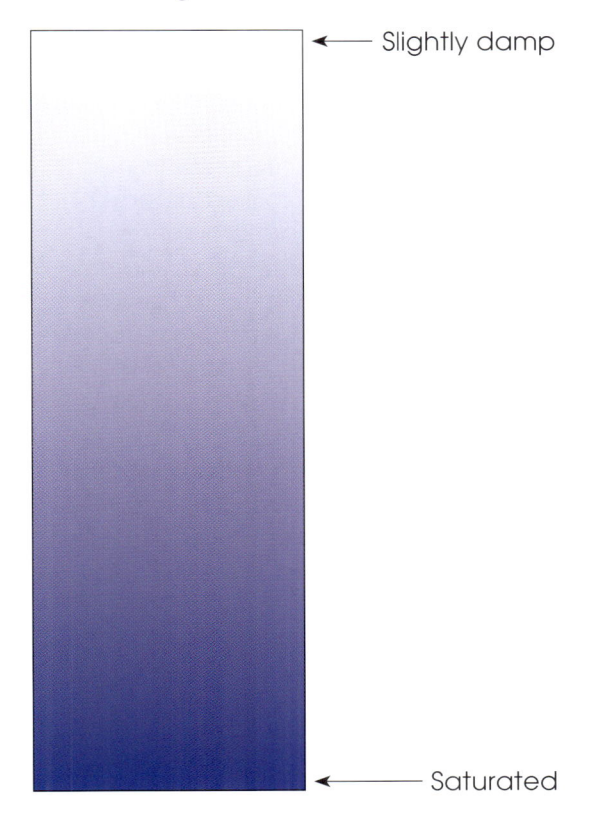

← Slightly damp

← Saturated

Note that the top of the sponge is a little damp but at the bottom it is saturated. If you now squeeze the sponge, water pours out – this is the **available water** i.e. the water easily taken up by the roots. When all this is used up we eventually get permanent wilting point (PWP) after which the plant dies. The sponge is still damp, yet you cannot squeeze any more out – this is the **unavailable water**, which cannot easily be released. By altering the type of sponge, i.e. increasing its pore size, we can make it drain more easily, but at the expense of less available water. If finer pores are present, then less water will drain, and hence a greater zone of saturation. So in many ways it is always a compromise, i.e. if you increase the air you decrease the water and vice versa.

One very important feature of the medium is the amount of air present after watering; this is called the air filled porosity (AFP). A simple method enabling you to calculate the AFP is given in Appendix 8.

Peat-based composts

Shredded peat makes a wonderful growth medium but you cannot take any old peat and use it in any old way. What you use needs to be fibrous and **not dusty,** i.e. the top layer from a peat bank, but never the 'blue' muddy peat deeper down. When I first started growing plants, I used to visit the peat banks in late spring when there was a dry spell, and used a rake to gather the surface peat broken up by the winter frosts. Once I had transported it home I would mix it with the correct chemical recipe to make either seedling or potting compost.

One interesting characteristic of peat-based composts is that they are affected by 'shrinkage' over a longer period, and the size of container affects the amount of air space. So a 2.5cm plug has 3%, a 10cm pot has 13% and a 15cm pot 20% air space. Peat particles are elastic and the swelling and contracting with moisture over time lowers porosity. This is one good reason to keep the compost moist! Air filled porosity (AFP) is fixed when you pot the plants and can decrease over time. Fortunately, vigorous root growth can maintain and even increase aeration. Anyone who works peat for fuel will be aware of this shrinkage, and when you dump out the compost from a 'dry' pot, you will certainly see a gap between the compost and pot wall where shrinkage has taken place.

I contacted a company based in Ireland for more information about their peat composts, since I was using around 300 x 80-litre bags per year. They said that the AFP of their **multipurpose** compost was usually around 8-12%. It should have enough fertiliser to last most plants for the first four to five weeks of growth; after this they would require additional feeding. Multipurpose compost is a compromise between what is ideal for germinating seedlings, and the medium suitable for growing on larger plants in pots and containers. Ideally, germinating seeds require finer compost with low fertiliser levels, while mature plants in large pots require much coarser compost with a higher fertiliser level. The multipurpose compost is a compromise between the two.

Characteristics of this **multipurpose** compost are given below;

- About 90% of particles are in the Grade range 10-15mm;
- The AFP is in the range 10-13%;
- The pH is in the range 5.5-6.0 using Dolomitic limestone as a neutralising agent;
- There is an added 'wetting agent' to aid wetting and rewetting;
- It contains vermiculite to increase water-holding capacity and act as a nutrient buffer;
- Liquid feeding should commence three to four weeks after potting for standard nutrient compost (and two to three weeks for the low nutrient)

In practice, I find some potting composts dry very quickly in glasshouse conditions but are fine for the outside pots where the greater AFP is an advantage in Shetland's wetter climate. All my glasshouse and tunnel plants are grown using multipurpose compost.

From what I have said already, most of the information should make sense, but there is also one important extra feature, namely an added 'wetting agent'. Wetting agents are critical for peat-based composts. A few Shetlanders still cut peat for fuel from certain local hills. Over the summer months there are generally more dry days than wet ones, and once the peat is cut and dried it is extremely hard to rewet. I have taken a dry clod of peat and put a few drops of water on it; the water just sits and might have soaked in by the next day (if it has not already evaporated). The wetting agents (which are no more than a glorified detergent), overcome this awkward problem. If you have difficulty watering your pots with the water 'running off' rather than soaking in, it may well be there is no wetting agent present – and you then have real problems! When you purchase a bag of compost always look for signs that wetting agents have been added. If not, then I would advise you to give it a miss and get some compost you know contains them.

There is also multipurpose compost 'with added John Innes', leading to a higher fertiliser reservoir due to the buffering capacity of the soil. Larger horticultural businesses can deal directly with the compost manufacturers to specify exactly what type of medium they want, whether it be a particular pH, AFP or fertiliser level. Rosa Steppanova makes specific composts tailored to her own needs. She is a particularly good perennial grower and sometimes when I visit her I come away thinking I know nothing! If you really want to make your own compost then you can use a cement mixer making sure that:

- The compost and chemicals are well mixed (but not for longer than is necessary otherwise you will damage the peat's structure);
- The peat is not too wet or else it will turn into little round 'lumps', which end up with the minerals coating the outside but none inside, i.e. it is not properly mixed. I know this from experience.

Alpines prefer soil + 30% grit to save them from waterlogging. Making up specialised composts is not a practical option for me, so I keep alpines 'dry' under the cold frames in winter instead.

Chemical formulation for peat-based composts

The simplest way to make your compost fertile is to use a 'Chempak' seedling or potting compost mix; all you have to do is add the chemicals in the packet to the correct volume of compost and mix it in the cement mixer as described above. If you want to save money, you can make up the chemical mix yourself using the raw ingredients – these are sometimes called 'straights'. Following are the suggested recipes given by GCRI (Glasshouse Crops Research Institute), which I have used successfully for several years.

Seed compost

To every cubic metre (1000 litres) of shredded peat add the following:

0.75 kg superphosphate;

0.4 kg potassium nitrate;

3.0 kg ground chalk, or calcium limestone.

Note that this compost is low in nutrients and is meant for seed germination. GCRI recommends adding 50% lime-free sand to the compost but I never found this necessary. Low nutrient compost is highly desirable for germinating species such as begonias and other salt sensitive types, but in real life I find multipurpose compost works pretty well for most plants. The ground chalk or calcium limestone is required to raise the pH from acidic to nearer neutral.

Potting compost

To every cubic metre (1000 litres) of shredded peat add the following:

0.4 kg ammonium nitrate (nitram);

1.5 kg superphosphate;

0.75 potassium nitrate;

2.8 kg ground chalk, or calcium limestone;

2.8 kg dolomitic (magnesium containing) limestone;

0.5 kg fritted trace elements 253A;

500g Aquamix G wetting agent granules.

This will give you a chemical mix at about one quarter the price of 'Chempak', but of course you have to buy these 'straights' in bulk. You can see there is a higher percentage of fertiliser and a slower releasing magnesium limestone. The fritted trace is essentially trace elements such as cobalt and copper dissolved in molten glass, and then rapidly cooled before being ground to a powder.

Compost bought one year can easily be used the following spring but do not keep it outside where it will get soaked, nor store it in a hot area where it will gradually dry out; the plastic bag contains lots of small holes through which the water can evaporate (dry peat is very difficult to re-wet).

Other types of Medium

Coir based

This is the waste produced from the coir fibre element of coconut husks, and is an attempt to reduce the use of peat-based compost, with peat being a finite (non-renewable) resource. As with all media, it has its own characteristics, which will mean new learning, so I shall stick with peat-based in the meantime. Coir may well take over from peat as more research goes on. One advantage is that it is longer lasting than peat and does not degrade as quickly. Soft fruit growers, who have started new trials, report excellent results; there is nothing like getting large harvests to persuade growers to change to something new. The '2011 Greenhouse Yearbook' states, "In the UK soft fruit sector, coir is beginning to look like the default growing medium". The main reason is that fruit growers can make a coir-based substrate last two to three years compared to the one to two years typically seen with peat. With fruit, the longer life of coir compensates for the higher purchase price. It always boils down to economics, especially in the commercial sector.

Coir is often supplied dehydrated and compressed, with the grower just adding water when ready to plant.

Above:
A coir sample before the addition of water.

Left:
A wetted coir sample sitting next to some multipurpose peat. The coir is lighter, coarser and with more fibres.

Hydroponics – small scale

Hydroponics literally means feeding plants using fertiliser solutions and without soil, the latter being substituted with a completely sterile medium. The original 'true' hydroponics was called nutrient film technique (NFT), where the feed solution was recirculated and the plants grown in feed solution running between two layers of plastic. The NFT technique is tricky to manage and led to the introduction of rockwool and perlite. These are both derived from heated or spun rock. Rockwool is used universally, however perlite gives good yields and gives much more leeway for the amateur grower. The media are sometimes called 'substrates' and there are lots of them, ranging from glass wool to pumice to river sand and expanded clay. Dennis Smith best summarises the advantages of rockwool and perlite in his book 'Growing in Rockwool':

> "Soil is often colder than the glasshouse atmosphere and is also an excellent medium for the growth of fungal and other diseases, which inevitably become established in an intensive cropping programme. Attempting to eliminate them completely by soil sterilisation is very difficult.
>
> Substrates like rockwool and perlite translate all of the disadvantages of soil into advantages. They allow fine control of the supply of oxygen, water and nutrients to the roots. They are lightweight, quick to warm up and can be economically heated to the optimum requirements of the crop, and initially sterile."

Hydroponics has been adopted in most commercial glasshouses because it is easily managed and high yielding.

How is hydroponics carried out?

Very simply by growing plants in sand, rockwool, perlite or some other sterile medium with sufficient air-spaces and liquid-holding capacity. For the amateur, perlite is ideal and easy to work with. If we have plants growing in a perlite bag or pot with feed dripping in at the top and a reservoir buffer at the bottom, we have an excellent combination of air/water balance with capillary action allowing movement through the bag to the roots. In essence, the perlite acts rather like blotting paper pulling the feed solution up to the roots from a base reservoir, itself being topped up once or twice a day. So 24 hours per day the plant can use exactly whatever water and minerals it requires; you just cannot achieve this level of accuracy by hand watering and feeding.

Right:
The left hand side tube of perlite was dipped into the blue solution about 30 minutes before the right hand side.

A simple guide to growing hydroponic tomatoes

Although this introduction uses tomatoes as an example, the same principles apply to most other plants

I normally propagate in rockwool cubes, but the plants can be brought on equally well in peat-based compost prior to planting. If using rockwool then you have to 'wet up' the cubes using a weak fertiliser solution since the rockwool has no soluble minerals in it whatsoever.

Take a large pot (8-10 litres), fill it full of medium grade perlite, set it in a cat litter tray or similar, fill it with feed solution until the tray is full with liquid, leave it overnight to soak thoroughly, then plant next day. Planting simply involves resting the rockwool cube on top of the perlite in the larger pot. If you have used compost, cut the base off the pot prior to resting it on the perlite. It really is as simple as that.

Above:
Why the smaller cubes are referred to as 'chocolate bar'!

Far left:
The stages in bringing on a tomato seedling are no different from that of the cucumber seedling; you can see the roots protruding from the small block. Notice how the small plug sits inside the chamber of the larger block.

Left:
Plants being grown in a bucket of perlite. The pots are sitting on trays, which act as a reservoir. Perlite growbags are no longer available and the pots are just as good, if not quite so convenient.

Right:
Tomato stems growing out of the rockwool cube, the drips feeding the plants, the foam tube acting as a 'dam' and the string wrapped around the plants for support. These plants are growing in perlite growbags.

Recently I have been growing four plants for my own use, feeding them once daily using a watering can, but several years back I had 12 plants. With this larger number of plants I used a drip system connected to a water pump (sitting in a barrel of feed solution), and the plants were growing in 25-litre growbags, three per bag. I had the pump activated by time switch to give two feeds at either end of the day. One season the tomatoes ran to 26 trusses and I had a lot of happy friends. Once the system is set up, it is just a case of swapping the pump from one feed barrel to the next alternately as each runs out; while one is being used the other can be warming up. The photo shows the rockwool cubes in which the plants are propagated, with the growbags wrapped in white polythene so the reservoir is held at the bottom. You can also see the polystyrene blocks between the growbags, which serve to hold the reservoir in place. The photo above shows clear polythene used as a wrapping just to make it easier to understand.

For those of you who want to keep it simple, the diagram below shows all that is needed. There are two blue 50-gallon drums; when one of the drums is being used, the other is warming up, though I do use a 60-watt fish tank heater to boost the temperature up to 15-20°C – that gets the roots excited! The feed solution (15°C minimum) gets pumped out of the pipe twice daily via an inline filter where it then flows into the drips going into the growbags (or pots).

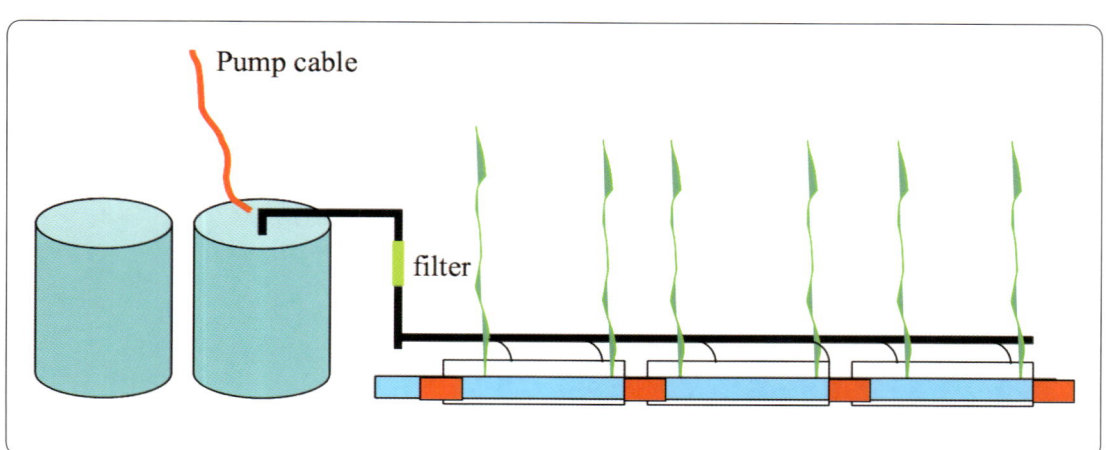

Above:

Perlite growbags, tubing, drips, 'dams' and solution reservoir ready for the plants. In reality you would not use dye or else your fruit would go blue.

Growbags are no longer available but this system will work equally well with a long trough lined with polythene in which you have large pots filled with perlite. The trough would have a u-shaped profile and be lined with white polythene. Once again, sit it on a polystyrene sheet to insulate it from the cold concrete. For really long troughs you would be better to have the whole trough on a slight slope, and put strips of polystyrene under the plastic at regular intervals to construct a series of little 'dams', so stopping all the liquid from running to one end. You then run the low density polythene (LDPE) pipe (coloured black) and insert one drip-tube to one plant.

Very simply, the feed solution is warmed – about 15°C is fine but not greater than 25 – then pumped twice-daily making use of a time switch, with a 10% minimum 'run off' (surplus). So if you were using 12 gallons per day you would look for 12 x 10% = 10/100 x 12 = 1.2 gallon 'run off' minimum. The 'run off' is the extra fluid which runs out of the end of the trough; I find a shallow cat litter tray ideal for catching the surplus. This 'run off' is vital as it always ensures there is plenty of feed reservoir in the bottom, and more importantly, keeps the levels of particular elements in balance, i.e. if the potash has a slightly higher uptake there is a fresh supply coming in twice daily.

Below:
A white collecting bucket sitting below the end of the row ready to collect the 'run-off'. Note the dark reservoir liquid being held in place by the blue polystyrene 'dam'.

You need to use a conductivity meter to check the strength of your feed solution. Conductivity meters were discussed in the last chapter.

If the weather is exceptionally hot and there is a high uptake of liquid, you could give a third feed but at half strength. In such situations you are better off damping down both the floor and the actual plants.

I usually feed fruiting tomatoes at a value of around CF 26, which is relatively high, but they are vigorous and producing fruit like mad.

I say more about the culture of tomatoes in Chapter 8.

For plants such as vines or fruit trees you will need to use a large heavy-duty container of about 100 litres. You may have to improvise the reservoir trays in which the large pots sit I wonder if they make cat litter trays for tigers or lions?

Hydroponic feeds

The hydroponics feed recipe shown in Appendix 7 was originally developed at Auchincruive around 20-30 years ago, when horticultural researchers were pioneering the use of perlite for the Scottish tomato growers in the Clyde valley. You can see that there are two concentrates involved, since the calcium source must be separated from the phosphate. At higher concentrations these will react to form a solid, which will simply sink to the bottom of the barrel, and two of the key minerals will then be lacking.

Hydroponic feed values for different crops

In Appendix 11, I have inserted a table giving nominal values for a range of different hydroponic crops you might want to experiment with.

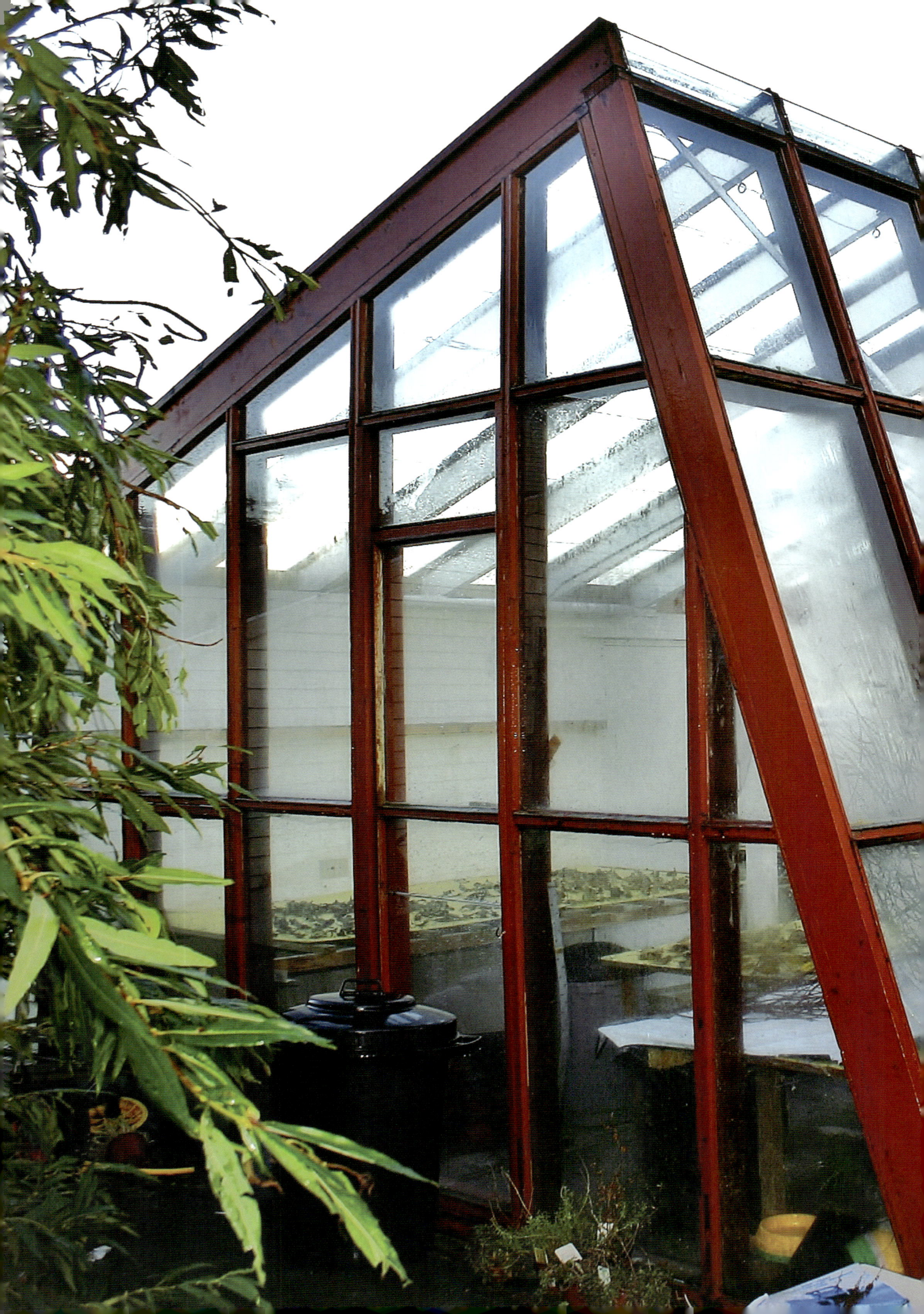

Chapter 7

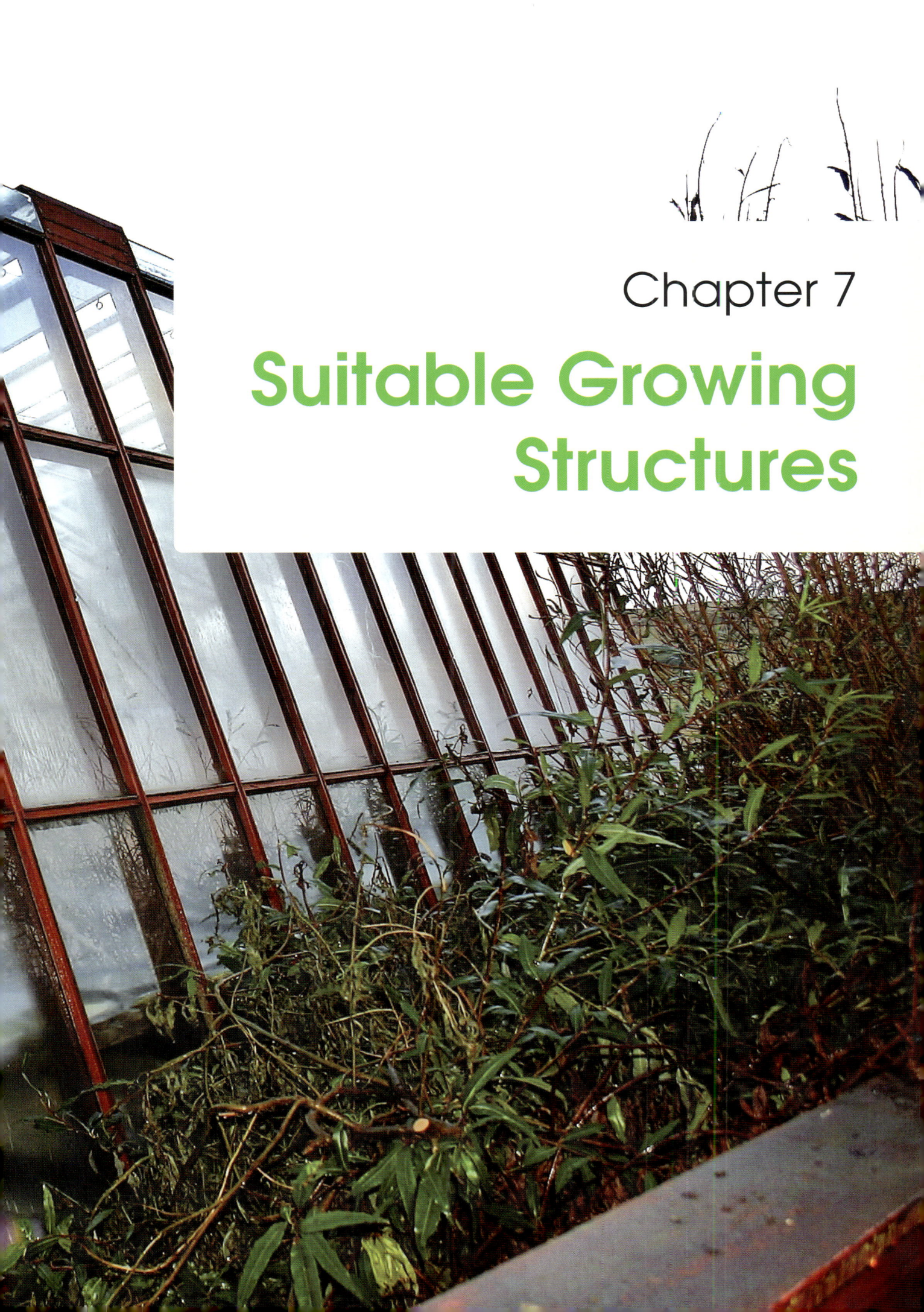

Suitable Growing Structures

Glasshouses

I have already discussed the weather in an island situation, particularly the wind. The fact that the five commercial windmills sitting on a hill a mile away from my house are the most efficient in the world (to date) says it all. Not only are there numerous gales, especially in late autumn, but also the annual wind speeds can at times exceed 100 miles per hour. In a nutshell, you should build according to the local conditions. My three glasshouses go back to 1990 and 1978 and no glass has been lost to date, at least by the weather; (I recall Craig Smith, a friend of my son, coming up very sheepishly to tell me he had accidentally thrown a snowball through one of the panes). You can buy small aluminium glasshouses from the mainland, which are fine if you are sitting in a sheltered town, and geodesic domes are sturdy. Ruby Jamieson has an aluminium glasshouse of dimensions 6 feet x 8 feet, but with extra shelving produces a great number of bedding plants. Her greenhouse is now about 23 years old, though her husband George, the shelf maker, had to bolt it to the concrete. Ruby's house sits in a very sheltered part of the village of Scalloway. Just out of interest, you do not need planning permission for this size of greenhouse, but check before you erect one since planning laws continually change.

Far more cost effective is to build your own. What you must bear in mind is that there is little problem holding it up – the real trick is holding it down!

Below:
Ruby Jamieson's 8 x 6 feet greenhouse; incredibly productive.

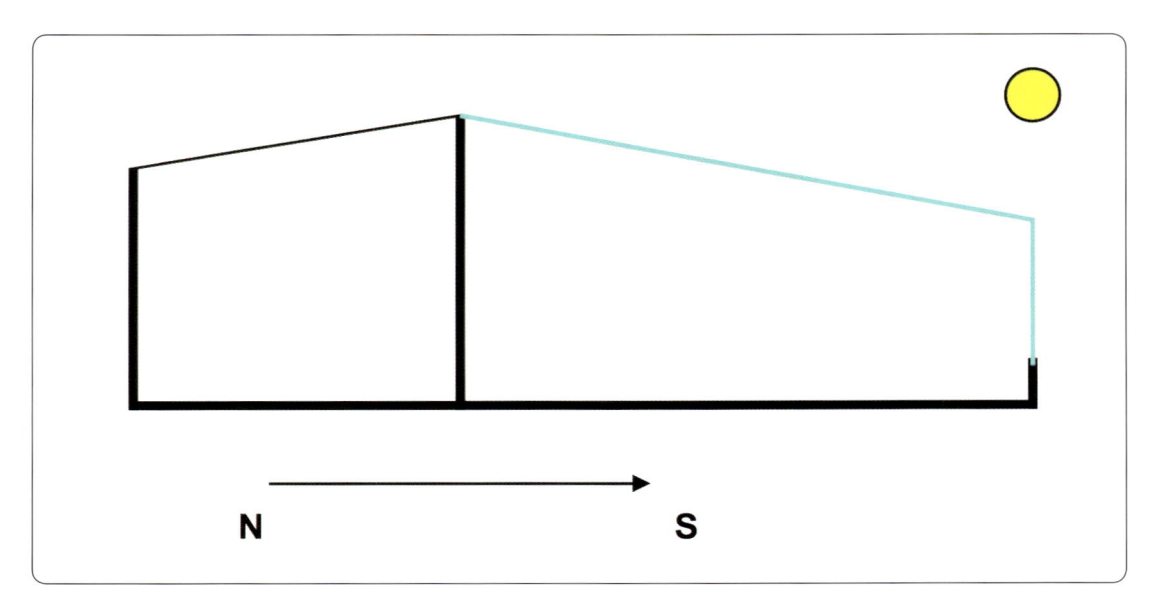

My glasshouses have all been built on the same principle – a store (at the north side) used primarily for storage and propagation, each with its own potting bench, with the greenhouse being a 'lean to' on the south side. This is shown in the diagram above.

The stores at the north side are essential. They all have both potting and storage facilities, allowing me to make up my fertiliser concentrates, whilst one of them has been converted into a large grow room with 60 or so fluorescent tubes.

The brick walls are ideal for attaching the wooden beams using 'bat straps'; if you get a builder to help you, he will know exactly what to do. If you are making a larger glasshouse then discuss the dimensions and structure with either a civil engineer or an architect. They will suggest having a structure with a central spine held by supports to the glasshouse floor. Make sure the wood is treated.

For longer beams use CLS specified timber since it is straighter and relatively knot free. The wood should be ordinary treated building timber, not hardwood or anything fancy. No matter what type of roof beam, a channel needs to be cut out using a router; this channel at either side of the beam is for 'bedding' the glass into. I always get this done by the wood merchant for little extra cost. The diagram below (not to scale) shows the idea; the glass (blue) is sitting on the silicon (coloured yellow), and the silicon sitting on the glazing strip (red). The glazing beads are not shown; they would rest on the silicon sitting on the upper surface of the glass.

The whole roof structure needs bracing and what I use are galvanised strips of steel called 'keel strap'. Though expensive, this metal is enormously strong and has the great advantage of not blocking out too much light.

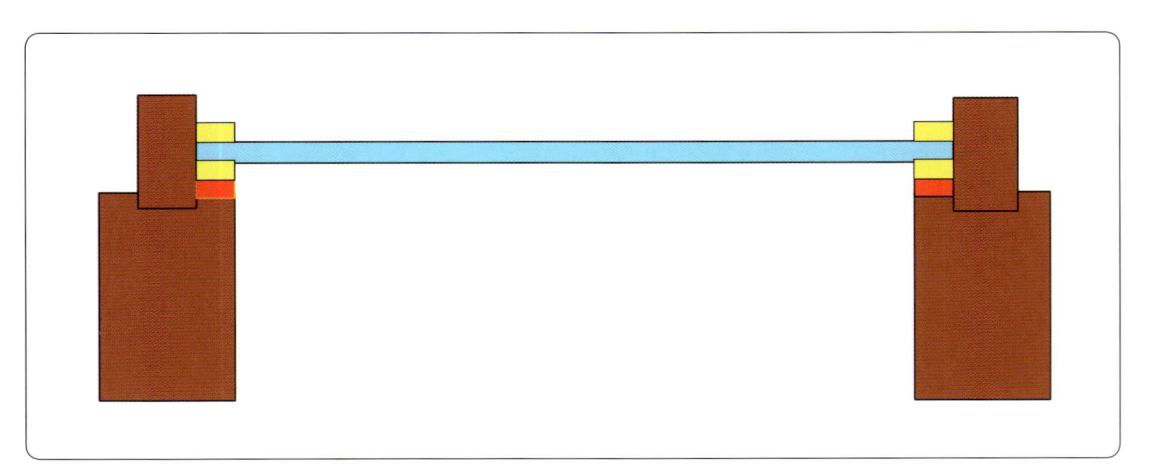

Above:
Store to the north, glasshouse facing south. Basic structure, end view.

Left:
Pane of glass sitting on a length of glazing strip (red) with silicon (yellow) below and above. Missing is the wooden bead keeping it firmly down.

Above:
The newest of my greenhouses; the outside still needs tidied up!

Now for a piece of advice which can save a lot of hassle. Get the roof beams painted with a good quality oil paint **before** you put them up; oil based paint is more durable than the 'water-based' in our harsher climate. One layer of undercoat and one of gloss is all that is needed, i.e. the roof beams can be put in place 'ready painted'.

Lay the floor incorporating the foundations at the same time. When you are setting up the concrete shutters for the glasshouse section, have a gentle gradient towards the bottom so any surplus water can run down and through small gaps in the front wall. If your glasshouse floor is level and a tap is left on accidentally, you can quickly find yourself in a paddling pool!

Once the walls have been put in place, the wall plates can be laid, and the beams tied down with long bat straps extending right down the wall as shown in the photo overleaf. If there is a strong wind, the wall will have to lift with the roof; if the wind is that strong I shall be looking for a rabbit burrow to hide in. For brickwork I use the wider 150mm blocks.

Once you start to erect the roof beams, the spacing is quite critical. If you are using 610 x 610mm sized glass, the gap between the beams of wood needs to be quite precise. Unless you are familiar with woodworking I would get a joiner to do this. I used 4mm thick glass for my newest house; this is strong without going 'over the top'. I purchased pristine sheets (of float glass). You can get old windows and start cutting, but it is rather like making your own compost – is it really worth all the trouble? You would be better off working overtime (if you can) and using the extra cash just to buy new. The attraction with glass is that it is 'forever', after a wash looks pristine, and gives high light transmission. I considered the possibility of using polycarbonate sheets. The sheets and all the fittings needed are very expensive (ending up costing at least twice as much as glass) but has the advantage of being virtually unbreakable. It looks nice, but can vibrate somewhat in windy conditions.

Left:
The bat strap fixed to both the wall and the floor, so holding the roof securely in place.

Below:
The roof beams connect to the front wall by means of nail plates.

Once the beams are up, you are ready to fit the glass. Fitting glass is not hard but you need to be fit and have decent staging to stand on. The most important thing is to be well organised with everything to hand since, especially on a sunny day, the silicone can cure within half an hour.

What you need are the following: general purpose **clear** silicone mastic; silicon gun; wooden beads; small galvanised nails; glazing strip; hammer; sharp knife; scissors, staple gun; and rag. **You need a dry day. This is paramount. If it is not dry the silicon will skid all over the place.**

Above:

The angle iron beam which supports the roof beams at their midpoint.

Right:

There are three bracing rods shown here; one along the front, one diagonal to the front wall, and one diagonal to the roof.

179

The method of fitting the glass is as follows:

1. Cut the glazing strip so it is a little longer than the beam span. Start to remove the backing strip and staple it in place along the timber channel. It will stick naturally so only a few staples are needed to fix it. Repeat for both sides;

2. Using the silicon gun squirt a layer from the bottom of the beam along the channels on both sides. Do not economise with the silicon. Now drop the first pane of glass carefully onto the silicon at the bottom of the run and gently press along both edges until you see the silicon squeeze out. You always work from the bottom up for each row of glass;

3. Squirt a layer of silicon along the top of the glass about 1cm from the edge. Now place the second pane so it overlaps the first by about 2.5cm; stretch and place one hand under the overlap then use your other hand to press on the top of it until you see the silicon flattening out. This silicon overlap makes the whole roof both airtight and much stronger (you are constructing a silicon sealed glasshouse);

4. You now fit a third pane in the same way;

5. When the glass is fitted all the way from the bottom to the top of the run, squirt a line of silicon along both edges, this time on top of the glass;

6. Finally, gently tap your beads into place with small galvanised nails. To speed things up I have the wooden beads pre-nailed;

7. Remember that the final top sheet may not be full width so have glass pre-cut prior to fitting.

You can do a lot of sheets in one day if you are really organised – that is the trick. Do remember that the silicon is fast drying so you cannot stop in the middle of a glazing run and have a cup of tea. It may seem a lot of work but you will end up with an exceptionally strong and drip free roof.

Above and left: These photos show the relationship between the glazing strip (black), silicon (below and above the glass) and the white wooden bead.

180

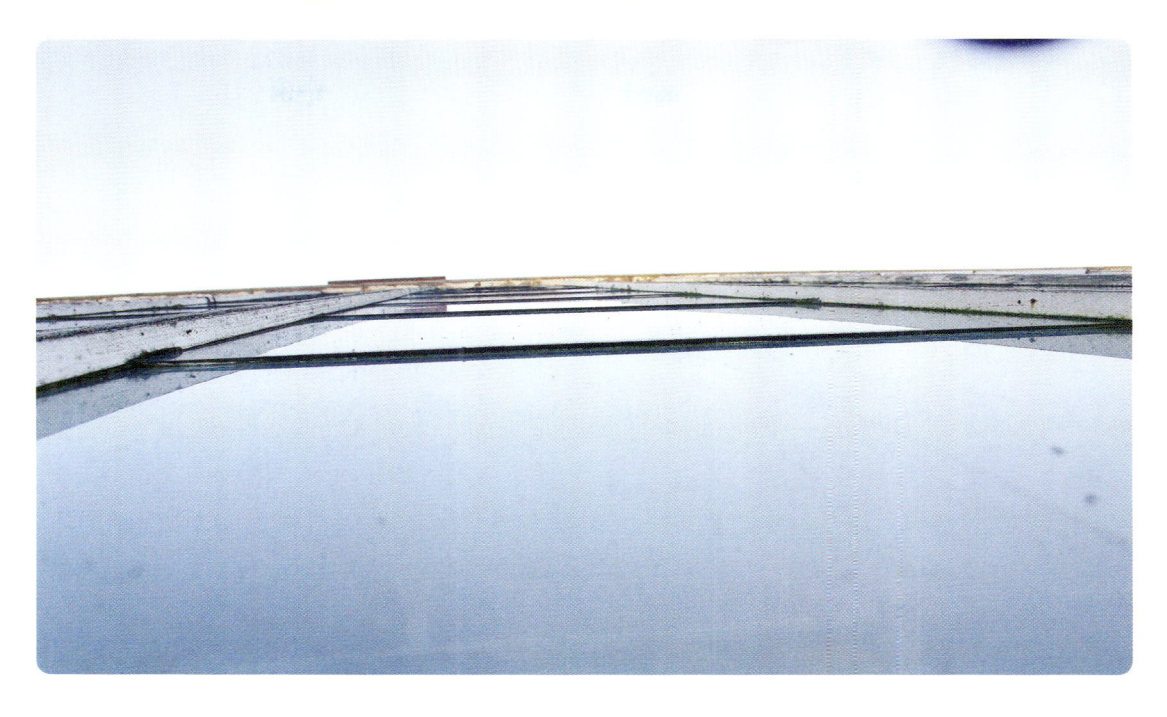

Above:
The glazing looks quite professional by the time you have finished. This photo shows a typical row of glass I put together around 10 years ago.

Below:
You can easily see the half matchstick keeping the two panes apart. The gap is then carefully filled with silicon.

Fitting glass to the sides

When it comes to fitting glass to the sides you need a slightly different approach. You fasten the glazing strip to the channel as before, and then squirt a run of silicon along both sides. Now fit the first pane to the bottom and gently press against it; once again you will see the silicon squeeze flat. The next pane will sit on **top** of the first, but now for something important – place matchsticks at either end of the top of the pane so that the second sheet of glass sits on them resulting in a slight gap (between the two panes). This is vital since it stops the two panes rubbing against each other in windy conditions. When the final pane is fitted you then squeeze another run of silicon along the outside edge of the glass, before fitting the two wooden beads. Finally, use another tube of silicon with a fine nozzle, and with a steady hand, squeeze a thin strip of silicon to fill the (matchstick) gap between the adjacent panes.

Cutting glass

Cutting glass is very easy providing you have a proper cutter. The one I use has a small reservoir of oil (3-in-1) in its barrel and this helps to lubricate the cutter as it moves over the surface. Make sure the glass is sitting on a towel or rag on a flat surface, and once you have estimated the cutter angle, cut with one steady constant movement. If you stop halfway it will not break cleanly. Sometimes this happens and then I use a second tool called a 'nibbler' (a broad nosed set of pliers) to remove any small projecting bits. Practice initially on some old glass and you will become very proficient. I have seen (very) senior citizens cutting glass effortlessly after a little practice. It is not that different from cutting bathroom tiles.

Doors

You will also have to consider what kind of doors you want and how the glasshouse is to be ventilated. This last part is crucial because you do not want to cook the plants but to grow them, and there is a great deal of difference. I use glass doors as shown left; each is very heavy and hung with stainless steel hinges. My newest glasshouse has sliding doors and these are certainly best if you can afford it. Whatever door you choose make sure there is plenty of glass since you want as much light entry as possible.

Left:
This is a seriously strong door glazed with 6mm glass. I would avoid glass altogether if you have children running about.

Below:
My smallest glasshouse has been producing crops for some 30 years or so. And the glass still remains squeaky clean; and no breakages.

Ventilation

Ventilation is critical but tricky to install and at this point you and the joiner need to figure something out. Although you can vent through the doors, assuming there is a breeze, on a calm day you have a major problem since you have to get the heated air out, and it only wants to go one way, i.e. up. If your glasshouse is not too large you could connect fans to clear plastic ducting sucking the heated air from the middle, but vented roofs are the logical answer. The pictures show the vents in my smaller greenhouse; you can see they are hinged at the front, with a rope pulley bringing about opening.

In my most recent greenhouse the vents are built into the roof of the store; from a construction point of view this seemed the easier option.

You can also get automatic vent openers.

Benching

With the exception of the cold frames, I grow all my plants on wooden benching. This has multiple advantages such as being out of the reach of rabbits and slugs, is easier to work with, and the plants are warmer compared to sitting on a concrete floor. The bench trestles (supports) are 50mm x 50mm (2in x 2in) rectangular sections with upright supports every 600mm (2ft). The bench spars are made from 50mm x 25mm (2in x 1in) treated whitewood with 150mm gaps. This is shown in the diagram below – not to scale.

I then cover the benches with thin 4mm plywood sheets, soak them with old paint then, when dry, roll a layer of plastic and then capillary matting over the top. This makes it easy to slide trays over the bench, with the capillary matting acting as a buffer when doing the watering. On a really hot day I soak the capillary matting to keep the humidity levels up. In my tunnels I have three sets of benches with two lanes between them. This provides a very high percentage of growing area, about 85%.

Above right:
The vents partly and more fully open. The ratchet and wheel is slow functioning but very strong.

Right:
Diagram of bench structure as mentioned in the text.

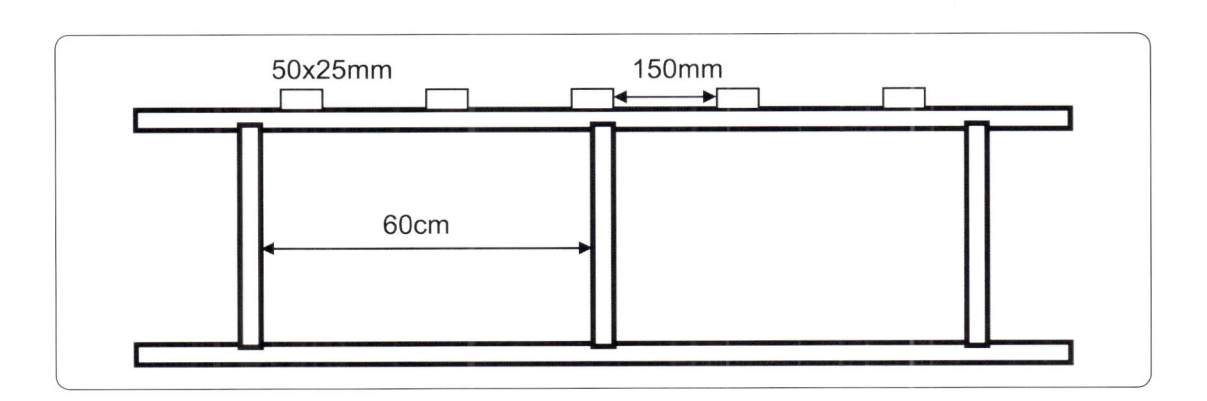

Water supply

I have at least three bib type taps fitted in each glasshouse. This greatly reduces the length of hoses needed for access; they are very cost effective. In my largest glasshouse everything is watered from the centre, whether it be direct from the cold-water tap (not in spring), tepid water being pumped from the heated barrel, or feed solution. Whether you can do your own plumbing or need to get a plumber in, get all the taps fitted at the same time; it takes very little time with push fit connections. Never use copper pipes. Also make sure you have a mains switch-off valve. You can never have enough taps in a glasshouse and when they are fitted with tap adaptors, you can simply unclip a hose from one tap and clip on to another.

Electrical fittings

You use electricity all the time in a glasshouse. In my own case it powers the propagator heat mats, the grow-rig tubes, pumps, water heaters, lights, and do not forget the radio. I have all the electrical sockets sitting reasonably high up along the back wall of the greenhouse. This allows for easy access but their position also means they are well out of the way when the daily watering and feeding takes place. Have these installed by a qualified electrician; the professionals are quick, and it takes them very little longer to fit six double sockets as compared to two. Before the electrician arrives make sure you have a full list of items to be done, rather than having to call him back to do something you overlooked.

Polytunnels

1. Commercial larger units

When I decided to put up my first tunnel in 2000, I did a little investigation to find the strongest brand on the market. A company called Clovis Lande was the winner and I ordered the model 'Highlande x-braced' designed to withstand 140mph wind loading. Essentially, a tunnel is a series of galvanised semi circular steel hoops, braced for extra strength. Over this is stretched polythene – I used the five-year type – although there are many types of polythene on the market. Recently I have seen a number of Shetlanders building small tunnels from plastic salmon cage hoops and heavy water pipes – and they seem to do just fine, although I would prefer to see some bracing at the gable ends. If you want to go for a larger structure, you really would be better (and safer) to purchase a properly designed steel unit.

Before you start, prior to getting a digger on site, make sure you know exactly what you want to do. I never wanted soil and, once removed, I had the digger driver spread fine gravel over the surface, also ensuring there was a trench surrounding the tunnel perimeter containing a field drainpipe and chips for drainage. He levelled the site with a small slope to help water run off. If you are not careful, you can easily end up with a swimming pool!

One thing to watch out for, especially if the digger is 'cutting and filling' into the side of a hill, is to leave plenty of room between the hill and the tunnel since, if there is a lot of snow (which falls down either side of the tunnel), you must have space to shift it otherwise it will build up and start putting pressure on the sides at the bottom.

These tunnels have been cleverly thought out; for instance the hoops have a slightly 'gothic' design with vertical sides.

Above:
A 20-metre Clovis Lande tunnel during construction. You can see the 'gothic arch' running along the centre; this helps break up the air currents and prevent an 'aerofoil effect'.

Right:
My larger 25-metre Clovis Lande tunnel under construction. The shutters will contain mass concrete producing a very heavy mass to keep it down should there be a hurricane.

Vertical sides enable you to work closer to the tunnel edge; in my case I have benches close to the plastic and taller plants do not end up rubbing against it. There is a little peak running along the length of the ridge – this helps to cancel the aerofoil effect of wind rushing over the roof surface. The galvanising is 'for ever' but I also replaced the nuts with stainless steel versions – then if I have to dismantle part of the structure for whatever reason it will be easy to unbolt.

My five-year polythene cover is now 10 years old and I think will do for a few more years yet which cannot be bad. Since our northerly climate is cooler, and with less sun, the potential for plastics lasting many years is certainly improved. Always ask the company for the best cover for our climate with strength being the number one priority; polytunnel covers are continually evolving and improving.

Built into these plastics are a number of chemicals called **inhibitors,** which prevent the plastic from becoming brittle due to UV degradation. My cover has an anticondensate coating on the inside and this helps to keep it clear and relatively drip free. The light transmission in a tunnel, with its relatively small section steel tubing, is very high indeed, far more than in the greenhouse with its larger wood beams. Modern polytunnel covers are much more than 'just a sheet of plastic'; some products consist of up to five separate layers, all extruded at the same time.

Quite remarkably, films can now be produced containing pigments that absorb UV light (which is not used in photosynthesis) and refluoresce it as blue, which the plants can use. This results in 2-3% more useable light reaching the crop. Blocking UV has also been shown to reduce spore production and spread of fungal diseases such as botrytis.

In the October 2010 issue of 'The Commercial Greenhouse Grower' the there was an article about a range of 'smart' films, which allows selective control of ambient light and temperature in a variety of climatic conditions. Independent tests on two spectral filter polythene films carried out in 2003 showed dramatic effects on soft fruit production. One gives a greater strawberry fruit size by reducing the internal temperature of the tunnel, while the diffusing nature of the cover allows up to 15% more usable light deeper into the plant foliage. Diffusing films cut out much of the infrared radiation so keeping the crops several degrees cooler. The other gave a 26% yield increase in raspberries. You must discuss your proposed crops with the tunnel manufacturer, and ask what they would suggest as being the most suitable plastic currently available.

One brilliant idea incorporated in modern tunnels is to secure the plastic around the edge of the tunnel by a 'grip strip' (not dip stick!), allowing easy tensioning when the plastic is a little warm. The profile and design of the strip means that the stronger the pulling force of the wind on the cover, the greater the grip. In the past, the method of holding the polythene down was to have it sitting in a trench filled with soil. Do not even consider that method today. The grip strip is expensive, but being an aluminium extrusion will last forever. I found that when fitting the cover it was very easy to get a decent tension on the cover, and each subsequent year the tension could be maintained simply by slackening the bolts securing the grip strip and tapping down with a hammer. Furthermore, by raising the grip strip above the ground and attaching a windbreak below, you will end up having a ventilated space all round the tunnel edge; you might want to have a windbreak of up to 1 metre high, depending on your location. You will lose a little heat but ventilation is just as important here as it is in a glasshouse.

Below:
A diagonal bracing bar, the white anti-hot spot tape sitting on the hoop, and the 'grip strip' running length wise along the bottom.

Above:
End views of single and double grip strip aluminium extrusions.

The dimensions of my first tunnel are around 5 x 16 metres. As well as the cost of the tunnel there is the concrete needed to hold the hoops in place. I ensured it would not lift whatever the weather by using twice the recommended quantity of concrete. Concrete is very cheap in the grand scale of things. For my newer tunnels I intend to simply run a concrete slab along each side with steel reinforcing rods binding it all together. It will require a bit more concrete but save the time needed to make individual square shutters for each of the 60 or so legs. There is one builder I know (who I shall not name to save embarrassment) who laid a slab of concrete, rested the tunnel on top of it, and the latter was last seen flapping around Iceland. True story!

Once the concrete holding the tube connectors is in place it is then a two-man job to erect the frame, not taking much longer than a couple of days.

Fitting the cover needs a few calm hours with at least three people. Make sure there is no wind because you have the ultimate sail. If it does 'take off', for goodness sake let go. Put it another way – imagine trying to hold onto a thousand umbrellas in a breeze! Prior to fitting the cover you will need to attach 'anti heat spot tape' to the steel to act as a barrier between the steel and cover. Whichever company you deal with will keep you right.

Although tunnels can be very strong indeed, you should try to have it positioned so it can get some shelter. Sitting on top of a hill is not an option! My first tunnel is well sheltered from most directions except north, so I made a windbreak using half telegraph poles concreted well into the ground, and between the poles I fastened windbreak. The original windbreak is still in place. The strongest parts of the tunnel are the gable ends so you should be aiming to get the tunnel pointed in line with what would be your strongest prevailing winds. The photos give an idea of how it all looks.

You will certainly need a water supply and, preferably, electricity. For the latter you only need to run small section armour plated cable from your garage or wherever to connect into a waterproof double socket, fixed to the wooden door lintel (in my case), handy but high up. This power is primarily to operate my water pump when the plants need to be fed.

One thing to keep in mind with larger glasshouses or tunnels is that you will only get out of it what you put into it, and there is a considerable amount of work involved.

A tunnel is a cost effective route achieving quality-growing space, and providing you operate within its limits, you can have a highly productive unit.

Left:
The outside of the tunnel.

Below:
Spring plants inside; lupins are to the right, violas to the left and mimulus plus lavender in the middle. The view is looking south.

suitable growing structures

Above:
The view inside the tunnel looking north.

Right:
The windbreak is simply half telegraph poles concreted into place, with the netting being attached to lengths of 100mm x 50mm wooden beams. This is still the original netting after some 12 years or so.

Pete's smaller tunnel, the Solar 'Splendid' is 3 x 6 metres and looks very attractive for the keen gardener. Structurally, it is more suited to a sheltered garden; I noticed that extra bracing wires have been incorporated. He said the cover could easily be removed for the winter, and this cover is now 10 years old. The walls are straight sided which allows the gardener to cultivate plants next to the tunnel edge. With careful scheduling you could be cropping over eight or nine months. Should you wish to reposition the tunnel, four people can easily carry it.

The second tunnel was a 6-metre wide curved structure (the 6 and 7-metre range) with chunky hoops, and far more rigidity. It looks as though it could cope with a high wind loading. The hoops are at 1.5-metre spacing, and the cover fits one panel at a time between each pair of hoops. The cover is held in place with some tensioned wire fixings and looks very solid. The cover has a seam at the bottom into which a steel rod is inserted, with the rod being held down by hooks. The single panels have the great advantage of being easily replaced, unlike more traditional tunnels where the whole cover is involved.

The frame bases are bolted to the concrete founds, once again prompting the adage of 'it is no problem to keep it up – the real trick is to hold it down'!

Left:
The windbreak giving shelter at the very exposed north side of the tunnel.

Below:
The Solar 'Splendid' tunnel bulging with crops. It sits in a more sheltered part of Pete Glanville's garden. You can also see some cloche hoops, which were covered with plastic in early spring.

2. Smaller tunnels.

'Solar Tunnel'

You may decide you want a more reasonably sized and manageable tunnel. There are plenty of smaller models on the market. One make commonly used in Shetland is the 'Solar Tunnel'. The local distributor, Pete Glanville, showed me the two versions he used on his croft; the key feature common to the 'Solar' range is a reinforced cover with tear resistant nylon mesh sitting between two layers of polythene. On the positive side you get a double-glazing effect coupled with fabric strength; negatively, you will get slightly lower light transmission. The strength and heat insulation factors will greatly outweigh the reduced light levels.

suitable growing structures

Above and right: The inside and outside of the larger, stronger tunnel in the 6-metre range from the Solar Tunnel company.

191

Polycrub tunnels

This is a brand new product to the market. It is based on using discarded sterilised salmon cage pipes to form the hoops, then cladding the outside with twin wall polycarbonate. Though much more expensive than a polythene cover, it would seem to be the ultimate in strength and heat insulation. I have seen a number of these in different areas of Shetland. This may well become a very popular product as I am regularly hearing about growers losing their polythene covers during windy periods.

Above:
The outside of the polycrub looks very different from those covered in polythene.

Left:
Peter Sinclair hard at work with some good looking crops starting to form.

Salmon hoop tunnel

Right and below: The outside and inside of a tunnel whose hoops have been made from old salmon cages. Simple but effective; I found little to complain about when inside.

Water pipe tunnel

Above and left: The outside and inside of a tunnel where the hoops were built from water pipes. Even during windy days I see no real problems occurring.

suitable growing structures

Cold frames

Cold frames are cheap and easy to construct, giving you in, effect, a 'mini-greenhouse', allowing you both to harden off plants as well as protect those which might struggle to grow outside. By using a cold frame you can bring on salad crops and strawberries at least a month earlier in spring and, just as important, a month later in autumn. This is a very cheap way to achieve a good quality growing area, and there is a quick payback time in which your initial costs are recouped; with the right plants and double or treble cropping it could be done the first season.

My design is efficient and, though not so convenient as a tunnel or glasshouse to work in, can be ideal for a great many species. Essentially the cold frame is constructed from 100mm x 50mm treated whitewood beams, joined at the tops with galvanised nail plates and at the sides with long thick screws. Channels were taken out of the main beams by the wood merchant to accommodate the glass. The glass is fitted without the silicon (dry glazed) though it is a good idea to have a layer of glazing strip for it to rest on. The glass sheets simply sit next to each other. The one problem I do find with the glass is that the plants sitting next to it tend to dry out fast, so with my new frames I intend using plastic covered panels, which can simply be removed and replaced with mesh when the sun gets stronger. The most difficult problem was achieving access and ventilation. I decided on a hinged roof so it could be opened during the day, allowing me to walk in and water at the same time. The cold frame is rectangular and better sitting on a slight slope long-ways, so the rain can simply run down and off the bottom. For the roof I use heavy gauge (tunnel) polythene. To fasten this use the grip strip already mentioned in connection with the tunnel.

Below:
A simple structure built using 100 x 50mm treated white wood. A bit inconvenient to use, but very cost effective.

I have mentioned the water run-off problem with cold frames – the second problem is with snow, which certainly does not run off. As you know, you can get one or two showers of snow, which is no big deal. However, with a long cold snap when the snow compacts time and again, you start to accumulate a deep layer, with the bottom evolving into heavy compacted ice. As more and more weight is added the inevitable calamity ensues. To overcome this I build a simple support into the middle of the cold frame roof. It is a nuisance but there is no alternative.

Above and left: Two views of my cold frames. The cat is keeping guard!

Stages in building a cold frame with 610mm (2 feet) glass panes

1. Start by building the two long sides. Work on a flat path. The main beams have been checked out to accommodate the glass as shown below. You will need 10 beams, 100mm x 50mm (4in x 2in) of treated wood with a check taken out as shown (not to scale). The blue line in the end view below shows where the glass will eventually sit.

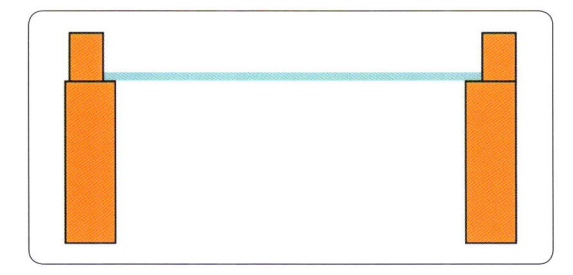

2. Join the beams together with 100mm galvanised nails (using pilot holes to stop the wood splitting). Make sure the channels to accommodate the glass are all on the correct side. Measure the diagonals to ensure it is square, then screw metal plates at the corners to make it rigid.

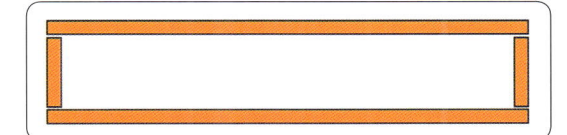

3. Now you need to insert struts between the top and bottom lengths to give support. Use 100mm galvanised nails again. These supports are 75mm x 50mm sections with no channel. These are shown in green in the diagram below (not to scale).

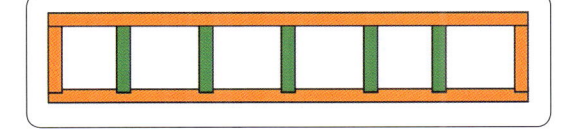

4. Now you need to make the end panels; they are built in exactly the same way as above except being half the length; with one of them you will have to leave a gap (doorway) so you can walk in and out.

5. Making sure you have someone to help you, take the panels to their final position and couple them together. What I did was to link the corners using galvanised metal nail plates and screws.

6. At this stage you now want to consider the floor of the cold frame. Simply use ground cover plastic, or ground cover plastic with stone chips spread over it, thereby holding it in place and preventing flooding.

7. You now need to consider the cold frame top. What I did was to have half of the roof as a permanent cover with the other half able to be opened by hand (as shown in the diagram below). Basically the brown areas show the fixed parts of the cold frames with the reds showing the vents – one in place and the other opened. You will need three or four hinges along the length; I find 75mm x 32mm flush hinges ideal, with all the screws being turboextra stainless steel size 4 x 40; stainless steel is vital in case you want to take the frame apart at a later date.

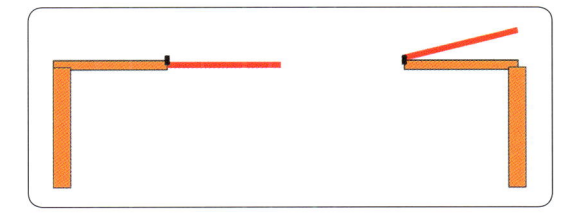

8. The opening vents need to be clad in thick horticultural polythene to make them transparent and lightweight. You could just as easily use twin wall polycarbonate although that would add a lot to the cost.

9. Once you have the lids and vents in place, it is time to fit the glass. If you assembled the sides fairly accurately you will be able to 'dry glaze', i.e. not using silicon. Prior to putting the glass in place I stapled on some glazing strip for the glass to sit against, holding the panes in place with wooden beading strips along the top of the pane and along the bottom.

I mentioned earlier that the plants near the edges of the cold frame tend to dry out more quickly than those nearer the middle. What fairly helps me is to have the plants sitting on capillary matting which spreads the water efficiently and also acts as a buffer, raising the humidity, particularly on sunny days.

Below:
This is my newest cold frame, based on fibreglass sheets hinged at the back. I have found it particularly useful for slowing plants down when they are coming ahead too fast.

suitable growing structures

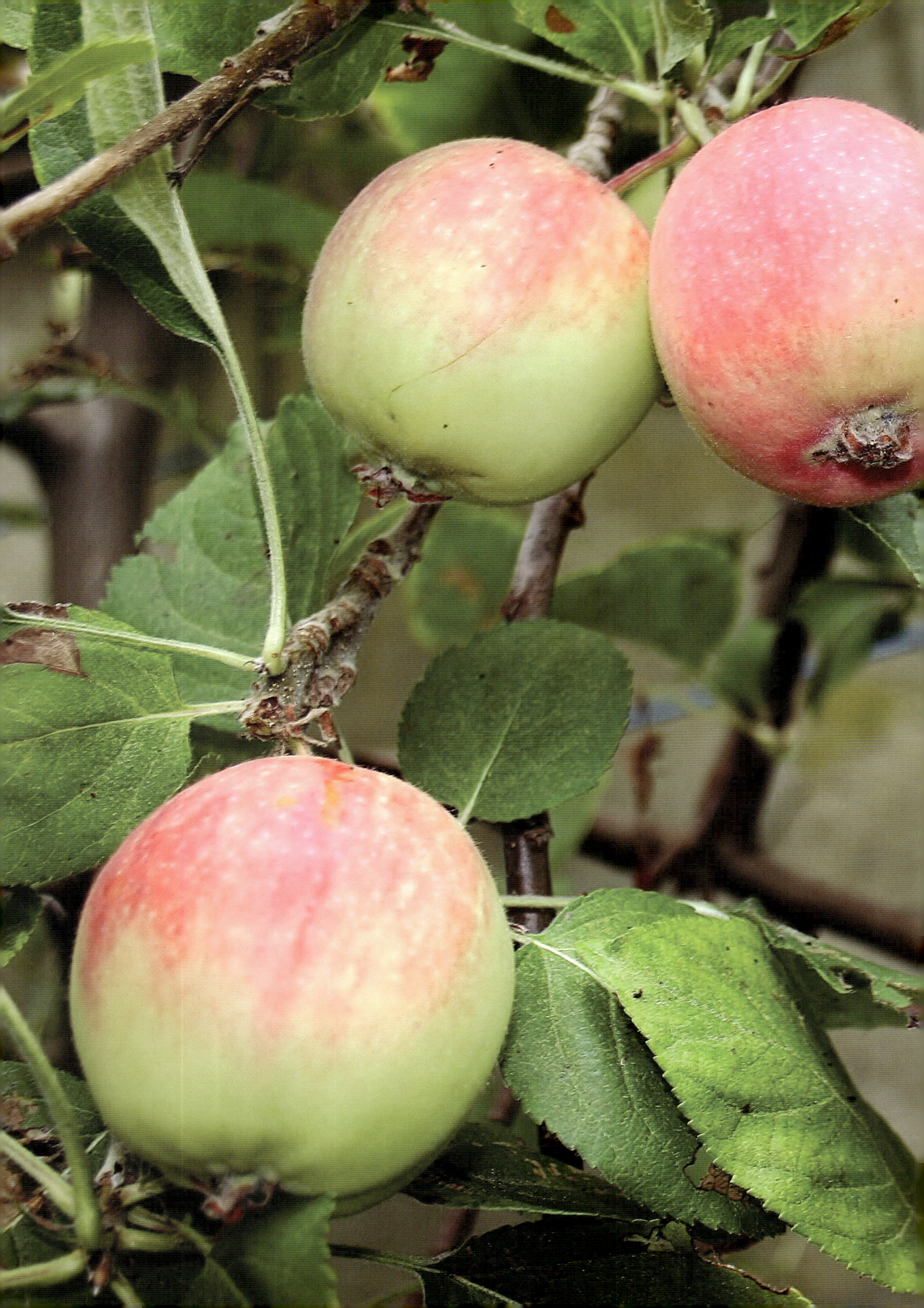

Chapter 8

Fruit Trees, Glasshouse Salads and Vegetables

Most fruits are easy to grow if you have a glasshouse or polytunnel to provide the few degrees of temperature lift necessary. In the mid 90s I was successful with peaches, plums, cherries, strawberries, grapes, apples, pears, raspberries, and blackberries; and of course gooseberries do fairly well outside. I am not a fruit expert but the notes below give a few pointers.

For this chapter I have used my own experience of some 20 years or so but have been given some extra information from Angus Nicol, Daniel Gear and Feri Bartai; they are all very experienced vegetable growers.

Angus Nicol

Angus has been growing fruit trees since the age of six. His garden at Frakkafield sits three miles from Lerwick in the deep valley called Dale, next to the main Shetland golf course. Despite being rather shaded from the morning sun in early spring, he has a rich diverse garden and is always experimenting; he is keen on grafting and a highly successful fruit grower. He is also a passionate beekeeper. As well as growing and selling plants, he does a lot of landscaping work, not to mention being a fully qualified canoe instructor and keen ornithologist. I regularly seek his advice. The cultivars he suggested worked admirably.

Feri Bartai

Feri is a keen and knowledgeable grower who has a smallholding down in Bigton, a small village near the south tip of Shetland, where he also grows food of the four-legged cultivar! As well as teaching cello, he is an avid reader. When he gets fed up reading books in English then he switches to those written in German, and if that gets boring then it is over to books written in Hungarian.

Daniel Gear

Daniel is an organic grower who trades under the name 'Lee-Lang', and cultivates around 10 acres on the east side of Shetland at South Nesting. I recall teaching Daniel how to grow lupins at the tender age of 10. Quite amusingly, he qualified with an honours degree in marine biology, and when I asked him, "Why the change to horticulture?" he answered, "I am fed up looking at fish!" He is still on a steep learning curve but his crops for 2011 were way ahead of those harvested in 2010.

Fruit trees; cultivars

Most fruit trees are grafted on to a variety of plant called a 'rootstock', and this governs the size of the final plant. Not many of us can accommodate a 40-foot apple tree in our glasshouse, and it does not look so smart sticking out through the roof! A popular size of rootstock for apples is M27, which leads to trees of 5-6 feet in height. The M27 is described as 'extremely dwarfing', with fruiting after two to three years. Next comes M9, which is said to be 'very dwarfing' with a height of 8-10 feet, but not fruiting until a year later than the M27. Besides this we get M26, MM106 and eventually MM111 and M2, reaching 25 feet (but yielding up to 360 pounds of apples)! There are other classes of rootstocks for different types of fruit ('Pixie' for plum and 'Giselle' for cherry – these are the most dwarfing and, therefore, most suitable for growing under cover). If you are unsure as to the correct combination then discuss with the fruit tree supplier – they will certainly keep you right.

Check whether the cultivar is self-fertile or not; I grew the cherry cultivar 'Stella' which needed no cross pollination and all I had to do (if there were no bees buzzing about) was to tap it in just the same way you would tap a tomato flower to help it to set. Cherry flowers are at their optimum for just one day. Angus has a cherry tree growing in his Frakkafield garden. He explained that he has had to have it protected because of problems with birds and rain.

However, the plums were a different kettle of fish, with two cultivars being necessary to achieve the pollination required. Very often the fruit tree supplier will give compatibility charts.

In order to produce decent yields, I grew the bigger trees and bushes in large 90-litre containers filled with perlite. I fed them hydroponically in almost the same way as feeding tomatoes (described in detail later on), except at a weaker strength of CF15. The (thornless) blackberry 'Waldo' went rampant and I was bouncing full of vitamin C when it was producing! The cherries (cultivars 'Stella' and 'Sunburst') were wonderful although the resident blackbirds had a field day when they started to ripen. Pride of place has to go to the plum trees ('Opal' and 'Kirks Blue'). Once you have eaten a freshly ripened juicy plum straight from the tree you will never eat a supermarket one again – you know, one of those tasteless things that nearly break your teeth! The only drawback was that the plums ripened over quite a short time span and it was therefore difficult for two people to get through 200+ plums in a fortnight!

Below:
My grapevine.

Right:
With the use of hydroponics the yields from my grapevine can be enormous.

Below:
Apple blossom on trees growing outside in Shetland. Photographed by Angus Nicol.

Left:
Angus Nicol can pick up to 500 apples from a selection of cultivars grown at Frakkafield. This variety is 'Greensleeves'. He never needs to see a doctor at any time!

You may need advice on training fruit trees, as well as pruning. I know that with the vine you simply cut back two thirds of the new growth at the end of the season, but for the others I asked Angus Nicol to come along and help.

One 'problem' I had was that the larger plants used enormous amounts of liquid in summer and I was having to alternate 50-gallon barrels of feed every day. The vine was so vigorous it seemed determined to get to the north end of the nearby airstrip before I cut it back severely! Unless you are very organised and have plenty of spare time, you would be better growing these larger plants in tunnel soil if possible.

I eventually gave the fruit trees to friends, partly because I did not have the time, but mainly because I needed more space for commercial production. My wife Christine was quite annoyed with me when I got rid of the plum tree. I shall return to some fruit production for our own use once I am better organised.

Right:
Another cultivar of Angus Nicol's apples.

Below:
My hydroponic plum tree; the fruit all ripened around the same time and it is difficult to eat 200+ plums in two weeks. Taste-wise they were stunning. The cultivar was 'Kirke's Blue'.

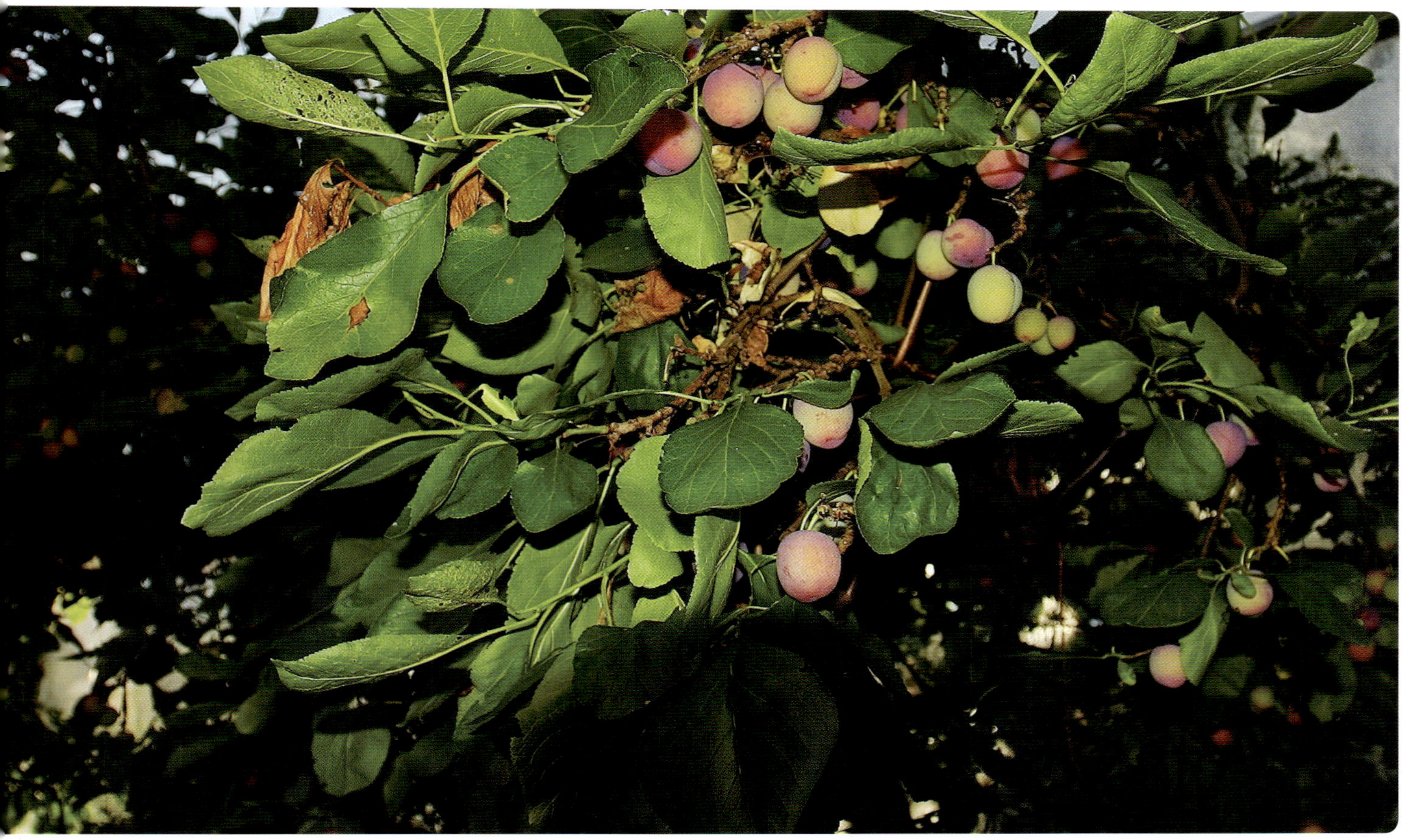
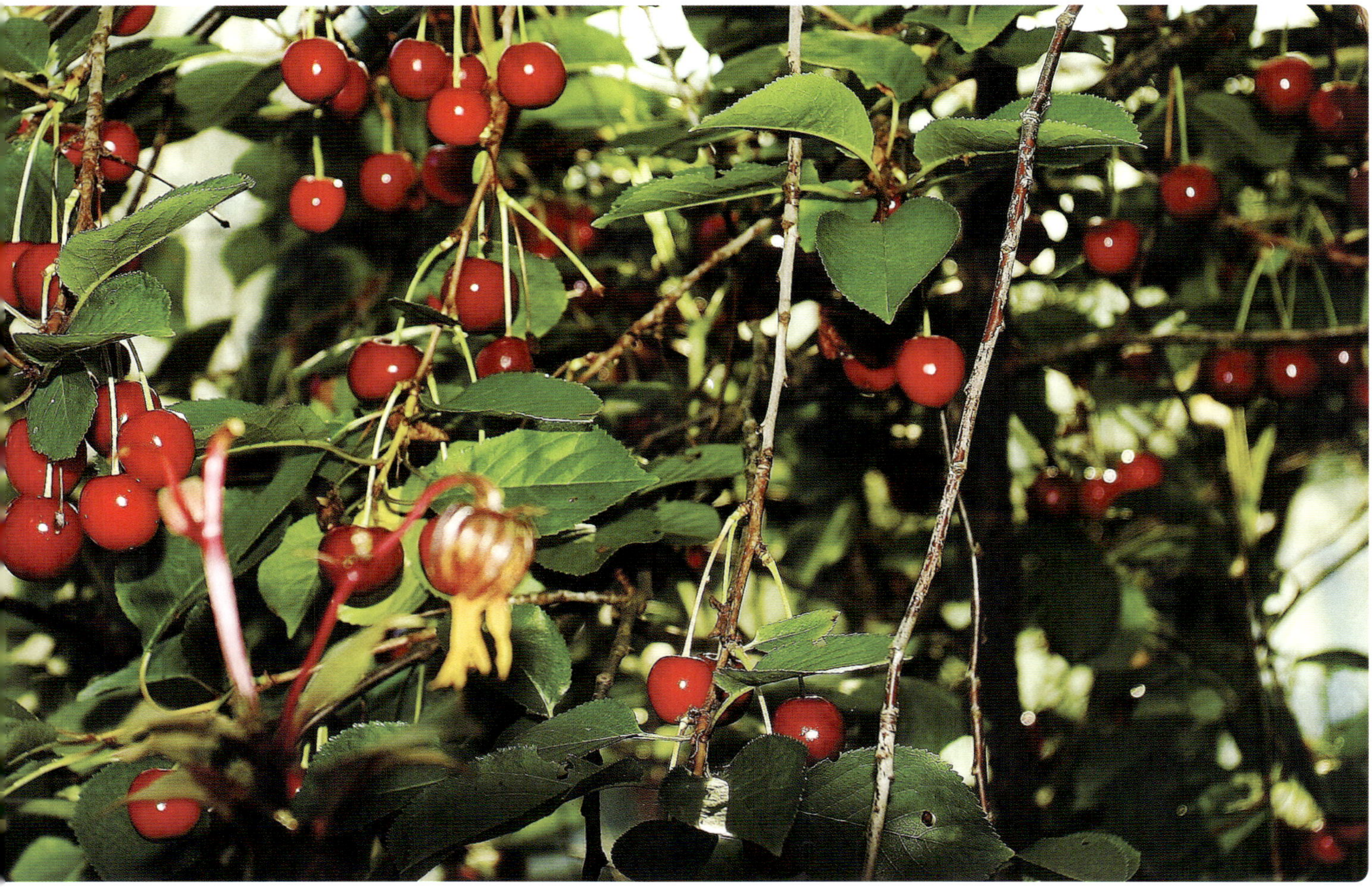

fruit trees, salads & vegetables

Above and opposite:

Some of Angus Nicol's fruit trees. Plum 'Opal'; cherry 'Morello'; and apple 'Katy'.

Strawberries

I used to grow *'Elsanta'* (a standard type) and *'Bolero'* (an everbearer). The latter produced fruit over a longer period of time although they tended to come in flushes. I recall one day (when there was a lot of fruit ripening) getting up early to pick the ripest, washing them, and taking them to the school where I worked. With the combination of good weather and high potash nutrition, the fruit were of premium quality. Joan Pottinger, one of my colleagues, said, "These are what strawberries used to taste like". On another occasion I took some pupils to see my crops as we were studying plant biology at the time. I looked at them and said, "Here are the strawberries – you are allowed **two** each." Someone came into the tunnel to tell me something, and when I turned round again all signs of anything red had vanished. Kids! The one problem I did suffer from was that of mildew in damp or calm conditions, however, my new tunnels have greater ventilation built into them, reducing this problem.

The strawberry crowns should be purchased for planting in early spring. Do not get them in autumn as you will lose several over the winter, and those grown and planted in early spring will certainly fruit the same year. Despite picking around 30kg of fruit from a 15-metre long row of plants grown hydroponically in 2004, I am not a strawberry expert.

I did have a problem with red spider mite. This is the danger of importing plants rather than growing plants from seed, but you do not have much alternative with strawberries since seed-sown plants are slow growing and time consuming, along with the fact you will be handicapped by lack of cultivar choice.

The current cultivars will be overtaken by new cultivars in the future. Keep looking at the catalogues and compare notes with any gardening friends. One grower told me that in 2010, 'Elsanta', despite fruiting a few days earlier, did not taste as good as 'Cambridge Favourite'; he also said he took runners each year from the most productive plants and dumped the oldest.

I grew my strawberries in 30-litre perlite growbags; these are no longer available, so you can either:

- Use peat compost growbags (used by a commercial grower on the Shetland Island of Yell) at 10 plants to a bag (5 each side);
- Grow in troughs filled with perlite;
- Grow in buckets filled with perlite.

I grow in troughs filled with perlite, and although it requires some extra work to set up, once in place, is easily managed and high yielding. To use this method you require long lengths of plastic gutter pipe; these are going to be the troughs. Get them supported on trestles, making sure there is a slight angle to allow liquid run off at the end, line with white polythene (black and white polythene is even better, black to the inside) and connect to the feed drippers. Make sure to have regular polystyrene 'dams', and a bucket or tray at the end of the slope to catch and measure the run-off (mentioned earlier). The diagram below shows the set up (not to scale); the purple squares represent the 50mm (2in) deep polystyrene dams, the yellow represents the perlite trough and the bucket at the end is to catch the daily run-off.

To stop the gutter from sagging, use angle iron supports, as shown below, or alternatively slats of wood. When adopting any of the three systems above, remember that when the media is full of feed solution it will be very heavy, be it peat or perlite. The last thing you want is for parts of the staging to collapse. Bear in mind that although it may cost more to install a stout support system, you only have to build it once. The plants will give you a crop over two seasons, and when you renew the plants, you simply replace the perlite (or peat compost) at the same time. Perlite is quite cheap. Make certain you order the medium grade and not the fine.

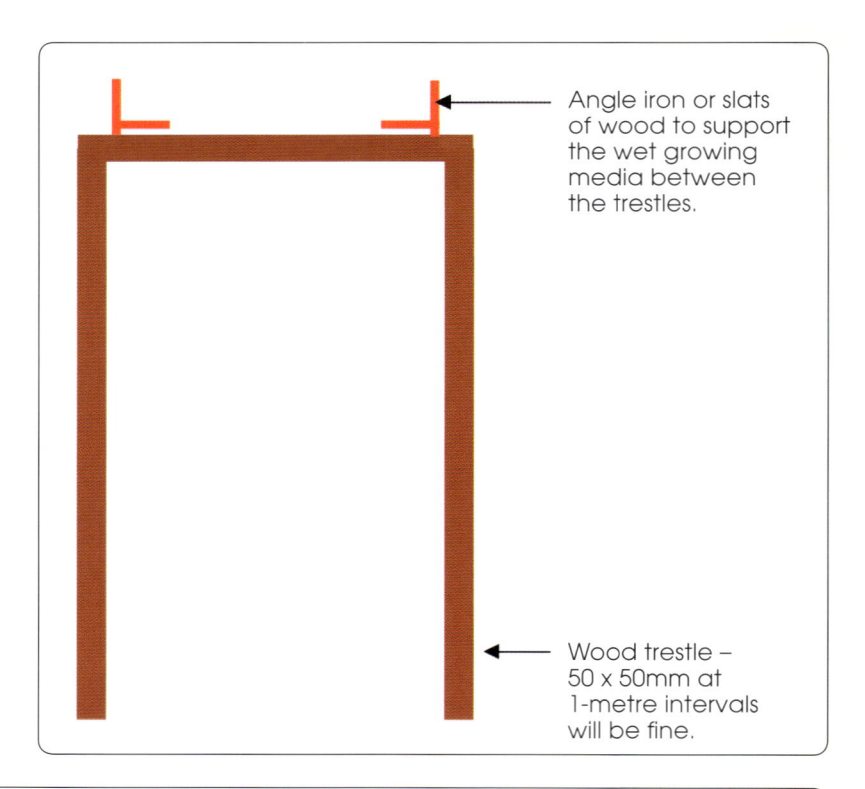

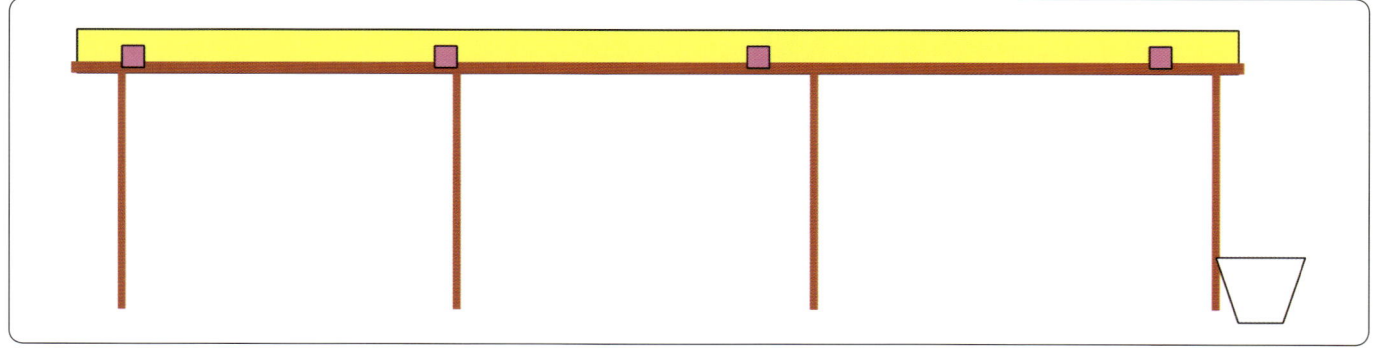

Angle iron or slats of wood to support the wet growing media between the trestles.

Wood trestle – 50 x 50mm at 1-metre intervals will be fine.

Once planted, use a high potash feed supplied at CF15 up to flowering, raising to CF20 from flowering to harvest, and once harvesting reduce to CF15. If there is a lack of insects then hand pollination will be needed, especially early in the season; this is time consuming but vital if you want to get nicely shaped fruit.

Strawberries grind to a halt after two years of fruiting, with lower yields and smaller fruit, so each year you should be rooting some runners to give you a succession of plants for the following year. Use the earliest runners to achieve maximum crown size to end up realising the heaviest yields. Make sure your new plants are kept flower and runner-free to help build up decent crowns; keep feeding during the autumn at CF15.

Every so often you should think about buying in new stock – these should have a quality registration to confirm that they are virus free.

Purchasing your plants

Purchasing can be expensive. If you were really keen, and had a few like-minded friends, you could share an order.

When you come to purchase strawberry plants you will typically see them on offer based on how they were graded. Essentially you find that the larger the crown the better the yield. The class A++ (18-24mm) are sometimes described as 'extra special'; these and the A+ 'extra' are often described as glasshouse plants. They are the most expensive but give the greatest yields, although they tend to produce in a more condensed harvesting period. You then drop down to grades A (standard) and B (potting).

Below:
The wet perlite growbags are very heavy hence the need for substantial support; you really do not want them growing on the ground. The other plant is a vine with the first tiny grapes beginning to appear.

Planting

You should try to get your plants delivered for a mid-April planting; this would give you a July harvesting. Major plant suppliers keep the plants in cold storage so there should be little problem getting them when the time is most suitable.

If you were to plant another crop at the start of June you would have another crop for September, although you may need to fine-tune this depending on your geographical location. If using perlite, remember to charge up the reservoir with feed solution the day before. When planting try to get the roots deep into the medium – I did not find this very easy and had to push the perlite apart to get the roots inserted. Make sure the base of the crown (where the roots begin) is level with the medium surface.

The grower of the strawberries above is David Henry. His crop is mainly the cultivar 'Elsanta' and is keenly sought throughout the Isles.

Raspberries

Raspberries can and do grow outside. I have seen them string-trained in a sheltered garden in Scalloway, but they realise their full potential when grown inside. Any shelter with decent light, giving a few degrees increase in temperature, will produce a substantial increase in yield. I had a great yield with the few plants I grew in my tunnel many years ago; they were grown in pots of perlite sitting in trays, and the fruit were large and succulent. One Shetland grower (using a small tunnel) said that in 2010 the crop was prodigious, the cultivar being 'Glen Moy', which has the attractive feature of being spineless.

The 'standard' varieties will fruit one year after planting, but the 'primocanes' (autumn types) should be picking fruit in the same year from August onwards. The 'standard' raspberries grow fruit on the previous year's growth; this is then removed after fruiting ,allowing the new canes to develop for the next season.

Blackberries

I grew these hydroponically in a large barrel; beautiful fruit with huge yields, although the plant took a lot of training. One plant is capable of producing 14kg (30lbs) of fruit, taking over a small greenhouse! These are grown in a similar way to standard raspberries where you remove the whole stem after it has fruited.

Glasshouse salads; Tomatoes

I already explained in Chapter 6 how to grow tomatoes in a hydroponics medium. The following notes give some guidance regarding the environmental conditions required, the use of peat-based compost growbags and the various cultivars I have grown over the years.

Tomatoes can grow very successfully in Shetland providing:

● You do not sow or plant too early;

● You provide a minimum night heat temperature of about 12 to 14°C.

Below: Blackberry 'Waldo'.

Although tomatoes are not hard to grow, they are tricky to grow well unless certain key conditions are met. I have only grown them hydroponically but the same basic ideas apply to peat-based medium. Many years ago I would telephone the late Robbie Norquay from Orkney for advice; he used peat-based growbags for his tomato crop. Here are a few pointers to keep you on the right tracks.

I would advise you sow from the middle to the end of March. Just sow as described earlier in the book; provide a minimum of 25°C to ensure emergence will be fast and even. By all means bring them on under lights but avoid planting before April unless you have a decent glasshouse capable of achieving and storing night temperatures of 12°C to 14°C. That will be early enough and you will still get loads of fruit, certainly before July. With decent culture, you can still be picking in November, although the fruit lacks the tastiness of the mid-summer trusses.

Make sure you use a small thermostatic fan heater or similar, which is able to maintain the night minimum temperature of 12°C. This will not only speed things up greatly, but also help to eliminate potential problems caused by botrytis. If you use a paraffin heater it is **vital** you use low sulphur paraffin otherwise you will generate sulphur dioxide, the precursor to acid rain. Also, make sure that the water or feed solution is warm, i.e. 15 to 20°C, by using a small aquarium tank heater.

The following notes refer to plants cultured in **peat growbags**.

Establishment is the tricky part. Make sure the growbag is sitting on a polystyrene sheet rather than on a concrete slab, to avoid heat loss. Obviously you need to plant into damp compost, but go easy with the watering in the first week or two; this will help to establish a strong root system, the precursor to a vigorous plant. When you plant do not remove the pot – simply and carefully remove the pot bottom with a sharp knife, and rest it on the exposed compost in the grow bag. There will be enough feed in the compost to get the plants started and to get the flowers to set, but once the first fruits are pea size, regular feeding is necessary.

You have to strike a balance between having the compost too dry and too wet. The peat compost should be wet enough so that when squeezed it releases a little water, but liquid should not be flooding out. Excess watering will lead to root death, with the plant going yellow and other strange colours, then you have to 'dry the compost back' to encourage new roots to grow – coupled with the risk of root rots setting in. This part of the process is tricky and one of the reasons I am so keen on perlite; you run much less of a risk with correctly managed hydroponics. There must be regular high potash feeding because the large fruit load puts a heavy demand on mineral requirements. Not enough feeding leads to large 'red water sacs' with no taste or 'flesh'; furthermore, the fruit will not keep well, and the parent plants will easily succumb to disease.

How many trusses? It all depends on the type of greenhouse you have, but do not adopt the mentality of stopping at five or six just because someone told you to. Tomatoes planted in mid-April should easily manage eight to 10 trusses. My glasshouse gets a lot of light and the plants have run to 26 trusses, demonstrating the potential of hydroponics. I usually remove the sixth truss since at that point the plant is carrying a heavy load; its removal gives the plant a breather, and allows the head to keep its vigour. Do make sure to give the plants a 'tap' at least twice a week when they are in flower, to enable the fruit to 'set' (this tapping releases the pollen enabling fertilisation and fruiting to take place).

The tomato plant is desperately trying to become a bush – one of the reasons it keeps on making axillary side-shoots (the little growths that form between the stem and main leaf stalks). You must remove these since you are trying to produce a (easily trained) long vine-like growth.

Cultivars

For several years in the past my main crop was F1 'Counter', giving lots of clean, round, medium-sized fruit which also tasted excellent. I then changed to F1 'Shirley' and although the first fruit are large, it can cope better with a slightly lower night temperature. There are lots of cultivars masquerading as 'cherry' types but the very inexpensive 'Gardener's Delight' is superb. Although the fruit is not the smallest, they are tasty and the plants give a huge (and I mean huge) yield. I have also grown yellow tomatoes but they tend to be very thin skinned and prone to irregular flesh, and some beef tomatoes that were real ugly beggars! There are lots of novelty types; I would forget these, and stick to one decent round cultivar, and each year grow one 'Gardener's Delight' at least.

In 2008, my tomatoes were planted in early June, ready for picking mid-July, and stopped at the 11th truss, ultimately giving me about 30-35kg from four plants. This was a totally cold grown crop, although the summer improved once June had passed. Tomatoes always grow better in a glasshouse than in a tunnel; the latter has too much temperature fluctuation, especially daytime versus night. Purely out of interest, I grew both F1 'Counter' and F1 'Shirley' in 2008, with the latter generating much more vigour and yield. The problem with 'Shirley' is that the first fruit are the size of apples; I have seen the bottom truss actually tear itself from the stem and sit rather sad-looking on the glasshouse floor!

The 'Counter' cultivar suffered a bit from blossom end rot, which is a physiological problem, i.e. the calcium was available at the roots, but the plant was unable to pull the minerals up the stem to the fruit. This can often happen in tomatoes if the humidity is too high or they have an environmental shock, which shows the importance of choosing the correct cultivar.

It is important to change the growing medium each year. This might just involve new growbags or digging out and changing the soil, depending on your situation. Tomatoes grown in the border in the greenhouse will give a lower yield but on the plus side are more tolerant of 'neglect'.

Feri Bartai said he was very keen on a cultivar called 'Matina', a potato leafed cultivar. He said they were both strong-growing and tasty.

I have tried a few of the hundreds of cultivars that are available and would make the following comments.

F1 'Shirley'. This is the tomato to grow; it has lots of vigour, can stand slightly lower temperatures and is heavy yielding. If there are any faults then it is that the first trusses of fruit are a bit large – sometimes the size of apples. Once you get to trusses two and three then the size moderates. It also tastes great.

'Alicante'. Why bother if you can use the above.

'Gardener's Delight'. This is an extremely good plant, particularly for a non-F1 hybrid cultivar. It is very high yielding with small fruit though not quite 'cherry tomato' size. It is fairly sweet if you like sweet tasting tomatoes (which I do not).

Yellow tomatoes. I have grown yellow tomatoes in the past and they have done reasonably well, but the main fault with them was the fact that the outer skin was very thin and so the fruit were liable to splitting. Apart from the cosmetic appearance I see very little to recommend them.

Beefsteaks. I grew beefsteaks a few years ago; they were big and ugly (and I mean ugly). Still, if that is what you want then there is nothing to stop you.

True-cherry types. The true small cherry type tomatoes are not hard to grow but the fruit is very sweet.

All in all, if you want a decent, sensible tomato then there really is little to beat 'Shirley'; if it ain't broke, why try and fix it?

Left: Hydroponically grown tomatoes. Can you see the top tomato on the nearest plant has a black base? This is 'Blossom End Rot' and has occurred due to environmental shock – maybe there was a day of mist, or too much heat.

Training the plants

Training tomatoes is easy providing you have a bobbin to hold the extra twine. They will need to be trained, and the trick is to start training them immediately rather than coming down one day and finding the plant on its side with a broken stem! Tie a slack loop around the base of the stem and then simply wind it up the stem between each pair of leaves. You will need something in the roof for the bobbin to attach to. If you had several plants you could have a length of supporting wire running along the roof beams – that is what I did.

Cucumbers

Cucumbers are much harder to grow than tomatoes but when you get conditions right they are extremely productive. The greatest danger with cucumbers is planting too early, and overwatering before a good root system has developed, resulting in both stem and root diseases. Unless you have good growing facilities I would avoid planting them before May. Here are a few pointers to keep you right.

To plant, carefully cut and remove the base of the pot and sit the plant on top of the (damp) compost. The roots can then go straight down. Initially you should water carefully and gently to encourage the plant's roots to spread through the growbag. Once the roots are established you will get vigorous top growth. Start feeding the plant at CF18, and once heavy fruiting is taking place increase this to CF20-22. If you are properly organised you should grow them in a perlite hydroponic medium (which they absolutely adore).

Try not to water too close to the stem – it is very prone to rotting. Never ever use cold water. Keep the feed strength slightly lower than that used for tomatoes and feed at least once a day. If it is a really hot day, give half-strength feed for the second irrigation, but concentrate more on damping down.

Now for the critical part – **remove all flowers** until the plants are at least 1.5 metres high, and also remove the side growths or 'laterals'. The first fruit are called 'stem fruit' since they form on the stem, and you should only allow a maximum of four to form. Keep the plant going until it hits the roof of your glasshouse, but before you pinch out the tip, leave the last three or four laterals in place. These will hang down to give the plant what is called an 'umbrella' habit, with the new fruit hanging down from the spokes of the umbrella. As the plant gets higher you will have to train it with a strong twine fixed to a bobbin holder hanging from a hook in the roof. When training make sure to have two turns of twine wrapped between each leaf break – if you do not there is a very real danger that the plant will collapse by sliding down the twine – a double turn prevents this.

Use the cultivar F1 'Tyria' if possible, since it is both an all-female hybrid (fertilised fruit tastes bitter and cannot be eaten) and also mildew resistant, critical in Shetland. If you cannot get 'Tyria' then try another F1, all-female with mildew resistance, such as F1 'Carmen'. If you cannot get one with mildew resistance then do not bother growing cucumbers at all. Do not confuse glasshouse cucumbers with outside or 'ridge' cultivars. There is a world of difference in taste and I would say the ridge types are barely fit for eating. Just my personal opinion.

One problem to watch for is spider mite – treat it by spraying the plant daily with water in the morning and try to keep the RH high and avoid excess dryness. If you do not have spider mite then try to keep it that way; the pest cannot fly so the only way it can appear is by being brought in on an infected plant. Be wary of introducing new plants to your greenhouse!

Left:
The F1 all female cultivar 'Tyria' produces superb tasting fruit, and is totally resistant to mildew attack.

Peppers

Before dealing with pepper cultivation, here is an amusing story: in 2008/09, I did a little supply work at Scalloway School. My colleague Tracey Regan proudly took me to the school glasshouse to show me her plants, including 'hot' peppers – there were probably insufficient to make half a curry for a mouse! The following year, I asked if she would like to grow peppers slightly differently. She said yes and I showed her how to grow them hydroponically. They grew and grew and grew until she ended up with a 'wall' of goodness knows how many kilograms of hot peppers. On a recent visit there were many fine plants growing, but not a pepper in sight. I cannot think why!

Below:
Tracey Regan's peppers grown in the very small glasshouse at Scalloway Primary School. This is a bell variety. You can see lots of greenfly which seemed to make little difference to the final yield. Photograph by Julie Jamieson.

Peppers seem to take forever to grow and produce fruit, yet when they do, you get a surprisingly large yield. The most critical thing is to get them sown early so they can be fruiting by late June/early July. I usually aim for around the middle of March with the seeds taking some five to six days to emerge. I bring them on in the grow room for as long as possible; if you do not have a grow room or grow rig, you would need to give a little warmth (assuming you were growing them in the greenhouse). It would make sense to section off a small part of the greenhouse and use that warmer area to full advantage to bring on your peppers, tomatoes and cucumbers. I certainly did that in the past. Religiously remove every white pepper flower you see forming until the plant is at least 40cm high; by allowing pepper formation at this stage the plant will remain small and, though the fruit may be early, your yield will be dismal. Start feeding at CF18 then to CF22-24 once you see vigorous growth kicking in.

The plants will certainly need training, since the fruit crop can get heavy, and in my early days of growing peppers many a branch full of peppers fell off. Rather than using string and bobbins, it is easier to train them using cross strings in the same manner as outdoor gardeners train their peas. Do plan your training method in advance as it will be essential.

Peppers are nearly always green prior to ripening (except for 'madras' which starts off shiny purple before going red); you can just as easily eat them green since some of them take a while to turn red or yellow or whatever. Be wary of some of the hot cultivars – they are almost painful to eat! I recall once growing a crop of hot peppers; I tasted one, burned my lips, and dumped the lot outside. A few days later someone visited and happened to mention they liked curries. To cut a long story short they ended up going with a bag and gathering up all the peppers from the midden, and left very happy! Purely out of interest, the 'hotness' of peppers is due to the presence of a substance called capsaicin and the hotness is measured using the Scoville scale. Someone once grew a chilli hybrid (the 'Infinity') with a value of over one million (1,176,182 SHU's or Scoville Heat Units). To put this in context, bell peppers have a value of zero, Tabasco sauce sits around 2,500 to 5,000, cayenne pepper 30,000 to 50,000, and Jolokia is 800,000 (incorporated into hand grenades used by the Indian military for counter terrorism). When the grower of the 'Infinity' pepper tasted a bit, he said, "It was all a bit worrying. The burn on my tongue lasted half an hour and the effects went on and on. At one point I was doubled over in pain and thinking about ringing the hospital. The worst was over by 11 o'clock, but it wasn't funny."

Peppers attract probably every pest known to man – greenfly, red spider mite and whitefly particularly adore them – be prepared! Once again you can see the advantages of bringing plants on from seed. They are also prone to botrytis, a fungus called Sclerotina, and various root rots.

On the left are two photographs of chillies, also grown by Tracey Regan in Scalloway Primary School. Photographs by Julie Jamieson.

Aubergines

I have never had much success with these. I tried a few plants hydroponically one year along with tomatoes and cucumbers; they grew until the 'hedge' was around 2 metres high. For whatever reason, the fruit were scarce and small, yet the other salads were highly productive. I do not like aubergines that much and never bothered with them again. I have grown a great many plants hydroponically, with aubergines being the only one a dismal failure. Strange!

Melons

I used to grow F1 'Sweetheart', a cantaloupe cultivar. It needs a lot of space and training, not to mention having to hand pollinate with a small brush. The fruit are small, only yielding a few mouthfuls, but they smell utterly gorgeous.

You can get a honeydew F1 cultivar under the name of 'Jade Lady', producing fruit of 1.5 to 2.5kg, with the flesh having high sugar content.

Vegetables and herbs

When I first started gardening some thirty years ago, I was of the mentality "if it could not be eaten you did not bother growing it". Having been commercial for a number of years now, I produce thousands of young vegetable plants but often never see the end result. The information below is partly my own but I must also acknowledge information given to me by Feri Bartai, Daniel Gear and Angus Nicol.

Although my three colleagues take things fairly seriously, a special mention must be made regarding my uncle, Tommy Goodlad, who is a relative amateur, yet with his enthusiasm and willingness to experiment, churns out as much good quality produce as anyone in Shetland. He is a devout believer in using seaweed – living 100 metres or so from the sea does help things along! I have included a photo of him holding two sacks of onions – not prize-winners – just large, decent onions; but here is the punchline – his onions are like that year after year after year!

He once said to me, "Each year there is always something which goes wrong." What he really meant was: "Each year most things go right." He keeps a basic diary (also including when he caught his first mackerel) particularly noting the cultivars and sowing dates.

Right:
My uncle Tommy from Scalloway; each bag holds eight or nine onions, all seaweed fed.

221

I have mentioned the limited growing season in Shetland. It amuses me when I read about growers in England planting first earlies, seconds and then main potatoes for instance. Here we get one shot at it; the 'earlies' are not that early (unless in a tunnel) so most growers just go for the main crop. The soil only warms up properly in mid-May – and that is already five months into the year. If you want succession over a long time interval, you have to use either cloches, tunnels or glasshouses to extend your season.

Since I started, there have been dramatic changes, partly with regard to the greatly increased number of cultivars available and changing consumer tastes, but also many people are now using both large and small polytunnels for culture and greatly expanding the crop potential.

Here are some comments regarding the various options available to budding kitchen gardeners.

Soil-grown

If you have decent soil then treasure it. Top quality soil is rather scarce in Shetland and at one point, when I felt my vegetable plot was a bit thin, I bought and spread some 30 or so tons of decent quality soil. I am not a pedologist (soil expert) but it goes without saying that you want a loam that is not too peaty and not too full of clay. There are advantages to having a slightly peaty soil and one with extra clay but that information is to be found in another book by another author.

Artichoke (Globe)

A lady from the east side of Shetland, Glenetta Smith, told me she had 'permanent artichoke roots' in her garden, given to her by a friend several years ago. She said they were often hammered with salt, since her house was quite close to the sea, but seemed to thrive whatever. I should imagine more people could grow them but they are probably perceived as being rather 'exotic' and possibly not to everyone's taste.

Beans, broad

The dwarf cultivar 'The Sutton' is recommended and can be grown outside, but needs some shelter.

Beans, French

Try the cultivar 'Prince', which also grows outside providing you have shelter.

Beans, French climbing

This is one which Feri spoke highly of, being a substitute for runner beans. The cultivar 'Cobra' sets very easily with tasty stringless fruit.

Beans, runner

I have never succeeded with this plant; too tender for outside, and it did not like the glasshouse. Feri said he produced large quantities of flowers but with poor setting, just the same as myself.

Beet leaf

I have grown and eaten cultivars such as 'Chard Bright Lights', which is a mixture of white, cream, yellow, orange, pink lipstick and red. They look a lot prettier than they taste; easy to grow. Certainly livens up the salad plate!

Left:
A nice stem of beet leaf grown in Debbie Scott's garden in Tingwall.

Beetroot

I used to grow 'Boltardy' many years ago; it never appealed to me in the boiled form but was delicious once pickled. Feri Bartai said he liked the cultivar 'Cylindra'. Later to mature than globe beets, it produces roots about 10cm long and is slow to bolt. 'Cylindra' has deep coloured flesh and a sweet flavour and has literally been designed for slicing; it is not unlike a dwarf cucumber, but red of course. Daniel Gear tried both 'Golden' and 'Egyption' with little success. The monogerm varieties such as F1 'Solo' are single seeded so need less thinning.

Borecole (Curly Kale)

I used to grow curly kale many years ago. Two things stood out in particular, firstly it was difficult to find caterpillars amongst the leaves and, secondly, it was strong tasting, perhaps not to everyone's taste. For the ultimate in bitterness then try 'Shetland Kale'; even the caterpillars struggle with that one!

Broccoli (sprouting)

This is becoming a very much more popular crop largely because it is fairly dependable; I have heard good comments about the cultivar 'Early Purple Sprouting'. Both the purple and white do well.

Brussel sprouts

The cultivar to use in Shetland has to be the cultivar F1 'Maximus' and first recommended to me by Feri Bartai. They come into production late autumn/pre-Christmas and are described as 'producing a high yield of round, smooth, well-flavoured buttons, good tolerance to a spectrum of fungal pathogens, and with a good shelf life'.

Cabbage

There are hundreds of cultivars of cabbages, one of my favourite vegetables. Christine sometimes makes a lovely dish called 'bubble and squeak' which is a fried mix of cabbage and onions in butter with added spices. Excellent!

Summer cabbage. I have grown 'Greyhound' (which is a pointed cabbage) in the past; I still see it advertised. Many growers get on well with the cultivar 'Primo', an early and compact ballhead; of course, when we speak about 'summer' cabbage in Shetland we are speaking about heads which are ready in August to September.

Winter cabbage. Here there is one superb performer, namely F1 'Tundra'. These can produce very large winter hardy heads (someone who gardens two miles to the west of Tingwall airstrip had a head weighing 10kg in season 2009). I hear its name mentioned a lot when I speak to other growers. I have also found the ballhead F1 'Impala' a fairly reliable cultivar to grow.

Red cabbage. The attractive feature about red cabbage is that they seem to be very 'pest resistant' which makes for easy culture, but unfortunately not everyone likes them. They do not survive the winter conditions and hard frosts, so should be used by late autumn. Some people like them in the pickled form. Just out of interest, the red contains more vitamin C than the green. The F1 cultivar 'Ruby Perfection' should grow well assuming the soil is half decent.

Savoy cabbage. I used to grow 'January King' many years ago without any real problem, but much prefer the ball type such as 'Tundra' mentioned above. With savoys, you always end up with slugs in between the (non-compact) leaves. Daniel Gear grows the F1 savoy 'Capriccio' successfully.

Left:
The old and the new sitting side by side. Shetland Kale (at the top) sitting next to F1 Savoy 'Capriccio'. These have been organically grown by Daniel Gear.

Calabrese

Rather like broccoli this plant is becoming popular; the one outstanding cultivar for Shetland is F1 'Marathon'. Feri Bartai spoke highly of the cultivar 'F1 'Fiesta', a cultivar that produces large domed heads. The beauty of calabrese is that numerous edible secondary side shoots are produced for eating once the centre head is harvested

Carrot

This is another mainstream vegetable which is easy to grow, but can give problems. One of the main problems is that it needs to be sown in late May/early June when, believe it or not, conditions for germination may be less than ideal, since Shetland often experiences the cold dry conditions known as 'the gabs o' May' about this time; this is discussed in Chapter 3 where Shetland's climate is considered.

Another big problem with carrots is the slow germination, since by the time you have sown the row and they are emerging some three or so weeks later, so too have a trillion weed seedlings. One way to avoid this problem is to 'fluid sow' the seeds. I experimented with this some 20 years ago and intend to return to it once my new vegetable plot is established. I have put some notes on fluid sowing in Appendix 5 but the gist of it is that you pre-germinate the seeds (so the roots are emerging), and then mix them into a thick gel so they are 'suspended', and then simply squeeze the gel out of a tube in rows on the soil – just like icing a cake!

I recall sowing carrot seed in deep trays of compost in the glasshouse and trying to prick them out directly in the soil; they were nice little plants but the 'hit rate' was very low. Another method would be to sow them in cardboard tubes and transplant the tubes, at which point you have to question how much effort are you willing to expend to achieve a carrot crop. Angus Nicol always uses a strip of polythene plus a little sand to cover the seeds with when sown. This helps keep in the moisture (and solar heat) so promoting a more even and slightly quicker germination.

The third problem is carrot fly. This is dealt with under pests and diseases.

'James Scarlet Intermediate'. This is a longer rooted carrot and one commonly grown in Shetland.

'Chantenay red-cored 2'. I used to have good results with this cultivar for many years; in fact the original seeds when I started were called 'Chantenay' – I cannot remember when the 'red cored 2' was added. This is a stump-rooted cultivar and ideal for shallow soils. I used to overwinter them in the garden shed in buckets of dry sand, which kept them in good condition, yet they were easily accessible.

'Autumn King'. Daniel Gear has had a lot of success with this cultivar; he has also had success with coloured types such as 'Solar Yellow' and 'Cosmic Purple', but did not fare so well with 'Lunar White', 'Red Samurai', 'Atomic Red' and 'Paris Market'.

F1 'Trevor'. This is an early Nantes type, which grew well for Maureen Cumming in Ollaberry. She grew some very successfully in 25-gallon blue barrels, with the extra height providing some deterrence to the carrot fly.

There are numerous new cultivars including multiple types of F1 hybrids. Many of these could be worth experimenting with but bear in mind that the 'earlies' will not give the heavy yield of the 'maincrop' cultivars; ideally you want a few earlies for late summer eating with the bulk as maincrop.

Out of interest, there are large quantities of carrots grown commercially in the south end of Shetland where the soil is naturally sandy.

Cauliflower

I am often quite amused by the charts supplied by the seed companies showing a matrix diagram of how, by growing different cultivars at different times, you can harvest a succession of cauliflower all year from January to December. I have experimented with this idea myself using different cultivars, but had little success, achieving no more than a five to six week spread of production. This is almost certainly due to the nature of Shetland's daylength where we have the two extremities of light levels at either end of the year. Since the cauliflower head is an actual flower, and flowering is both photoperiodic (i.e. related to daylength) and temperature-dependent, there is obviously a link. Research carried out on cauliflower development found that if early cultivars are sown late they produce 'button heads' and late cultivars sown early give leafy growth and produce curds very late.

Cabbage root flies absolutely love cauliflower. All brassicas are prone to root fly (save for red cabbage and Shetland Kale) and there is a section dealing with them in Chapter 9, 'Pests and Diseases'.

I cannot remember all the cultivars I used to grow, and the bulk of them will now be superseded, however 'All the Year Round' certainly grew well in the 80s and 90s and I still see it advertised; one favourable year they were the size of saucepans and I had to give many away to friends; I never really took to blanching vegetables for the freezer for there always seemed to be something missing when thawed and reheated. The photograph below shows a fine selection of heads of the cultivar F1 'Aviron', harvested by Daniel Gear in September 2011. Just out of interest, Moles Seeds describes it as "*Vigorous with good curd production. Suited to colder autumn and later work, and thrives across the UK. Sow mid spring for cutting July to November*". Another cultivar Daniel likes is 'Optimist'.

Feri Bartai spoke highly of the 'Romanesco' group, which he describes as being "reliable and growing over a long period". Successional sowings gave him results from June to September. This is a 'cauliflower variant' which is sometimes called a 'broccoflower'. For the mathematicians amongst you, the curds form lots of perfect little logarithmic spirals (natural fractals) with each bud being composed of a series of smaller buds, all arranged in yet more spirals. The maths is boring, but it really is a most attractive head!

One thing to note about cauliflowers is that they are not the easiest plants to grow, and even some of the large commercial growers can have problems, depending on the season.

fruit trees, salads & vegetables

*Above:
A lovely tray of organic cauliflower grown at Lee Lang's nursery at Nesting. I had to bend back some of the leaves to expose the curds for photographing.*

The Scottish Agricultural College advised me that if my soil was verging on the acidic side, I could have problems with molybdenum deficiency coupled with clubroot susceptibility. However, they said that if I wanted to "have a go" then possibilities include 'Plana', 'Fargro', 'Nautilus' and 'Frement'. They also mentioned a cultivar called 'Clapton' with good clubroot resistance, though late in maturing.

Finally, the Indian sub-continent is passionate about cauliflower; apparently West Bengal alone has 57,000 hectares dedicated to it, with a total production of 1.67 million tonnes; plenty of potential 'cauliflower and cheese sauce' dishes over there, but they probably spoil it by making curries! Bet you didn't know that!

Celery

Most people I speak to seem to hate celery. I love celery as part of a salad but there has to be a bottle of mayonnaise present. They are quite easy to grow, with the sowing date being important, but remember they are frost sensitive. I sow around mid-February and then prick the seedlings out about the start of April. The seed is cheap but take care to sow it thinly – do you really want to prick out 2000 plants? I grew 'Golden Self Blanching' fairly easily.

Celeriac

This lesser known vegetable is a delicious winter vegetable with a celery flavour and is excellent in stews. Feri Bartai uses the cultivar 'Prinz' which is fairly reluctant to bolt, though you have to make sure to harden it off properly. It does not take kindly to root disturbance so it is better sown as single seeds into small cells. The large, round root has crisp, white flesh, which can be eaten raw in salads, sliced or grated.

Chicory

I grew this many years ago with the intention of using the roots as a coffee substitute. I cannot remember much about it so the taste could not have been overwhelming! Out of interest, it is one of the key ingredients of 'Camp' coffee, made in Paisley.

Fennel, Florence

This is easy to grow, and I recall picking decent 'bulbs' many years ago. It tastes extremely like aniseed, which is not to everyone's liking.

Kohlrabi

Feri Bartai told me he found this very easy to grow, being ready for harvest after ten weeks, and with a nice turnip taste.

Leek

Leeks are easy to grow and good to eat. Like many vegetables, the sowing time is critical and to get decent plants you really need to sow in February, the earlier in the month the better. The seedlings come up quickly although it may take two to three weeks to achieve complete emergence depending on the cultivar. Nothing seems to happen for a while, and then suddenly you have decent seedlings. Similarly when planted in the soil – nothing much, then they charge on. The period when 'nothing is happening' is when they are putting down their roots. The roots always need to come first to achieve a decent plant. I have always used 'Musselburgh' and these tend to be almost foolproof. I did contact the Scottish Agricultural College a few years back regarding other cultivars and they stated that F1 seed (at five times the cost) would not be cost effective, the main advantage of the expensive cultivars being increased uniformity. This feature might be essential if you were supplying the market, but not for your own kitchen. If you wanted to go down the F1 route then the Scottish Agricultural College recommends experimenting with cultivars such as 'Porbella', 'Lancelot' (Elsoms Seeds) and 'Conora' (Yates Seeds).

Below:
A fine row of leeks grown by Tommy Goodlad on the hill above Scalloway harbour.

Lettuce

Lettuces are easy to grow; those I particularly like are the 'cut and come again' mixed babyleaf types. I tried to grow 'Iceberg' cultivars in the past, but found it took a long while for them to heart up. Daniel Gear likes 'Lollo Rossa', which is a non-hearting type with waved and serrated red tinged leaves. Another cultivar mentioned is the iceberg cultivar 'Dublin', with relatively quickly maturing solid heads. If sown 'little and often' a long cropping period will follow.

Onion (salad)

I recently grew some of the salad type F1 'Guardsman' with good results. The real trick regarding many of the salad type plants is to try and get successions of crops so they are maturing over a long period. You need to be organised to end up picking over a long season. Another good cultivar is 'Summer Isle'.

Onion (maincrop)

Daniel Gear asked me to bring on some onion plants from seed. I had tried 'Rijnburger 5' once or twice before with poor germination rates, but he wanted me to try F1 'Takmark'. The latter was superb with quick, even germination, and the seedlings stood up like rows of little soldiers. Another cultivar mentioned is 'Bedfordshire Champion'. My uncle, Tommy Goodlad from Scalloway, is the master onion grower. His success is due to using seaweed extract (discussed later on in the book). In 2010 he used 'Globe' (heat treated to kill the flower embryo and preventing the plant bolting), 'Setton' and 'Stuttgarder Stanfield' as onion sets; he said that they all did well. One problem many growers have in our 'less-than-dry' climate is the actual winter storage; sometimes the necks are a bit thick and that does not help matters. My uncle simply puts them in a net bag and hangs them up in a dry cupboard, then removes them as required.

Below: Tommy Goodlad's onions. It is nice to see the narrow necks.

Parsley

Easily grown but slow to germinate; one little trick is to buy a plant from a supermarket and then transplant into the garden. This saves a lot of time if you have forgotten to sow the seeds early on.

Parsley, Hamburg

Hamburg parsley is an unusual vegetable with parsnip-flavoured roots and edible parsley-flavoured leaves, and one that Feri Bartai recommends highly. The roots can be left in the ground over winter and used when needed.

Parsnip

This plant is very under-rated and tasty, making excellent soups amongst other things. As mentioned earlier, use primed seeds to speed things up. Cultivars doing well in Shetland include 'White Gem' and primed 'Palace'. They seem to be relatively pest free and can be quite expensive in the shops.

Pea

Cultivars suitable for the Northern Isles include 'Feltham First', 'Sugar Snap' and 'Kelvedon Wonder', the latter being earlier to yield a crop.

Potato

I have not grown many potatoes primarily because of lack of garden space. Angus Nicol is successful growing potatoes, and what is significant about his choices is that they all have a good resistance to 'tattie blight'. Cultivars showing some resistance include 'Cara', 'Kondor', 'Orla', 'Markies', 'Valor', and 'Remarka'; a recent development has been the arrival in the UK of the Sarpo potato cultivars such as 'Mira' and 'Axona' – I say more about them in Chapter 9 in the section dealing with 'tattie blight'.

To produce an early crop, cover the ground with black polythene eight weeks prior to planting, and sprout the tubers in a warm, light place. Change the cover to clear polythene after planting.

My uncle in Scalloway plants his tatties at the start of March in his tunnel, with his first crop being eaten around mid-June using the cultivar 'Orla', although he said the taste did not appeal to him. For outdoors he used the cultivars 'Kestrel', 'Shetland Black', 'Catriona', 'Epicure' and 'Red Duke of York'.

A purple potato that growers claim is extra healthy is the 'Purple Majesty'. It has a distinctive deep colour, and contains up to 10 times the level of antioxidant, anthocyanin, compared with white potatoes.

Daniel Gear has good results with 'Sarpo Axona' (blight resistant), 'Rooster' and 'Cara'.

Maureen Cumming concentrates on growing her potatoes in 25-gallon blue barrels. She gives the plants protection when they first come through, as they are that bit higher off the ground. She keeps them fairly deep in the barrel and then 'earths them up' as they grow. The sheltered location of the barrels means she has to take note of the moisture levels, watering as and when required. The blue barrels contain a mixture of her own (clay) soil with peat and sand, with seaweed added in winter, and during growing time carefully applying 15:15:20 fertiliser. She found that excess fertiliser led to 'watery' tatties, and three plants per half-barrel gave the optimal yield. Three varieties that did well for her were 'Admiral' (from Thomson and Morgan), 'Records' and 'Edzell Blue'.

Below: What exotic plant do these flowers belong to? A Shetland black potato of course!

Rhubarb

Easy to grow from seed, but make sure to harden-off the young plants; they are very tender compared to the adults and I recall having to resow the first time I grew them in an unheated glasshouse. I had no problems growing 'Victoria' from seed.

Spinach

Easy to grow and horrible to eat! I do not care how much iron it contains – give me raw liver any day! When Christine asked me to grow some I would always tell her I had run out of seeds (though I may have had a large packet in the fridge). Popeye, who apparently eats a full tin at one go, could only have been a cartoon character. I forget which varieties I grew so you can see how impressed I was with them!

Swede

A really nice winter vegetable. The one to go for here is 'Marian', resistant to both clubroot and mildew diseases, but can be prone to cabbage root fly. Others recommended are 'Best of All' and 'Gowrie'. I love them mashed with a little butter and pepper.

Turnip

Not much to say here; I used to grow 'Purple Top Milan' which has been around for decades. Some cultivars seem less prone to pests, with 'Atlantic' coming out quite well, being a quick-maturing, bolt-resistant Purple Milan type. Daniel Gear found 'Atlantic' to be very fast growing and also did well with 'Goldana' and 'Snowball'.

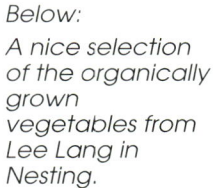

Below:
A nice selection of the organically grown vegetables from Lee Lang in Nesting.

Tunnel grown crops

Tunnels are particularly valuable when growing plants in Shetland because at one fell swoop you mimic the climate found in the south of England. Well-built tunnels will cope with the gales, and I have said a few things about them in Chapter 7. My first tunnel is now some 10 years old and still has its first covering of polythene in place, though there have been a few repairs, particularly along the folds formed when the film was transported here.

From the start I decided I did not want soil-grown crops, but instead concreted the floor and covered it with benches and large containers. The benches were used to support pots, with growbags or containers used for fruit trees. I grew all the fruit and salad hydroponically, but they could just as easily have been grown in compost. A proper hydroponics system has the edge for ease of management and realises huge yields. I used a perlite medium with the feed solution being pumped out from plastic storage barrels (blue in the photos); this process has already been described.

Courgette

This is an easy-to-grow crop; the trick is to harvest them before they get too big. One problem I often met when growing these in my tunnel was that of blossom rot at the end of the fruit during damp spells with little air movement. The fungus is attracted to the higher sugar levels in the flower, and this spreads to the end of the fruit; I would nip the flower off before this happened. I regularly used the cultivar F1 'Ambassador' with good success.

Tomato

These do not do well in (single skin) tunnels in Shetland. I remember once planting the same cultivars of tomatoes in the tunnel and glasshouse at the same time to see how they did. The tunnel-grown ones struggled compared to the very nice plants coming on in the (unheated) glasshouse. The tunnel's relatively cold nights are not at all to their liking. It may be that some of the newer cultivars could do better, but I would always give the glasshouse priority for this crop. The 'polycrub' tunnel with its double wall should grow them much better, as shown in the photo below.

Below:

Tomato 'Piccolo Dattero' F1, grown by Susan Davidson in a Nortby Polycrub tunnel. These are very attractive fruit, better than I used to grow using my single skin polythene tunnel. Photograph by Emily Robertson.

Cucumber

You will have difficulty growing the 'true' greenhouse cucumber in a tunnel, however, the 'ridge' cultivars such as F1 'Burpless Tasty Green' or 'Masterpiece' do fairly well. Do be aware that these are different beasts from true indoor cucumbers such as F1 'Tyria' – the taste and quality of which puts them in a league of their own. In fact, I would go as far as to say that outdoor ridge cucumbers are 'sub standard' vegetables.

Sweetcorn

These grow well in tunnels, but do take up a lot of space simply to yield no more than two cobs per plant. They need to be grown as a 'block' of plants to allow cross-pollination. Greenfly used to be a pest once they moved inside the cob; I was only aware of them when I dehusked the cob prior to eating. One year I was selling some young plants but only had mini-sweetcorn labels, which I forgot to amend; a few weeks later a grower, who had bought them, came and said to me: "Goodness, if these are the small ones, I would not like to see the size of the big ones!"

*Right:
Linda Glanville picking some very healthy looking organically grown lettuce.*

Herbs

Many herbs are dead easy to grow, as well as being fast in delivery. These include peppermint and spearmint, chamomile, chives, dill, marjoram and sage. I am sure many of these would do fine outside in the garden but I find it more convenient to keep them in the tunnel in a decent-sized pot. I have not had much success with basil (the cultivar 'Sweet Genovese' was recommended to me) – more than likely I was trying to bring it on too early in a cool glasshouse. If you grow basil then leave the sowing for as late as possible.

Some more ideas regarding fruit and vegetables

Organic or not?

I cannot imagine anyone being at odds with organic principles because, in a way, you are working alongside nature. So I never spray my edibles with any synthetic pesticide, and if problems arise will use either nicotine or derris, or some of the natural predators which you can buy in small quantities.

However, I have mixed feelings about the nutritional aspect. The big problem I find with organic fertilisers, whether cow muck, chicken manure, seaweed or whatever, is that you have no idea of the rate of release of minerals. If you are growing fruit for instance, we all know that high potash levels are imperative. Good old cow muck will have potash but how much? Two scenarios can follow – either the plant is getting too much, or more likely not enough. As I said earlier, this was one of the problems I found with slow-release fertiliser; I was not sure what the release rate was, and I do not have time or the inclination to carry out mineral analysis (despite my love of chemistry). When you mix up a fertiliser solution containing 300ppm of potash you know exactly what the plants are getting.

However, the one very desirable effect with applying organic matter to the soil is that it improves its structure.

Genetically Modified (GM) seeds

I have even more of a quandary when it comes to GMO (genetically modified organisms). Of course there is the danger of having one crazy scientist doing very silly things, but is the idea of taking a tattie blight resistant gene from one type of potato plant and inserting it into another susceptible cultivar so very wrong? Think of the thousands of tons of copper-based fungicides which would no longer have to be used.

Genetic modification has been going on for a long time in the field of biotechnology, and many of the medical drugs we use both effectively and cheaply come from GM bacteria. So a vital lifesaver such as thyroxin can be made cheaply and in volume, as compared to the tiny amounts derived from the processing of tonnes of abattoir offal in the past.

As with many things, if common sense is used, it could be to everyone's benefit.

I am well aware that many readers may not agree with these thoughts.

fruit trees, salads & vegetables

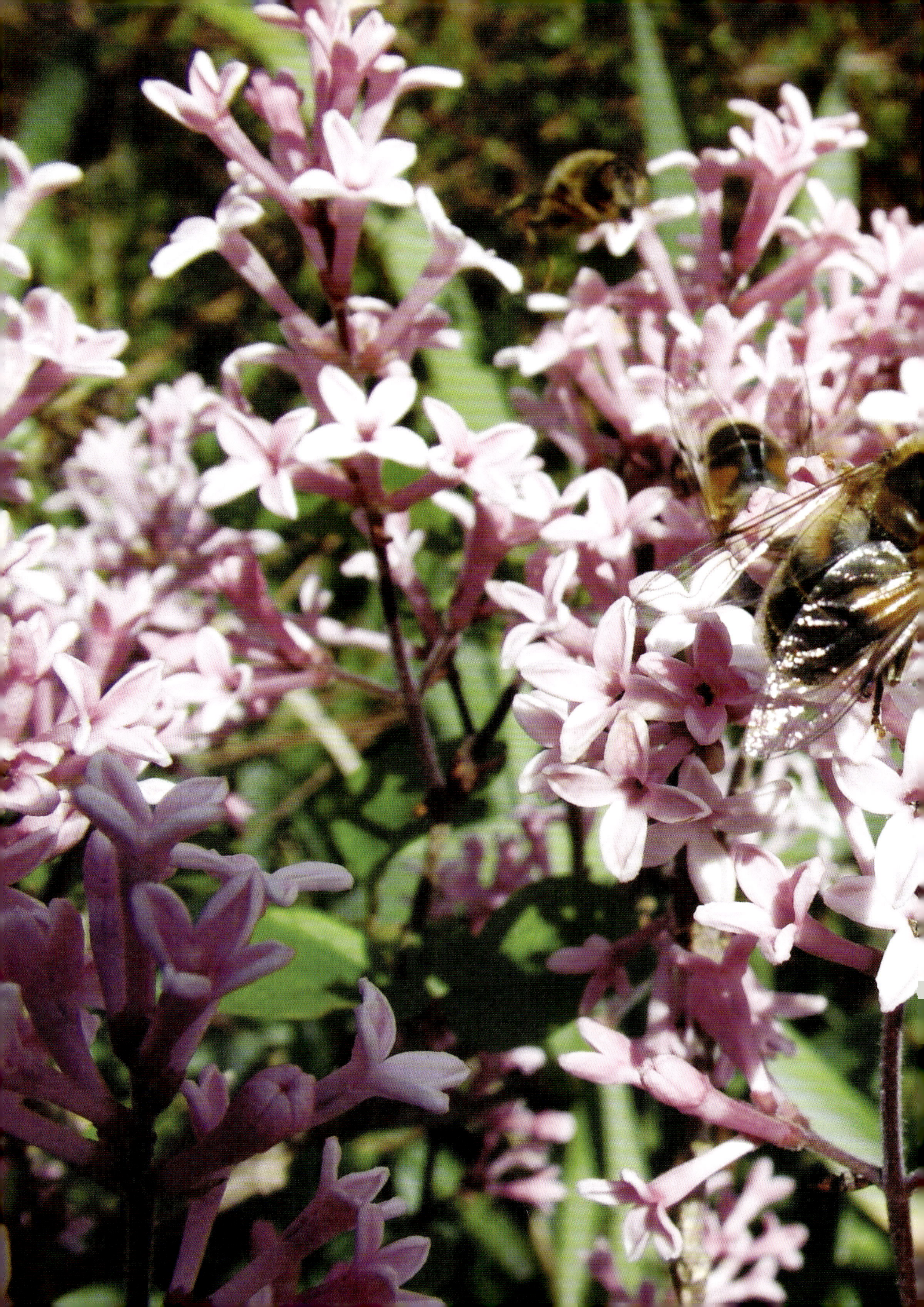

Chapter 9
Pests, Diseases and Weeds

pests, diseases & weeds

Do not get these mixed up. A **pest** is some kind of organism that will attack any sort of plant whether it is healthy or otherwise; a **diseased** plant is one that is ill and has been infected by a virus, bacterium or fungus. Healthy plants can also be attacked by these last three but are less likely to succumb. Let me state that although I am not a dedicated organic grower, I will not use pesticides on my food crops because there are alternatives. I can only speak meaningfully about the problems I have encountered, but shall also add comments about the experiences of some of my colleagues. A **weed** is simply a plant in the wrong place – I have had to treat tomato seedlings as weeds in certain circumstances.

Physiological problems

Take care not to confuse pests and diseases with physiological problems – these are really the effects of a faulty environment – be it related to light, temperature, atmosphere, water supply or nutrient levels. A plant will wilt if some pest or disease has damaged its roots, but the same will also happen if it is short of water! Many injuries can be caused by physical or chemical damage and some are not that obvious. Below is a brief summary of the key physiological disorders extracted from the RHS publication 'Garden Pests and Diseases', to which I have added my own comments.

Too little light leads to thin weak plants prone to diseases. As I said earlier, there is nothing worse than forcing a plant with heat and insufficient light; it becomes 'leggy'.

Too high a temperature leads to scorching, scalding and flower withering; the scorching is often the result of insufficient ventilation, so the leaves cannot transpire (sweat). Imagine if you were hot and could not sweat; this is why breathable clothing is so popular.

Low temperature causes young soft foliage to becomes silver or white, and frost, of course, kills tender plants. It needs extreme cold for frost to develop in a glasshouse; it requires minimal heat to keep it at +1°C: the 100-watt tubular heaters I mentioned earlier are the simple answer.

Too dry an atmosphere causes poor growth, bud drop and leaf burning. You will know this is a common problem in houses with central heating but it often happens in the greenhouse. You need to try to raise the humidity on 'blue-sky' days by soaking the floors and capillary matting to keep the air 'buoyant'. The poor growth arises as a result of the leaf stomata (leaf sweat pores) closing and then photosynthesis slowing down and possibly stopping due to lack of gas exchange. Misting or fog units are another alternative for raising the moisture levels and one I am considering for the future. Acute shortage of water obviously causes wilting, with irrigation leading to recovery, but if this happens too often the plant may not recover; if you keep forgetting to water, the plant will die and it will be your fault!

Sporadic supplies of water can lead to damage of certain fruits and potatoes. Regular watering is always going to be best.

At the other extreme, excess moisture is fatal, leading to the onset of all types of disease, especially root rots and botrytis; once again make sure to ventilate – the greenhouse windows should become dry during the daytime. Excess moisture can also induce mineral deficiencies, the classic example being 'blossom end rot' of tomatoes where the fruit develop abnormally due to a lack of calcium being taken up from the roots, despite plenty being available in the growth medium.

Waterlogging through overwatering is disastrous eventually leading to root death and subsequent disease; pick up the odd pot and check the weight, and keep a look out for plants with abnormally coloured leaves – they will nearly always have been overwatered.

Mineral salts; shortage of any one leads to various mineral deficiencies while excess leads to root scorching. Stick to the recommendations on the feed packet or use a conductivity meter.

Pests

Pests include all the creepy crawly organisms whose key function in life is usually to destroy the plant you are trying to grow. There are myriads of these but I just want to mention some of those you are most likely to meet in Shetland, and to say a little about how you might combat them. A second group of pests are the large 'grazers' such as sheep and rabbits; rabbits have been discussed in Chapter 4.

I am lucky in that there are many insect pests I have never even seen, far less been bothered with. I have never come across a whitefly for instance, but know they are tricky to eliminate. Like all other forms of life, insects are not capable of 'spontaneous generation', so unless you are unlucky enough to live next door to someone whose greenhouse or garden is infected with these other species, they are just not going to appear out of thin air. This is why it has been five or six years since I last saw a spider mite.

One of the main attractions in bringing on everything from seed is that there are no pests or viruses present. Conversely, I would never purchase plants from a car boot sale. If you do, then carefully check the leaves and the roots. Surprisingly many of the plants in the supermarkets will be pest free, since the suppliers know better than to sell infected plants.

In a nutshell, if you haven't got a pest, then don't bring it in!

Dealing with pests

Before dealing with particular pests I want to say a bit about pest control in general. There are two modes of attack; the first is using natural 'organic' based protection, and the second using synthetic pesticides.

A. Organic based strategies.

These include using physical methods, naturally occurring insecticides, biopesticides, and predators such as ladybirds.

1. **Soaps and oils:** These damage the exoskeletons of insects leading to spiracle (breathing tube) blockage with the insects suffocating. One product I used for a few years was *'Majestic'* which is a contact spray containing natural plant extracts. The principle is that, once sprayed, the insects have difficulty moving coupled with their breathing holes (spiracles) becoming blocked leading to suffocation. I eventually gave it up as it was impossible to hit all the pests, and everything became so sticky.

2. **Natural plant-derived insecticides:** If you wish to stay within organic guidelines you could use plant-derived insecticides such as derris or pyrethrum. I will, on occasions, use nicotine shreds to fumigate, and although organically approved, it is a scheduled poison and has now been withdrawn. The beauty of fumigation is that the smoke gets everywhere, and when I return next morning the floor is covered with greenfly or whatever I have been targeting. The idea of putting old cigarettes into water and spraying the solution is not that daft.

3. **Biological control:** Biocontrol really means using one organism to combat another, always better than using boxes of chemicals. Almost all gardeners know that ladybirds are good news as they enjoy eating aphids – that is a form of biological control we all know about; Shetlanders may be unimpressed with my example since there are no ladybirds present here! However, you will certainly have hoverflies in your garden – these are natural predators; hoverfly larvae feed on greenfly. I have a biological control book produced by Koppert Biological Systems in 1992 in which they proudly quote some 15 products; looking up their website recently, I saw there are now no less than 56! I do not see any products suited to cabbage root fly; they will have hit the jackpot when they crack that one! If you have introduced predators, then you should stop spraying the aphids, as the predators will need food for survival. If you have hoverfly for combating greenfly it may seem for a time as though the greenfly are getting worse, but eventually things will settle down once a predator-prey relationship has been established; the point is that the greenfly will not be eliminated, but rather kept in balance.

4. **Biopesticides:** This somewhat overlaps with biological control and is the future path for pest management; we are going to find these appearing more and more as a real alternative for conventional chemicals. There are three main groups, including 'microbials' (mentioned earlier with regard to the cabbage white butterfly), 'botanicals' describing extracted plant compounds, and finally 'semiochemicals', which are primarily pheromones (insect hormones). With biopesticides there is neither chemical residue nor harvest interval. The key advantage of these biopesticides is, because they have a more complex mode of action, resistance is very unlikely. Purely out of interest, it appears that there are 16 biopesticides now registered in the UK as compared to the USA's 200!

I mention below the use of bacteria for cabbage white butterflies and vine weevil, and there is the ongoing development of fungal products to target white flies

B. Synthetic pesticides

There are dozens of pesticides on the market; although many have different names, the active ingredients tend to be similar. They are grouped into either those with **contact action** where the active molecule merely has to touch the pest to cause death, or **systemic action** where the molecules flow through the plant's sap to be ingested by the insects that are doing the feeding. The five categories following include the bulk of the pesticides available at present.

1. Organophosphates and carbamates. These are cholinesterase inhibitors, i.e. they stop nerve action; some of their molecules form the basis of nerve gases. Highly toxic to mammals.
2. Pyrethroids and chlorinated hydrocarbons. Destabilise nerve cell membranes.
3. Macrocyclic lactone. Affects gamma amino butyric acid (GABA) dependent chloride ion channels which inhibit nerve transmission.
4. Chloronicotinyls. Damages nervous systems.
5. Insect growth inhibitors. Prevent growth of chitins, which is the main component of insect shell or skin.

The table below shows some of the armoury available for greenfly, and by the time this book is printed many will be out of date, and removed from the market. It is enclosed purely out of interest.

Some insecticides registered for chemical control of aphids, listed by chemical class.

Pesticide Class	Trade name/Common name	Comment
Organophosphate	Duraguard ME	Microencapsulated extended release
	Knox-Out GH	
Carbamate	Closure 76WP	
	Mesurol 75W	
Pyrethroid	Talstar GH	Pyrethroids work best when combined with other products.
Chlorinated Hydrocarbon	Thiodan 50WP	Sometimes combined with a pyrethroid product

Some of the organic treatments used for aphid control

Botanical	Fulex Nicotine (nicotine)	One of the very old products, but still effective against aphids.
Soaps and Oils	M-Pede (insecticidal soap)	Soaps and oils kill by contact so thorough coverage is needed.
Mycoinsecticides	BotaniGard ES, WP	Most effective against aphids when combined with other insecticides.
Other	Avid (abamectin)	To suppress, young immatures must be contacted.

Insects quickly develop resistance so you may have to use pesticides containing active ingredients with different modes of action. Some affect the nervous system of the animal, and some work by preventing the animal from producing a new external skin or shell. They should all be treated with great care, especially those acting on nerve function, because they will certainly affect your nerves as well. This is one of the main reasons that sheep dip has been banned. I know that when farmers were treating their flocks, I could smell it in the air, and the dipping troughs were about a mile away! As far as resistance goes, the gold medal must go to the Colorado beetle (*Leptinotarsa decemlineata*), having managed, in the space of 50 years, to develop resistance to 52 different compounds belonging to all major insecticide classes, including cyanide!

Many of these substances will be unavailable for the amateur but if your insecticide is not working, look at the label, see what the active ingredient is and its mode of action, then try to get another product with a different ingredient; the latter is usually obvious with the label saying 'Contains xxxxx'. For example, if Orthene was not successful then you need not bother using Dithio as they are both organophosphate based.

There are thousands of different insecticides and it is hard to keep track of them, bearing in mind that they are often replaced with more efficient versions, and some of them end up being taken out of circulation due to some problem that has arisen.

Some examples of products available for amateur use are given below; you can see there is a poor selection available for the gardener compared with the commercial grower, partly for practical reasons and partly for health and safety. And it seems to be getting worse with the EU removing some products which have been used for generations, such as the organic insecticide Derris. Apparently the EU has now banned sulphur dust, used to prevent storage rot, yet permits its use as a fertiliser.

I currently use a product called 'Gazelle', primarily to combat aphids. It obviously works fast with a name like that! Its action is both contact and translaminar (moves through leaves), so is useful for plants with lots of foliage where you cannot guarantee hitting 100% of the pests. The active ingredient is acetamiprid, which has been derived from the neonicotinoid group. Yes – related to nicotine – the same compound millions of people inhale presumably to get rid of the greenfly in their lungs! This move was essential since my last product ('Ambush C') was pyrethroid based, and eventually having no effect on the greenfly at all, i.e. they had developed resistance.

I apply the 'Gazelle' at the rate of 1 gram per litre using a knapsack sprayer, and it dissolves easily in water to give a blue solution. It is rainfast (i.e. will not be washed off by rain) in two hours, and has a 'knock down' (lethal) period of 20 minutes for some species of aphid.

Trade name	Active Ingredient
Mulltirose concentrate	Myclobutanil
Provado (various)	Imidacloprid and thiocoprid
Greenfly killer	Deltamethrin
Vitax PY sprays and powders	Pyrethrums
Bayer Kybosh	Permethrin and natural pyrethrum
Westland Plant Rescue RTU	Thiamethoxam and abamectin

'Gazelle' is also effective in controlling many other insects and is outstanding against piercing, sucking and chewing pests such as thrips, leaf miners, leafhoppers, mealybug, beetles and weevils (specific species), leaf midges, scales, whitefly, fly species (e.g. cherry, sawfly and sciarid) and capsids.

No one willingly wants to use these chemicals; for instance I never treat any edibles with pesticides, but sometimes you have no choice when it comes to non-edibles. If there are only one or two plants affected you can throw them out, but you do not want to lose a whole crop.

Specific pests and their control

1. Greenfly (aphids)

There are around 30 different species which can turn up in the greenhouse! These are parasitic insects and can breed asexually, so the female can generate immense numbers when the conditions are right. They suck the sap and the plants can cope with some loss, but in large quantities the plants are literally bled dry. They can also deposit sticky honeydew, which makes a tremendous mess – especially on peppers – which then need to be washed (as I know from experience). Finally, they can spread viruses, so plants can become infected with TMV (tobacco mosaic virus) for instance. As if life were not bad enough, later in the year some of them change sex, develop wings then really get around.

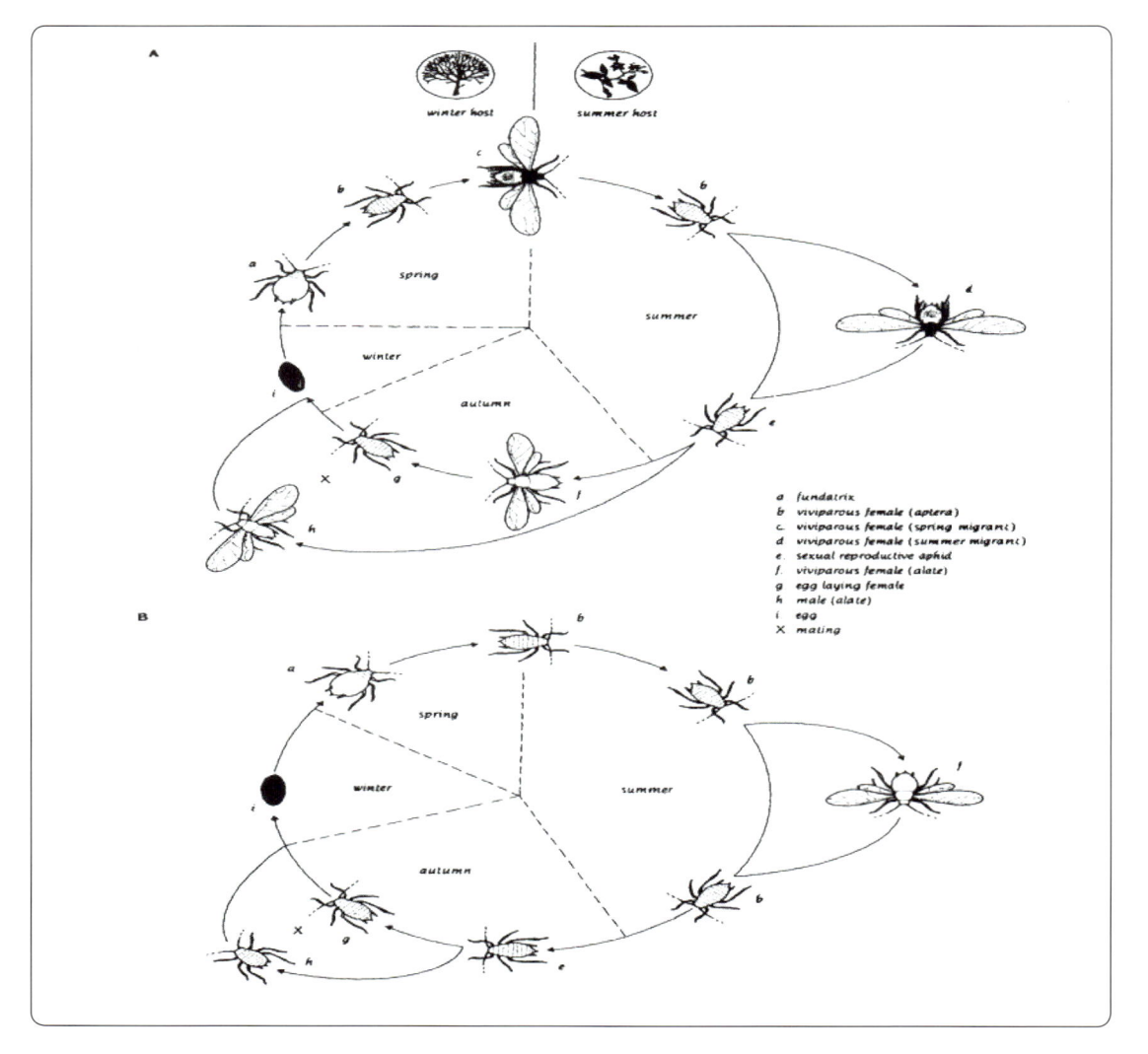

Left:

Aphid life cycle. Reproduced with kind permission of Koppert UK.

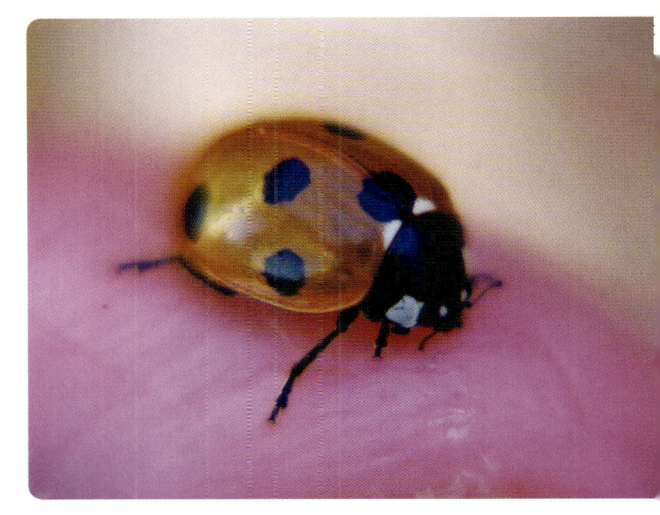

If you have aphids then hope that hoverflies appear; these lay eggs and the larvae feed on aphids; eventually you will get a 'status quo' where the hoverflies keep the aphids in balance.

The diagram on the previous page (with permission of Koppert UK) shows the complexity of the greenfly life cycle, and my only reason for including it is to show that nothing in nature is ever as simple as it seems.

Everyone in Shetland will meet greenfly, especially if you have roses or similar host plants nearby; insects occurring naturally in a place are said to be 'endemic'.

One biological control predator commonly sold to tackle greenfly is *Aphidolites*. It is possible to purchase it in small quantities for the amateur gardenere.

There are dozens of aphicides on the market, some of which have already been mentioned in the table above. Once again, if one substance does not work make sure to replace it with another whose active ingredient is different.

Above:
A greenfly.

Right:
Three natural predators of greenfly: top – a ladybird which, unfortunately, is not native to Shetland; middle – a lacewing; bottom – a hoverfly caterpillar, which clearly has a greenfly in its jaws.
Photographs by Angus Nicol.

245

2. Slugs

Slugs will eat most green things but positively love dahlias and salads, and if they find a tray of primrose seedlings then disaster follows. Although the 'traditional' metaldehyde pellets are easily used, my colleague Angus Nicol praises dry bran which slugs cannot digest, and when eaten, swells up and kills the slugs. Do not leave slug pellets anywhere near pets, particularly dogs and cats. One of our friends lost her pet dog as a result; some dogs will eat anything – as I found out with our pet retrievers. Not many of you will have heard of 'Ferramol' slug killer, containing the active ingredient ferric phosphate; a newer version has been brought out called 'Ferramol Max', three times more concentrated. Environmentally these are light years ahead of the traditional pellets, both having a very small effect on the non-target organisms, and degrading into naturally occurring nutrients.

Another method of slug prevention is to put a copper strip around the base of the plants you want protected; slugs do not like being in contact with copper. I should imagine the copper strip found in twin and earth cable would be fine. Electricians will have plenty of spare scraps especially if they are rewiring a building.

You have to be particularly wary when new seedlings are emerging, or when you have just planted some brassicas. I would recommend broadcasting a few slug pellets at this time since the large slugs can give small plants a hammering. It is not so bad when the plants are larger. This is one of the reasons I like cabbages with tight heads – the slugs cannot get 'in between' the closely packed leaves and riddle it with their droppings. With a loose headed cabbage like a Savoy there are always slugs stuck in between the leaves. Every garden will have slugs whether hiding in the edges or amongst the organic debris. Combating slugs is common sense since the more rubbish lying around the garden for them to hide in the worse the problem will be.

One feature of the pests which helps in location is the slimy trail they leave after crawling along; when you see this, a slug will be close by. Very often you will find them attached to the underside of a plant pot.

There are also nematodes available for controlling slugs such as 'Nemaslug'. Nematodes are incredibly tiny thread-like worms found naturally in the soil, but not related at all to the earthworm; those in 'Nemaslug' use the slug's body as a breeding chamber.

3. Caterpillars and cabbage white butterfly

If you are growing any plants from the brassica family, these butterflies will flutter around and get particularly interested in your cabbage patch. When the cluster of eggs first hatch things do not seem too bad. But just as the caterpillars grow at an exponential rate, so does their feeding. If you do not watch out, you can end up with plants with only the stalks of the leaves being left – I have seen this happen (not in my own garden, I might add).

Despite the eggs being coloured bright yellow they are not easy to find; the best plants are targeted first, usually under the leaf with cauliflowers being their meal of choice and red cabbage at the bottom of the menu. A simple plan is to **regularly** check the leaves to identify where a batch has newly hatched, as the leaf will have a little clear 'window' at that area. When very small, the young larvae only manage to eat the underside of the leaf leaving the rather transparent upper epidermis still in place. At this stage they are clumped together and easily squashed. Once this cluster becomes mobile, they spread out and then it is much more difficult to tackle the problem.

If you do not have the time (as is usually the case), the second course of action is to cover the plants with fleece or grow them in some large frame covered with a strong fine mesh. This will protect against cabbage root fly, carrot fly, cabbage white butterfly, pea moth, cutworm, cabbage whitefly, leaf miners and many species of aphids. It also has the advantage of acting as a windbreak yet allowing rain to pass through and give ventilation. The company maintains it will last for 10 years. I know one local grower who has covered frames with it and has had excellent results. The smaller of my two new tunnels is going to have an 'Enviromesh' cover primarily to be used as a 'hardening-off' area.

For a larger patch the simplest method of control is simply to treat with a bacterial biocontrol with the wonderful name of 'Bacillus thuringiensis'; this can simply be sprayed on and will infect the caterpillars. This bacterium acts by producing toxic proteins which react with the cells of the gut lining. This paralyses the digestive system, and the infected insects stop feeding within hours and subsequently die from starvation.

I know of one or two people in Shetland who have used this successfully, and for those with, say, even two or three hundred cabbages, it really is a no-brainer.

4. Cabbage root fly

These are nasty. Root flies are the larvae of a small bluebottle-like insect, *Delia radicum*, which hatches in late spring, and then flies to the nearest brassica plant to lay its eggs next to the stem; the emerging grubs burrow down and feed on the roots; say no more! About twenty years ago I had some gorgeous cauliflowers growing in my garden. One sunny day they all wilted and when I pulled one up for examination, the plant just lifted clean out of the soil with barely a root fibre left; with good roots it would have been a 'tug-of-war'. All these large plants subsequently died, and to say I was shocked is an understatement. I know it is not a cause for celebration when you find cabbage white caterpillars on the leaves, but at least you can see and easily treat them! Be in absolutely no doubt that if you grow brassicas then root fly will appear. It might not be there first time round but will eventually appear just as day follows night.

There are lots of ideas as to how to combat this pest. One of the most frequently quoted is using a piece of carpet underlay around the base of the stem of the plant so the insect cannot get to physically lay her eggs – some people soak this in creosote and the smell is presumably repulsive. One grower I know maintains that rotting seaweed placed at the base of cabbage plants will repel cabbage root fly. Sheila Gear, in her book 'Foula, Island West of the Sun', stated that the crofters planted their kale plants at the end of April or the start of June in order to 'avoid infestation from a fly which was believed to lay its eggs only in May!'

Below:
If you have not seen the caterpillar in this photograph you should try and get out more often. Photograph by Angus Nicol.

The mesh mentioned earlier with regard to cabbage white butterflies would enable you to kill many birds with one stone. Making a large timber frame would be no big deal, and the mesh could be fitted to the roof with panels soon after planting (and the risk of snow had passed) yet you would still be able to enter and do the weeding. One of my friends, an organic commercial grower, is considering going down this route. Fleece certainly works although it is rather difficult to remove when you want to get some weeding done. There are two or even three generations of this fly in a year, and if you can avoid the first, the second will not be so bad since the plant roots will be that much larger. If you had a small garden you simply could scale down their ideas. Ideally you want fleece with a maximum mesh size of 1.3mm.

In November 2011, I spoke to Dr Rosemary Collier from the Crop Centre at Warwick University regarding the state of play with root fly. She said physical protection was undoubtedly the best, but some commercial farmers growing brassicas had their plants or modules pre-dipped with such products as 'Dursban WG' (containing chlorpyrifos), although this is soon to be banned; others resorted to some sort of fleece protection.

She also said that there was a lot of interest being shown in a new product called 'Spinosad' (sold under the trade names *Tracer*, *Spintor*, *Laser*, *Conserve* and *Success*). This is one of the new so-called biopesticides. It is derived through the fermentation of a naturally occurring organism, and is highly active at low use rates both by ingestion and contact. Advantages include speed, long residual control coupled with no special handling or use restrictions; and it is organically approved.

Looking at the 'Tracer' label from Dow Agrosciences, it is described as "a selective insecticide for use in field vegetables and fruit crops for the control of caterpillar pests, and useful control of cabbage root fly and thrips". Its effect is to act on neuro-receptor sites of the insect, i.e. it is a nerve poison. Apparently, symptoms appear almost immediately, with complete mortality occurring within a few hours. The application rate is 12ml in 1 litre of water per thousand plants as a root drench, followed by a maximum of two sprays to the foliage of the plants. The jury is still out regarding its efficacy.

Left:

Adult cabbage root fly. Photograph courtesy of Warwick University Crop Research Centre.

Top two photos: Public enemy number one. There can be dozens of larvae eating one root.

Right and below: You can see the dramatic difference in root size and leaf growth between the predated cabbages compared with the unpredated.

Bottom right: These are cabbage root fly pupae formed from the grubs above. They are in a winter sleep mode (hibernation) called diapause. I was told they would need at least 15 weeks to emerge as adult flies, so needed a lot of patience.

249

5. Leatherjackets

Leatherjackets are an enormous problem in Shetland; they are the young larvae of crane-flies or 'daddy-long legs', and are also known as 'stoorie worms'. You know they are bad news for agriculture when the local authority gives out 'stoorie worm' grants to help combat the problem! The larvae are grey-brown grubs with tough skin, which particularly like grass roots. One of my crofting neighbours told me one year there had been a lot of rain and the arable areas were sodden. This brought the pest to the surface attracting about 100 or so gulls which stayed and fed for 'several days'. Another example was in the village of Hamnavoe where one of my friends was having no success with her lawn. She had it treated with 'Cyren' and told me the pests surfaced in thousands.

'Cyren' is an excellent pesticide but unless you know what you are doing, get someone qualified to help you. The active ingredient in the insecticide is a substance called chloropyrifos; this is a type of anticholinesterase and extremely toxic. **On no account get it on your skin.** Cyren can be applied at any time from the beginning of November up to the end of March where high populations are detected or damage is first seen. Early treatment is recommended.

The larvae can develop very fast in pot plants and I have seen heavy infestation in as little as six to eight weeks. Many plants are susceptible; some that come readily to mind are various campanula, ornamental grasses and shasta daisy (*Chrysanthemum leucanthemum*).

6. Carrot root fly

I have not encountered these but they can be disastrous; once again larvae burrow into the roots and the whole plant suffers. My garden is high on a hill a far distance away from other gardens and it may just have been too far for the insects to migrate. There are fleeces available, with another option being to rotate your crops. I have heard good reports from gardeners using the cultivar F1 'Flyaway' and see another new cultivar called F1 'Resistafly'. To quote Moles Seeds: "Flyaway is well known for its tolerance of carrot root fly. Whilst not resistant it is not attractive to the egg laying flies and the maggots do not grow well on it."

Uncle Tommy Goodlad said that once he started 'watering' his carrots with seaweed extract he had no more troubles during 2009 and 2010 but said it might just have been coincidental. He said there was a stench when the 'brew' was applied; possibly the fly did not like it either?

Left:

Stoorie worms cause damage simply as a result of their vast numbers, and can completely destroy grassland.

The Shetland-based seaweed company 'Bod Ayre' maintain that a sprinkling of seaweed dust along the rows keeps carrot fly away.

Another suggestion is to have a mesh 'fence' surrounding the carrot plot. Since the fly stays below two feet (in theory) it should not get to the plants.

Finally, windy sites apparently have fewer problems with this pest, presumably because the flies cannot move around so easily. Wind certainly has a magical effect of getting rid of midges.

7. Red spider mite

In the past I have lost strawberries and cucumbers due to this pest, and it is particularly fond of raspberries. Like aphids, it sucks the juices out of the plant but is very much smaller and is an arachnid (spider family) rather than insect. It also has a very much more complex life cycle. A highly magnified adult is shown below. The fine silk webs are easier to see than the actual pest. When you have seen it once, you will easily recognise it again.

I have seen cucumbers going from dark green to an almost bleached colour over a few weeks in some crops due to the presence of red spider mite.

Since I dislike pesticides I have tried:

- Regular spraying with water (as they dislike high humidity) with partial success; Angus Nicol is a bit more forceful with the water but you must be careful not to damage the plant. A fireman's hose is not an option!

- Spraying with natural soaps and waxes with limited success; I used 'Majestic' (mentioned earlier) with limited success. Soaps are good on a number of insects because they breathe through their skin so while they can cope with water, soap asphyxiates them. Everything does get rather 'sticky' unfortunately.

- You could introduce the parasitic predator *Phytosieulus*, which eats the spider mites for food. This is the route adopted by commercial growers. You can easily order it on the Internet. Biocontrol is becoming important in many areas of horticulture and agriculture these days.

Top two photos:
I found these spider mites in a tunnel to the west side of Shetland. After you have seen them once, they are easily identified another time. It is the fine webbing which gives the clue as to what it is.

Bottom:
This is a magnified photograph taken by Angus Nicol. In real life you will find them hard to see unless using a small magnifying glass.

8. Vine weevil

There are many types of weevils but the one normally referred to by UK gardeners is the black vine weevil. These are devastating. The culprit is a beetle whose larvae eat and destroy roots, not unlike a cabbage root fly. The root damage is only part of the problem since root rots then get established. You rarely see the adults as they are nocturnal. They eat green leaves, leaving either holes or very often crescent shaped notching on the leaf margins. I have certainly lost cyclamen and primroses to this pest, and apparently they are very fond of rhododendrons.

I have come across a bacterial product which tackles vine weevil, however you need to consider the average soil temperature in Shetland and how the product would behave at cooler values. Very recently a microbial product, based on *Metarhizium anisopliae*, has been introduced for vine weevil control in soft fruit and ornamentals; the organism is basically a fungus pathogenic to insects. In essence the insect larvae becomes mouldy. There has also been the introduction of one strain of the parasitic nematode worms, *Steinernema kraussei*, specially bred to operate at temperatures as low as 5 degrees, and kills the pests within a few days. Most nematode worms prefer a soil temperature above 12°C.

One friend used a chemical called 'Suscon Green' mixed into his compost, although it has now been taken off the market. For the amateur gardener, there are insecticides that can be used – the one that comes to mind is 'Provado' Vine Weevil killer; read the instructions very carefully before you use it. If you suspect your plant is suffering from vine weevil damage, carefully dig it up or remove it from the pot and carefully look at the roots – the grubs are a creamy white with brown heads and easily seen and removed if need be.

One fascinating fact regarding black vine weevils (*Otiorhynchus sulcatus*) is that they are all female so breeding is parthenogenetic; scientists believe all the males died out during the last ice age, which I find remarkable.

Top:
Vine weevil larvae wriggling in a pot of mossy saxifrage.

Left:
A vine weevil adult I found crawling over some saxifrages.

Below:
Typical adult vine weevil damage; rather unsightly, but it is the larval killing of roots which does the real harm.

pests, diseases & weeds

9. Gooseberry sawfly

I am only mentioning this because I know Angus Nicol has problems with it. It is easily treated but can very quickly reduce a plant to bare stems. Dust the plant with Derris dust in mid-May when it is damp; this usually dispatches the first generation and seems to give good control. The eggs are laid on the underside of leaves along the veins, usually near the centre of the bush; the over-wintering adult lives in the soil

Pest summary

The main pests affecting Shetland plants include:

- Cabbage white butterflies – look for the small, hatched caterpillars or eggs and remove, or else do not bother planting. If not removed, your plants will be reduced to a stump;

- Cabbage root fly – use a barrier to deter the adults from laying their eggs. Note they also affect all crucifers, including plants such as turnips and swedes;

- Slugs – remove and treat, or suffer the consequences. They love hiding under plastic trays and pots. You may well see the slimy trail on the damaged plant leaves;

- Greenfly – spray with insecticides or use pyrethrum-based powder or a nicotine wash, which is approved by the organic growers, or leave to natural predators;

- Vine weevil – these particularly like primulas and cyclamen. Incorporate a suitable insecticide when potting up or treat with Provado Vine Weevil killer. Nematodes can be effective in the (warmer) greenhouse;

- Red spider mite – very tricky. Try to keep the glasshouse or tunnel atmosphere buoyant and not too dry. Wash leaves possibly on a weekly basis but beware of ending up with botrytis. Predators could be the best solution.

Above:
Gooseberry sawfly.
Photograph by Angus Nicol.

Diseases

Fungi, viruses, nematodes and bacteria all cause diseases; you are certainly going to be bothered by fungi and it is worthwhile knowing a little about them.

Scientists who study fungi are called mycologists and there is much for them to research, as there are about 100,000 species. The most important fact about all fungi is that, although they are normally thought to be like plants, they are animal-like in respect to their nutrition. They obtain their energy either as parasites, symbiotically (as sharers) or finally as saprophytes (decomposers). The next important fact is that they reproduce by producing astronomic numbers of spores; for example, what we call a mushroom is really the fruit body able to release millions of spores **every single minute** once the cap opens. Finally, all fungi have an extensive root system (called the mycelium) built from individual strands called hyphae. Large quantities of hyphae give rise to the 'furry' growths we find on rotting foods such as bread and cheese.

Fungi have played a key role in the history of mankind. The most obvious part is their use in the making of bread and alcoholic beverages, but there is also their involvement in the making of some cheeses, the value of penicillin and other antibiotics, and their importance in anti-haemorrhaging drugs and hallucinogens. The fungus Fly Agaric (the 'Noddy' mushroom) is an interesting species; if you eat the skin you go on a high, if you eat the flesh you die and so presumably if you eat the whole plant then you die happy!

Conversely, fungi have caused much grief by affecting us with ringworm, athlete's foot and thrush, not to mention all the food that has decayed due to fungal infections.

I have a book called 'Plant Pathology' by George Agrios (costing over £60) with over 600 large pages, so you can appreciate there is a lot to this subject.

Beneficial fungi

Certain species of fungi have developed a sharing (or symbiotic) relationship with many plants, and these species are collectively known as mycorrhizas. This sharing process can be seen when a grower has planted some trees. This relationship takes some time to establish, and we find there is often a two or three-year lag before the trees really benefit. The result is delayed but welcome vigorous growth. Mycorrhizal fungi effectively create a second root system for the plant; these roots act to increase the plant's own root capacity over 700 times. In 1cm^3 of soil something like 20 metres of fungal roots can exist, sourcing and transferring nutrients and water. Scientists have determined that around 90% of all land-based plants will form an association with mycorrhizae. This is a huge subject in its own right.

The compost heap

We all know about compost heaps, and the fact that dead plant remains, when sufficiently rotted, contribute towards the well-being of the next generation of plants springing up from the soil. Irrespective of whether we are speaking about the carbon cycle, nitrogen cycle or whatever, fungi play a key role in the process. I have mentioned compost heaps earlier in the book.

Harmful fungi

Fungi are a source of many diseases, but remember bacteria and viruses can also cause diseases. Usually we think that if a plant is diseased then it is not doing so well, but plants can also suffer for other reasons and I have already spoken about physiological problems. A fungal disease is the effect of a fungus feeding on a living plant; sometimes the symptoms of mould or whatever is fairly obvious but not always. There are thousands of plant fungal diseases, but I intend just saying a little about the few that you will certainly meet in Shetland.

Botrytis

Botrytis cinerea is also called 'grey mould', very often seen in infected strawberries; the 'fluff' normally associated with it is the fungal root system or mycelium. The pathogen also causes spotting and rotting of leaves and fruit, and stem botrytic rot is particularly harmful – sometimes I get it on my tomato plants and if it is not treated then the stem will rot right through and everything above is killed off. The spores are everywhere, but only germinate when the conditions are very humid. To be more precise, if the relative humidity is greater than 96% for three nights in a row in the warmer season, then the spores will develop and then, for example, you get the signs of 'ghost spotting' in tomatoes. If you are serious about growing tomatoes, a decent RH meter is a vital tool. Incidentally, tomato fruit do not succumb to spotting once the skin has gone shiny. The spores are everywhere. The fungus is also very partial to the sugar that remains in the old flower petals at the calyx end of the fruit (as I mentioned earlier regarding courgettes).

Botrytis is a disease of damp glasshouse conditions so if you do not ventilate sufficiently during the day, or do not give a little heat at night, then it (with a lot of other infections) is guaranteed.

A typical botrytic infection on a tomato plant showing both early (below) and advanced (top) levels.

*Right:
This pin mould on these raspberries is the same organism which attacks bread if the conditions are right.*

Essentially botrytis is a symptom of high humidity and bad glasshouse management.

Mucor

Mildew (powdery)

Mildew affects all sorts of plants. It is characterised by the appearance of spots or patches of a white to grey powdery growth and is most common on the upper surface of the leaves. It only grows on the tissue surface, and feeds by sending tubes below. Powdery mildew seldom kills the plants but uses up their nutrients, reduces photosynthesis, increases respiration and transpiration, and reduces growth. These diseases are caused by many species of the family *Erysiphaceae*; there are over 100 species of mildew, with some of them being far more serious in warmer climates.

I grew cucumber plants many years ago, and saw them changing from green to white in a very short time, just as though they were covered in snow. There was obviously a subsequent loss in photosynthesis and hence yield. The particular species of mildew affecting my plants needs humidity above 90% to germinate, so once again try to keep venting. Ironically, cucumbers grow at their best at 90% RH, so, as with many aspects of horticulture, it is a case of compromising. Although the resulting coolness may slow the plant's growth, the plants will look green and healthy and that is what matters. If you grow cucumbers in Shetland it is imperative you use a mildew resistant cultivar such as 'Tyria' F1.

Glasshouse cucumbers (as compared to the outdoor 'ridge' types) are prone to so many diseases that it makes you wary of growing them at all, but with correct husbandry in summer they can be high yielding.

Mildew was also occasionally a problem with strawberries grown in my polytunnel. I contacted a fruit consultant, Colin Stirling, and he said: *"Powdery mildew makes the fruit very 'seedy' and apart from dull has a white powdery appearance. The cultural control for powdery mildew is to avoid big variations in day/night temperatures especially hot dry (atmosphere) days and cool moist nights. Once mildew starts it just spreads, irrespective of conditions."*

This reminds me of an amusing story involving the Whiteness and Weisdale SWRI (Scottish Women's Rural Institute) who visited me in 2009. Amongst other things, I had emphasised the need to reduce glasshouse humidity with regard to disease prevention and so on. We then returned to the house for a cup of tea (they supplied the excellent home bakes), and the obligatory 'question and answer time'. Mrs Florence Grains said she was having problems with mildew on her Michaelmas daisies, so I rambled on again about opening vents and air movement; Mrs Grains graciously let me finish, then said rather disconcertingly in the broadest Shetland accent, 'But dey're ootside'. To say there was a roar of laughter is an understatement. There is nothing like making a fool of yourself for getting brought down to earth!

The following week I paid her a visit and gave her two remedies: one is very similar to baking soda (sodium bicarbonate), namely potassium bicarbonate, a spray of which helps to clean the leaves; and I also gave her some 'Nimrod' fungicide.

Below:
Powdery mildew.

Tattie blight

This disease is the reason that so many Irish people are found in the USA. I have not grown potatoes for several years now; the following comments include some notes given to me by Angus Nicol.

If you see potato leaves with brown or black patches at the tips and margins, your plants are probably starting with tattie blight. In moist conditions you may also see a delicate white growth as well. The brown patches can also develop on the stems. The blight fungus, *Phytophthora infestans*, which actually grows through the leaves' pores at the start of infection, causes the blackness. This disease gradually spreads causing the whole plant to eventually rot and, just to add insult to injury, can then spread to the tubers, and these end up with a reddish brown rot under a discoloured skin. Warm damp calm conditions are fatal; the sort of conditions we can get in Shetland during a misty summer period. More specifically, a minimum night temperature of 10°C with 75% relative humidity for 48 hours leads to a 'blight period' where the risk of infection is high. Although many people, including myself, dislike the idea of spraying with chemicals, there is not much option unless you use blight-resistant cultivars. Those recently introduced to the UK are the 'Sarpo' potato cultivars such as 'Mira' and 'Axona'. Bred in Hungary, these cultivars are claimed to have extremely good and durable resistance to blight. I have seen them on sale where they are described as "*having unprecedented blight resistance, huge yields of tasty, floury tubers. Grows well in a range of soil types and has vigorous weed suppressing foliage.*" I have also seen the cultivar 'Axona' which is described as: "*Very similar to Mira in all respects, particularly with outstanding blight resistance, but the tubers are more regular in shape and the flesh is slightly more creamy*".

I know some of the commercial farmers spray on a regular basis in Shetland – being surrounded by sea does not do much for keeping the atmosphere dry. One of the traditional sprays is a copper sulphate based compound called Bordeaux mixture: this is still permitted for organic growers – do remember its function is primarily protective. When the fungus grows it releases organic acids causing the copper to be released and the disease is then destroyed. Another product available for gardeners is 'Mancozeb' (Dithane 945). Tuber infection can be limited by earthing up soil around the stem, coupled with prompt removal of infected foliage. The fact that these spores can remain dormant is a good reason for rotating your crops, making sure you remove and destroy all the tubers that can act as a source of disease for the following year. Another line of defence for commercial growers is to spray with 'Zineb' or 'Maneb' (or their modern substitutes), repeating at 14-day intervals depending on the wetness of the season. If you are serious about growing potatoes, and have a large crop, then I would strongly advise you contact the Scottish Agricultural College to check what chemicals and timing would be appropriate for Shetland.

The Potato Council states "successful blight control is best achieved through prevention rather than cure". No fungicide currently on the market can be regarded as totally effective at stopping blight. All blight fungicides are protective although some of them have a limited curative function, providing they are applied very soon after infection.

The global annual costs of the disease are estimated to be in the region of £3.5 billion. Although the scientists have found resistance in the laboratory, the field trials are what really matter. Professor Jones who is in charge of the project stated, "We have isolated genes from two different wild potato species that confer blight resistance".

Anti-GM campaigners criticised the trials, saying it was possible to grow blight-resistant potatoes using conventional methods.

Blight can affect tomatoes but mercifully the higher temperatures experienced in the greenhouse help to keep the blight at bay.

Some typical symtoms of tattie blight.

Damping-off

We experience 'damping-off' every time we sow seedlings using unsterilised compost, sowing the seeds too dense, or keeping the seedlings in an enclosed container where the humidity gets too high. It is typically caused by two key fungal pathogens, *Pythium* and *Phytophthora*, and the resulting effect is narrow stemmed seedlings which keel over, and that is that! Once started, it can easily spread. Some growers give the compost a drench with a fungicide such as 'Filex', but for the small-scale grower this can be prohibitively expensive. If you are careful when sowing there should not be too many problems; the only species I sometimes find awkward are those densely sown such as lobelia and alyssum. One useful tip is that as soon as the seedlings have germinated, then get them immediately under some good quality lighting which will also help to dry the foliage. The extra energy helps them grow better and they are then better able to resist the pathogen. I largely eliminated damping-off as a problem once I started to grow my plants as plugs using artificial lighting. I would say that if you were growing seedlings too early without the aid of supplementary lighting, you stand a very high chance of suffering from this disease; if you do not have decent facilities you would be better off buying plugs later in the season. 'Chestnut compound' is also used as a treatment/preventative.

Clubroot

This is sometimes called 'finger and toe' because of the distortions caused to the roots of plants affected, particularly members of the *Cruciferae* such as brassicas and turnips; in fact the scientific name of clubroot is *Plasmodiophora brassicae*. I had a slight problem with it when I first started growing vegetables some 30 or so years ago. One of the main problems is that the spores can remain dormant in the soil for up to 20 years, which can be a real nuisance since so many of the vegetables we grow are part of this large family.

Right:
Damping off; you can see the infected seedlings have fallen over and the base of the stems are narrowed.

There are a few things you can do if your soil is affected:

- Grow Clubroot resistant cultivars such as the swede 'Marian';

- Try to grow in soil whose pH is slightly above neutral (7.0 to 7.5); or try raising your soil pH with the addition of lime in the calcium carbonate form;

- As far as cabbages, cauliflowers and brussel sprouts are concerned, I was advised by a consultant to prick out the seedling into a small cell, pot up into a half-litre pot, and grow on until I had quite a large transplant (hardened-off of course). When I planted it out, I tried to keep the root ball intact; the theory is that even if some of the roots get infected there are still plenty in the sterile ball to keep the plant going. This is one solution, and although it means a bit more work I always ended up with a good crop;

- Commercial growers have a great deal of success using a fertiliser called calcium cyanamide (trade name 'Perlka'). Its key role is to prevent long-lived spores from germinating;

- If it is present in your soil don't spread it; clean your boots before visiting other growers.

Just out of interest the 'Grower' magazine (Oct 16, 2003) stated that Syngenta were promising clubroot resistant varieties 'by 2005'. They said that a naturally occurring clubroot resistant gene had first been identified 16 years ago; the company had been working intensively on the selection and evaluation of the gene. They said that the first commercially available crops would be white cabbage in 2005 followed by cauliflower and brussel sprout varieties in the following seasons. I see the National Vegetable Society (NVS) currently offering the clubroot resistant cabbage varieties Kilaton F1 and Kilaxy F1 for sale, as well as the cauliflower Clapton F1.

Feri Bartai tried some of the Bod Ayre product called 'Sea-Feed Granular Plant Food' to combat a new outbreak of clubroot in his garden and found a huge improvement with only traces of clubroot present.

Root rots

These can affect many plants including tomatoes, and is one reason NOT to grow tomatoes in unsterilised soil. The rots include brown root rot, corky root rot and phytophthora root rot to name but three; all are caused by different species of fungi. Many growers can grow tomatoes in soil by grafting the required cultivars onto a root rot resistant rootstock. Stick to growbags or hydroponics. Cucumbers are very prone to root rots, and unless you have good growing facilities, it is not a good idea to try to grow these too early in the season.

Left:

Typical club root growths. Photograph courtesy of the Royal Horticultural Society.

pests, diseases & weeds

Many years ago I was having some root problems, particularly after a few days of summer mist followed by bright sun, so I contacted Fred Bell, a consultant based in Guernsey. This is a summary of what he said.

1. Healthy plants make and lose root hairs all through the year.

2. A sudden change from very sunny conditions to very dull ones (such as misty/sunny conditions), heavy deleafing, or a heavy fruit pick will lead to high root hair loss.

3. New healthy roots are white and furry. Older roots are cream or pale brown.

4. If the outer sheath comes off and the roots look like an electric cable then this usually means you have an infection of brown or corky root rot (*Pyrenocheaeta lycopersici*). Normally an application of Filex or Aaterra will cure this. The roots below these infections are basically useless.

5. Vigorous rooting types are better but will eventually get the same problems if the conditions are such that root rots are encouraged.

Tobacco mosaic virus

This was a serious disease of tomatoes in the past and one you or I will probably never encounter. I mention it because most tomato varieties carry the symbol 'TMV resistant', and is one reason we should appreciate modern plant breeding.

Other plant diseases

There are dozens of other plant diseases, including all the rusts and smuts which are particularly harmful to cereal farmers; one called *Sclerotina*, and there are *Alternaria* leaf spot, basal rots, brown root rot, corky root, *Didymella*, *Verticillium, Fusarium,* anthracnose and, believe me, many more.

Finally, you may have heard of the devastating effects of 'Dutch Elm disease'. What is interesting about this problem is that a type of bark beetle carries the infectious spores from tree to tree. This complex arrangement typifies the life cycles of many fungal species.

Control of plant diseases

As far as greenhouses are concerned, the best control is glasshouse management coupled with good hygiene.

- Use good quality clean seeds; often these are fungicide treated.

- Grow disease resistant cultivars; for instance the Swede cultivar 'Marian' is clubroot resistant with this disease being common in Shetland. If you use soil then it has to be sterilised – and this is easier said than done!

- Use peat-based compost wherever possible; it tends to be relatively sterile, and currently is much cheaper than the newer composts such as coir.

- Try as much as possible to keep the glasshouse clean and tidy.

- You should be exercising good hygiene coupled with cleanliness, a good practice for any sort of animal or plant husbandry. Plant pathologists have suggested simple hygiene and disinfecting routines can cut inoculum levels by 70-80%.

- Sweep away dead leaves and rubbish, and try to prevent moss and algal build up. Try using a firm brush; I personally often use a pressure washer at the end of the season. Also get rid of diseased plants or cut away and dispose of diseased parts. This can take some time but is a good recipe to help success. Sometimes a clean water wash between crops is a good idea because it prompts the spores to germinate and they then die.

- There are excellent horticultural sterilants such as 'Jet 5', which is effective and relatively non-toxic. This should certainly be considered if you are a commercial grower.

- Try to get rid of puddles; this will help to lower the humidity. This is one reason that the concrete floors of my glasshouses are sloping.

Use resistant cultivars

Plant genetics has resulted in growers being able to grow different kinds of plants with wonderful colours, shapes, yields and tastes, simply by crossbreeding. I am NOT speaking about genetically modified organisms (GMO). I was once at a talk where the grower said that F1 seeds were too expensive; that grower will never succeed. I would never have been able to grow cucumbers if the mildew resistant cultivars such as 'Tyria' had not come on the scene.

Obviously there are huge amounts of research relating primarily to the main food crops; I have already mentioned the cucumber F1 'Tyria' regarding its resistance to mildew.

I recently looked up a company called Rijk Zwaan to see what they had in the way of tomato cultivars. One of their range, 'Capriccia', interested me so I looked it up. This is what it said. "Tomato 'Cappricia' RZ *F1 Ff For Si TSWV Va Fol Sbi ToMV Vd*". You will easily understand that 'RZ' is the company's name, and the symbol 'F1' means it is a hybrid. But what about all the hieroglyphics? These indicate the plant's ability to combat different disease organisms. So *TSWV* equates to tomato spotted wilt, *Va* and *Vd* stands for two species of verticulum wilt, *Fol* stands for fusarium wilt and so on. Unless you are a commercial grower you do not need to worry what these diseases are; just accept that your plant stands a much greater chance of thriving.

Try using biostimulants. I have already mentioned these in Chapter 5 dealing with plant nutrition. Professor Geoff Dixon states in an article in the 'Grower' magazine: "these substances encourage benign microbes which are antagonistic to the disease parasite." All very complicated but, of course, Shetlanders have inadvertently been using biostimulants for years – 'tang' (seaweed). I am not going to repeat what I said earlier regarding the benefits of seaweed extract, but simply to quote Maxicrop's statement: "*Our biostimulant (seaweed extract) can be compared to an immunisation injection, ensuring the plant's defence systems are in a higher state of readiness ...*"

Shetland's very own 'Böd Ayre' products will have exactly the same virtues.

Use smart films. Believe it or not, scientists have developed a range of polythene films which have been modified to block out certain types of light radiation. Quite remarkably, this reduces certain fungal activity, in particular that of botrytis and powdery mildew. I wrote about this in Chapter 7 when I discussed polytunnel construction.

Using fungicides. If you have a disease outbreak where you are faced with the prospect of losing a crop or a very valuable plant, then it could be worth using one of the multiple fungicides on the market. There are many different types, each with its own spectrum of activity. Some are preventative such as 'Aaterra' and 'Filex', whereas others such as 'Fongarid' (active ingredient furalaxyl) are curative. Furalaxyl was overtaken by Metalaxyl-M. 2011 and its wet summer led to many outbreaks of downy mildew, including some strains showing resistance to Metalaxyl-M. You also have to be very careful thinking about using many of them on food plants. I tend to avoid using fungicides, but if I have stem botrytis on a tomato plant I will sometimes paint the stem with a little 'Derasol' rather than lose the whole plant. Also be aware that some of the older products such as 'Rovral' are becoming less efficient as the pathogens build up resistance, not unlike many of the super bugs, which are causing so many problems in modern hospitals.

Just recently I purchased a new fungicide called 'Switch', which is extremely effective at combating *Botrytis* (and also *Alternaria, Ascochyta, Colletotrichum, Fusarium, Gloeosporium, Monilinia, Mycosphaerella, Nectria, Penicillium, Sclerotinia, Stemphylium* and *Ventura*; do not worry about all these names – they are only included to show the versatility of the fungicide). I have been advised to spray at 0.5 grams per litre of water, with a 7-day gap between applications, and a maximum of three applications. It has many advantages including one of the ingredients (Fludioxonil) remaining on the leaf surface giving protection, and the second ingredient (Cyprodinil) both remaining on the leaf surface as well as moving within the leaf providing curative activity.

I see that a company called Everiss has a type of slow release product, which releases both fertiliser and fungicide simultaneously; this allows growers to do away with the regular sprays and drenches, as well as enabling better protection of the roots

Biological control of fungi

In 2009, a new product called 'Serenade' was introduced. It is essentially a suspension of a naturally occurring strain of bacteria used to control plant diseases, including blight and botrytis. This bacterium (*Bacillus subtilis*) is known to be hostile towards many fungal plant pathogens, instigating nutrient competition, site exclusion, colonisation, and attachment of the bacteria to the fungal pathogen. It is also thought it may invigorate the plants immune system, as well as interfering with fungal spore development.

This product is organically approved, and can be used up to 20 times a year with zero harvest intervals for all crops. Quite remarkable! This is showing how disease control is going to be achieved in the future!

Fargro's 'Prestop' is a bio-fungicide based on *Gliocladium* spp used for tackling root diseases *Botrytis* and *Didymella* in various crops.

The April 2012 issue of 'The Commercial Greenhouse Grower' contains information about two newly introduced biopesticides. One is called T34 which contains *Trichoderma*, and targets the disease *Fusarium*; the other is called AQ 10 and contains *Ampelomyces quisqualis* – it combats powdery mildew mycelium (roots). I only mention these to show how fast this field of knowledge is progressing.

Weedkillers

No one really wants to use these chemicals, but sometimes there is no option. I have an area in my new nursery where the grass was infested with masses of dockens. I asked for help from the Scottish Agricultural College(SAC) and was given good advice. In the past, if I found dockens, I would successfully dig them up in early spring when the ground was still wet and the root (with a good heave) would slide out; that is fine if you just have the odd one to deal with. The SAC recommended a weedkiller called 'Grazon 90', which kills the dockens but leaves the grass to carry on growing. A substance attacking one group of plants only (in this case broadleafs) is said to be a 'selective herbicide'; I would have had to use something else (such as 'Acumen' or 'Alistell') had there been clover among the grass. There is no way I could ever have eliminated them just by digging. I contacted Dow Agrosciences (the manufacturer) regarding rainfastness; they replied saying "it was unaffected by rain two hours after application". I recall spraying dockens one day, and a freak shower of rain passed over 30 minutes or so later; despite this, one hour later, the leaves were all starting to curl up and look scorched, so the chemical was obviously absorbed by the leaves rapidly and keenly.

Speaking of dockens reminds me of a story in which the late Duncan Houston (a well known local crofter), was reported as saying, "Dockens; they're so tough you could put them on the mantelpiece and they would still grow". This was uttered in the broadest Shetland dialect of course.

There are thousands of herbicides on the market, but the one you may be most familiar with is the one called 'Roundup', whose active ingredient is glyphosate. 'Roundup' is said to be a 'broad spectrum non-selective systemic herbicide', i.e. it is effective against most plants, and moves through the plant's tissues right down to its roots; it then acts on various enzymes preventing the plant

Below (from top):
Public enemy number one and its nemisis.
Immediately after spraying with Grazon 90.
Two days after spraying.

pests, diseases & weeds

from making amino acids, essential for the plant's well-being. After spraying, leave it for five days to let the chemical have its full effect. You will soon know if you have succeeded because the first signs of action are a 'dulling' of the leaves. Surprisingly, two weeks later the area you have treated can then be sown with grass seed or whatever. It is a relatively safe product compared to the products containing, say, paraquat.

Whichever herbicide you use, here are a few pointers to observe from my own experiences:

- Label your watering cans or sprayers with permanent labels or markers; otherwise you will be cleaning them endlessly, and spray assemblies are difficult to completely sterilise. I would be very nervous about using these for anything else – and plastic watering cans and sprayers are relatively cheap in the grand scheme of things. Some growers, including myself, use a red watering can for this purpose;

- Be extremely careful with spray 'drift'. On a windy day spraying is nonsensical, because the bulk of the chemical will be floating away and then you suddenly find your bushes not looking so pristine. I nearly always use a coarse spray with the larger heavier droplets staying within a smaller area;

- Check how the chemical behaves in rainy weather. The 'Grazon' I used is supposed to be 'rainfast' after two hours though in reality it is much quicker. Grazon 90 seems to be absorbed by the leaves very quickly, especially those of nettles. In the case of 'Roundup' you are looking at about four to five hours. If it does not say on the packet, just email or telephone the manufacturer, and say you need technical advice;

- Make sure you are spraying at the correct time of year, or when the plants are about the right size. There is information available which will show you the optimal size the weeds need to be for most effective control. You do not want the crowns to be too small, whilst also not too large

- If you are organised and have a larger garden, then it could be very worthwhile contacting agricultural suppliers for bulk quantities of the herbicide. 'Rouncup Pro Biactive', used at 20ml per ltre of water, gives me something like 250 litres of powerful herbicide. Of course it lasts several years;

- Make sure you use the correct dilution – too weck will be ineffective whereas too strong will be wasteful (and not necessarily any more effective);

- There are 'residual herbicides' such as 'Ronstar'. Essentially you sprinkle the granules (which dissolve) or spray the liquid on the potted plant surface, leaving a residual layer on the surface of the pots or soil. 'Ronstar' works by the germinating seeds absorbing a lethal dose of the herbicide as their shoots push through the surface layer. As you can imagine this provides a tremendous advantage for nursery stock growers.

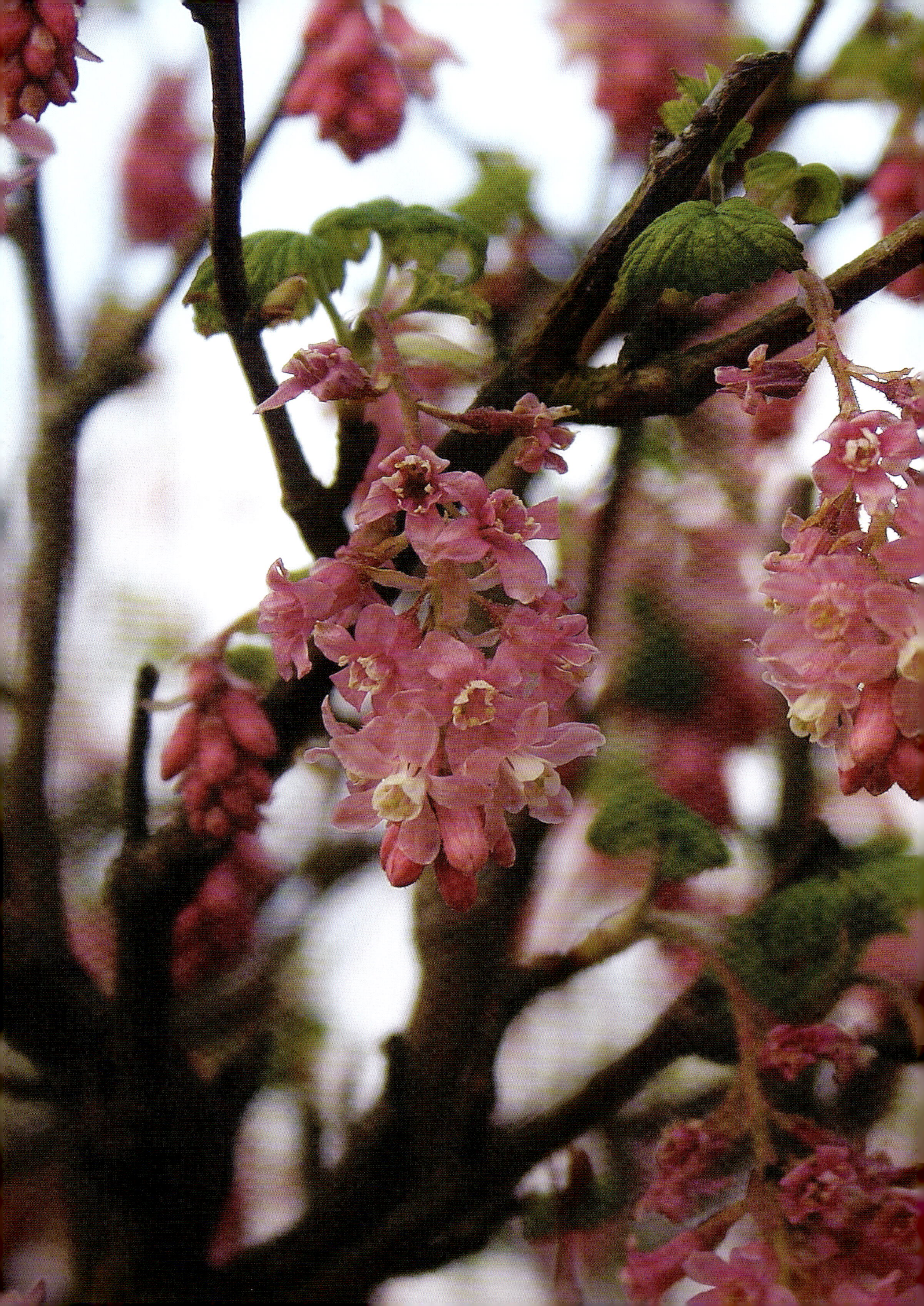

Chapter 10
Appendices

Appendix 1

The two seed supplier websites are:

- www.molesseeds.co.uk
- www.jelitto.com

Other websites I regularly look at include:

- www.leagardens.co.uk
- www.greenhousegrower.com
- www.lowsofdundee.co.uk
- www.fastech-phtester.com
- www.ballbookshelf.com
- www.ibsbuyersguide.co.uk
- www.vitax.co.uk
- www.botanicoir.com
- www.perlite.org
- www.rhs.org.uk
- www.solartunnels.co.uk
- www.koppert.com

Most of these are self-explanatory.

Appendix 2

Building a heated propagator

Having at least one or two decent propagators is absolutely vital if you want to produce lots of seedlings or take cuttings. It is essentially a box full of sand with an electric blanket in the middle, and a thermostat giving control. You can become really smart by lighting it from above, so helping the seedlings grow furiously.

If you decide to build one yourself it is VITAL that you make sure there is proper earthing, and also RCD devices; this should be the norm for all glasshouse electrics. If you are not familiar with electrics, **consult an electrician**.

I originally constructed two sand-based propagators in which I did the bulk of my propagation. The dimensions used for these are –

Small propagator; 32 x 56 x 5 inches (81 x 142 x 13cm).

Large propagator; 102 x 30 x 7 inches (260 x 76 x 18cm).

One important thing to remember is that these will virtually last forever. My larger one was 20 years old before I had to replace the cable, and it has saved me thousands of pounds. By the way, cats positively love lying on the warm sandy bed, and mice are even worse since they eat up the seedlings. I am not joking.

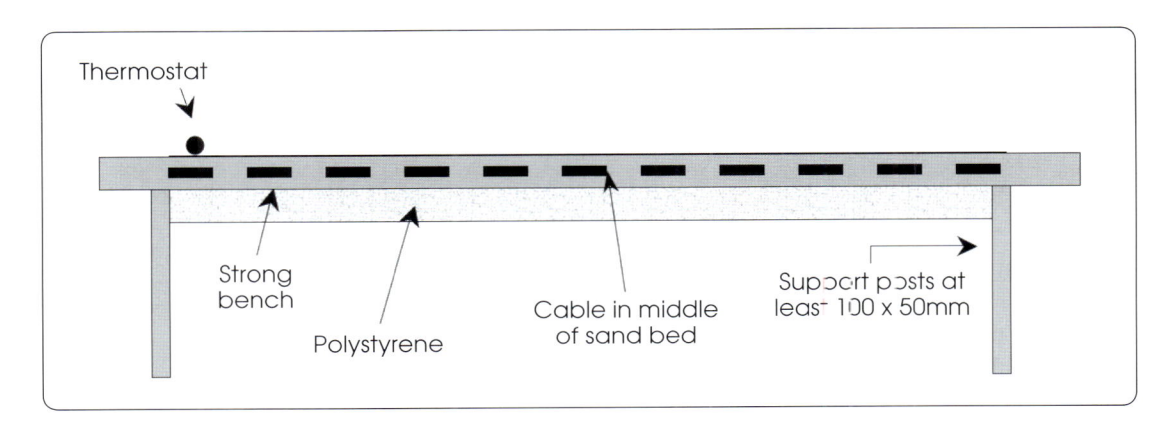

More recently I moved away from sand-based propagators to metal conducting ones, the only single reason being that sand is extremely heavy. In my present ones, the cable sits on a polythene sheet resting on 50mm Kingspan. A thin galvanised sheet rests on top of the cables and this spreads the heat evenly over the surface. The photo above shows the various layers i.e. Kingspan, polythene, cable, metal sheet, capillary matting. I have around 300 square feet of propagation space.

One problem you will meet is that although you may be getting good root growth, particularly at night early on in the season, the air temperature can become very low and plant growth sluggish. I have my propagators arranged not only so that it is insulated against heat loss at night, but also so that on warm days the hinged lid can be folded back allowing full access to the sun.

Above:
Showing the upper galvanised metal sheet having been raised with the yellow heat cable sitting on white polythene, and it in turn sitting on a 50mm Kingspan sheet. The red electrical tape holds the heated cable in place.

Left:
A rod-type thermostat. You cannot see the actual rod – it projects out into the propagation bed behind it.

Appendix 3

Germination results

I have germinated a lot of seeds over the years; each time I tried a different cultivar, the result went into my database for future reference. This means that if a particular cultivar is suppose to emerge, say in six days, and has not appeared by eight or nine days there could well be a problem, such as the seeds being non-viable. Bear in mind that many seeds germinate over a long period with just a few 'coming all at once'; i.e. the days quoted are when the first seedlings showed. Unless it says so, most seeds would have been germinating in my grow room at about 20-22°C. The symbol % given in a few cases means the approximate percentage germination. V stands for vermiculite (coarse unless it says otherwise). The symbol SD stands for Jelitto's recommended sowing directions, and GN stands for 'Gold Nugget' or Jelitto's primed seed. Many of the other comments should be obvious.

Remember that this table only relates to the germination details and does not say how well the plants thrived after pricking out and potting up.

KEY

V = vermiculite
d = days
SD = sowing directions as given in the Jelitto website
GN = Gold nugget primed seeds supplied by Jelitto
% = Percentage germination
3/cell = seeds sown as threes, or fours
Med = medium
Surface = surface sown
OW = overwinter
Emerge = root emerging from the seed

SPECIES / CULTIVAR	Days and %
Achillea 'Cassis Red' fine V	3d
Achillea millefolium medium V	3d@21c
Achillea sibirica med V vigorous	2d
Aethionema grandiflora fine V 90% germination watch botrytis	7d
Ageratum pinch out growing point when larger	5d
Alyssum montanum 'Gold Ball' 60%	3d
Alyssum montanum 'Mountain Gold' 100%	3d
Alyssum sulphureum very erratic	5d
Alyssum white	7d
Anacyclus pyrethrum 'Silver Kisses' SD15	2-3d
Anaphylis marguerite 'Pearl Everlasting'	5d
Anchusa azurea 'Feltham' did not thrive	9d
Anemone hupehensis did not thrive	9d
Anemone multifida 'Rubra'	11d
Anthemis carpatica 'Karpatica' 3/cell med V	6d
Anthemis tinctoria 'Kelwayi'	7d
Antirrhinum 75% yield light to germinate	4d

SPECIES / CULTIVAR	Days and %
Aquilegia alpina med V	11d
Aquilegia buergeriana 'Calimero' GN did not thrive	9d
Aquilegia caerulea 'Biedermeier' GN high %	11d
Aquilegia caerulea 'Danish dwarf'	20d
Aquilegia canadensis GN	11d
Aquilegia sibirica GN	11d
Arabis blepharophilla ' Red Sensation' thin V + light	4d
Arabis caucasica compacta 'Snow Cap' thin V + light	5d
Arenaria montana GN med V SD 15	6d
Armeria maritima 'Splendens' (sea pink)	3d
Artemisia absinthia SD 15	2d Emerge
Artemisia dracuncula (tarragon)	2d Emerge
Aryncus sylvestris looks good at Scalloway	
Aster alpinus 'Trimix' did not thrive	9d
Aster sibiricus SD 16	4d
Astilbe 'Bella Mix' good germination B/C	6d
Astilbe chinensis var. pumila surface + light	4d Emerge
Astilbe chinensis var. 'Showstar' surface + light	4d Emerge
Aubrietia med V watch slugs & waterlogging over winter	4d
Bacopa 20°C.	3d
Bellis	4d
Bergenia cordifolia 'New Hybrids' fine V 22°C. SD20	6d 90%
Bidens med V	2-3d
Bouteloua gracilis SD 16	2d Emerge
Brachycomb	1-2d
Buphthalmum (oxeye) SD 15 med V	6d
Buphthalium salicifolium 'Alpengold' SD 15 med V	5d
Cabbage	5d
Calamintha grandiflora	6d GN
Calceolaria surface + light	5d Emerge
Calendula med V	3d
Caltha palustris	10d GN
Campanula carpatica	8d Emerge
Campanula carpatica 'Blue Clips'	8d Emerge
Campanula cochlearifolia (c.pusilla)	4d Emerge
Campanula garganica SD 15	5d Emerge GN
Campanula glomerata	4d
Campanula 'Isabella' INDOOR PLANT	5d Emerge
Campanula persicifolia 'Grandiflora' (Blue Bells)	5d Emerge
Campanula poscharskyana	11d Emerge GN
Campanula punctata	7d GN

SPECIES / CULTIVAR	Days and %
Campanula punctata rubrifola	6d
Campanula takesimana	6d GN
Cardamine pratensis (lady'smock)	4d
Carex buchaanii ('Red rooster')	Long time
Catanache alba did not thrive	5d
Catanache caerulea SD 15 did not thrive nor overwinter well	5d
Celeriac small seed	7d+
Celery	7d+
Centaurea rupestris did not thrive	7d
Centaurea dealbata did not thrive	7d
Centaurea montana scarify and soak seeds	5d
Centaurea uniflora	4d
Centranthus ruber var. *coccineus* 'Rosenrot' red valerian	7d
Cerastium (Snow in summer)	3d
Cerinthe glabra SD 16	8d
Cerinthe major 'Purpurascens' (Purple Bell) SD16	6d
Chamomile nobilis surface sow	2d
Cheiranthus med V	4d
Chrysanthemum leucanthemum SD15	5d++
Chrysanthemum leucanthemum 'White Knight' SD15	6d++
Chrysanthemum maximum 'Sonnenschein' Rosa recommends	5d++
Chrysanthemum maximum nan 'Snow Lady' expensive but high germination	5d++90%
Chrysanthemum coccineum 'Super Duplex' did not thrive	5d
Clematis orientalis	9d
Clematis tangutica	7d
Coleus	3d Emerge
Coriander cool immediately it is through	4-5d
Cortaderia selloana 'Pink Feather'	2d
Cortaderia richardii much slower growing	c5d
Corynephorus spiky blue quick growing	4d Emerge
Cosmos 20°C. med V	2d
Cyclamen Laser 90% germination Sierra 75%	21d
Dahlia med V 15-20°C	3d
Delospermum cooperi expensive did not thrive	5d
Delospermum sutherlandii ' Peach Star'	2d Emerge
Delospermum sutherlandii	4d
Dianthus alpinus	3-4d
Dianthus arctic fire	5d
Dianthus barbatus 'Midget' too late for an annual	5d
Dianthus 'Confetti'	3-4d

SPECIES / CULTIVAR	Days and %
Dianthus deltoides 'Arctic Fire'	4d
Dianthus deltoides 'Brilliancy' did not OW	4d
Dianthus deltoides 'Microchips'	5d
Dianthus deltoides 'Nelli'	5d
Dianthus deltoides	4d
Dianthus 'Flashing Light'	5d
Dianthus 'Ideal'	3-4d 98%
Dianthus 'Ipswich Pink'	4d
Dianthus knappii (yellow)	3d
Dianthus plumarious 'Sweetness' SD15	5d
Doronicum mag	6d
Doronicum orientale 20°C. Thin V. Expensive seeds	7d
Echinacea purpurea 'Magnus' large seedling	4-5d
Echinops ritro did not thrive in peat compost	3-4d
Endive med V	3-4d
Eragrostis spectabilis bad for root damage - forget	2d
Erigeron aurantiacus Stoorey and slug problems	6d
Erigeron 'Azure Fairy' Stoorey and slug problems	2d
Erigeron glaucus. Stoorey and slug problems	6d
Erodium – scarify and soak	5d
Erysimum allioni (orange) easy but tall plant	4d
Erysimum helvetica poor % germination	4d
Euphorbia polychroma GN no cover but press into compost	6d
Euphorbia rigida into fridge first	16d
Fennel sweet zifa med V	4d
Festuca glauca	5-6d
Gazania 15c med V	3d
Gypsophila repens rosea	4d
Helenium 'Helena Mix' did not thrive	7d
Heliotrope	4d
Hemerocallis 'New Hybrids' (day lily) - 3 years to flower!	11d
Hesperus matronalis med V	5d
Heuchera americana 'Dale's Strain' GN expensive	5d
Hosta New Hybrids	11d
Incarvillea dlelavayi Not for peat based	6d
Iris setosa med V	9d
Isotoma or *laurentia* 20c dark for first 7 days; expensive seed, pink quicker	4d+
Kniphofia did not thrive in peat compost	9d
Kniphofia 'Firedance'	12d GN
Kniphofia uvaria 'Border Ballet'	12d GN
Lavaterra 20c Med V	10d

SPECIES / CULTIVAR	Days and %
Lavandula stoechas	7d GN
Leek	up to 28d
Lemon balm fine V	6d
Liatris spicata 'Goblin' med V	6d
Lilium formosa princeii slow and erratic	5d
Linaria aeruginea 'Neon Lights' SD15 fine V	7d 90%
Linaria alpina	5d 90%
Linaria purpurea GN	3d
Linum perennis 'Blue Sapphire' did not thrive	7d 50%
Livingstone daisies	7d
Lobelia bedding type	8-9d
Lobelia sessilifolia thin fine V	8d
Lupin 'Gallery' med V	3d
Lupin 'Ice' slow erratic germination	slow
Luzula lucius even and quick	9d
Luzula (Star grass)	9d
Lychnis alpina surface + light	5d
Lychnis arkwrightii 'Orange Gnome'	9d
Lychnis flos jovis nana 'Peggy'	10d
Lysimachia atropurpurea in fridge for month needs <5°C to germinate	5d 50%
Lysimachia punctata GN slow but steady grower	7d 90%
Lythrum salicaria (purple looserife) slow but steady grower	5d
Malva moschata GN did not thrive in peat compost	3-4d
Matricaria	2d
Meconopsis cambrica fine V	12d
Meconopsis betonicifolia 'China Blue'	7d
Mimulus stick to raw seed	2d
Monarda citriodora	4d
Myosotis	5d
Nasturtium	1-2 wks
Nemesia use raw seed watch ventilation and fungal problems	6d
Osteospermum med V 20°C	5d
Pansy 'Matrix'	5d 90%germ
Papaver alpinum fine V SD 15	3d
Papaver nudicaule SD 15	5d
Parsley	9-10d
Pennisetum setaceum 'Fountain grass'	3d 90%
Peppermint	5d
Petunia	5d
Plantago major 'Variegata'	17d

SPECIES / CULTIVAR	Days and %
Primrose primed	4d
Primula bulleesiana GN surface sown very small	9d
Primula denticulata 'Runsdorf-Hybrids' (Nepal Mix)	9d
Primula pubsescens (Auricula)	10d
Prunella grandiflora 'Freeland' mix	5d 99%
Prunella grandiflora rubra Did not thrive in peat compost	6d 75%
Pulsatilla (violet) need chalky soil	7d GN
Sage med V English sage	3-4d
Salvia 'Salsa Series' bedding med V	7d
Saponaria ocymoides 'Snow Tip' chill first – unreliable flowerer	8d
Saponaria ocymoides vernalisation vital overwinter	8d 90%
Saxifrage arendsii (white)	9d
Sedum acre 'Octoberfest'	2d Emerge
Sedum 'Czar's Gold'	6d
Sedum kamtschatica	3d
Sedum oreganum	2d
Sedum pulchellum	3d
Sedum reflexum SD 4/15	2d Emerge
Sedum spurium 'Coccineum' (Purple Carpet)	3d
Sedum spurium 'Summer Glory' very nice	2d 90%
Sedum telephium 'Emperor's Waves' late and tall but OW fine	2d
Sedum ternatum	6d
Semperivivum 'Winter Hardy' GN	2d 90%
Silene acaulis poor germination	6d
Silene uniflora 'Compacta'	5d
Silene uniflora 'Robin Whitebreast'	5d
Silver grass	4d Emerge
Solanum med V watch mice with berries	5d
Solidago cutlerii SD 15	5d
Spearmint	6d
Spergularia not attractive very small	3d
Stachys macrantha	4d
Stipa capillata ' Lace Veil' SD 16	8d++
Stipa 'Pony Tails'	2d
Sweet pea 'Cupid'	5d
Tagetes	2d
Tarragon	1d Emerge
Thyme	5d
Trifolium rubens	6d
Uncinia egmontiana poor germination	17d++
Uncinia rubra med V <5°C for a month	17d++

SPECIES / CULTIVAR	Days and %
Verbascum phoeniceum 'Violetta' less vigorous than wedding and 16 candles	4d
Verbascum chaixii 'Sixteen Candles' predated	5d
Verbena sow slightly dry	5d
Veronica gentianoides BC	7d
Veronica officinalis	4d
Veronica porphyriana	2d
Veronica prostrata 'Nector'	9d
Veronica spicata 'Blue Bouquet' Expensive seed	95% 5d
Viola 'Avalanche'	6d
Viola GN *soraria* 'Freckles'	F
Viola soraria 'Dark Freckles' GN	c7d
Viola soraria 'Rubra' GN	c7d

Appendix 4

Building a plate sower

Plate sowers should work well for most of the pelleted seeds.

Basic rules regarding drilling.

1. Drilling so many holes at the same time causes the drill to heat up and melt the plastic, so drilling must be done under water to ensure a clean hole. This is very important. Even under water it is essential to remove the drill regularly to allow the drilling fragments to escape, especially when using one of the small pilot drills with thicker Perspex. For the pilot holes use 1.5mm drill with a small 12v model-maker's drill.

2. With larger holes use a pilot hole initially. Mark the hole's position with a small dot using permanent marker, as the holes are impossible to see under the water.

3. Always use **2mm Perspex** for the **top sheet**. This means that the surplus pellets are easily swept away with the **antistatic brush**.

4. Once hole is finished then use what is called a 'Roebuck' type drill to form a concave shape on the surface.

Pellet sizes. Each species is different in size, and each size falls into a range. The trick is to get the largest and smallest of the range to fit into the hole without two sitting side by side. In general this should be extremely uncommon.

Species	Top diameter	Bottom diameter	Comments
Onion moles	4.0	4.5	
Calceolaria	1.5	4.5	
Campanula carpatica	2.5	4.5	
Ageratum	2.5	4.5	
Dianthus	4.5	4.5	Direct into P40; raw seed flat and curled hence large pellet
Lobelia multiseed	2.5	4.5	Wide spread of sizes
Lobelia single seed	3.0	4.5	This holds around 8 to 10 seeds
Leek		4.5	4.0 also fine share with onions
Cabbage	2.5	4.5	Should manage 96% easily; 3.0 a bit too large
Petunia	2.0	4.5	
Geranium	3.5	4.5	Wrong shape – ok if tail up
Gazania	2.0	4.5	Need to get tail up
Pansy	2.0	4.5	Did not work seed are too irregular to work properly
Mimulus	1.5	4.5	
Strawberry	1.5	4.5	
Begonia	1.5	4.5	
Antirrhinum	2.0	4.5	

Plate sowers; dimensions

These have been based on the Plantpak P180s, the P5 and P 40 units (the cut versions).

P180s

Base plate 4mm x 60cm x 37cm.

Top plate 2mm x 305mm x 585mm; the 305mm is the critical size here.

P5 and P40s

Base plate 4mm x 293mm x 420mm.

Top plate 2mm x 265mm x 432mm; the 265mm is the critical size here.

Note that the top plates are slightly longer. The space at the end will be used to contain surplus seed to the side in between 'drops'. Before you start you need to squirt a strip of silicon round the edge of the top plate. This silicon barrier prevents the seeds rolling off the edge.

Using a plate sower

With practice you can sow many seeds precisely and quickly; I regularly sow around 10,000 brassica seeds using this device so that each 'strip' ends up with around 20 small plants for the potential customer.

You need to be organised; I sow standing up with the device at neck level. The sower is to the left of the bench and the seed tray containing the compost is to the right.

1. Making sure the holes in the upper and lower plate are out of line, I clip four bulldog clips to the corners to keep both plates secure.
2. I fill the upper tray with a decent amount of seed along one edge. Remember the silicon strip will keep them in place.

appendices

Above:
Green 'graded' seed and ungraded seed. You can see that the former is much more regular.

Above right:
Plate sower top plate 'charged' with green seeds. By sliding the top plate slightly to the right the two holes line up and the seed drop into position.

Right:
The seeds after the drop, not perfect but pretty good. The seeds are then covered with compost, watered and then covered in cling film.

3. Keeping the sower at a slight angle, I gently move the sower back and fore – you will see the seeds filling the spaces in the upper sower. I do this over a very large tray to catch any seeds which spill over the edge of the sower.

4. I then keep the sower level and gently sweep the seeds back in the other direction using a wide carbon antistatic brush.

5. I carefully position the plates above the seed tray, and when in position release the bulldog clips and move the top plate to line up with the base plate.

6. A gentle tapping will release all the seeds. Before taking the sower away get the plates back out of line and replace the bulldog clips.

7. The instructions above may seem a bit elaborate but you will become quite fast with experience. I can sow quite accurately around 500-600 seeds per hour.

279

Top:
After three days or so in the grow room at around 22°C you can see the seedlings emerging and pushing up the cling film. At this stage I immediately remove the film and get the seedlings out to a cold frame or cool tunnel.

Above left:
Emerging seedlings.

Above right:
Fully emerged.

Left:
10 or so days later after sitting in the cold frame; you can see the main leaf now growing out of the centre of the shoot between the cotyledons.

Appendix 5

Guidelines on fluid sowing (fluid seed drilling) of seeds

I tried this 25 years ago and it is one technique I intend to return to very soon. Essentially it involves pre-germinating seeds in ideal conditions (such as you might get in a bathroom cupboard), suspending them in a jelly medium, and then extruding lines of jelly strips (containing the germinated seeds) on to the soil. Carrot is a good example since in normal Shetland conditions it may take three or more weeks to germinate in the soil, and by that time the soil has become littered with weed seedlings. Inside the bathroom cupboard it may be three or four days. The main stages are:

1. Soak the dry seeds in tepid water in a bowl for 3-4 hours, giving longer if the seeds were large like peas or beans;
2. Using a fine kitchen sieve, strain the seeds;
3. To germinate use a flat plastic tub or dish, put some toilet tissue on the bottom covered by a layer of cotton cloth. Add water until the tissue has been fully wetted, and then gently brush the seeds over the cotton;
4. Cover loosely with a lid or a piece of cling film to raise the humidity;
5. Once there is a high % of germination, make ready the gel. If you were using laponite then make up a 2-3% solution. When it has thickened stir the seeds carefully into the gel. They should remain suspended.

Once the jelly strips have been extruded then cover with a little soil to stop drying out. The ideal extruder should not be dissimilar to a cake icer used by bakers.

Below:
Dry carrot seeds prior to soaking and germination.

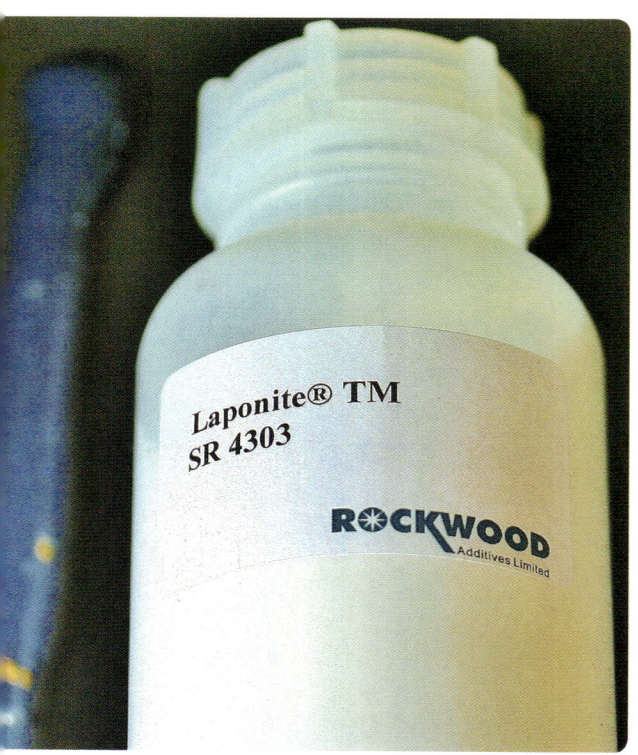

It is very important to use the correct jelly; be wary of wallpaper paste, which may contain harmful fungicides. You will know when the jelly is thick enough since the seeds will be suspended in it.

One suitable product is called 'Laponite' from a company called Laporte. This product has many advantages: when pressure is applied to the gel it becomes fluid and allows the suspension of seeds to flow easily through the drilling apparatus; it is inorganic so does not rot; it is clear so the seeds are easily seen; and finally it is ideally suited to soft water such as we have in Shetland.

Some higher yields for fluid-drilled compared to dry seeded crops include carrot (+ 22%), celery (+36%), parsley (+107%) and tomato (+12%); and these results have probably come from areas with better climates than Shetland.

Above:
Carrot seeds after 72 hours, having been soaked for the first four hours. They are sitting on a fine cotton cloth with moist toilet tissue underneath.

Left:
Laponite gel. You can just make out carrot seeds suspended in the gel on the left of the photograph.

Below:
A line of gel containing germinated seeds.

Appendix 6

Making a plug extractor

1. Use a 4mm thick piece of Perspex – no thinner.

2. Mark out precise positions or use existing template.

3. Start off drilling with 1.5mm bit and then move up to 2.5 then 3.0 then 3.5. Make sure to drill under water as before.

4. Screw a 1 inch x no. 10 round headed poz drive screw into each position trying to keep each as vertical as possible.

Use the same principle to form a dibber to aid sowing the seeds precisely in the middle of the cell.

Above:
The apparatus above works just as well as a plug extractor or a dibber to make indents in the soil.

Right:
A different size of dibber was used to assist the sowing of these Livingstone daisy seedlings..

Appendix 7

Bedding feeds formula masses

To make up a solution giving 200N: 100P: 200K (all mg per litre)

1. Add the following to 100 litres of warm water; 6.7 kg ammonium nitrate, 9.1 kg potassium nitrate and 3.3 kg mono ammonium phosphate.

2. This will take a while to dissolve (possibly 24 hours) but the warm water will help. You may also wish to add some dye; a popular colour is blue. This is your concentrated solution.

3. To feed the plants you now dilute this 200 times. Of course adding half the quantities of the chemicals would give you the same strength of feed if you were to dilute it 100 times. Once I start feeding, the dilute blue in the feed solution tells me that feed is being added, though I always use a conductivity meter to get an accurate dilution.

If feeding on a hot sunny day, immediately wash the foliage with fresh water to avoid leaf scorch. The beauty about using drip irrigation is that this is avoided.

The feeds formulae below have been taken from the ADAS liquid feeds table. The masses are given at 80% for each component – the full amount is more difficult to dissolve (at 100%)

1. Balanced feed 1-1-1. The amounts needed for the three key ingredients are

    Potassium nitrate @ 8.272Kg

    Monoammonium phosphate @ 6.16Kg

    Ammonium nitrate @ 5.68Kg

2. High Nitrogen feed 2-1-1. The amounts needed for the three key ingredients are

    Potassium nitrate @ 5.2Kg

    Monoammonium phosphate @ 3.84Kg

    Ammonium nitrate @ 10.48 Kg

The above amounts are to be dissolved in 100 litres of water to give a very concentrated solution. The concentrate has then to be diluted at approximately 180 times, prior to feeding the plants, but **check value with conductivity meter**; around EC = 2.0 will be strong enough.

Formula for making up hydroponic 'long haul' feed solutions

This formula was first devised at the Scottish Agricultural College based at Auchincruive near Ayr.

Concentrate A	Amount per 25 litres
Calcium nitrate	6.3 kg
Potassium nitrate	5.2 kg
Iron EDTA	200 grams
Ammonium nitrate	225 grams
Manganous sulphate	44 grams
Borax	40 grams
Zinc sulphate	18 grams
Copper sulphate	3.6 grams
Ammonium molybdate	1.2 grams

Concentrate B	Amount per 25 litres
Potassium nitrate	5.2 kg
Mono ammonium phosphate	2.7 kg
Magnesium sulphate	4.05 kg

Once you have weighed out the ingredients simply throw them into the two barrels and then add 25 litres of water to each. It will take a day at least to completely dissolve; solution A is a brown tinge whereas B is completely clear. If you find difficulty weighing the copper and molybdenum sources just take them to the science department of your local school – they will have accurate balances – and take a box of chocolates as well!

To use, simply take equal amounts of A and B and mix them in a large barrel of water. Roughly 1.5 litres of each will give an EC value of around 2.0 in a 200-litre barrel but you must double check this with a conductivity meter.

Appendix 8

Calculating air filled porosity (AFP)

The following notes have been based on information found in the book 'Ball Plug and Transplant Production'

1. For proprietary mixes the AFP should be available from the manufacturer.
2. Collect a suitable container with a plughole in the bottom. A litre plastic jug would be ideal.
3. Fill the container up to the one litre mark, tapping it down to settle the media.
4. Fill another one-litre jug with water and slowly add water to the media in the first jug. It may take a little waiting until the media becomes completely saturated. **Note the amount of water added**.
5. Remove the plug and **collect and measure the water**, which drains out.

Results

   a. Media added = a ml
   b. Water added = b ml
   c. Water drained = c ml

Total porosity % = $b/a \times 100$ =

Aeration % = $c/a \times 100$ =

Water holding capacity % = total porosity − aeration =

Appendix 9

Taking cuttings

Each year I propagate a large number of trees and shrubs very simply and effectively. Easy plants include various **willows** (of which I have four cultivars) and **flowering currant**, and I have had some success with **grape (vine)** and **honeysuckle**. A really good plant is **black cottonwood** (*Populus trichocarpa*). You essentially take your cuttings in early spring just before the buds have opened, insert the cut twig into a pot of peat-based compost, give it a watering to settle the compost around the stem, set it on a **warm** bed (from about 13-15°C but absolutely no more than 20°C) and then try to avoid excessive moisture loss by covering the rooting plant with some polythene. Hardwood cuttings taken in autumn and placed outside in a prepared bed of gritty compost/earth will give good results, though the trick is not to do what Angus Nicol did when he was a small boy – pull them up every day to see how they were doing! Rosa Steppanova takes all her hardwood cuttings in spring (usually March) with much higher success rates; she trims the cuttings and then pushes them through thin black plastic sheeting, leaves them for a year, and then pots into 2, 3 or 4 litre pots.

Although taking cuttings from the varieties mentioned above works easily, do not believe that all plants are easy; many are notoriously difficult.

Right:
Black cottonwood cuttings ready for soil insertion and rooting.

Stage 1 – take your cutting

You are best to take your cuttings using proper secateurs.

Stage 2 – insert the cutting into the pot of compost

Stage 3 – put the pot onto a warm surface and wrap in a clear polythene sheet; cut the corners of the bag to reduce condensation

Within a fortnight the roots will start appearing, certainly in the case of willows.

Flowering current is another tree easily rooted; and very pretty!

Far left:
Cuttings enclosed in a polythene bag to keep relative humidity high

Left:
New white roots forming at the base of the cutting; these only took around 10 days.

Left:
The stem of a six-year-old black cottonwood tree, very thick and chunky. This plant thrives particularly well since the resinous sap is disliked by rabbits and other large herbivores.

Below:
Flowering current.

Appendix 10

Shetland's weather

I downloaded this weather summary from the Internet. It confirms what the locals know anyway, particularly the wet and dark winters.

- The average temperature in Shetland is 7.2°C (45°F).
- The average temperature range is 9°C.
- The highest monthly average high temperature is 14°C (57°F) in July & August.
- The lowest monthly average low temperature is 1°C (34°F) in January & February.
- Shetland's climate receives an average of 1003mm (39.5in) of rainfall per year, or 84mm (3.3in) per month.
- On average there are 243 days per year with more than 0.1mm (0.004in) of rainfall (precipitation) or 20 days with a quantity of rain, sleet, snow etc. per month.
- The driest weather is in May when an average of 52mm (2.0in) of rainfall (precipitation) occurs across 15 days.
- The wettest weather is in December when an average of 118mm (4.6in) of rainfall (precipitation) occurs across 25 days
- The average annual relative humidity is 84.0% and average monthly relative humidity ranges from 79% in May to 88% in November.
- Average sunlight hours in Shetland range between 0.5 hours per day in December and 5.3 hours per day in May.

There are an average of 1038 hours of sunlight per year with an average of 3.0 hours of sunlight per day.

Appendix 11

Optimal hydroponic feed values using the formula given in Appendix 7

Table showing nominal CF values for a range of hydroponic crops

Asparagus	14-18	Lettuce Fancy	3-8
Basil	10-14	Lettuce Iceberg	6-14
Beans	18-25	Melons	10-22
Beetroot	14-22	Parsley	8-18
Blueberry	18-20	Pea	14-18
Broccoli	14-24	Radish	12-22
Capsicum (pepper)	20-27	Roses	18-26
Carnation	12-20	Spinach	18-35
Carrot	14-22	Squash	18-24
Cauliflower	14-24	Strawberry	18-25
Celery	15-24	Tomato	22-28
Chives	12-22	Turnip	18-24
Cucumber	16-24		

Appendix 12

Building a strong potting bench

In a nutshell, you build four trestles from 200x50mm treated wood with 75x75mm supports. You then cover the bench with lengths of 200 x 50mm treated wood; it is makes sense to fasten the legs at the bottom to the concrete floor. Remember there will be some nice storage space under the bench. The diagram below is not to scale.

Now you can do one of two things; you can either cover the bench with plywood to give a smooth surface, or much better to have it covered with thin stainless steel, bent at 90 degrees so the back of the stainless steel sits against the wall at the back of the bench; this will keep squeaky clean year in year out. This is shown in the diagram below – use 1.5mm stainless steel. You should also screw a wooden lip at the front of the bench – this keeps the compost in place. A piece of wood 25x100mm should be fine.

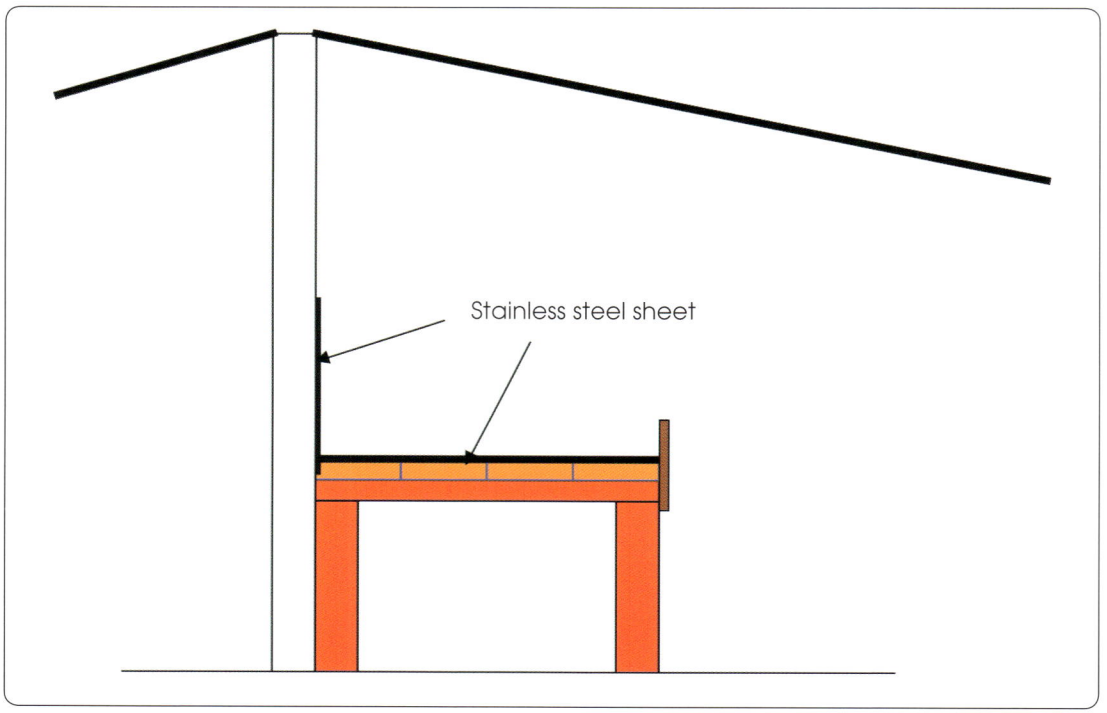

Stainless steel sheet

Left:
My larger potting bench. It can easily support six large bags of compost if needs be. Note the retaining plank stopping spillage onto the floor. The main planks are 150 x 50mm. I have not fitted the stainless steel yet.

appendices

Right:
My smaller potting bench. The heavy bench is covered with a thin sheet of stainless steel; around the edge you can see the wooden lip preventing compost spillage.

Appendix 13
Recommended reading

Besides the websites I have mentioned you should try to get a copy of Collins practical gardener 'Bedding Plants' by Martin Fish and of course the 'Bedding Plant Expert' by Dr D.G. Hessayon. Both these books come as part of a series and for the cost they are superb.

Two basic guides for propagation are 'RHS Propagating Plants' by Alan Toogood and 'Plant Propagation' by P.D.A.McMillan. 'Nursery Stock Manual' by Lamb, Kelly and Bowbrick is really more a book for the professional and is published by Grower Books.

If you want to set up an irrigation system either for your greenhouse, tunnel or garden, then you should be getting in touch with LBS Horticultural Supplies, and acquire one of their catalogues. Their products are not cheap (for instance you can get much cheaper pumps from Screwfix) but they give very good advice whether it has to do with sprinkler systems, drip irrigation, filters, timers and hoses. Certainly when I wanted an overhead sprinkler system their advice was excellent.

If you want to find out more about nutrition then the 'Bible' is 'Media and Mixes for Container Grown Plants' by A.C. Bunt, but only get it if you know some chemistry.

For those of you who are really serious about nutrition you should be thinking about getting MAFF/ARC 'Diagnosis of Mineral Disorders in Plants'; there are three volumes; volume one looks at Principles, volume two deals with Vegetables and volume three deals with Glasshouse Crops. They are expensive.

'Media and Mixes for Container Grown Plants' as mentioned at the end of Chapter 5.

'Growing in Rockwool' by Dennis Smith, one of the Grower Books. This is quite advanced but the same principles apply to perlite.

A book I cannot recommend highly enough is 'Herbaceous Perennial Plants' by Alan Armitage. As well as being thoroughly informative, it is also very amusing. Regarding *Leontopodium* (Edelweiss) he said that after being at the 'Sound of Music' film he was ready to be stunned by the beauty of that mystical plant. A little later he then says that bringing it down to lowland gardens has done nothing for it, and you should "enjoy the movie and let well enough alone". Exactly my own sentiments when I saw what the seed turned into! The book runs to over 1100 pages. Shop around and you can get it for about £40. A great investment!

I have mentioned 'Hardy Plants in the North' by the late John Copland in the text.

You should also get hold of 'The Impossible Garden' by Rosa Steppanova; a visit to Lea Gardens on the west side of Shetland is always an inspiration. What always amazes me is how weed-free it all is. I sometimes ask Rosa for advice and she is always very generous with her help. I recall when I first started growing perennials and told her I was struggling to grow columbines; she said "What species is it?" I could see the bemused look on her face when I replied, "Are there more than one?"

It is also worth getting the Royal Horticultural Society 'Encyclopaedia of Perennials', both an attractive and a modern guide.

Once again you will be hard pressed to get any better books on fruit and vegetables than the 'Expert' series ('The Fruit Expert', 'The Vegetable Expert' and 'The Greenhouse Expert') and Collins 'Kitchen Garden'.

If you look up Amazon you will find hundreds of books about growing vegetables, salads etc.

As you can imagine there are hundreds of books dealing with pests and diseases, and of course you can get a lot of information from the Internet; the books mentioned below are some of my own guides.

'Biological Control in Plant Protection' by Jelyer et al. ISBN 1-874545-28-6. This book is a Royal Horticultural Society guide, and a must for the organic grower, full of stunning photos.

Koppert Biological Systems. This company produces a regular digital newsletter free of charge; you should think of visiting their website.

'Collins Guide to The Pests, Diseases and Disorders of Garden Plants' by Buczacki, Harris and Hargreaves. ISBN-10 0002200635 and ISBN-13: 978-0002200639

I have the older (shorter) version of this book and it is superb. The modern editions are more expensive with more photos and obviously much more up to date.

'A-Z of Garden Pests and Problems' by Ian G Walls ISBN 0 907812 66. This book is now some 30 years old and you should be able to pick it up cheaply on the Internet.

Clockwise from below:

Clematis montana 'Rubens'; Aquilegia x hybrida 'McKana's Giants'; Armeria; heather with bee;, Tulips; Dicentra spectabilis; Digitalis 'Candy Mountain.

Jubilee Flower Park

293

Clockwise from below:

Nemesia; Dianthus 'Ideal'; Petunia 'Mirage Reflections'; Lilium 'Jetfire'; Felicia heterophylia 'The Blues'; Chrysanthemum leucanthemum 'Alaska'; Montbretia 'Lucifer'; Gladiolus tristis; Dianthus nana giganteus 'F1 Super Parfait cultivar'.

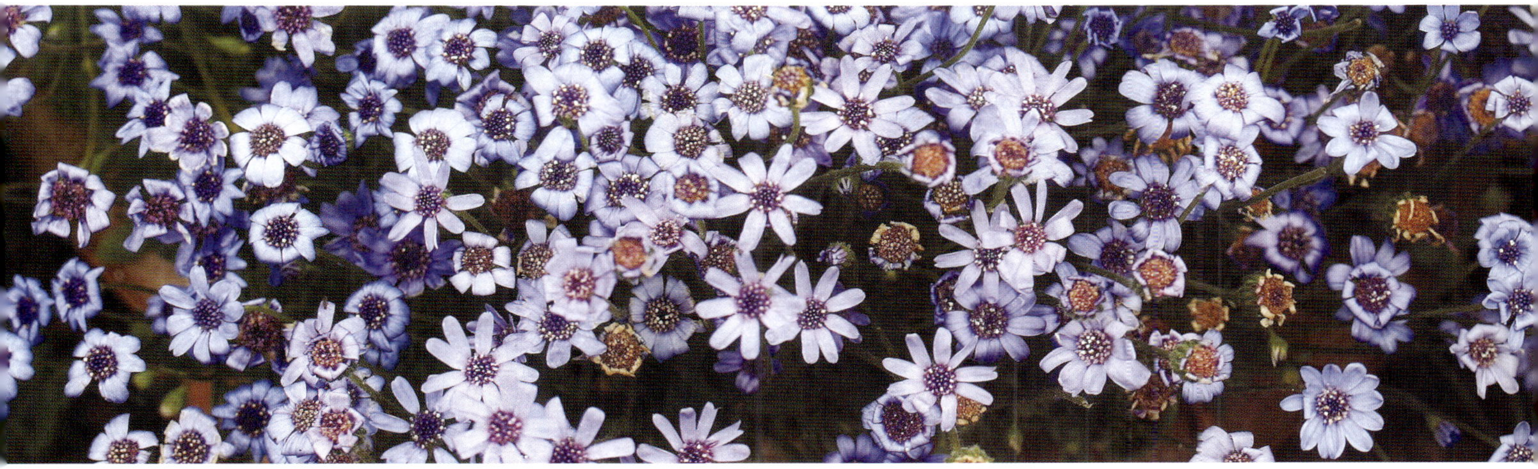

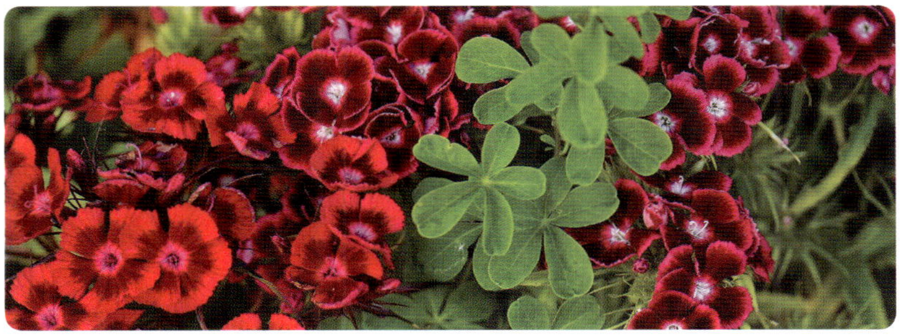

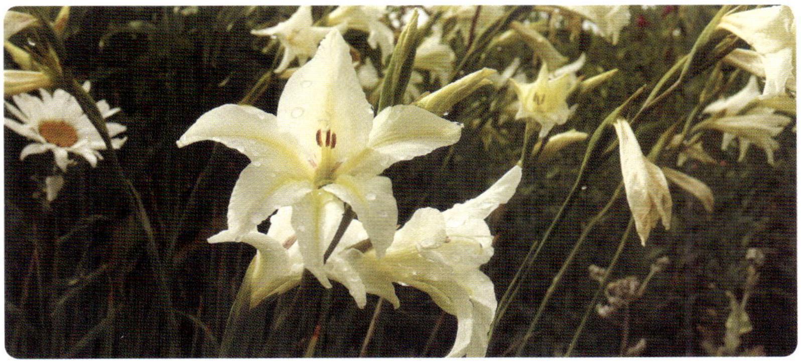

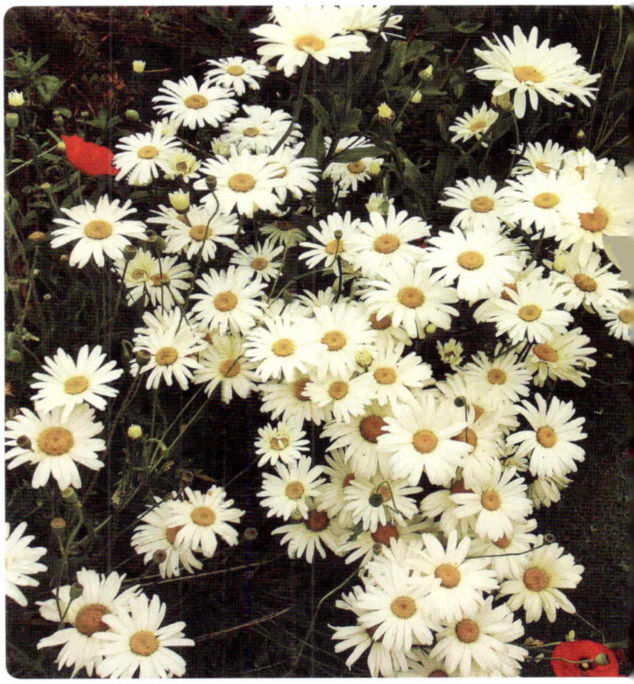

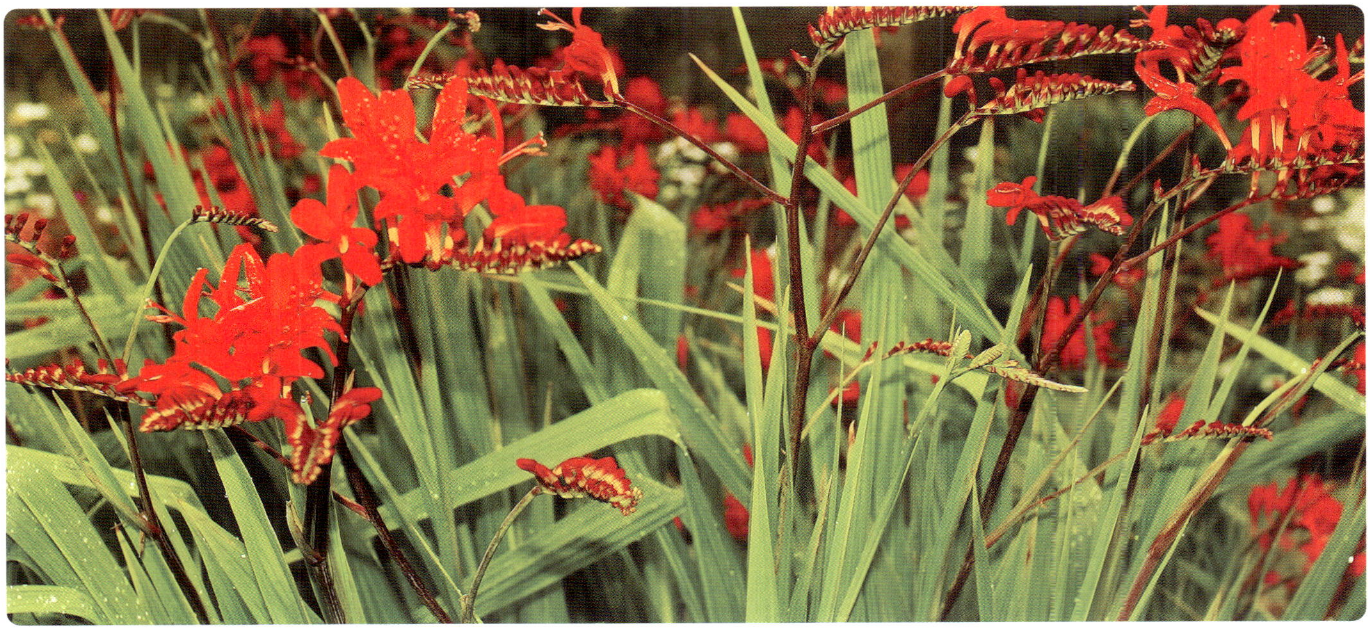

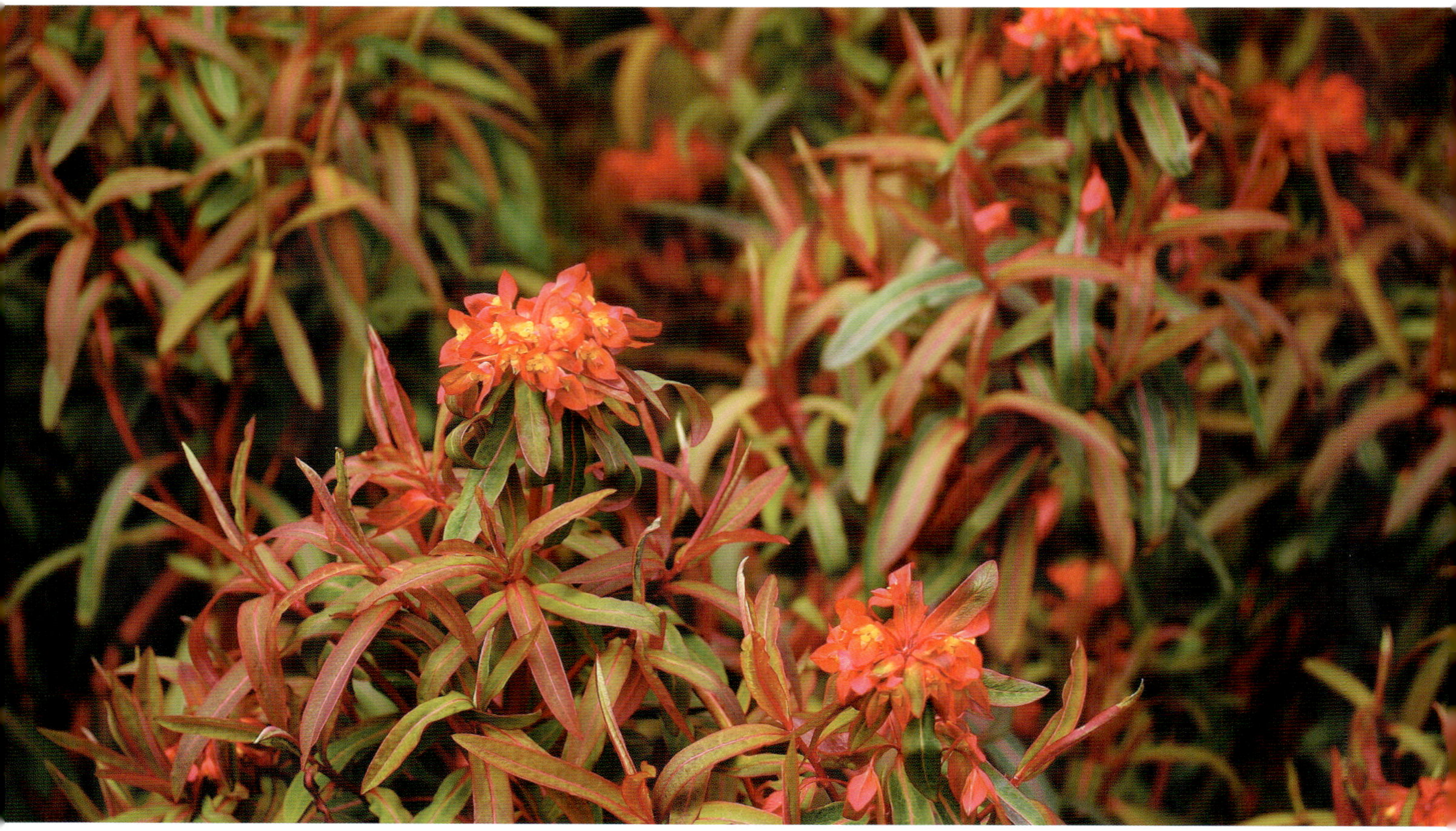

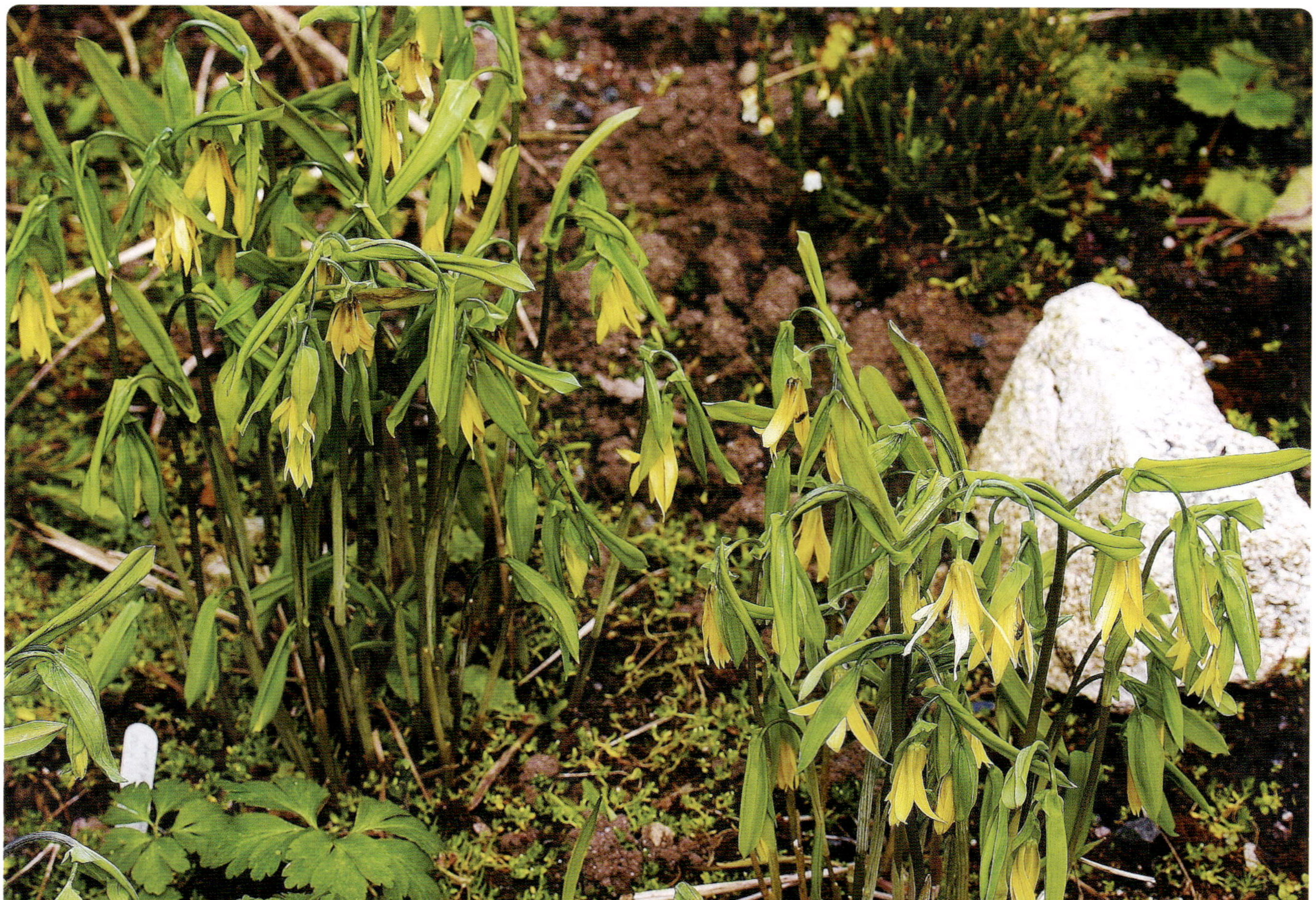

Clockwise from left:
Euphorbia griffithii 'Dixter'; Rhododendron yakushimanum 'Ken Janeck'; Fritillaria meleagris; Lunaria; Meconopsis 'Lingholm'; Ulvalaria perfoliata.

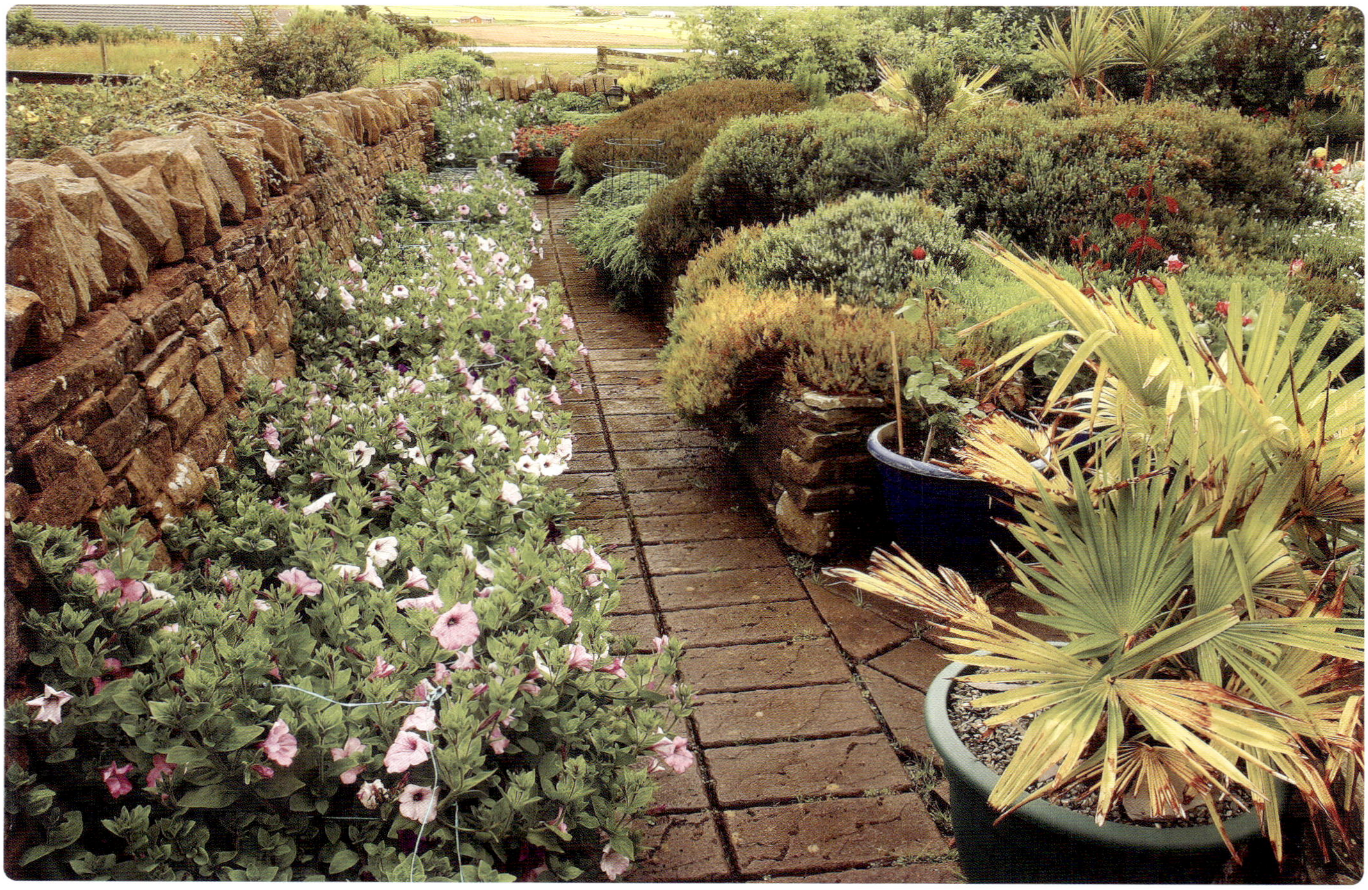

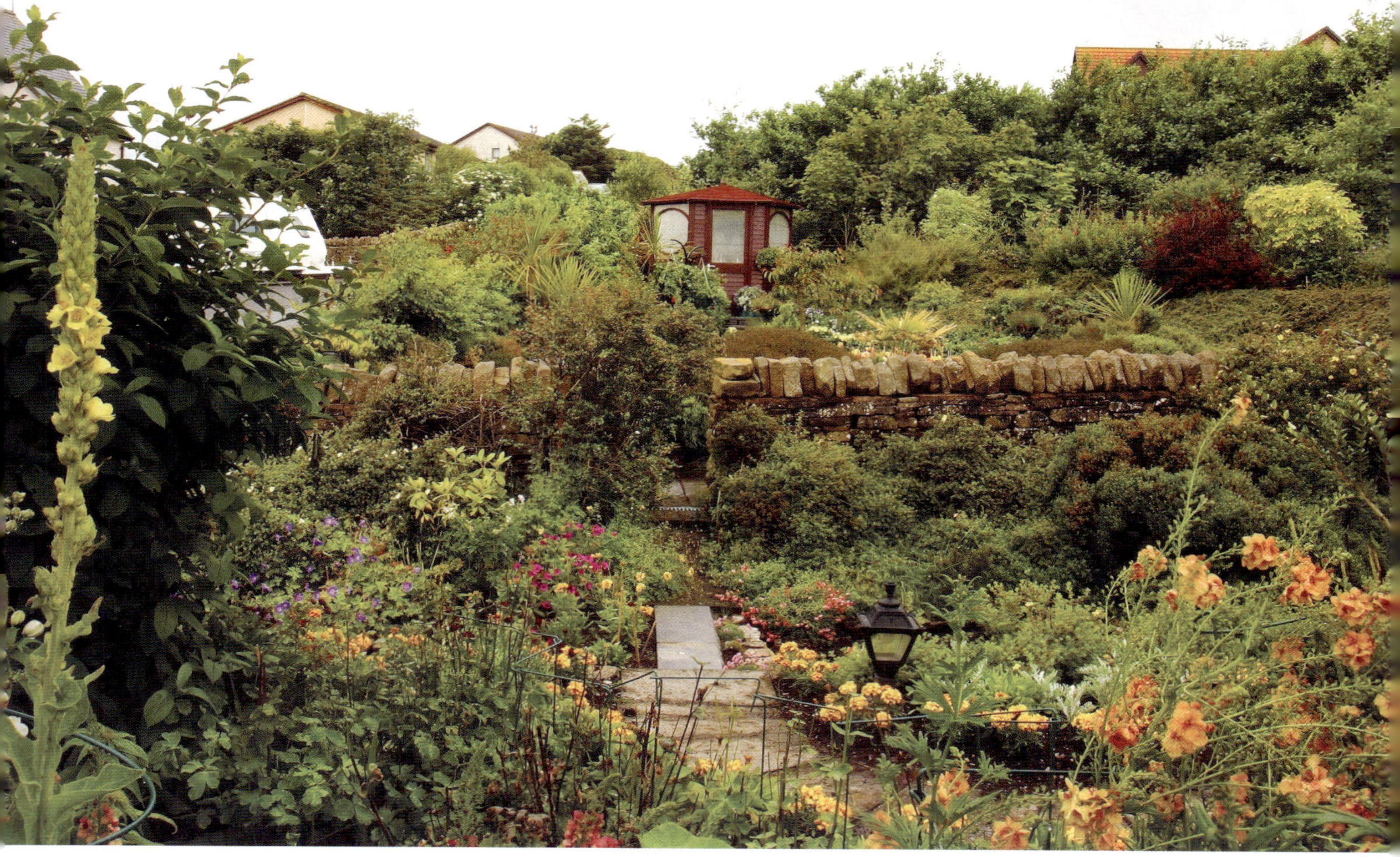

Opposite:
Two views of Adam's garden.

This page, clockwise from below:
AL red variegated fuschia;
small flowered petunia;
osteospermum; begonias.

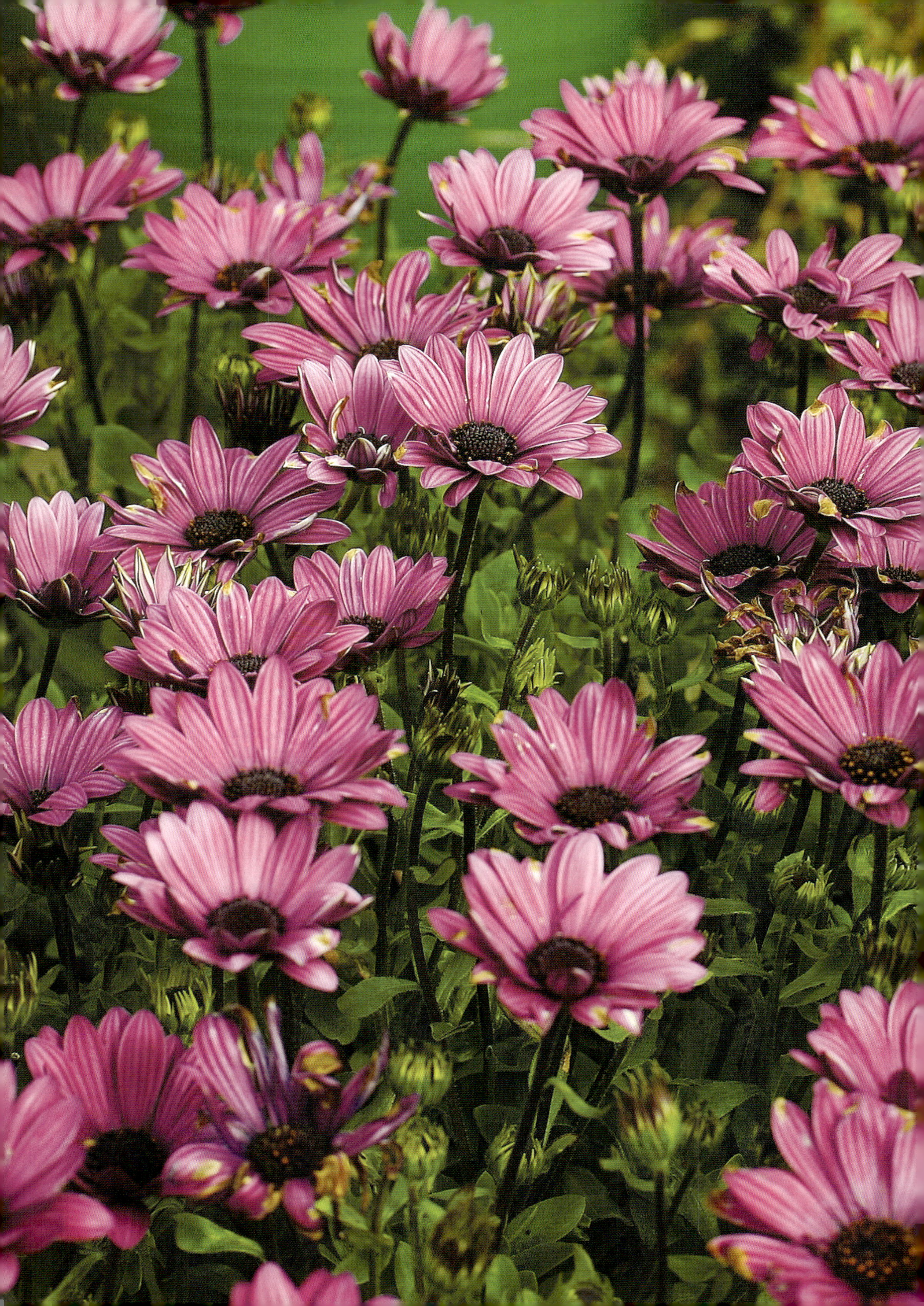

Index

Figures in **bold** indicate a photograph or illustration.

Achillea A. 'Cassis Red' 271
    A. clypeolata 83
    A. filipendulina 'Gold Plate' 97
    A. millefolium 83, **97**, 271
    A. millefolium 'Cassis' 97
    A. millefolium 'Summer Berries' 97
    A. millefolium 'Summer Pastels' 97
    A. sibirica 83, 271
    A. sibirica camtschatica 'Love Parade' 97
Aconitum A. napellus 97, **97**
Aethionema grandiflora 271
    'Grandifolium' 83
African marigold 75, **75**
    see also Tagetes erecta
Ageratum 63, 271
Air filled porosity (AFP) calculation 285
Ajuga A. pyramidalis 97
    A. reptans 'Burgundy Glow' 97
Alchemilla A. alpina 97
    A. mollis 'Thriller' 83, 97
    A. robustica 97
Allium A. aflatunense 97
    A. christophi 97
    A. moly 97
    A. obliquum 83
    A. ostrowskianum 97
    A. triquetrum 97
Alyssum A. montanum 'Mountain Gold' .. 83, 97, 271
    A. montanum 'Gold Ball' 83, 271
    A. saxatile 'Gold Queen' 97
    A. sulphureum 83, 271
    'Crystal' annual 63, **63**
    'Snowdrift' annual 63, 271
Anacyclus pyrethrum 'Silver Kisses' 271
    pyrethrum var depressus 83
Anaphalis margaritacea 'New Snow' 83
Anaphylis marguerite 'Pearl Everlasting' 271
Anchusa azurea 'Feltham' 271
    azurea 'Loddon Royalist' 97
Anderson, Liam 95
Anemone A. blanda 97
    A. hupehensis (japonica) 97, 271
    A. nemorosa 97
    multifida 'Rubra' 271
Anthemis A. tinctoria 'Kelwayi' 98
    A. tinctoria 'Sancti-Johannis' 84, **84**
    A. tinctoria 'Sauce Hollandaise' 98
    carpatica 'Karpatica' 271
    tinctoria 'Kelwayi' 271
Anthriscus sylvestris 98
Antirrhinum 271
    'Appeal' 64
    'Cheerio' 64
    'Chimes' 64
Aphids 244, **244**, 245
    life cycle 244
    treatment 245
Apples 205, **205-208**

Aqilegia A. alpina 98, 272
    A. buergeriana 'Calimero' 98, 272
    A. caerulea 'Biedermeier' series 98, 84, 272
    A. caerulea 'Origami' series 98
    A. chrysantha 98
    A. flabellata 'Cameo' series 98
    A. 'McKana' 98
    A. 'Musik' 98
    A. vulgaris var stellata 'Barlow' series 98
    A. vulgaris var stellata 'Greenapples' 98
    A. vulgaris 'Winky' series 98
Aquilegia A. caerulea 'Danish dwarf' 272
    A. caerulea 'Dragonfly' 84
    A. caerulea 'Origami' 84
    A. canadensis GN 272
    A. sibirica GN 272
Arabis A. alpina 'Snowcloud' 98
    A. blepharophylla 'Red Sensation' ... 84, **84**, 98, 272
    A. procurrens 'Glacier' 98
    caucasica compacta 'Snow Cap' 272
    procurrens 'Glacier' 84
Arenaria montana 84, 272
Armeria A.maritima 'Alba' 98
    'Joystick' 85
    maritima 'Splendens' 272
Artemisia absinthia 272
    dracuncula (tarragon) 272
Artichoke 222
Aryncus sylvestris 272
Asilbe A. chinensis var. pumila 98
    A. japonica 98
Aster A. novi belgii 'Alice Haslam' 98
    alpinus 'Trimix' 272
    sibiricus 272
Astilbe 98, **98**
    'Bella Mix' 272
    chinensis var. 'Showstar' 272
    chinensis var. pumila 272
Astrantia major 98
    maxima 98
Aubretia A. deltoidea 99
    x culturum 'Cascade' 85
Aubrietia 272
    x cultorum 'Cascade' 85

Bacopa **64**, 109, **109**, 272
    'Abunda' 64
    'Bluetopia' 64
    germination 29, **29**
    'Snowtopia' 64
Beans, broad 'Sutton' 222
    French Climbing 'Cobra' 222
    French 'Prince' 222
    runner 222
Bedding feed formula masses 284
Beet leaf 'Chard Lights' 222, **222**
Beetroot, 'Boltardy' 223
    'Cylindrica' 223
    'Egyptian' 223
    'Golden' 223
    'Solo' 223

Begonia 'Non-stop' 64, **64**
Bellflower, see Campanula
Bellis perennis 65, **65**, 272
    'Rominette' 65
    'Tasso' 65
Benching 183, **183**
Bergamot, see Monarda
Bergenia B. cordifolia 'New Hybrids' 272
    B. stracheyi 99
Bidens 65, 272
Biosept 143
Biostimulants 262
Blackberry 213, **213**
Borecole (curly kale) 223
Botrytis 255, **255**
Bouteloua gracilis 272
Brachycomb 65, 272
Brassica culture 31
Bugle, see Ajuga
Buphthalium salicifolium 'Alpengold' 272
Buphthalmum (oxeye) 272
    B. speciosum 99
Busy Lizzie, see Impatiens
Buttercup, see Ranunculus

Cabbage 272
    red 223
    root fly 247, **248**, **249**
    savoy 223
    summer 223
    white butterfly 246
    winter 223
Calabrese, 'Fiesta' 225
    'Marathon' 225
Calamintha C. grandiflora 'Elphin Purple' 85
Calceolaria 272
Calendula 272
'Fiesta Gitana' 65
Caltha palustris 272
Camassia C. leichtlinii 99
    C. leichtlinii ssp suksdorfii 'Caerulea' 99
    C. quamash 99
Campanula 85, **85**
    C. alpestris 99
    C. carpatica 86, **86**, 272
    C. carpatica 'Blue Clips' 272
    C. carpatica 'Pearl' 86
    C. cochlearifolia 86, 99
    C. cochlearifolia (c.pusilla) 272
    C. garganica 86, 272
    C. glomerata 99, 272
    C. lactiflora 99
    C. latifolia 99
    C. latiloba 99
    C. persicifolia 86, 99
    C. persicifolia 'Grandiflora' 272
    C. poscharskyana 86, 272
    C. punctata 86, 272
    C. punctata rubrifola 273
    C. rapunculoides 86
    C. rotundifolia (harebell) 86
    C. takesimana 86, 273
    C. turbinata 99
    'Isabella' 86, 272

Candytuft, see Iberis
Capillary matting 135, 136, **136**
Carbamates 242
Carbon dioxide controller 123, **123**
    enrichment 123
Cardamine pratensis (lady'smock) 273
Carex 93
    buchaanii ('Red rooster') 273
Carnation, see Dianthus caryophyllus
Carrot, 'Autumn King' 225
    'Chantenay red-cored 2' 225
    'James Scarlet Intermediate' 225
    'Trevor' 225
Catanache alba 273
    C. caerulea 86, 99, 273
Caterpillar cabbage white 247, **247**
Catnip, see Nepeta
Cauliflower 227, **227**
    'All The Year Round' 226
    'Aviron' 226
    'Clapton' 227
    'Fargro' 227
    'Frement' 227
    'Nautilus' 227
    'Plana' 227
    'Romanesco' 226
Celeriac 273
    'Prinz' 227
Celery 273
    'Golden Self Blanching' 227
    sowing 32
Cell units 24, **24**
Celosia 66
Centaurea C. dealbata 99, 273
    C. montana 99, 273
    C. rupestris 273
    uniflora 273
Centranthus C. ruber (red valerian) 86
    C. ruber 'Pretty Betsy' 99
    C. ruber 'Snowcloud' 99
    C. ruber var. coccineus 273
Cerastium (Snow in summer) 273
    C. tomentosum 99
Cerinthe glabra 273
    major 'Purpurascens' 273
Chamomile nobilis 273
Cheiranthus 273
Cherry 208, **208**
Chiastophyllum oppositifolium 99
Chicory 228
Chlormequat 69
Chrysanthemum carinatum 'Bright Eyes' 66, **66**
    coccineum 'Super Duplex' 273
    leucanthemum 'White Knight' 273
    maximum 'Sonnenschein' 273
    maximum nan 'Snow Lady' 273
    paludosum (Marguerite) 66
    parthenium 'Santana' 66
Cineraria (flower) 81, **81**
    'Cirrus' annual 66
    'Siver Dust' annual 66
    see also Senecio cruentus
Clematis orientalis 273
    tangutica 273

Clubroot	259, 260, **260**
Coir	166, **166**
Cold frames	195, **195-198**
Cold frames construction	197
Coleus	80, **80**, 273
Columbine, see Aquilegia	
Compost analysis	151
coir, preparation	165
garden	143
heap	254
peat based	163
potting, preparation	165
seed, preparation	165
Conductivity meter	138, **149**
meters, calibration	150
units	149
Copland, John	94
Coreopsis	99
Coriander	273
Cortaderia	93
richardii	273
selloana 'Pink Feather'	273
Corydalis	100, **100**
C. flexuosa	100
C. lutea	100
C. solida	100
Corynephorus canescens	93
spiky blue	273
Cosmos	**66**, 273
'Cosmic'	66
'Sonata'	66
Courgette 'Ambassador'	232
Cow parsley, see Anthriscus sylvestris	
Cranesbill, see perennial Geraniums	
Crocosmia C. 'Lucifer'	100
Cucumber	218, **218**
'Burpless Tasty Green'	232
'Carmen'	217
germination	15, **15**
'Masterpiece'	232
'Tyria'	217
Cultivar resistance	262
Cuphea ignea	80
Cuttings	285, **285**, 286
Cyclamen	273
persicum cultivars	80
Cyren, use of	250
Dahlia	**67**, 273
'Figaro'	67
'Redskin'	67
Damping off	259, **259**
Daylength neutral plants	54
Delospermum cooperi	273
sutherlandii	273
sutherlandii ' Peach Star'	273
Delphinium	101
Dessication	124
Dianthus	68, **68**
alpinus	87, **87**, 273
barbatus	68
barbatus 'Midget'	273

caryophyllus (carnation)	68
chinensis	68
chinensis x barbatus	68
'Confetti'	273
D. deltoides 'Arctic Fire'	87, 101, 273, 274
D. deltoides 'Vampire'	101
D. plumarius	87
D. spiculifolius	87
deltoides 'Brilliancy'	274
deltoides 'Microchips'	274
deltoides 'Nelli'	274
'Flashing Light'	274
'Ideal'	274
'Ipswich Pink'	274
knappii (yellow)	87, 274
plumarious 'Sweetness'	274
Dicentra D. 'Bountiful'	101
D. 'Pearl Drops'	101
Digitalis	87
D. purpurea	101
D. purpurea albiflora 'Suttons Apricot'	101
D. purpurea 'The Shirley'	101
Dimorphotheca	104
Diseases of plants	254
Doronicum	101
orientale	87, 274
orientale 'Little Leo'	87
Drip irrigation assembly	145, **145**
Echinacea purpurea 'Magnus'	274
Echinops bannaticus	101
ritro	274
Elephants ears, see Bergenia	
Empot-12	46, **46**
-15	46, **46**
Endive	274
Eragrostis spectabilis	274
Eremurus E. robustus	101
E. stenophyllus	101
Erigeron	87
'Azure Fairy'	274
E. aurantiacus	274
E. glaucus	274
E. speciosus 'Azure Fairy'	87, 101
E. speciosus 'Pink Jewel'	101
Erodium	274
E. chrysantha	101
E. macradenum	101
E. manescavi	87
E. manescavii	101
E. reichardii	101
Eryngium E. alpinum	101
E. bourgatti	101
E. varifolium	101
Erysimum E. allioni	87
E. allioni (orange)	274
E. 'Bowles Mauve'	101
E. 'Constant Cheer'	101
E. helveticum	87, 274
'Jenny Brook'	101

Euphorbia E. amygdaloides 'Robbiae' 101
    E. polychroma 88, 274
    E. rigida 88, 274
    E. x martini 101

Feed, dilution 146, **146**, **147**
    diluter 147
    injector 147
    making your own 139
    organic 141
    preparation 146
    proprietary 138
    slow release CRF 140
    timers 148
Feeding 136
Fennel sweet zifa 274
    Florence 228
Festuca 93
    glauca 274
Fleabane, see Erigeron
Flowering 53
Fluid seed sowing 281
Fluid sowing 281, **281**
Fluorescent lighting 116
    economics 122
Foam flower, see Tiarella
Forget-me-not, see Myosotis
Forsyth, Joanna 95
Foxglove, see Digitalis
Foxtail lily, see Eremurus
Francoa sonchifolia 101
French marigold 76, **76**
    see also Tagetes patula
Frost protection 124
Fruit trees, sizes 203
Fuchsia 88, **88**
Fungi, bacterial control 263
Fungicides 263

Gaillardia 101
    'Arizona Sun' 68, **68**
Gazania 274
    'Kiss' 69
Genetically modified (GM) seeds 234
Gentiana G. Septemfida 88
    G. sino-ornata 88
    sino-ornata 102
Gentians 102, **102**
Geranium (Cranesbill) 89, **89**, 102
    (pelargonium) 'Summer Showers' 69
    (pelargonium) 'Video' 69
    G. cantabrigiense 'St Ola' 102
    G. cinereum 'Ballerina' 102
    G. cinereum 'Lawrence Flatman' 102
    G. macrorrhizum 102
    G. 'Orion' 102
    G. phaeum 102
    G. pratense 'Mrs Kendall Clark' 102
    G. pratense 'Striatum' 102
    G. psilostemon 102
    G. sanguineum 'Max Frei' 102
    G. subcaulenscens 102
    G. x riversleaianum 'Mavis Simpson' 102
    G. x riversleaianum 'Russel Pritchard' 102
    sanguineum 89

Germination 19, **19**
    results 271
Geum G. chiloense 102
    G. chiloense 'Lady Stratheden' 102
    G. chiloense 'Lady Stratheden' 89
    G. chiloense 'Mrs Bradshaw' 102
    G. chiloense 'Mrs Bradshaw' 89
    G. coccineum 102
    G. 'Oranges and Lemons' 102
    G. rivale 102
Glass, cutting 181
Glasshouse benching 183
    doors 182
    electrical fittings 184
    environment 54
    ventilation 183
    water supply 184
Glasshouses 175
    fitting glass 180
Glazing 180, **180-181**
Gloxinia sinningia 81
Godetia 45, **45**
Gooseberry sawfly 253, **253**
Grapes 204, **204**, 205
Grasses 93, **93**
Gray, Ruby Anne 95
Grazon 90 .... 264, **264**
Greenhouse structure 175, **175-179**
Grip strip 187, **187**
Grow room 118, **119**, **120**
Growing rig 116
Growing rigs 117, **117**, **118**
Growth media 163
Growth regulators 46
Gunnera G. manicata 103
Gypsophila G. cerastoides 89
    G.r epens rosea 89
    repens rosea 274

Hand sowers 16, **16**
Hardening off 47, 124
Heathers 92, **92**, **93**
Helenium 'Helena Mix' 274
Heliotrope 69, 274
Helleborus H. corsicus 103
    H. niger 103
    H. orientalis 103
Hemerocallis 'New Hybrids' 274
Herb seeds 30
    sowing 32
Hesperis matronalis 103, 274
Heuchera americana 'Dale's Strain' 274
    H. americana 'Dale's Strain' 89
    H. americana 'Melting Fire' 103
    H. sanguinea 'Mtetallica' 103
    H. sanguinea 'Purple Petticoat' 103
    H. sanguinea 'Ruby Bells' 89
Hosta 103
    New Hybrids 274
Houseleek, see Sempervivum
Humidity control 33
    meter 55, **55**
Hydroponic feeds appendices **7**, **11**, 284, 287
    optimal feed values 287
Hydroponics 167

Iberis I. aurosica 103
    I. sempervirens 103
Impatiens 70, **70**
    'Accent' 70
    culture 28
    'Dezire' 70
    'Expo' 70
Incarvillea delavayi 274
    I. delavayi 'Deli Rose' 103
    I. mairei 103
Inkster, Diane 95
Inula I. ensifolia 103
    I. helenium 103
    I. hookeri 103
    I. orientalis ` 103
    I. orientalis 'Grandiflora' 103
Iris I. chrysographes 103
    I. pumila 103
    I. reticulata 103
    I. setosa 274
    I. setosa 103
    I. sibirica 103
Isotoma (Laurentia) 69, 274

Jacob's ladder, see Polemonium
Jamieson, Ruby 95

Knautia macedonica 103
Kniphofia 274
    'Firedance' 274
    K. 'Flamenco' 103
    K. hirsuta 'Firedance' 89
    K. hirsuta 'Traffic Lights' 103
    K. uvaria 'Border Ballet' 89
    uvaria 'Border Ballet' 274
Knotweed, see Persicaria
Kohlrabi 228

Labelling 22
Lady's mantle, see Alchemilla
Lamb's tails, see Chiastophyllum oppositifolium
Lamium maculatum 'White Nancy' 103
Laurentia, see Isotoma
Lavandula stoechas 275
Lavaterra 70, **70**, 274
Lavendula stoechas 103
Lawn problems 128
Leatherjacket 250, **250**
Leaves 49
Leek 228, **228**, 275
    and onion culture 31
    'Conora' 228
    'Lancelot' 228
    'Musselburgh' 228
    'Porbella' 228
Lemon balm 275
Leslie, Adam 95
Lettuce 233, **233**
    'Dublin' 229
    'Lollo Rossa' 229

Leucanthemum L. vulgare 'White Knight' 103
    L. 'White Knight' 89
    L. x superbum 'Alaska' 103
    L. x superbum ''Crazy Daisy' 103
    maximus 'Dwarf Snow Lady' 89
Liatris spicata 'Goblin' 275
Light emitting diodes (LEDs) 122
Light feeding plants 151
Light requirement 54
Lighting and plant growth 116
Lilium formosa princeii 275
Linaria aeruginea 'Neon Lights' 275
    alpina 275
    purpurea 275
Linula L. aeruginea 104
    L. alpina 104
    L. purpurea 104
Linum perennis 'Blue Sapphire' 275
Livingstone daisies 275
    see also Mesembryanthemum
Lobelia 71, **71**
    bedding type 275
    compact cutivars 71
    culture 28
    sessilifolia 275
    trailing cutivars 71
Lobularia, see Alyssum
Long day plants 54
Lungwort, see Pulmonaria
Lupin 90, **90**
    'Gallery' 275
    'Ice' 275
    L. 'Gallery' 90
    L. 'Lulu' 90
Lupinus L. Russel 'Gallery 104
    L. Russel 'Lulu' 104
Luzula 275
    'Lucius' 93, 275
    sylvatica 'Select' 93
Lychnis alpina 275
    arkwrightii 'Orange Gnome' 275
    arkwrightii 'Orange Zwerg' 90
    flos jovis nana 'Peggy' 275
    L. chalcedonica 104
    L. coronaria 104
    L. coronaria 'Albc' 104
    L. flos-cuculi 90
Lysimachia L. atropurpurea 275
    L. atropurpurea 'Beaujolais' 90
    L. punctata 275
Lythrum salicaria (purple looserife) 275

Macronutrients 137
Malva moschata 275
Marguerite 66, **66**
    see also Chrysanthemum paludosum
Matricaria 275
Meadow rue, see Thalictrum
Meconopsis betonicifola 'China Blue' 275
    cambrica 275
Medium feeding plants 151
Melon 'Sweetheart' 222

Mesembryanthemum (Livingstone Daisies)	71, **71**
Michaelmas daisy, see Aster	
Mildew, powdery	255, **256**
Mimulus	275
M. cupreus	90, 104
M. luteus	90, 104
Mineral absorption	51
Monarda citriodora	275
didyma	104
Monkey flower, see Mimulus	
Monkshood, see Aconitum	
Montbretia	100, **100**
see also Crocosmia	
Mowat, Kit	95
Mucor	255, **255**
Mullein, see Verbascum	
Myosotis	275
'Blue Sylva'	104
'Magnum'	72, 104
palustris	72
scorpoides	104
'Sylva'	72
'Victoria'	72
Nasturtium (Tom Thumbs)	72, 275
Nemesia cultivars	72, 275
Nepeta racemosa	104
Nerine	104, **104**
Onion	221, **221**, **229**
maincrop 'Bedfordshire Champion'	229
maincrop 'Globe'	229
maincrop 'Rijnburger 5'	229
maincrop 'Sturrgarder Stanfield'	229
maincrop 'Tamark'	229
salad 'Guardsman'	229
salad 'Summer Isle'	229
Organic or not	234
Organophosphates	242
Osmosis	138, **138**
Osteospermum	72, 275
jucundum	104
Overwatering	133
Overwintering plants	123
Oxalis O. adenophylla	105
O. enneaphylla	105
O. florabunda	105
Pansy	78, **78**
'Matrix'	275
Papavar P. alpinum	105, 275
P. nudicaule	275
P. orientale	105
P. orientale 'Royal Wedding'	90
P. rupifragum	105
P. somniferum	90
Parsley	230, 275
Hamburg	230
sowing	32
Parsnip 'Palace'	230
'White Gem'	230
Pea 'Feltham First'	230
'Kelvedon Wonder'	230
'Sugar Snap'	230

Pearl everlasting, see Anaphalis margaretacea	
Pelargonium, see Geranium	
Pennisetum setaceum 'Fountain grass'	275
Penstemon	106
P. alpinus	90
P. heterophyllus 'Zuriblau'	90
P. strictus	90
P. x mexicale 'Sunburst Amethyst'	90
P. x mexicale 'Sunburst Ruby'	90
Pepper	219, **219**, **220**
Peppermint	275
Perlite capillarity	167, **167**
grow bag arrangement	170, **170**
troughs	210
Persicaria P. affine 'Darjeeling Red'	105
P. affine 'Donald Lowndes'	105
Pest treatment, biological control	241
biopesticides	241
contact action	242
plant derived insecticides	240
soaps and oils	240
synthetic pesticides	242
systemic action	242
Petunia	275
cultivars	72-74, **73**, **74**
culture	26
plugs	27, **27**
'Wave' culture	26
pH	154
adjustment	158
and solubility	156, **156**
importance	155
of liquids	154, **154**
paper	157, **157**
soil testing	157
Photosynthesis	49, **49**
Physalis alkekengi	105
Physiological problems	239
Phytophthora infestans	259
Pinks, see Dianthus	
Plant structure	47
Plantago major 'Variegata'	275
Plate sower	17, **17**
construction	277, 279, **279**
use	278
Plug cell units	24
Plug extractor	283, **283**
Plug production	24
Plug sowing	25, **25**
Plums	207, **207**, **208**
Polemonium P. caeruleum 'Blue Pearl'	105
P. caeruleum 'White Pearl'	105
P. carneum	105
P. yezoense 'Purple Rain'	105
Polydrip trays	134, 135, **135**
Polytunnel environment	56
Polytunnels 'Polycrub'	192
'Solar Tunnel'	190
commercial	185
Poppy, see Papavar	
Potato, blight	257, **258**
'Cara'	230
'Catriona'	230
'Epicure'	230

flower	230, **230**
'Kestrel'	230
'Konder'	230
'Markies'	230
'Orla'	230
'Red Duke of York'	230
'Remarka'	230
'Shetland Black'	230
'Valor'	230
Potentilla P. atrosanguinea var.argyrophylla	91
P. crantzii	105
P. megalantha	105
P. nepalensis 'Helen Jane'	91
P. nepalensis 'Miss Wilmott'	91, 105
P. nepalensis 'Ron McBeath'	91, 105
P. nepalensis 'Shogran'	91
P. neumanniana	91
P. x tonguei 'Yellow Queen'	105
Potting bench	44, **44**
construction	288, **288**, **289**
Potting up	44-46
Pricking out	41
guidelines	42
Primrose	276
Primroses	152, **152**, **153**
Primula bulleesiana	276
denticulata 'Runsdorf-Hybrids'	276
P. acaulis	105
P. auricula	105
P. beesiana	91, 105
P. bulleyana	91
P. denticulata	91, 105
P. elatior	105
P. integrifolia	105
P. japonica	91, 105
P. juliae	105
P. luteola	105
P. prolifera	105
P. pulverulenta	105
P. rosea	105
P. veris	105
P. viallii	91
P. vulgaris 'Arctic Series'	91
P. x bulleesiana	105
P. x pubescens 'Exhibition Series'	91
P. x pubescens (auricula strain)	105
pubsescens (Auricula)	276
Propagator construction	269, **269**
Prunella grandiflora 'Freeland'	276
grandiflora rubra	276
Pulmonaria P.officinalis	
'Cambridge Blue Group'	105
Pulsatilla (violet)	276
vulgaris	105
Pyrethroids	242
Pythium	259
Rabbits	125
Ranunculus R. aconitifolius 'Flore Pleno'	105
R. gramineus	105
Raspberries, 'Glen Moy'	213

Recommended reading	291
Red spider mite	251, **251**
Red valerian, see Centranthus ruber	
Red-hot poker, see Kniphofia	
Rhododendron	107, **107**
Rhubarb 'Victoria'	231
Rockwool cubes	168, **168**
Root hair damage	52, **52**
Root rots	260
Root structure	48, **48**
Root zone temperatures, optimal	43
Roots	48
Rosmarinus R. officinalis	105
Rudbeckia	105
Sage	276
Salvia 'Salsa Series'	276
splendens 'Salsa'	74, **74**
Sandison, Helen	95
Saponaria S. ocymoides	91, 106, 276
S. ocymoides 'Snow Tip'	91, 276
S. officinalis	106
Savoy	224, **224**
Saxifraga S. arendsii	91, 106, 276
S. oppositifolia	106
Scabiosa	106
Schizanthus	81
Schizostylis coccinea	106
Scotch marigold, see Calendula	
Sea holly, see Eryngium	
Sea pink, see Armeria	
Seaweed	141
extraction	141, **141**, **142**
Sedge, see Carex	
Sedum	91, **91**
Sedum 'Czar's Gold'	276
S. acre 'Oktoberfest'	91, 106, 276
S. aizoon	91, 106
S. album	106
S. cauticola	106
S. dasyphyllum	106
S. hybridum 'Czar's Gold'	91, 106
S. kamtschaticum	91, 106, 276
S. middendorffiarum	106
S. oreganum	91, 106, 276
S. pulchellum	91, 106, 276
S. reflexum	106, 276
S. selaskianum	91, 106
S. spathulifolium	106
S. spectabile	106
S. spurium	91, 106
S. spurium 'Coccineum'	276
S. spurium 'Summer Glory'	276
S. telephium	91, 106
S. telephium 'Emperor's Waves'	276
S. ternatum	276
Seed, germination, light dependent	35
sowers	16
types	14, **14**
Seedlings	43, **43**

Seeds, 'coated' 13
    'detailed' 13
    estimating numbers 14
    pelleted 13
    plate sower 17
    'primed' 13
    raw 13
    'slick coated' 13
    sowers 16
    sowing 16
    storing 15
Sempervivum 92, **92**
    'Winter Hardy' 276
Senecio cruentus (flowering cineraria) cultivars ... 81
Shasta daisies, see Leucanthemum
Shelterbelts 126
Shetland, compressed season 113
    cooler temperature 115
    moister air 115
    weather statistics 287
    wind 115
Short day plants 54
Shredder 23, **23**
Sidalcea S. candida 'Bianca' 106
    S. malviflora 'Rosanna' 106
    S. malviflora 'Purpetta' 106
Sieve 22
Silene S. acaulis 106, 276
    S. maritima 'Robin Whitebreast' ... 106, 276
    S. schafta 92, 106
    S. uniflora 'Compacta' 92, 106, 276
Silver grass 276
Sisyrinchium augustifolium 106
Slugs 245
Snapdragon, see Antirrhinum
Snow-in-summer, see Cerastium
Solanum 276
    pseudocapsicum 82
Solidago 106
    cutlerii 276
SON-T lamp 121, **121**
Sowing bench 17, **17**
    dates 36
    temperature guidelines 35
Spearmint 276
Spergularia 276
Spinach 231
Spinosad biopesticide 248
Spurge, see Euphorbia
Stachys macrantha 276
    S. macrantha 'Robusta' 106
    S. officinalis 'Rosea' 106
    S. officinalis 'Superba' 106
Stage of growth 53
Stems 49
Stipa capillata ' Lace Veil' 276
    'Pony Tails' 276
    S. capillata 93
    S. tenuissima 93
Stonecrops, see Sedum
Strawberries 'Bolero' 109
    'Elsanta' 109
    planting 212
    purchase of 211
Strawberry 212, **212**

Streptocarpus 82, **82**
Supplementary lighting 121
Sutera, see Bacopa
Swan river daisy, see Brachycom
Swede 'Best of All' 231
    'Marian' 231
    'Snowball' 231
Sweet pea 75, **75**
    'Cupid' 276
Sweet rocket, see Hesperis matronalis

Tagetes 276
    erecta (African Marigold) 75
    patula (French Marigold) cultivars 76
    signata 76
Tanacetum densum ssp amani 106
    haradjanii 106
Tarragon 276
Thalictrum aquilegifolium 106
Thermometer 20, **20**
Thyme 276
Thymus serpyllum 106
Tiarella T.polyphylla 'Filligran' 106
Toadflax, see Linaria
Tomato 216, **216**, 232
    'Alicante' 215
    'Beefsteak' 215
    'Counter' 215
    'Gardener's Delight' 215
    'Matina' 215
    'Piccolo Dattero' 232
    'Shirley' 215
    training 217
Tomatoes 213
Trace elements 137
Transpiration 51
Trifolium rubens 276
Trollius T. chinensis 'Golden Queen' 106
    T. cultorum 'Orange Globe' 106
    T. x hybridus 106
Tropaeolum speciosum 106
Trough construction 210, **210**
Tumbling Ted, see Saponaria
Tunnel view 56, **56**
Tunnels 185, **185-194**
Turnip 'Atlantic' 231
    'Goldana' 231
    'Purple Top Milan' 231
    'Snowball' 231

Uncinia egmontiana 276
    rubra 276

Vegetable mix 231, **231**
    seeds 30
Ventilation 183, **183**
Venting 54
Verbascum phoeniceum 'Violetta' 277
    V. chaixii 'Sixteen Candles' 92, 277
    V. chaixii 'Wedding Candles' 92
Verbena 277
    tenuisecta 92

Vernalisation	53	Walterson, John and Bertha	95
Veronica V. gentianoides	107, 277	Water absorption	51
V. officinalis	277	pump	144, **144**
V. officinalis	107	quality	156
V. porphyriana	277	storage	146
V. prostrata	107	temperature	34
V. prostrata 'Nector'	277	timers	148, **148**
V. spicata	107	Watering	144
V. spicata 'Blue Bouquet'	277	cans	144
Vine weevil	252, **252**	drip irrigation	145
microbial control	252	hoses and lances	144
Viola	77, **77**	plants	133
annual cultivars	77	Waterlogging	124
'Avalanche'	277	Websites	269
V. cornata	107	Weedkiller 'Grazon 90'	264
V. odorata	107	'Roundup'	264
V. soraria	107	Wheel sower	18, **18**
V. soraria 'Dark Freckles'	277	Wind damage	123
V. soraria 'Freckles'	277	Windbreaks	126, 127, **127**, **190**
V. soraria 'Rubra'	277		
x wittrockiana (Pansy) cultivars	78	Yarrow, see Achillea	
		Zinnia	79